SUBVERTING SOCIAL INEQUALITIES

Gender as a Social Reality

AAP Insights in Women's and Gender Studies: Reshaping Identities

SUBVERTING SOCIAL INEQUALITIES

Gender as a Social Reality

Akanksha Srivastava, PhD
Disha Maheshwari, PhD
Chitra Krishnan, PhD
Editors

AAP APPLE ACADEMIC PRESS

First edition published 2025

Apple Academic Press Inc.
1265 Goldenrod Circle, NE,
Palm Bay, FL 32905 USA

760 Laurentian Drive, Unit 19,
Burlington, ON L7N 0A4, CANADA

CRC Press
2385 NW Executive Center Drive,
Suite 320, Boca Raton FL 33431

4 Park Square, Milton Park,
Abingdon, Oxon, OX14 4RN UK

Library and Archives Canada Cataloguing in Publication

CIP data on file with Canada Library and Archives

Library of Congress Cataloging-in-Publication Data

CIP data on file with US Library of Congress

ISBN: 978-1-77491-814-2 (hbk)
ISBN: 978-1-77491-815-9 (pbk)
ISBN: 978-1-00356-341-9 (ebk)

ABOUT THE BOOK SERIES: AAP Insights in Women's and Gender Studies: Reshaping Identities

Series Editor:
Chitra Krishnan, PhD
Associate Professor, Symbiosis Center for Management Studies, Noida, Symbiosis International Deemed University, Pune, India
E-mail: ananya.chitra@gmail.com

AAP Insights in Women's and Gender Studies: Reshaping Identities is more than just a collection of books; it is an interdisciplinary journey, breaking down disciplinary borders to delve into the complexities of gender from an intersectional perspective. This approach offers readers a rich tapestry of insights that span academic, cultural, and geographical boundaries. The belief is in the power of knowledge to drive substantial impact. The series aims to bridge the gap between academic rigor and practical application, providing tools that empower educators, researchers, students, and activists to spark change and advance the cause of gender equality around the world.

Diversity is at the core of the series, proudly showcasing narratives from researchers, activists, and practitioners who are at the forefront of influencing gender dialogue. Discussions encompass a wide range of topics, including intersectionality, international feminism, LGBTQ+ rights, and more.

Each volume in the series aims to exemplify an unwavering commitment to thorough academic research and profound analytical exploration. There is a resolute conviction in the potential of knowledge to effect meaningful change. The AAP Insights in Women's and Gender Studies: Reshaping Identities series hopes to serve as a guiding light of enlightenment, equipping readers with the tools to embark on a profound voyage of exploration, empathy, and proactive engagement.

The book series broadly considers the contributions from the following fields:

1. Women's Empowerment for a Sustainable Future
2. Narratives of Empowerment: Women Redefining Identity

3. Queer Perspectives: Unveiling Diverse Gender Realities
4. Intersectionality and Activism: Challenging Systems of Oppression
5. Global Gender Realities: Stories from Around the World
6. Challenging Gender Norms: Exploring Fluidity and Nonconformity
7. Historical Perspectives: Tracing Women's Contributions and Struggles
8. Feminism Beyond Borders: Solidarity and Social Change
9. Bodies and Identities: Reclaiming Autonomy and Agency
10. Evolving Masculinities: Breaking Free from Traditional Roles
11. Education and Empowerment: Transforming Gender Norms in Learning
12. Health and Wellness
13. Economic Empowerment
14. Technology and Gender
15. LGBTQ+ Rights and Activism

Join us in reshaping identities, challenging norms, and advancing the discourse on gender and identity. Together, we can make a profound difference in the world.

BOOKS IN THE SERIES TO DATE

- **Subverting Social Inequalities: Gender as a Social Reality**
  Editors: Akanksha Srivastava, PhD, Disha Mahfeshwari, PhD, and Chitra Krishnan, PhD
- **Gender Equality and Leadership: Transforming the Organizational Culture**
  Editors: Mubashir Majid Baba, PhD, Chitra Krishnan, PhD, and Neelni Giri Goswami, PhD

ABOUT THE EDITORS

Akanksha Srivastava, PhD
Associate Professor, School of Education, Sharda University, Greater Noida, India

Akanksha Srivastava, PhD, is an experienced academician, writer, and editor with over 15 years of experience in the education industry. She is currently working as an Associate Professor with the School of Education, Sharda University, Greater Noida, India. She has worked on a variety of projects, including nonfiction books, academic articles, and technical reports. In addition to her work as an editor, she is also an accomplished author. Her research interests include the intersection of inclusion with a focus on women's experiences, on which she has published extensively. As the editor of this volume, Dr. Srivastava brought together a diverse group of scholars to explore the various themes and topics related to the history of gender and sexuality in Europe, Asia, Africa, and USA. Dr. Srivastava holds a doctoral degree in Education and a master's degree in English and Anthropology.

Disha Maheshwari, PhD
Assistant Professor, School of Education, Sharda University, India

Disha Maheshwari, PhD, is currently working as an Assistant Professor at the School of Education, Sharda University, India. She was a Commonwealth Scholar at the Centre for Applied Linguistics, University of Warwick, Coventry, England. At Sharda University, she teaches courses on gender studies, communication, and research methodology in education (qualitative) at the undergraduate and postgraduate levels and on pedagogy at PhD level. She has presented her research work around the world, including at Cambridge, Stockholm, Hong Kong, Warwick, Oslo (virtual), Tamilnadu, Punjab, etc. Her areas of interest are gender and education, discourse and identity, and higher education pedagogy. She worked as a research assistant on the project "ELT Survey of India" from February 2016–May 2016 at the University of Warwick, UK, funded by the British Council. She also worked as a project associate on the project "Children and Teachers as

Co-Researchers: Exploring Young Learner Classrooms in India," funded by the Rand D Project Grant, University of Delhi, India. She was awarded her PhD in Education from the University of Delhi, India.

Chitra Krishnan, PhD
Associate Professor of Human Resource Management and Behavioral Science, Symbiosis Centre for Management Studies, Noida, India

Chitra Krishnan, PhD, is an Associate Professor of Human Resource Management & Behavioral Science at the Symbiosis Centre for Management Studies, Noida, India. She is a teaching professional with over 16 years of national and international experience. She possesses excellence in teaching and research. Before her academic career, she worked in industry in various positions of responsibility. She has been actively involved in rigorous academic pursuits in the field of higher professional education to enhance skill sets that promote the holistic development of learners. She has a number of publications in acclaimed journals at the national and international levels and has also participated in many national and international conferences. She is passionate about writing and has seven books to her credit with international publishers. She has been impaneled as a member of the review committees for conferences and journals of repute. Her area of interest includes human resource management, organizational behavior, talent management, diversity management, employee satisfaction, knowledge management, artificial intelligence, and emotional intelligence.

CONTENTS

CONTRIBUTORS

Manvi Arora
School of Social Work, University of Montreal, Canada

Joshi Raghavan Edassery
UTAS, IBRA, Oman

Abel Ebiega Enokela
Department of Guidance Counselling, Faculty of Education, Ambrose Alli University, Edo State, Nigeria

Seema Garg
AIBS, Amity University, Noida, Uttar Pradesh, India

Kritika Gosain
School of Education, Sharda University, Greater Noida, Uttar Pradesh, India

Yesim Kakalic
The University of Warwick, England

Shikha Kapoor
Professor, Amity International Business School, Amity University, Noida, Uttar Pradesh, India

Rekha Kaushal
Department of Education, School of Humanities, Social Sciences, and Education, GD Goenka University, Haryana, India

Chitra Krishnan
Symbiosis Center for Management Studies, Noida, Symbiosis International Deemed University, Pune, Maharashtra, India

Disha Maheshwari
School of Education, Sharda University, Greater Noida, Uttar Pradesh, India

Jasmine Mariappan
UTAS, IBRA, Oman

Kiran Nair
Abu Dhabi University, Abu Dhabi

N. C. Narayanan
Indian Institute of Technology–Bombay, Mumbai, Maharashtra, India

Tram Ngoc Ngo
Faculty of Foreign Studies, Vietnam Maritime University, Vietnam

Nhung Hong Thi Nguyen
QA Higer Education, QA Limited company, The United Kingdom

S. Rakendu
Indian Institute of Technology–Bombay, Mumbai, Maharashtra, India

Neelam Rana
Indian Institute of Technology–Bombay, Mumbai, Maharashtra, India

Mohamed Riyas
UTAS, IBRA, Oman

Amila Rupasinghe
Senior Lecturer, Faculty of Education, Horizon Campus, Knowledge City, Malabe, Sri Lanka

Supriya Lamba Sahdev
Department–Management, ISBR Business School, Bangalore, Karnataka, India

Stephanie Schnurr
Baden-Wuerttemberg Cooperative State University and The University of Warwick, Germany

Ashutosh Sharad
ISBR Business School, Bangalore, Karnataka, India

Marianna Slutskaya
The University of Warwick, England

Akanksha Srivastava
School of Education, Sharda University, Greater Noida, Uttar Pradesh, India

Ashika Srivastava
Georgia Institute of Technology, Georgia

Vivian Steurer
Baden-Wuerttemberg Cooperative State University and The University of Warwick, Germany

Abdulla Thanseer
UTAS, IBRA, Oman

Thanuja Maithrie Witharana
Deputy Commissioner of Educational Publications, Educational Publications Department, Ministry of Education, Sri Lanka

FOREWORD

Subverting Social Inequalities: Gender as a Social Reality, co-edited by Dr. Akanksha Srivastava, Dr. Disha Maheshwari, and Dr. Chitra Krishnan, is true to its title and refreshing to read as the chapters are analytically robust, lucid in style, maintain logical flow, and bring nuanced insights on a wide range of thematic areas. The overarching concern of this anthology is to examine two crucial areas of gendered realities—Education and Workforce.

The sociocultural and political landscape for gender equality in India today is determined by a complex mixture of the new and the old. Numerous modern institutions of governance, judiciary, and politics rest on the base of the traditional gender norms biased against women as well as sexual and gender minorities. Despite gender stereotypes, modernization, industrialization, globalization, and urbanization have led to some irreversible changes for women—some positive and some problematic. On one hand, opportunities for better education for the mass of girls and women have expanded, but this does not translate into jobs/careers. Over the last quarter of a century, the decision-making power of women in the local self-government has increased, and nearly 2 million women elected representatives in the urban and rural local self-government bodies have crossed the boundary of domesticity, and all political parties are enthusiastically putting up candidates for the reserved seats for women in the rural and urban PRIs, but the same politicians vehemently oppose women's reservation in the state legislative assembly/ legislative council and the parliament.

Women's Challenges in the 21st Century

Women are entering male-dominated sectors, aspiring for promotion, and challenging opportunities, but they have been targets of a strong backlash with increased violence within and outside the home, acute wage differentials, and discrimination and sexual harassment in the workplace.

The fundamental rights of the Constitution of India guarantee equality, liberty, and dignity, but religion-based family laws pursue double standards in the most intimate relations such as marriage, divorce, custody, and guardianship rights, right to residence, inheritance, and property. Reforms in legislation over the last four decades, either through the judicial route or through the legislative route, do not match the ground reality that is devoid of intersectional justice and a level playing field for all genders.

Gender binaries are challenged by the LGBTQIA+ community in an organized fashion, but in gender-responsive budgetary discourses, neither their voices are to be found nor any provision made to reduce the gender gap in crucial areas of education, health, employment, skilling, decision-making, and combating gender-based violence. Migration, environmental degradation, climate calamity, and the recent pandemic have had a gender differential impact in terms of loss of employment, income, and livelihoods; erosion of reproductive health services, high maternal and child deaths; increased malnutrition, the loss of access to education, digital divide, forced child labor, and forced child marriages.

In this background, the timely publication of this book gains great significance in identifying the roots of hurdles and major challenges in approaching gender equality and finding solutions to them.

"Gender and Education" of this edited volume captures lived experiences of gender-based socialization within the formal system of education: with special reference to transgender and gender-diverse learners in the classrooms, un-gendering at school via engagements with teachers and students, global perspective on the gender difference in mathematics performance, gender, and information and communication technology, the girl-child education assessed through the lens of gender-illiteracy nexus in Nigeria and gender bias, internalization and reinforcement in classroom discourse captured through an in-depth case study of communicative English classrooms in Vietnam.

"Gender and Workforce" of the book reflects on the obsolete and archaic gender norms and stereotypes that perpetuate the gender base of the division of labor in households, the labor market, and the macroeconomy. A nuanced understanding of workplace discrimination is captured by chapters across cultures. On the one hand, industrially advanced countries such as Germany and the USA continue to pursue gender-unequal policies and practices covertly when it comes to educated middle-class women, while ruthlessly exploiting migrant workers in dead-end jobs without any scope of professional mobility. On the other, postcolonial economies such as Sri Lanka and India pose a disabling ecosystem for women in the workforce that prevents women from taking up leadership positions. The paradox of gender equality in the corporate world is marked by women being paid less than men and facing worse working conditions, microaggression on a day-to-day basis, lower promotion opportunities, and workplace discrimination.

The major strength of the book is the intersectional perspectives in deconstructing the feminization of stigmatized occupations in the waste sector in Kerala, gendered professional identities in academia, challenges to educational leadership faced by the Sri Lankan Educational Administrative Service Officers, and the nature of inequalities in industrialized countries such as America and Germany.

Chapters in this volume bring forth profound and meaningful perspectives and focus on the dualism regarding gender concerns. Since the post-1975 International Women's Year, most countries have implemented a series of progressive measures and affirmative actions, but they have mainly benefited a small minority of women. In this context, the practical gender needs, as well as the strategic gender needs of women, need to be examined with the touchstone of the Convention on the Elimination of All Forms of Discrimination Against Women (CEDAW) adopted by most nation-states.

Indian Women in the Globalized World

During the Indian freedom movement, the political involvement of women was remarkable in fighting colonialism. In independent India, both Indian men and women were granted the 'right to vote' 75 years ago. Indian women have been active as voters. But the political culture is rife with misogyny, casteism, colorism, communalism, and social inequalities, money, and muscle power. Public-private dichotomy ('Public' for men and 'private' for women) also comes in the way of women's work participation and active political participation and representation in the decision-making of public spaces.

Goddess-worshipping Indians have no qualms in the pre-birth elimination of girls and female infanticide. This paradoxical situation of women in India is alarming. On one hand, they are worshipped as goddesses, while on the other hand, burnt for dowry. Boys are more desirable and seen as a support for parents in their old age as necessary to continue the family lineage. Girls are considered an unwanted burden yet used for serving their brothers and men and suffer in silence as atrocities such as abuse, violence, rape, early marriage, trafficking, and danger for women in public spaces. Discriminatory practices such as child marriages, dowry, honor killing, witch hunting, and gender-biased sex selection indicate profound vulnerability and inequality towards girls and women in Indian society.

Globalization of the Indian economy and neoliberalism have dramatically influenced social life in India. The expansion of the middle class is said to have occurred as a consequence of this process. Based on ethnographic research among lower middle-class families in West Bengal, India, the author examines the apparent paradox between women's positive perceptions of empowerment and the overall negative impact of structural adjustment policies on women. Many scholars argue that globalization has been detrimental to women due to growing structural gender inequalities, but many respondents identify greater opportunities to challenge pre-existing patriarchal norms through the role models available in the globalized media. While there are increasing inequalities for households, women do not consider these to be gender disadvantages, emphasizing instead the opportunities for greater independence. The author pays particular attention to the confluence of the pro-women consumer discourses of the global market with earlier developmental notions of the public role of women.

Dimensions of Women's Subordination

Women encounter more obstacles than men in education, training, and the acquisition of resources, and often are treated unequally in their terms and conditions of employment. Gender segregation, and the structure on which women's relatively subordinate position in the workforce is based, keep women working at lower-level jobs, concentrating power in the hands of men. The roles of men and women have been different for most of human history since prehistoric times. In hunter-gatherer societies in the past, hunting had been largely a male preserve while gathering a female role. Other roles were often carried out by only one of the genders. However, differences in roles did not imply disparity of status.

Socially constructed markets perpetuate segmentation on the grounds of caste, class, race, ethnicity, religion, ableism, and gender. The subordination in recent times is most clearly seen at the overall level in two dimensions: lateral subordination, where women-dominated sectors and occupations have lower status and are given lower values than male-dominated sectors and occupations, and subordination in the vertical dimension, where women as a group are to be found at a lower level in the hierarchies than men. It has been seen that countries with high employment rates of women have high segregation rates. As more women enter the labor markets they are recruited into sectors and work tasks that already are defined as 'female jobs,' and they are doing service jobs earlier performed in the household and now transformed into market work. A consequence of gender segregation is uneven economic conditions. Empirical studies estimate that gender segregation explains a large proportion of the gender wage gap.

When building families, men are usually learning their trade or occupation, and establishing their position in the labor market. Women still have responsibility for care, both at home and in the market. She, therefore, plans a larger part of her life around a combination of gainful employment and her responsibilities in the home and for the family. She does these using different strategies for both caring for the family and maintaining her employment.

Women in the World of Work

"Work" can be defined as the physical or mental effort or activity directed toward the production or accomplishment of something. For the framing of development policies, national-level statistics are in the principal data input, but this is largely impaired by the undercounting of women, both as workers and those available for work. The first barrier is of course the definition of work vis-à-vis women's work. We continue to relate work only to remunerative aspects of work as work. Indian women are engaged in two kinds of work; one that produces an income and the other that does not. They are known as paid and unpaid work respectively. Even where women are doing market-oriented work, the special characteristics of women's work make such work 'invisible,' for example, home-based piece rate workers. The census concept of 'work' overemphasizes production for exchange and although it does include some non-market production for own consumption such as cultivation where men are also involved, it excludes by a strange logic other types of production for own consumption such as livestock maintenance (done mostly by women) and hence these figures do not correspond with the non-market output in the national accounts.

The lack of freedom of choice, power and material resources, traditional gender roles, and norms, stand – in the way of development, as is evident in most parts of the world. Significantly, a large proportion of women in the world live in poverty, and efforts to reduce poverty are inseparable from the aspirants for greater quality. Research indicates that gender equality in the long run has led to a reduction in poverty. Unequal power structures for women and men constitute an impediment to economic growth and democratic development. Equal opportunities for women and men to own land and assets, earn money, and participate in working life, are essential for sustainable and democratic development in the long run. These verses collected over years of training workshops on Gender at Work vividly capture the paradox of gender equality in the world of work:

The family picture is on HIS desk.
Ah, a solid, responsible family man.
The family picture is on HER desk.
Umm, her family will come before her career.

HIS desk is cluttered.
He's a hard worker and a busy man.
HER desk is cluttered.
She's a disorganized scatterbrain.

HE is talking with his co-workers.
He must be discussing the latest deal.
SHE is talking with her co-workers.
She must be gossiping.

HE's not at his desk.
He must be at a meeting.
SHE's not at her desk.
She must be in the ladies' room.

HE's having lunch with the boss.
He's on his way up.
SHE's having lunch with the boss.
They must be having an affair.

The boss criticized HIM.
He'll improve his performance.
The boss criticized HER.
She'll be very upset.

HE got an unfair deal.
Did he get angry?
SHE got an unfair deal.
Did she cry?

HE's getting married.
He'll get more settled.
SHE's getting married.
She'll get pregnant and leave.

HE's having a baby.
He'll need a raise.
SHE's having a baby.
She'll cost the company money in maternity benefits.

HE's going on a business trip.
It's good for his career.
SHE's going on a business trip.
What does her husband say?

HE's leaving for a better job.
He knows how to recognize a good opportunity.
SHE's leaving for a better job.
Women are not dependable.

Several studies show that women are more often overqualified for their jobs than men. Other studies show that women have less influence over their work organization and content than men. Women also generally have a greater degree of monotonous, repetitive motion in their work. Further, studies show that occupations where women predominate have a lower status than male-dominated occupations, even if the occupations require equivalent education and training. In workplaces with as many women as men, in apparently the same occupation, the women often perform different tasks, which most of the time are classified differently in status and pay. The work women almost always perform is valued lower.[1]

The paradox of gender equality and the employment market is most pronounced. Do we see the confluence of employment and empowerment for women in the informal sector?

Theoretical and empirical debates about the relation of women to class/caste/ethnicity/race/religion and work, and the implications of these relations for theories of male domination and women's oppression as well as for other systems of social domination, continue to be important sources of theories and investigations of gender identities, roles and powers in the field of women and gender studies, as well as in history, sociology, anthropology, and economics. They also have important implications for epistemology, metaphysics, and political theory in the discipline of philosophy, and consequently other disciplines in humanities and the social sciences. Clarity about gender issues in work informs policy measures, labor legislations, social security, and the overall status of women in the household, community, and economy.

[1] A/HRC/44/51: Women's human rights in the changing world of work – Report of the Working Group on discrimination against women and girls, UNHRC (2020). https://www.ohchr.org/en/documents/thematic-reports/ahrc4451-womens-human-rights-changing-world-work-report-working-group (accessed on 22 May 2024).

What emerges from the chapters written with an inter-disciplinary perspective in this book is, that a precondition for women's human rights in terms of the right to education, employment, justice, and dignity is the redistribution of power and resources. This book serves as an important resource for policymakers, political and development practitioners, employers and educationists; and of course students, research scholars, and teachers.

I congratulate the editors of this valuable publication, Dr. Akanksha Srivastava, Dr. Disha Maheshwari, and Dr. Chitra Krishnan, and the contributors of chapters for their grounded research, robust analysis, powerful message, and delineating pathways for change.

—Prof. Vibhuti Patel, PhD
Vice President, Indian Association for Women's Studies

PREFACE

As we enter the 21st century, social inequalities continue to persist in various forms across the globe. While these inequalities are rooted in historical, cultural, and economic factors, they are also perpetuated by social norms and expectations that shape our everyday lives. Gender inequality manifests itself in a variety of ways, including unequal access to resources, limited opportunities for education and employment, and discrimination and violence against marginalized groups. While progress has been made in some areas, gender inequality remains a significant barrier to social, economic, and political advancement for many individuals and communities. One of the most pervasive and enduring forms of social inequality is gender inequality.

Despite various efforts to promote gender equality, women and non-binary individuals continue to face discrimination, violence, and exclusion in many aspects of life, such as education, employment, healthcare, and politics. These inequalities are deeply embedded in social structures and cultural norms, and they are often reinforced by power dynamics that favor men and traditional gender roles.

However, it is important to recognize that gender is not just a biological characteristic or personal preference. Rather, it is a social reality that shapes our experiences, expectations, and opportunities in life. Gender is not just about being male or female; it is a complex and multifaceted phenomenon that involves norms, values, beliefs, and behaviors related to femininity, masculinity, and other gender identities.

In this book, we explore the ways in which gender operates as a social reality and how it intersects with other forms of social inequality, such as race, class, sexuality, and ability. We examine how gender is constructed and maintained through various social institutions, such as the family, workforce, and education system. We also analyze the ways in which individuals and groups subvert gender norms and challenge gender inequalities through activism, art, and other forms of resistance.

Chapter 1 explores the internalization of gender ideology and construction in classroom discourse. Deploying a sociocultural linguistic approach to explore the role of gender in identity construction, it is found that despite the institutionalization and goal-driven nature of classrooms, classroom discourse is permeated with gender internalization and stereotypes. The construction and reinforcement of gendered identities and ideology are negotiated through various discursive strategies associated with Vietnamese masculinity and femininity. This chapter confirms the significant influence of gender norms in professional contexts and fine-grained discourse analysis's role in revealing the implicit manifestation of gender expectations and bias existing in educational contexts.

Chapter 2 attempts to explore the intersection of professional identity and gender identity construction by two women professionals in academia by investigating experiences of gender-based harassment and discrimination. The qualitative method of narrative inquiry is used to explore narratives of sexist behavior and gender discrimination in the workplace. It explores how gendered remarks cause self-doubt in the way these two women construct their professional identities. The paper aims to identify the ways in which patriarchal articulation of professional identity leads to a feeling of marginalization as working professionals. It also highlights the resistance strategies employed in the construction of professional identity while also carefully avoiding the risk of being labeled 'difficult women.'

Chapter 3 explicates how education as a system explicitly socializes the learners into a carefully scripted version of gender through the ethos and practices of the educational institutions in multiple ways. These claims are based on first-hand experiences of transgender and gender-diverse learners and their systemic engagement with educational institutions.

Chapter 4 assesses the gender-illiteracy nexus in Nigeria in relation to girl-child education through the lens of conflict theory. It examines the role gender plays in determining access to education in the country. Gender disparity spreads through the socialization process as individuals come in contact with socialization agents like family, education, peer groups, and mass media. These agents of socialization could impart or reinforce learned gender-based behaviors that could be disadvantageous to the girl child and her educational rights, by and large.

Chapter 5 looks at how and to what extent technological boon in the 21st century has made way for another kind of gender disparity which is digital. Half of the female population of the world lacks access to technology and is thus walled off from the globalized world. Gender disparities are evident in the difference in male and female technological abilities, female participation in the IT industry, and difference in technology utilization by both genders.

Chapter 6 explores the assumption that boys outperformed girls in the achievement of mathematics as they are biologically different. Gender differences in mathematics and science interests can be observed in early childhood.

With the onset of adolescence, gendered patterns arise, concurrent with the development of gender identity and adult gender roles. Mathematics anxiety, which has been witnessed more in female students, is one of the predominant factors that affect mathematics performance. Gender issues still exist in mathematics in developed countries, including Canada, the UK, and the USA. To improve outcomes for both genders in the subject of mathematics, the milieu of the classroom environment, teachers' attitudes, the learning style of the students, pedagogical strategies, outside classroom experiences, and activities should be offered to encourage mathematics instruction to be addressed wisely.

Chapter 7 Gender-segregated schools in Sri Lanka have ingrained certain gender norms inside students. Boys and girls exhibit diverse gender role behaviors due to traditions, value systems, mini-cultural backgrounds, and the socialization process in single- and mixed-gender schools. As a country that withholds various cultural and traditional values, the influence of the school environment based on gender is a significant factor in shaping society and its qualities, values, and attitudes toward gender equality. The chapter evaluates the advantages and disadvantages of both same-gender and mixed-gender schools and analyzes how socialization in both settings affects the development of gender stereotypes, prejudices, and discrimination. Furthermore, this chapter examines the effect on gender equality in single-gender versus mixed-gender (coeducational) schools in Sri Lanka.

Chapter 8 brings to the surface the gendered practices and discrimination that exist in many German workplaces. Through exploring employees' lived experiences, we provide insights into the language of gender (in) equality and the ways in which gender is produced. Drawing on 20 interviews and using discourse analysis, we identify and describe some of the discursive processes through which those affected by gender equality issues make sense of them on the personal, organizational, and societal levels. Findings illustrate that these levels are interconnected and that there is considerable variation in the ways in which professionals talk about their experiences of gender equality policies and practices at work.

Chapter 9 deals with the informal waste sector in India predominantly which sees a large number of women working, while the formal waste management system run by the urban local bodies is dominated by men. Kerala being one of the first states in the country to shift to a state-wide decentralized model of waste management has managed to create livelihood opportunities for around thirty thousand women in the formal waste management sector. The feminization process replaced municipal sweepers (who are predominantly men) and engaged Haritha Karma Sena women to carry out the collection, segregation, and processing of waste. With this, waste management in the state improved many folds, receiving awards and accolades from across the world, along with large cost savings for urban local bodies. Associated with the feminization process is the issue of precariousness, especially low and unstable income, lack of social security benefits, decent working conditions and bargaining power, high health risks, social stigma, and discrimination. These are typical traits of informal work. Yet women undertake and continue to be part of such jobs. We studied such differentiated and complex realities to identify and explain what facilitates such processes through an empirical study of Haritha Karama Sena in the solid waste sector in Kerala. The study also adds to the literature on the gendered division of labor in the waste sector.

Chapter 10 analyzes various sources of contemporary discourse in terms of Gender studies and primarily tries to put across a nuanced and modern-day approach toward gender equality. The central theme of the chapter is that all stakeholders should focus on creating equitable conditions rather than inorganically demanding for equality. This would be the organic way to achieve the reality of Gender Equity. Here, we also appreciate the progress made by different communities across the World in the past century in terms of contribution towards a strong female workforce but also identify differential levels of progress. Therefore, we need to have a segmented approach to understanding specific problems and delivering customized solutions. Finally, we argue that women are not the only stakeholders in the quest for Gender equality there are Members of the LGBTQIA+ community and also the society at large because there is a high degree of positive correlation between women's workforce participation and economic growth.

Chapter 11 explores the gendering of professional mobility by focusing on the experiences of a non-elite migrant – a Turkish woman who immigrated to Germany in the early 1970s. The migration of women was frowned upon and viewed as immoral by large parts of Turkish society. The move to Germany challenged hegemonic gendered expectations and practices, including the gender order and its underlying ideologies. By unpacking the discursive processes through which notions of mobility and work are gendered in and through her stories, we provide insights into the complex ways in which gender is produced, reproduced, and either naturalized or challenged.

Chapter 12 analyzes the role of gender in Indian immigrants' perspectives on what is known in the United States as the "American Dream." While mainly associated with wealth and success, the American Dream is said to be different for each person. However, this chapter intends to look more closely at the underlying differences in what this pursuit entails when gender roles and norms come into play specifically for Indian immigrants. Through a series of semi-structured interviews, this research aims to draw upon the real-life experiences of an Indian couple who immigrated to the United States and has lived there for almost twenty years.

Chapter 13 emphasizes the fact that Women leaders face many barriers in their leadership journey. This chapter will discuss the barriers faced by Sri Lankan women leaders in the Sri Lanka Educational Administrative Service. First, a literature review is done to reveal the barriers for women leaders. Then a sample of women leaders would be interviewed to see their experience with these barriers. Mainly, the effects of institutional and individual mindsets of stereotypes will be discussed. Further, current real-world cases would be presented at the end. Moreover, suggestions to identify the barriers will be given in the chapter.

Chapter 14 explores the concept of gender equality, its root causes, and its impact on various aspects of society, including education, employment, entrepreneurship, and politics. The article explores the significance of unpaid care work in the examination of gender differences in labor outcomes and emphasizes the necessity for governments, civil society organizations, and people to engage together in addressing gender inequality. The paper also presents a literature review on the topic of gender equality, covering various studies and reports on the subject. Ultimately, the paper argues that achieving gender equality is essential for creating a more just and prosperous society and that it requires a sustained and collaborative effort from all stakeholders

Chapter 15 deals with Female entrepreneurship which is a growing field of research, since it is crucial to the corporate environment. There are many challenges and risks involved in the entrepreneurial journey. It is far harder to be an entrepreneur and a woman. This study explores and examines the evolution and challenges of women entrepreneurs, a lot of literature on it, the difficulties and challenges they encounter, and various programs and schemes of government introduced for the promotion of women entrepreneurship in India with the case of a few successful women entrepreneurs in India.

Chapter 16 addresses that "Equal rights for men and women are a basic human right and a prerequisite for a peaceful, wealthy, and sustainable world." The Preamble, Fundamental Rights, Fundamental Duties, and Directive Principles of the Indian Constitution all mention the idea of gender equality. Per the Constitution, the government is permitted to enact laws supporting discrimination against women. Long-term progress is required to eradicate discrimination against women and provide equal opportunities for both education and employment. Gender equality is crucial because it promotes economic development. International organizations describe gender equality in terms of economic development and human rights, notably women's rights.

We believe that by recognizing and subverting gender inequalities, we can create a world where everyone has the opportunity to thrive, regardless of their gender identity or expression.

ACKNOWLEDGMENTS

Writing and editing this book was a personal and emotional journey for all of us. It made us visit and revisit various aspects of our lives where we negotiate our identities as women under the immense control of patriarchal social norms. Working on this book has helped us understand our shared experiences as women in a gender-unequal world and also in some ways understand the ways in which we can negotiate these inequalities.

We are forever indebted to Dr. Prakash Iyer from Azim Premji University for the idea of this book. His lecture on 'Subverting Gender Inequalities' at Sharda University and my interaction with him germinated the idea for this book. We are also grateful to Prof. Vibhuti Patel for graciously accepting our request to write the foreword for our book. She has succinctly brought out the distinct features of this book while sharing her insight on various themes of the book.

We are grateful to our lovely contributors who have helped us explore the issues related to gender inequalities across the globe. This book would not have been possible without the support and contribution of many of our loved ones. We are also grateful to our families for supporting us through the journey of this book.

Finally, we are grateful to each other for the handholding, support, and words of encouragement whenever one of us needed them.

—Disha Maheshwari, PhD
Akanksha Srivastava, PhD
Chitra Krishnan, PhD

INTRODUCTION

As we move into the 21st century, social inequalities continue to exist in various forms worldwide. While these disparities are tied to historical, cultural, and economic factors, they are also sustained by societal norms and expectations that influence our daily lives. Gender inequality is evident in numerous ways, such as unequal access to resources, restricted opportunities in education and employment, as well as discrimination and violence faced by marginalized groups. Although some progress has been achieved, gender inequality still serves as a major obstacle to social, economic, and political progress for many individuals and communities. Among the most widespread and persistent forms of inequality is gender inequality.

Despite numerous initiatives aimed at advancing gender equality, women and non-binary individuals continue to experience discrimination, violence, and exclusion across many sectors, including education, employment, healthcare, and politics. These inequalities are deeply ingrained in societal structures and cultural norms and are often reinforced by power dynamics that prioritize men and uphold traditional gender roles. However, it's crucial to understand that gender is not simply a biological attribute or a matter of personal choice. Instead, it is a social construct that shapes our experiences, expectations, and life opportunities. Gender goes beyond the binary concept of male and female; it is a complex and multifaceted phenomenon encompassing the norms, values, beliefs, and behaviors associated with femininity, masculinity, and other gender identities.

Gender is often thought of as a binary concept, with individuals categorized as either male or female based on their biological sex. However, many people identify as non-binary or gender non-conforming, meaning they do not identify exclusively as male or female or do not conform to traditional gender roles and expectations. Gender is also a performance (Butler), something that we "do" (ref). Overall, gender is a complex and multifaceted concept that plays a significant role in shaping individuals' experiences and opportunities. It is important to recognize and respect the diversity of gender identities and expressions, and to work towards a more equitable and inclusive society for people of all genders. Gender is a socially constructed concept that varies across cultures and over time.

Gender can influence various aspects of life, including self-identity, relationships, career choices, and access to resources and opportunities. Gender identity is a personal and deeply felt sense of one's gender, which may or may not align with the gender assigned at birth based on biological sex. It turns out to be one of the most important factors responsible for the ways in which our social experience and in lieu identities are constructed and negotiated in our communities. One's gender would determine to a large extent the kind of opportunities, or their lack thereof, criticism, and appreciation the individuals will receive during their lives. Gender inequalities refer to the unequal treatment or opportunities individuals may experience due to gender identity. These inequalities can manifest in various ways and affect people of all gender identities, although they often disproportionately impact women and people who identify as non-binary or gender non-conforming.

In this book, we delve into how gender functions as a social reality and intersects with other forms of inequality, including race, class, sexuality, and ability. We explore how gender is shaped and sustained by various social institutions, such as the family, the workplace, and the education system. Additionally, we analyze how individuals and groups defy gender norms and challenge gender-based inequalities through activism, art, and other forms of resistance.

Subverting Gender Inequalities

Subverting gender inequalities involves actively challenging and dismantling gender-based biases, stereotypes, and discrimination, and promoting equality and equity for people of all genders. Here are some ways to do so:

1. **Challenge Gender Norms and Stereotypes:** This involves questioning and challenging traditional gender roles and expectations, and promoting more diverse and inclusive representations of gender in all aspects of life. This can include advocating for non-binary or gender-neutral language, challenging sexist jokes or comments, and promoting positive portrayals of diverse gender identities in media and popular culture.

2. **Promote Gender Equity in Education:** This can involve advocating for equal access to educational opportunities for people of all genders, and working to eliminate gender-based biases in academic and career fields. This can include promoting programs and initiatives that encourage girls and women to pursue education and careers in science, technology, engineering, and math (STEM)

fields, as well as promoting diversity and inclusivity in all educational environments.

3. **Advocate for Policies that Promote Gender Equity:** This can involve advocating for policies that address gender-based discrimination and bias, such as policies that promote equal pay for equal work, provide parental leave and other family-friendly policies, and protect against harassment and discrimination on the basis of gender or gender identity.
4. **Support Gender-Diverse Individuals and Communities:** This involves promoting supportive and inclusive environments for people of all gender identities, and working to eliminate discrimination and stigma against gender-diverse individuals. This can include supporting organizations that advocate for gender equity and diversity and promoting inclusive policies and practices in workplaces, schools, and other institutions.

Overall, subverting gender inequalities requires a long-term commitment to promoting gender equity and challenging systemic biases and discrimination. It involves working towards a more inclusive and equitable society for people of all gender identities.

This book focuses on how gender-based inequalities are perpetuated and negotiated in two main spheres: education and the workforce. The chapters come from various geographic, socio-economic, and cultural backgrounds, providing a wide range of areas where gender inequalities and the opportunities to subvert them exist. It is important to first acknowledge and understand the ways in which gender inequalities permeate society in order to create opportunities to negotiate or challenge them.

Gender and Education

After families, educational institutions play one of the most significant roles in shaping one's identity. Educational institutions are the places where students learn to negotiate their lives as 'boys' and 'girls.' It is another domain where the social norms and stereotypes with respect to gender are maintained, produced, reproduced, and challenged. Gender differences are significant even before individuals can enter them, i.e., with reference to the access to these places: who has access to educational institutions, and what kind of institutions are open to individuals of different genders? Gender differences also come in the choice of subjects/discipline, behavioral expectations, distribution of chores and activities, role assignment, and expectations with respect to academic performance among various other issues.

Gender and education are closely intertwined, as gender can significantly impact access to and experiences within educational systems. Historically, there have been gender-based barriers to education, with girls and women often facing systemic discrimination, social and cultural norms, and economic constraints that limit their educational opportunities.

Over the past few decades, progress has been made in terms of gender equity in education, but significant disparities still exist in many parts of the world. In some regions, girls are still less likely than boys to attend school, and women are less likely to pursue higher education or enter certain fields, such as science and technology.

Gender also plays a role in how individuals experience education. Research has shown that girls and boys may have different learning styles and preferences, and may face different challenges and biases from teachers and peers. Additionally, gender-based stereotypes and expectations can impact academic achievement, with girls and women often facing lower expectations and more limited opportunities for leadership and advancement.

Overall, addressing gender disparities in education requires a multifaceted approach that involves addressing social and cultural norms, promoting equal access to educational opportunities, and ensuring that educational institutions are supportive and inclusive of all genders.

Gender and Workforce

In the context of the workforce, gender has historically played a significant role in shaping individuals' career opportunities and trajectories. Women, in particular, have faced significant barriers to entry and advancement in many fields, including gender bias, stereotypes, and discrimination. However, in recent years, there have been significant efforts to promote gender equality in the workplace through initiatives such as diversity and inclusion programs, equal pay legislation, and the advancement of women in leadership positions. The patriarchal norms for heterosexual men and women in the family can create challenges in the workplace for women and other gender minorities as well. There are various dominant factors such as s Leadership styles, Gender Bias, Work-Life balance, Communication Style, and emotional expression that play a major role in making these norms socially acceptable and normal. Leadership styles can be a major challenge. Men who are accustomed to leading and making decisions in their families may also exhibit similar behaviors in the workplace. This can manifest as a tendency to be more assertive, dominant, and directive in their leadership style. Gender bias is equally responsible for workplace discrimination. Men who subscribe to traditional patriarchal norms may hold conscious or unconscious biases against women, which can affect their behavior and decision-making in the workplace. This can manifest as discrimination in hiring, promotion, and pay, as well as micro-aggressions and hostile behavior towards women in the workplace.

The concept of work-life balance as constructed by society creates unrealistic expectations for women in the workplace. Historically, the concept of work-life balance has been defined in terms of the needs and expectations of male workers, as they have been the primary breadwinners in many societies. However, as gender roles have evolved, so too understands the work-life balance for both men and women. One of the key differences between the concept of work-life balance for men and women is the role of caregiving. Women have traditionally been responsible for taking care of children, elderly relatives, and other family members. This has led to a greater need for flexibility in their work schedules to accommodate their caregiving responsibilities.

On the other hand, men have traditionally been expected to focus primarily on their careers and have not faced the same pressure to balance their work and family lives. However, as more men take on caregiving responsibilities, the concept of work-life balance for men is evolving as well. Men who prioritize their role as the breadwinner and head of the household are neither expected nor are likely to take on caregiving responsibilities or seek flexible work arrangements. This can perpetuate the idea that caregiving is a woman's responsibility and limit women's opportunities for advancement in the workplace. Another difference is related to societal expectations and gender stereotypes. Women are often expected to prioritize their family and personal lives over their careers, while men are expected to prioritize their careers over their personal lives. These expectations can influence how men and women perceive and manage their work-life balance. In conclusion, while the concept of work-life balance is important for both men and women, the differences in societal expectations and caregiving responsibilities can impact how the concept is understood and managed by each gender. Communication styles can cause barriers to inclusion. Men who are socialized to be emotionally stoic and suppress vulnerability may have difficulty expressing emotions and building strong relationships with colleagues, particularly with women and members of other marginalized groups. The concept of emotional expression can be a challenge for both men and women in the workplace, but the specific challenges they face may differ. For men, there can be a societal expectation to display a limited range of emotions, such as anger or confidence, while suppressing other emotions like sadness or vulnerability. This can lead to difficulties in expressing themselves fully in the workplace, which can impact their ability to build relationships, collaborate with others, and manage stress.

On the other hand, women can face a double standard when it comes to emotional expression. They may be penalized for being too emotional or perceived as weak, while also facing pressure to be warm and nurturing in their interactions with colleagues. This can lead to a narrow range of acceptable emotional expressions for women in the workplace, and they may need to carefully navigate their emotions to avoid negative stereotypes or backlash. Overall, the challenge of emotional expression in the workplace can impact both men and women, and it is important for organizations to foster an inclusive culture that values emotional intelligence and recognizes the diverse ways individuals express themselves. This can limit their ability to work effectively in diverse teams and create a more inclusive workplace culture. The socially constructed perceptions of competence give an added advantage to one specific gender. Men who are socialized to equate masculinity with competence and authority may be more likely to be perceived as competent and authoritative in the workplace, even if their actual performance does not warrant it. This can perpetuate gender-based stereotypes and limit opportunities for women and other marginalized groups to advance in their careers.

It is important to continue to examine and address issues related to gender and the workforce to ensure that everyone has equal opportunities to succeed and contribute to society. There are several strategies that can be employed to subvert gender issues in the workforce. Like promoting gender diversity. Employers can promote gender diversity in the workplace by actively recruiting and hiring women, as well as individuals from other underrepresented groups. This can be achieved through targeted outreach efforts, diversity and inclusion programs, and training for hiring managers to recognize and overcome unconscious biases. Ensuring pay equity between men and women is a critical step in addressing gender issues in the workforce. Paternity leaves should be increased for the fathers. Paternity leave helps to promote gender equality by acknowledging that parenting responsibilities should be shared between both parents. When fathers are given the opportunity to take time off work to care for their children, it helps to break down traditional gender roles and encourages more men to take an active role in child-rearing. Offering more paternity leave to fathers is not only good for families, but it can also have positive impacts on workplace productivity, employee retention, and gender equality. Employers can conduct regular pay audits to identify and address any disparities, as well as establish transparent pay scales and performance metrics to ensure fair compensation. Offering flexible work arrangements, such as work from home, job sharing, and flexible schedules, can help support employees in balancing work and family responsibilities, which can be particularly important for women. These arrangements can also increase productivity, engagement, growth, and retention. Employers can provide training and education to help employees recognize and overcome unconscious biases and promote a culture of respect and inclusivity. This can include workshops, seminars, and online training programs focused on diversity, equity, and inclusion. Mentorship and sponsorship: Providing mentorship and sponsorship opportunities for women can help support their career development and advancement. This can include formal mentorship programs, as well as encouraging senior leaders to advocate for and promote women in leadership positions.

By implementing these strategies, organizations can help subvert gender issues in the workforce and create a more equitable and inclusive workplace for all employees but it would be incomplete without positive initiatives and acceptance on the part of the families, policies, and education system. The second section of the book is an attempt to bring to the surface the issues and challenges being faced globally, in the work culture, when Gender becomes the limiting factor. We have tried to share a comprehensive view of the issue as the chapters bring forth the picture from developing as well as developed nations. These nations, although diverse geographically, demographically, politically, and also economically yet social inequalities with specific reference to Gender, is a universal evil and need to be addressed with utmost urgency.

Through this book, we hope to provide a comprehensive and nuanced understanding of gender as a social reality and inspire readers to act toward a more just and equal society. Through a range of case studies and theoretical perspectives, we aim to provide readers with a deeper understanding of the complex and dynamic nature of gender inequality and how it can be subverted and transformed. We also explore the role that individuals, communities, and institutions can play in challenging and dismantling gender inequality and promoting social justice and equality for all.

CHAPTER 1

GENDER BIAS, INTERNALIZATION, AND REINFORCEMENT IN CLASSROOM DISCOURSE: A CASE STUDY OF COMMUNICATIVE ENGLISH CLASSROOMS IN VIETNAM

NHUNG HONG THI NGUYEN[1] and TRAM NGOC NGO[2]

[1]*QA Higer Education, QA Limited company, The United Kingdom*

[2]*Foreign Language Department, Vietnam Maritime University, Vietnam*

ABSTRACT

Gendered bias and internalization play a crucial role in the way classroom discourse is constructed and contribute to the reproduction of gendered expectations and inequalities. This chapter investigates the processes in which gendered expectations and bias are reproduced and reinforced in the discourse of communicative English classrooms in Vietnam. Conceptualizing gender from a constructionist perspective, where gender is perceived as performativity, the chapter deploys a sociocultural linguistic approach to explore the role of gender in identity construction and negotiation between interlocutors (both teachers and students). The findings show that despite the classroom contexts, where goals are well-defined and pedagogically influenced, the speakers share the same gendered internalization and mutually construct the expected gendered values in Vietnam. It is also found that the construction and reinforcement of gendered bias and stereotypes are negotiated through some discursive strategies associated with Vietnamese masculinity and femininity. The

Subverting Social Inequalities: Gender as a Social Reality.
Akanksha Srivastava, Disha Maheshwari, Chitra Krishnan (Eds.)

chapter echoes the argument from previous linguistic and gender studies highlighting that workplaces (classrooms, for this case study) are sites for not only the construction of professional identities but also gender positioning and identity.

1.1 INTRODUCTION

The issue of gender inequality in Vietnamese education has been one of the most robustly debated research areas of recent years following the national attempt to promote gender equality throughout the country (UN Women, 2021). To contribute to this effort, this chapter explores and sheds light on a relatively under-researched site (gender and Vietnamese classroom discourse) as a classroom is considered a place where social ideologies and many hidden messages are formed, reinforced, and bequeathed. Employing Butcholtz & Hall's (2005) sociocultural linguistic approach, this chapter argues that gender plays a significant role in the construction of Vietnamese teachers' professional identities in their classroom interaction. The chapter firstly outlines critical theoretical foundations, such as normative gender ideologies in Vietnam and issues around gender and classroom discourse, followed by the advantages of a sociolinguistic approach framework. We also offer analyzes of several classroom excerpts which inform our findings before ending with a brief discussion of implications and some recommendations for future research.

1.1.1 VIETNAM AND GENDER IDEOLOGY

Confucianism has had a heavy and long-standing impact on gender practices in Vietnamese culture. It sets standards for men and women, leading to women suffering from great unfairness and discontent (Nguyen, 2014; Truong, 2016). Vietnamese women have a long history of being underestimated physically and intellectually under the heavy influence of Confucianist ideals of 'men superior, women inferior' (Vu & Pham, 2021). This mindset has been conveyed through many old sayings and proverbs; for example, 'men have broad shoulders/women have weak legs and arms' (đàn ông sức dài vai rộng/đàn bà chân yếu tay mềm), or 'A blessed family is one where the son outperforms his father' (con hơn cha là nhà có phúc). In the second saying, only the sons and the father are mentioned; the performance of females in a family, while it could be excellent, is not taken into consideration. Such undervaluation is also found in Drummond and Rydstrøm's (2004) work, where they indicated that in the past, Vietnamese women were mainly illiterate and stayed at home while men had access to education, resulting in male dominance in socio-political and economic affairs; and that of Vu and Pham (2021) stating that "...women's life accomplishments are judged by their marriage. Men occupy public space while women's 'sphere' remains the home."

It is the misconception of women's abilities that leads to the undermining of women's position in many aspects of life, especially in their own family (Vu & Pham, 2021; Institute of Linguistics Vietnam, 2022). In a typical Vietnamese nuclear family, the husband comes before the wife (as in the saying 'husband and wife are like cuckoos/husband goes first, wife follows' (vợ chồng như đôi chim cu/chồng thì đi trước, vợ gật gù theo sau)) and the husband should be the person who makes decisions on almost every issue (Nguyen, Nguyen, & Do, 2021). This deeply rooted mistaken belief that a woman is less competent than a man also casts its shadow on unmarried women. Vietnamese folklore has this famous saying "trâu đi tìm cọc, chứ cọc không đi tìm trâu" (it is the buffalo who looks for the stake, not the vice versa), indicating that females (the stakes) should passively stay and wait for males (the buffaloes) to choose them as wives or girlfriends. A woman who does the opposite will be perceived as violating the 'Hạnh' virtue – one of the four crucial social standards for Vietnamese women explained below.

Apart from attaching such an inferior social position to females, Confucianism imprints obligations as well as expectations that women have to follow, otherwise they will be considered a failure or an embarrassment to the family (Mjåland, 2015). The Three Obediences and Four Virtues (Tam tòng, Tứ đức) are among the most deeply embedded sets of moral principles and social codes that have put constraints on Vietnamese women's leeway since the feudalism period. Within the three Obediences (tam tòng), women are supposed to act with unquestioning obedience in regards to their fathers before marriage, their husbands when married and to their oldest sons when their husbands die (Drummond & Rydstrøm, 2004). The four virtues (tứ đức) include Công (labor and contribution), Dung (appearance & manners), Ngôn (speech), Hạnh (conduct and inner beauty). Each of the four elements describes a standard that a Vietnamese woman needs to train herself upon, like life targets from birth (Figure 1.1).

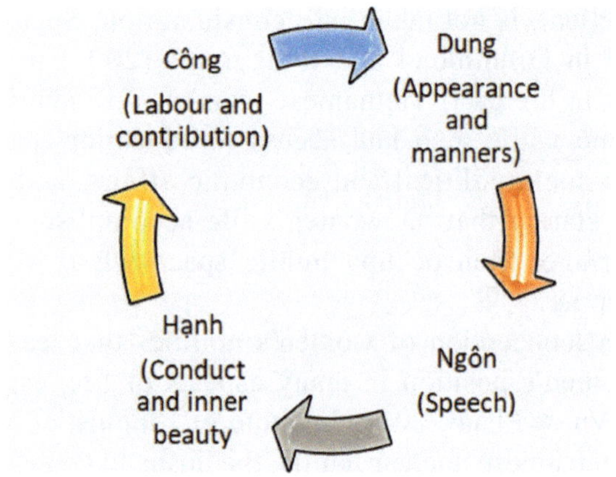

FIGURE 1.1 The four virtues of Vietnamese women.

Firstly, 'Công' covers both housework and work outside the home, though it is often misunderstood as referring only to the former. In fact, the term originally promoted the idea that women should focus on "domestic roles involving housework, care of children, and deference and support for their husband's family" (Jiang, 2009, p. 234). However, in modern society, where the job market has become more open to females, 'Công' gets a broader denotation, putting more responsibilities on women's shoulders, inferring that women have to "giỏi việc nước, đảm việc nhà" (excel at national affairs and duteous at housework) simultaneously. The second virtue, 'Dung,' focuses on a woman's graceful appearance and posture. While the former reckons her appearance to be "humble, decent, and modest" (Drummond & Rydstrøm, 2004), the latter requires her to have decent behaviors, for example "đi đứng khép chân, ngồi phải kín đáo" (walk and sit elegantly). As for the third virtue 'Ngôn,' a woman is educated to be a soft speaker, and her speech should reflect her goodwill and obedience. There are many old sayings that emphasize the importance of 'Dung' and 'Ngôn,' for example, "một khen đi đứng nhẹ nhàng/ hai khen ăn nói dịu dàng dễ nghe" (one compliments on walking softly/ two compliments on speaking softly and pleasantly).

Lastly, the virtue 'Hạnh' acts as a strict code of conduct aiming not only at a woman's morality but also at her purity. On the one hand, it cultivates a model of a highly righteous woman with 'đức hạnh,' meaning kindness, tolerance, and a beautiful soul (Baoninhthuan, 2015). On the other hand, 'Hạnh' implies 'tiết hạnh,' requiring girls to preserve their purity until marriage and be loyal to their husband once wed, as in the saying "đã cho vào bậc bố kinh/ đạo tòng phu lấy chữ trinh làm đầu" (as stated in the sutra/

a woman's virginity is of foremost importance). This second connotation of 'Hạnh' should be well practiced and can be observed through Vietnamese women's 'Ngôn,' where talking about sexual matters and sex education for young girls is largely avoided and ignored by their mothers (who are perceived as being better communicators than fathers on the subject) (Bui, 2020), or their 'Dung' when they are expected to dress "kín cổng cao tường" (high walls with a closed gate, or dressing discreetly) in public places.

This section has extensively discussed the normative gendered expectations in Vietnam, including the cultural and ethnographic backdrop essential to the exploration of how gender stereotypes and bias can influence the way Vietnamese people talk and behave. Additionally, the analysis in this chapter draws on previous findings regarding normative features of masculinity and femininity speech styles, such as directness, competitiveness, and goal-orientation being associated with males while females are associated with indirectness, collaboration, and person-orientation (Holmes & Schnurr, 2006; Schnurr, 2013; Schnurr & Holmes, 2009). By examining gender discourse in classrooms from various perspectives, we aim to approach and explore the dynamic construction and manifestation of gender in this context.

1.2 GENDER AS A SOCIAL CONSTRUCT AND DOING GENDER THEORY

The conceptualization of gender in this chapter follows poststructuralist views where gender is not seen as being strictly biological but as a socially constructed phenomenon (Butler, 1988; McDowell, 2018). Under this line of literature, gender is considered to be an activity (West & Zimmerman, 1987), a performance (Butler, 1988), whereby performing or conforming to certain stereotypical gendered associations of masculinity or femininity, speakers establish the impression of being a man or a woman. Since these gender associations of masculinity and femininity are diverse and perceived differently throughout various contexts, this chapter echoes the requirement to consider them in plural form rather than singular form (henceforth masculinities and femininities) (Schnurr, 2013).

Conceptualizing gender as performativity and as something we do rather than we innately possess offers more dynamic ways for examining how gender is performed and negotiated through language compared to essentialist views of the concept. Earlier studies in language and gender under essentialism aim to elucidate how differently men and women speak, linking this to their fundamental biological sex differences. In other words, this body of research resides in sustaining the division between men and women due to their biological differences and hence their distinctive use of language. Gender is therefore considered to be something deterministic, implying a "pre-existing discourse" to gender (Nguyen, 2017, p. 152). Studies under the essentialism approach to gender and language have been challenged due to their simple mapping of linguistic items to their functions and the amplification of differences while overlooking similarities in language use between men and women (Nguyen, 2017).

Theorizing gender as performativity contests the deterministic nature assigned to it in essentialism, emphasizing the dynamic process of establishing and negotiating gender positions in talk. Rather than seeing gender as something being predetermined and fixed prior to a dialog, gender is realized as a discursive and constant process of constructing and negotiating between participants in an interaction. In other words, during the unfolding of a conversation, interlocutors constantly draw on a range of discursive linguistic strategies to construct their identities and negotiate the talk's pragmatic functions, and such linguistic choices also index their gender positioning (Holmes & Schnurr, 2006; Schnurr & Holmes, 2009). This approach accentuates the fact that speakers can draw on various linguistic repertoires associated with femininities, masculinities, or both to achieve their pragmatic purposes, not being restricted to a certain set of linguistic or social expectations prescribed by their sexes.

1.3 GENDER DISCOURSE IN VIETNAM EDUCATION AND CLASSROOM TALK

As part of an ever-increasing research body of pedagogy and equality in classrooms, research has expanded regarding questions of the best pedagogical practices to how teaching is essentially based on understanding and enacting social phenomena (such as gender); in other words, questioning how teaching practices are governed around teachers' and students' understanding of their world (their socio-political contexts, culture, and norms) (Blaise, 2012; Vu & Pham, 2020; Vu & Pham, 2021). For example, Vu & Pham (2020, 2021); Ngo (2007); and Brundrett & Thuy (2018) have highlighted how Confucian gender norms and bias still permeate textbooks for primary and high schools in Vietnam, regardless of some positive signs for gender equality. Researchers also discovered that staff in managerial positions and teachers whose perceptions and attitudes could be transferred to lesson planning, classroom activities, and curriculum are subjected to both conscious and unconscious bias despite their united support for the government commitment to gender equality in education (Vu & Pham, 2020, 2021; Brundrett & Mai, 2017). This chapter resonates with such a mainstream viewpoint; however, it looks into classroom discourse and in-class interaction to see how embedded gender bias and expectations can be reinforced and penetrate classroom talk.

Research on gender and classroom discourse has approached this interconnection from various angles to draw practical pedagogical implications for enhanced learning outcomes. From examining the role of gender in features of class discourse between male and female teachers (Monsefi & Hadidi, 2015), to male and female students' linguistic behaviors (Blaise, 2012), to the interactional treatment teachers choose for students of different sexes, the findings generated in this body of literature have provided an ample collection of features of gendered discourse in the classroom. For example, previous studies investigating the gender and classroom discourse from students' perspectives have observed that male/boy students tend to be given noticeable attention and therefore can contribute significantly more in the classroom interaction than their female/girl counterparts (Nielsen & Davies, 1997). With regards to male/female teachers, previous studies have also highlighted the congruency between normative gendered conversational styles and teachers' linguistic behaviors in the classroom. Specifically, while male teachers' classroom communication tends to demonstrate authorization with greater power exertion where short display questions are made, female teachers' classroom interactional styles move towards a nurturing and supportive environment where students' peer cooperation is promoted and referential questions are regularly used (Dhillon & Kaur, 2021).

1.4 HUMOR AND GENDER IDENTITIES

As one of the strategies regularly deployed in many professional and institutional contexts, humor is essentially influenced and constructed by gender stereotypes (Schnurr & Omar, 2021). For humor to work (receiving or successfully bringing off humor), speakers need to understand the existence of many common grounds relating to controversial or sensitive topics, such as race, sex, politics, and so forth (Schnurr, 2010). Gender, regularly in the form of gender stereotypes or bias, can therefore prevail when speakers construct or participate in humor in talk.

Previous studies have pointed out different types of humor and how women and men tend to differ with regards to their humor variation. Teasing humor, in particular, has been found to be one of the remarkable linguistic strategies due to its ambiguity (Haugh, 2017). Since being interpreted broadly on a continuum, teasing humor can be perceived as "playful or done in jest [or] it can easily slide into being characterized as aggressive" (Haugh, 2017, p. 204). Due to this dynamic nature of teasing humor, it has been a valuable linguistic resource for leaders and tends to be used to exert social control, deliver criticism, and establish solidarity (Schnurr & Holmes, 2009; Schnurr & Omar, 2021). As a less challenging and potentially face-threatening type of humor, self-denigrating humor is considered an affiliation-building type and tends to be deployed largely by women (Hay, 1995). Studies have shown that women tend to deploy self-denigrating humor to display their identities as approachable and friendly people, therefore enhancing the rapport between speakers in talk, whereas men lean towards more challenging types of humor as discussed previously (Schnurr & Holmes, 2009; Schnurr & Omar, 2021).

1.5 DATA COLLECTION AND ANALYTICAL APPROACH

Based on social constructivism, this current chapter uses qualitative methodology to investigate the process when gender bias and internalization contribute to Vietnamese teachers' identity construction and negotiation with their students. The data was collected from two widely-known and highly-regarded English centers in Haiphong, Vietnam, namely ABC and English for all (these names have been changed for confidentiality purposes). These two institutions were chosen for their reputations and their highly interactive communicative English courses for undergraduate students, which meet the requirements of studying classroom discourse in this chapter. A group of four Vietnamese teachers (four females and one male) aged 25 to 30, each having a minimum of three years teaching experience, were selected as participants as this specific age group (with a certain level of experience in the field) is more willing to employ innovative teaching methods and is able to reflect well on their pedagogy. A total of 48 hours of classroom interaction were recorded and transcribed, through the excerpts of which the enactment of gender and identity construction of these case studies are explored and analyzed in detail.

This chapter relies on Conversation Analysis (CA) conventions to produce transcripts through which close attention to interaction features was examined. It is, however, noted that the analysis does not follow CA analytical framework, as closely examining micro elements in interaction, such as turn-taking and sequence management, is not the focus in this chapter. Rather, we investigate the process of gender identity negotiation where many cultural and gender social norms are enacted, as well as how such interactions between interlocutors demonstrate gender bias, internalization, reinforcement, and contestation within the classroom context. To achieve such aims, this chapter uses a sociocultural linguistic approach (Bucholtz & Hall, 2005) which will be elucidated below.

Bucholtz & Hall's (2005) sociocultural linguistic approach to identity construction offers a holistic analytical framework in which the understanding of identity construction can be examined through five broad principles, namely emergence, positionality, indexicality, relationality, and partialness. The advantages of this framework lie in its emphasis on the multifaceted characteristic of identity construction, where many complex layers of one's identities are claimed to be simultaneously established and constructed in talk (positionality principle). These layers involve macro/local categories, speakers' specific cultural and ethnographic positions, and the relevance stances indexed due to contingent roles and positionings taken/abandoned in talk. Furthermore, the discursive nature of identities is strongly highlighted, owing to the relevance of different identities that emerge in an unfolding conversation. Speakers' identities, therefore, are not fixed and remain unchanged from the beginning till the end of a conversation, but are indeed partial since they are constantly shifting and reconfigured at different moments in an interaction.

Bucholtz & Hall's (2005) sociocultural linguistic approach fits nicely with the research aims of this chapter, as it allows a micro analysis of identity construction in the interaction while at the same time acknowledging the macro social and cultural contexts in which the talk occurs. Moreover, through its five broad principles, the dynamics and multifaceted nature of identity construction can be examined (the interrelationship between speakers' professional, situated, and gender identities). Additionally, during our analysis, three main questions are used to detect the linguistic strategies the participants deployed and the role gender plays in these classroom extracts:

1. What kinds of verbal acts are the interlocutors aiming to perform? (Discussing, giving instructions, evaluating tasks)
2. How are such verbal acts performed? (How are instructional questions formed? Or how is feedback delivered?)
3. By performing these kinds of verbal acts in particular ways, what situated and social identities are at play, and what are their connections with gender norms and order in the Vietnamese context?

1.6 DATA ANALYSIS

The construction of good English language teacher identities and the enactment of Vietnamese femininity.

The extracts presented in this section demonstrate how Vietnamese femininities and gender expectations are intricately intertwined and become relevant in various classroom activities. Situated within common pedagogical teaching activities, such as giving follow-up feedback, facilitating students' dialogue, and participating in open discussions with students, it has been observed that gender norms and gender order play a significant role in helping the teachers construct their professional as well as gender identities. Specifically, it has been found that many layers of Vietnamese femininity (the four virtues discussed in the previous section) are enacted to portray these teachers as good English teachers, and such representation has indexed their gender positioning as Vietnamese women. Extract 1.6.1 captures the discussion between Jane and her whole class on the advantages of being a teacher. The extract illustrates how Jane portrays herself as an approachable teacher and constructs her gender identity being aligned with expected Vietnamese femininity by using a personal narrative in a whole-class discussion.

EXTRACT 1.6.1 Open Discussion and the Connection with Vietnamese Femininity Virtue "Công" (Jane's lesson 27/03)

90 91 92	T	What I like most about my job is that I can feel young when I teach (.) young people because it's a lot of fun and secondly, I love my job because I have a very flexible time.
93	Ss	Flexible (.) flexible↑
94	D	Thời gian linh hoạt flexible
94		Flexible timing flexible
95 96	T	Flexible time it means that if I don't have any class at school (.) I can stay (.) at home and prepare the meal or um do some housework
97	D	Yes
98 99	T	And three I: I only have (0.5) classes at my university (.) in the morning (.) in the morning so I can spend all the afternoon at home

T: Teacher; D: Diya; L: Leen; Ss: other students.

In her sharing at the beginning of the extract, among many observations, Jane chooses to immediately emphasize that '[I] feel young when I teach young people' (line 90 and 91). Her involvement with the students (young people) is part of the rewards she gets from teaching and gives the students a sense of being valued. A teacher interacting with her students in such a manner helps the individuals in the classroom feel better as a person, which supports the implication from previous studies that female conversational speech styles often revolve around person-orientation (Schnurr, 2012). Moreover, deploying such an affective statement helps Jane minimize the power relation between teacher and students. In other words, it narrows down the distance and at the same time strengthens the close rapport between them.

As the conversation unfolds, the teacher shifts her personal identities as someone is sharing about her job to her professional identity as she explains the phrase 'flexible time' in line 95 and 96, once again switching back to her personal identity when she adds the third reason in line 98 and 99. It is noticeable how she spends her off work time cultivating a typical image of a Vietnamese wife and mother whose value is determined by a set of social expectations. Examining this extract, the effect of 'Công,' one of the four virtues, is evident. Instead of choosing other leisure activities, she chooses to "stay at home" and take care of the house and her family ("prepare the meal" and "do housework"). By aligning closely to the virtue 'Công' which pictures a woman who can fulfill responsibilities both in and outside the home, it can be clearly seen that the teacher's normative, unmarked gender identities of being a Vietnamese woman are explicitly constructed. The following extract illustrates similar person-orientational aspects of common female speech styles during a teacher-student dialogical sequence.

Extract 1.6.2 demonstrates how teacher Jane provides feedback to her student, Mae. The extract occurs after Mae's presentation on the topic of 'your daily routine.' What is particularly interesting about this extract is the way the teacher constructs and conveys the feedback to the student.

EXTRACT 1.6.2 Giving Feedback to the Students and the Connection with Vietnamese Femininity Virtue "Ngôn" (Jane's Lesson 14/03)

T →	I must say that it's a very nice speech very nice talk about um daily routine
→	and um (.) I love it because you said that you loved your job and I also love
→	my job so I love someone who loves the job ((smiley tone))
M	Hihi ((Mae giggles))
T	Understand? Just kidding however, I think there are some problems with
	your grammar like I um to check the email you should say to check email
	and some problems with the verb tenses and I say that again that you need to
	pay attention to your final sounds like because /bɪˈkɒz/ uhu ok but it is

20	M	Best là tốt I think it is best
20		Best is good I think it is best
21	T	You did a good job I think that I need to send you some more grammar
22	M →	exercises for you to bring [home] for your self-study
23		[Yeah]
24	M →	Yeah, thank you teacher

T: Teacher; M: Mae.

Giving feedback is potentially a face-threatening act, as through this activity, the student's face can be made vulnerable depending on certain levels of criticism or suggestions to improve performance from the teachers (Hadden & Frisby, 2019). Teacher Jane in this extract had structured her feedback in such a way that shows great consideration for the student's face while, at the same time, getting her constructive comments across. In particular, the teacher's main feedback content is captured from lines 15 to 19 where details for improvement are made explicit to the student, including grammar, verb tenses, and final sounds. However, this turn (from line 15–19) is not located immediately after the completion of the student's presentation, only appearing after the teacher's compliment from lines 10 to 13. It is apparent that the teacher has conveyed the feedback quite indirectly by providing the compliment, "It's a very nice speech, very nice talk." Moreover, the repetition of the positive adjective "nice" shows how the teacher positively orients to the student's performance and hence enhances the student's face as someone who performs well in the class.

The teacher's indirectness strategy comprises a compliment and the use of jocular humor during her elaboration on the strength of the student's speech. From lines 11 to 13, the teacher overtly mentions the connection between the student and herself, stating "you said that you loved your job and I also love my job, so I love someone who loves the job." By projecting alignment and similarity (Bucholtz & Hall's, 2005) adequation and distinction relation, relationality principle), the teacher's compliment and extended turn not only constitute an endorsement of the student's face but also downplay the status differences between Jane and the student. Through such positioning and approach, Jane gives an impression of herself as someone who is friendly, close, and shares things in common with the student. It is also noted that, by coupling a strong sentimental statement with a smiley tone (line 13), the teacher manages this feedback sequence just enough to retain her professional face while getting her social face across at the same time. In other words, while her portrayed identities, which convey someone who is friendly, close, and has things in common with the student, are mobilized, her expertise and professional face are not threatened or damaged.

Drawing from this extract, the teacher's indirectness (to mitigate face threats) and rapport-oriented approach to feedback have portrayed Jane as a good English teacher and a friendly and approachable person to students, while also evoking her gender positioning. Being indirect and soft-spoken has been indicated (Session 1.1.1) as one of the four important virtues in Vietnamese femininity, and therefore by aligning with such a way of conduct, Jane has simultaneously constructed and reinforced her unmarked gender identities as an elegant and well-mannered Vietnamese woman. The coming two extracts (1.6.3 and 1.6.4) demonstrate how the virtue "Hạnh" and normative ideas of gendered behaviors emerge as relevant aspects in the classroom activity.

Extract 1.6.3 takes place during a presentation session in Joy's class. In this task, the whole class is divided into smaller groups, with each being appointed a specific situation. The students are given 15 minutes of allotted time to discuss and are invited to act out their situation once the time finishes. Mya and Jay in Extract 1.6.3 are acting out their situation of "a couple's first-time dating."

EXTRACT 1.6.3 Acting out the Given Situation and the Connection with Vietnamese Femininity Virtue "Hạnh" (Conduct) (Joy's Lesson 24/03)

40	M	Tut tut tut ((mimicking telephone calling))
41		(1.0)
42	J	Hello Mya
43	M	Hello Jay
44	J	How are you today?
45	M	Uhm I am fine thank you (.)
46	J	Uhm I am fine ah I am:
47	T →	I miss you ((smiley tone))
48	J	>I miss you<
49	T+Ss	Hahaha
50	J	Do you have free time tonight?
51	M	Oh yes, I am free tonight
52	J	I uhm can I invite you or ah can I invite you have dinner this-tonight
53	M	Yes, ok see you tonight
54	J	Yes, bye bye
55	M	Bye bye

T: Teacher, M: Mya; J: Jay; Ss: other students.

What is of significance in this extract is the way Joy intervenes and her use of teacher-initiated humor through students holding the floor. Joy's joke is constructed with a rather strong affective turn (line 47), "I miss you" with a smiley tone, introduced swiftly in between Mya and Jay's ongoing play sequence from line 40–46. Notably, the teacher's turn is essentially constructed to complete Jay's turn in line 46 when Jay seems slightly confused, through his stretching sound "I am." From professional identity construction viewpoints, by using humor to facilitate and support the students' work, Joy's intervening indexes a stance of professionalism, portraying her as a responsive and supportive teacher. However, this humorous affective turn has not only aided pragmatic functions (supporting and facilitating learning) but also infers prominent multi-layered gendered implications.

Firstly, the teacher's timely and rather strong affective utterance to join in with Jay (a male student) reflects relevant Vietnamese norms regarding typical love relationships and promotes expected gendered behaviors towards men and women. As demonstrated previously, it is widely accepted in Vietnamese society that men should "make the first move," as described in the famous proverb, "Trâu đi tìm cọc, chứ cọc không đi tìm trâu" (It is the buffalo (men) who should look for the stake (women), not the vice versa). Women who do not conform to this will be considered ill-mannered and consequently fail to fulfill their Vietnamese virtue, "Hạnh" (conduct and inner beauty). The teacher's turn here therefore does not simply carry its pragmatic function but also can be interpreted as the reinforcement of such gendered beliefs and norms assimilated in Vietnam. Structuring her turn promptly with such an affective stance indexes Jay's gender positioning as someone who complies with Vietnamese stereotypical gendered behaviors.

Furthermore, the internalization of these gender stereotypes toward Vietnamese males and females' accepted behaviors in romantic relationships is jointly constructed by all the speakers in this extract, not only the teacher. Jay's immediate adoption of Joy's suggestion shows his alignment with the teacher along with his prompt embrace of the expected gendered role of being a man in a romantic relationship. Moreover, it is worth noting that the play was discussed and planned between Mae and Jay prior to this extract. The way the entire play sequence is structured, such as making Jay the caller and Mae the recipient, indicates a shared common understanding between both students about what constitutes a typical, common first date and the gender performance/hierarchy implied by such perceptions. The gender bias and expectation that Vietnamese men should take the lead in love and relationships (making the phone call (line 42), openly sharing their feelings (line 48), and inviting the ladies to dinners (line 52) are clearly demonstrated and reinforced in this extract. In other words, this extract has shown how intricately gender internalization and bias become relevant in the classroom conversation and how multi-layered identities are shaped through such orientations. Not only do the participants construct their professional identities as teachers and students in this institutional context, but their gender identities are also formed by fulfilling the stereotypical roles expected of Vietnamese masculinity and femininity.

The involvement of gender bias toward Vietnamese men and women's behaviors is similarly observed in Extract 1.6.4. This extract takes place during the initial stage of Hope's lesson where homework checking is typically carried out. The insertion of the teacher's code-switched, jocular turn in between the teacher and Bay's dialog around Bay's missing her homework demonstrates the process of an identity shift and the construction of gender identities.

EXTRACT 1.6.4 Homework Checking and the Connection with Vietnamese Femininity Virtue "Hạnh" (Conduct and Inner Beauty) (Hope's Lesson 27/04)

1	T	Can I see your reading writing Ok Bay what's wrong?
2	B	Em làm rồi nhưng mà em để ở nhà anh King mất rồi I have done it but I have left it at King's house
3	T	Ôi ôi em lại để nhà King à (.) em làm gì ở nhà King mà để quên ở đấy? ((Teasing tone)) Oh, oh you have left it in King's house (.) what did you do in King's house that made you forget your homework there? ((Teasing tone))
4	Ss	Ha ha ha
5 6	T	So can you call him can you call him so he can um he can bring your homework is he coming?

T: Teacher; B: Bay; Ss: other students.

In this extract, the noticeable linguistic behaviors of switching code from English to Vietnamese and the deployment of teasing humor index certain affective stances and construct Hope's multiple identities. When being asked to present her written homework, Bay, in line 2, has explained the reason for missing her homework, stating that, although she has completed it, she has unfortunately left it in one of her male friends' house, King. Bay's reasoning is shortly followed by Hope's response using a code-switched, teasing-toned question (line 3). Drawing from Hope's turn, it can be interpreted that what is particularly noticeable for Hope is the fact that a female and male student (Bay and King) have visited each other for studying, which is considered rather uncommon behavior. The teacher's turn here is structured in two parts. While the first part expresses the teacher's surprise at Bay's explanation for her missing homework, the second part jokingly questions King and Bay's activities that led to Bay's current classroom issue (failing to present homework as it has been left at King's place).

The teacher's surprise reactions and teasing humor mark the shift from her default professional identity (a teacher) to occupy her new interactional role of a witty, playful joke-maker. From a pedagogical perspective, choosing to respond to students' failed tasks with cheeky teasing humor can be seen as a less negative option compared to other more hostile methods (Pomerantz & Bell, 2011), for example punishment or dismissal from the class. Therefore, by choosing such linguistic behavior, Hope firstly portrays herself as a forgiving and empathic teacher who can bring innuendo and joking into play. Moreover, drawing from the positionality principle, which highlights the fact that multiple identities can simultaneously be enacted in the same interaction, it can be observed that the local dimension of Hope's gender identities is also constructed.

Enacted from Vietnamese femininity and the concept of Hạnh (conduct and inner beauty), Hope's teasing humor is indeed established on a gender ground which promotes the normative gendered behavior of maintaining distance between two unmarried opposite-sex individuals. This gendered behavior is stressed more heavily towards Vietnamese women (among four crucial feminine virtues) and requires them to maintain such a distance; otherwise, their behaviors can be regarded as inappropriate (Nguyen, 2014). By raising and questioning Bay's action within a teasing frame, the teacher has managed to implicitly deliver her pedagogical challenge from gender expectations rooted within Vietnamese femininity. This linguistic behavior not only shows her understanding of the typical, acceptable behaviors of Vietnamese women, but also, by deploying such an approach, Hope constructs her own Vietnamese woman identities.

The use of teasing humor in this extract has demonstrated how using humor can index an affective stance to construct multiple identities and, through such a process, the rapport between the teacher and the students is enhanced (indicated by the whole class's laughter in line 4). The following extract, on the other hand, illustrates other functions of teasing humor and its implications in the teacher's identity construction.

The construction of "teacher knows best" and the enactment of Vietnamese masculinity. This extract occurs after Emily's presentation of "qualities that a good friend should have" and marks the turn to a follow-up, post-presentation discussion between Jack and Emily. During this discussion, Jack challenges and asks for clarification on one of Emily's main points (Extract 1.6.5).

EXTRACT 1.6.5 Teacher-Student Discussion and the Enactment of Vietnamese Masculinity (Jack's lesson 01/03)

T	Ok very good (.) So you don't like someone (.) you don't like someone who often talks bad behind your back↑
E	Yes (0.5) true friends never did that
T →	Yeah, what about you↑ ((Smiley tone))
	((Whole class laughs))
T →	Do you sometimes talk bad behind your friends↑
E	Sometimes I um
T	You talk yeah (.) you talk bad
E	I am not a liar
T →	You are not a liar (.) So you think it is not good right↑ (.) It is not a good habit to talk bad about people
E	Just some time
T →	Just some time↑
E	Yes
T →	How many times a day↑ ((Whole class laughs)) How many times a day↑
E	The day↑
T →	How many times a day (.) One day (0.5) How long, how long do you spend↑ (1.0) How much time do you spend talking bad↑
E	One minute
T →	One minute (.) are you sure↑ One minute or one hour↑ One minute or one hour make sure one minute or one hour
E	15 minutes
T	15 minutes (.) Everyday 15 minutes (.) So from tomorrow please stop doing that (.) Spend 15 minutes learning English
E	Yeah
T	Ok↑ If you want to talk bad about someone (.) talk bad about me in English (.) but in English ((joking tone))
E	Every girl
T →	Every girl↑ No my wife doesn't
E	Are you sure↑
T	I am sure
E →	I don't think so
T	You don't think so but I know (.) Ok kidding just kidding (.) next one (.) what's about you Alice↑ You have a lot of friends↑

T: Teacher; E: Emily.

Initiating a teasing sequence with consecutive questions to reinforce the Vietnamese gender stereotype that gossiping is typically associated with Vietnamese women is the remarkable strategy deployed in this extract. The teasing sequence begins in line 390 when Jack formulates his direct, confrontational question, albeit mitigated within a teasing humor frame. This question acts as a challenging pedagogical question and simultaneously indexes an evaluative stance which portrays Jack as a person who holds a stereotypical perception about Vietnamese women. On the one hand, it is a common practice for teachers to elicit and create more English-speaking opportunities for students in the lesson's production phase (Presentation-Practice-Production) (Bui & Newton, 2021). On the other hand, Jack's question carries more than solely the pedagogical implication since, by challenging the moral claim Emily established (true friends do not talk behind each other's back), Jack also orients Emily to common stereotypical behaviors of Vietnamese women, including gossiping and being nosy. Therefore, Jack's linguistic behavior of asking the mitigated teasing question indexes not only epistemic stances of pedagogy but also gender norms and stereotypes.

The indexicality of the teacher's epistemic stances progressively gains power in the subsequent turns. Within the teasing frame established in turn 390, in the following turns, by posting consecutive questions and seeking confirmation answers from Emily (line 392, 396, 399, 401, 404, and 407), Jack gradually establishes and reconstructs the Vietnamese female stereotypical attribute of being inquisitive. The questioning sequence revolves around Emily's perception towards her admitted gossiping behaviors ("So you think it is not so good, right?"), to the frequency of such behaviors ("how many times a day, how long"), to his correctional question ("are you sure? One minute or one hour?"). It can be interpreted that such a direct and confrontational linguistic approach is derived from a predetermined, ideological gendered bias towards Vietnamese women. That is, gossiping and talking badly behind someone's back are typically Vietnamese female behaviors, and therefore, by being a female student in this class, Emily cannot be an exception. By indexing this gender epistemic stance through his linguistic certainty that results in Emily changing her answers (admitting her gossiping behavior in line 398 and correcting the duration of her behavior in line 409), Jack portrays himself as a person who knows best.

The enactment of Vietnamese masculinity is twofold here. Firstly, regardless of being mitigated slightly within the teasing frame, the humor deployed seems purposeful as it is used to ascribe a rather negative normative gendered behavior observed in Vietnamese to a female student in class. Jack's competitive and challenging sequence can potentially become a face-threatening situation for Emily and indeed was not positively received by her (her contestation in line 419). Through constructing his identity as the knower and an authoritarian, Jack simultaneously does gender by drawing from speech styles that are "indexed for power and authority and for masculinity" (Schnurr, 2013, p. 138). Secondly, the negative perception inferred through his evaluative statement (line 396 and 397) and his wife's exclusion (line 416) also distances Jack from such behavior and simultaneously orients himself to the masculine standards of Vietnamese men, such as being "goal-oriented" rather than "people-oriented." This therefore constructs his gender identity as a Vietnamese man.

1.7 DISCUSSION AND CONCLUSION

The classroom extracts taken from a classroom context in this chapter have demonstrated how gender bias and ideologies in Vietnam can materialize and manifest in classroom discourse. The ways classroom discourse is structured and the employment of various linguistic behaviors by the four Vietnamese teachers have exhibited the subtle ways in which gender can play a role in the construction of the identities of these teachers. Our findings echo previous studies that confirm and advocate the crucial role of gender identities in constituting institutional talk (Holmes & Schnurr, 2006; Schnurr, 2009, 2013; Schnurr & Holmes, 2009; Schnurr & Omar, 2021). That is, although gender identity construction is not primarily the main focus in professional workplaces, gender norms and stereotypes tend to be under the auspices of the transactional and relational purposes of workplace life (or in our cases, classroom life) and can be potentially pertinent at different points of the conversation.

In addition to providing empirical findings on the manifestation of gender in English communicative classrooms, our findings have illustrated that the teachers employ various types of humor, including teasing humor (Extracts 1.6.4 and 1.6.5), self-denigrating and jocular humor (Extracts 1.6.2 and 1.6.3), to not only construct their professional identities but also to establish gender by drawing from certain speech elements associated with normative gendered speech styles/behaviors. Specifically, teachers' use of indirectness and expressive statements for rapport building in the analysis is in line with feminine conversational styles (people-oriented tendency) found in previous studies. Additionally, what is more significant is the enactment of local and ethnographical dimensions of gender that are context-specific and relevant to Vietnam's gender ideologies. For example, the gendered expectations and biases (men must take initiatives in romantic relations and women should keep distant from males to avoid inappropriate behaviors) are discursively emerged and have been negotiated in the classroom discourse.

Our analysis puts forward not only the discursive linguistic strategies deployed by the teachers to construct multi-layered professional and gender identities, but also how gender internalization and manifestation are mutually understood and negotiated by speakers in these educational contexts. The teacher's quick, unmarked turn and the male student's swift taking up of a gender role (Extract 1.6.3) is one of the examples that demonstrates how gender understanding and internalization are consciously and subconsciously at play in classroom talk. This also reflects the processes through which gender ideologies and order are conjointly created and reinforced, as well as the tendency of classroom dialogical sequence being shaped by how teachers and students are perceived and judged through their compliance with normative gendered speech styles/behaviors. We also aim to highlight the benefits of Butcholtz & Hall's (2005) sociocultural linguistic approach. By allowing us to produce a more nuanced analysis drawing from micro elements to macro social and cultural categories, the framework has advanced our understanding of gender in classroom discourse and identity construction.

Sharing its unique sociocultural position and analytical approach, this chapter hopes to contribute to the book's overall theme with a case study of four Vietnamese teachers in their communicative English classrooms. Through our micro-analysis of classroom excerpts, our aim is to demonstrate the implicit construction of gender identities and the processes of how embedded gender bias and expectations can penetrate classroom discourse. By drawing readers' attention to the internalization and implicit reproduction of gender bias in professional educational contexts, we seek to raise teachers' and educators' awareness of these issues in regards to establishing gender equality in classrooms. We also hope that future research can foster this gender manifestation and evaluate its pedagogical implications in greater detail (Table 1.1).

TABLE 1.1 Transcriptions Conventions

Basic Conventions		**Other Conventions**	
.	Falling intonation	↑	Prominent rising intonation
,	Continuing contour	↓	Prominent falling intonation
?	Questioning intonation	> <	Quicker than surrounding talk
(2.0)	Pause of about 2 seconds		
(…)	Pause of about 1 second	→	Feature of interest. This is placed in the left-hand margin to draw attention to a feature the analyst wishes to highlight.
( )	Pause of about 0.5 second		
(.)	micropause		
[]	Overlap		
:	Sound stretching		
(( ))	Other details		
aaaa	Translation		

Source: Adapted from Richards (2006).

KEYWORDS

- **conversation analysis**
- **data analysis**
- **social constructivism**
- **Vietnam and gender ideology**

REFERENCES

Baoninhthuan. (2015). Nghĩ về "Công-Dung-Ngôn-Hạnh" ("Considering "Cong-Dung-Ngon-Hanh"). Retrieved from: https://baoninhthuan.com.vn/news/69775p0c30/nghi-ve-congdungngonhanh.htm (accessed on 19 June 2024).

Blaise, M. (2012). *Playing it Straight: Uncovering Gender Discourse in the Early Childhood Classroom*. New York: Routledge.

Brundrett, M., & Thuy, M. T. D. (2018). The challenge of ensuring gender equality in Vietnamese and English high schools. *International Journal of Comparative Education and Development, 20*(1), 2–15.

Bucholtz, M., & Hall, K. (2005). Identity and interaction: A sociocultural linguistic approach. *Discourse Studies, 7*(4–5), 585–614.

Bui, T. L. D., & Newton, J. (2021). PPP in action: Insights from primary EFL lessons in Vietnam. *Language Teaching for Young Learners, 3*(1), 93–116.

Butler, J. (1988). Performative acts and gender constitution: An essay in phenomenology and feminist theory. *Theatre Journal, 40*(4), 519–531.
Dhillon, N., & Kaur, G. (2021). Self-assessment of teachers' communication style and its impact on their communication effectiveness: A study of Indian higher educational institutions. *SAGE Open, 11*(2), 21582440211023173.
Hadden, A. A., & Frisby, B. N. (2019). Face threat mitigation in feedback: An examination of student feedback anxiety, self-efficacy, and perceived emotional support. *Communication Quarterly, 67*(1), 60–75.
Haugh, M. (2017). Teasing. In M. Attardo (Ed.), *The Routledge Handbook of Language and Humor* (pp. 204–218). Routledge.
Hay, J. (1995). *Gender and Humor: Beyond a Joke.* (MA Thesis). Victoria University of Wellington, New Zealand.
Holmes, J., & Schnurr, S. (2006). 'Doing femininity' at work: More than just relational practice. *Journal ofSociolinguistics, 10*(1), 31–51. https://doi.org/10.1111/j.1360-6441.2006.00316.x.
McDowell, J. (2018). Men's talk in women's work: Doing being a nurse. In F. Bargiela-Chiappini & S. Harris (Eds.), *The Handbook of Workplace Discourse* (pp. 361–372). Routledge.
Mjåland, J. H. (2015). *The Changing Face of Shame: Relationships, Marriage and Globalisation in Contemporary Vietnam. Based on Life Story-interviwes in Contemporary Haiphong City, Vietman.* (MA Thesis). University of Agder, Norway.
Monsefi, M., & Hadidi, Y. (2015). Male and female EFL teachers' politeness strategies in oral discourse and their effects on the learning process and teacher-student interaction. *International Journal on Studies in English Language and Literature (IJSELL), 3*(2), 1–13.
Nguyen, Q. N., Nguyen, T. M. P., & Do, T. L. H. (2021). Gender biases in resettlement processes in Vietnam: Examining women's participation and implications for impact assessment. *Impact Assessment and Project Appraisal, 39*(3), 206–217.
Nguyen, T. T. H. (2017). Language and gender studies: past and current approaches and debates. *VNU Journal of Foreign Studies, 33*(6), 150–157.
Nguyen, T. V. (2014). Confucianism "Three Obediences and Four Virtues" theory and its impacts on Vietnamese women nowadays. (Ph.D. thesis). Ho Chi Minh National Academy of Politics Hanoi. Retrieved from: https://123docz.net/document/3015236-effects-of-the-three-obediences-and-four-virtues-ethics-on-vietnamese-women-in-the-present-time.htm (accessed on 19 June 2024).
Nielsen, H. B., & Davies, B. (1997). The construction of gendered identity through classroom talk. In A. LiPuma & T. Melia (Eds.), *Oral Discourse and Education* (pp. 125–135). Ablex Publishing.
Pomerantz, A., & Bell, N. D. (2011). Humor as safe house in the foreign language classroom. *The Modern Language Journal, 95*(s1), 148–161.
Richards, K. (2006). *Language and Professional Identity: Aspects of Collaborative Interaction.* New York: Palgrave Macmillan.
Schnurr, S. (2009). Constructing leader identities through teasing at work. *Journal of Pragmatics, 41*(6), 1125–1138.
Schnurr, S. (2010). Humor. In F. Bargiela-Chiappini & A. Haugh (Eds.), *Interpersonal Pragmatics* (Vol. 6, pp. 307). Walter de Gruyter.
Schnurr, S. (2013). Chapter 6: Gender. In *Exploring Professional Communication: Language in Action* (pp. 128–149). London: Routledge.

Schnurr, S., & Holmes, J. (2009). Using humor to do masculinity at work. In N. Norrick & D. Chiaro (Eds.), *Humor in Interaction* (pp. 101–118). John Benjamins Publishing Company.

Schnurr, S., & Omar, N. A. M. (2021). Leadership and humour at work. In *The Routledge Handbook of Language, Gender, and Sexuality* (pp. 197-211). New York: Routledge.

Truong, N. A. (2016). Những người ngồi mâm dưới (Those who sit in lower mats). Retrieved from: https://vietnamnet.vn/nhung-nguoi-ngoi-mam-duoi-324352.html (accessed on 19 June 2024).

UNWomen. (2021). *Country Gender Equality Profile Viet Nam 2021*. Retrieved from: https://asiapacific.unwomen.org/en/digital-library/publications/2021/10/country-gender-equality-profile-viet-nam-2021#view (accessed on 19 June 2024).

Vu, M. T., & Pham, T. T. T. (2021). Still in the shadow of Confucianism? Gender bias in contemporary English textbooks in Vietnam. *Pedagogy, Culture & Society, 31*(3), 477–497.

CHAPTER 2

A NARRATIVE INQUIRY INTO INTERSECTIONS OF PROFESSIONAL IDENTITY AND GENDER IDENTITY CONSTRUCTION IN ACADEMIA

DISHA MAHESHWARI and AKANKSHA SRIVASTAVA

School of Education, Sharda University, Greater Noida, Uttar Pradesh, India

ABSTRACT

Gender discrimination and harassment are common workplace issues faced by most women around the world that lead to decreased psychological and physical well-being (Fitzgerald & Cortina, 2018). This paper attempts to explore the intersection of professional identity and gender identity construction by two women professionals in academia by investigating experiences of gender-based harassment and discrimination. The qualitative method of narrative inquiry is used to explore narratives of sexist behavior and gender discrimination in the workplace. It explores how gendered remarks cause self-doubt in the way these two women construct their professional identities. The paper aims to identify the ways in which patriarchal articulation of professional identity leads to a feeling of marginalization as working professionals. It also highlights the resistance strategies employed in the construction of professional identity while also carefully avoiding the risk of being labeled 'difficult women.'

Subverting Social Inequalities: Gender as a Social Reality.
Akanksha Srivastava, Disha Maheshwari, Chitra Krishnan (Eds.)

2.1 INTRODUCTION

Individuals are constantly constructing and negotiating their identities in their respective social environments. Maheshwari (2019) writes that "One cannot claim a singular static identity as an individual exists within a situation of dynamic and multiple identities" (p. 253). She writes that identity is continuously constructed and reconstructed in interaction with members of society. According to Weatherall (2000), the identification of a person as belonging to one of two gender groups is a fundamental guide to how they are perceived, how their behavior is interpreted, and how they are responded to in every interaction and throughout the course of their life.

Thus, an individual's understanding of societal gender stereotypes and norms plays a major role in every interaction (Holmes, 2008). One's identity is produced and reproduced through a nexus of subject positions which include not only how we position ourselves, but also how we are positioned by others within gendered discourses in academia. The idea for this paper emerged from the various discussions that the co-authors participated in, positioned as female academicians. Here, the identity as both 'female' and 'professionals working in academia' is crucial as they help situate the paper in the discourses of identity construction as 'women' and as 'academicians' in a patriarchal society.

Co-writing the paper also indicates the shared nature of our experiences as women working in the higher education sector. The main purpose of the in-depth examination of these autoethnographic narratives is to critically voice how the experiences of gender discrimination took place and affected the researchers in their academic endeavors and professional identity construction and negotiation. This approach gives agency to the individual by acknowledging the social construction of experiences of gendered discourses and social practices at work and thereby allowed exploration of contextual and personal nuances of the experience.

2.2 INTERSECTION OF PROFESSIONAL IDENTITY AND GENDER IDENTITIES

Gender identity and professional identity are two distinct aspects of a person's identity. Gender identity refers to a person's internal sense of their own gender, whether they identify as male, female, both, neither, or another gender identity. Professional identity, on the other hand, refers to the way a person sees themselves in relation to their chosen profession or career.

While gender identity and professional identity are separate concepts, they can intersect and influence each other. For example, a person's gender identity may impact their career choices and the way they navigate their professional environment. Transgender and non-binary individuals may face unique challenges and discrimination in the workplace due to their gender identity, which can impact their professional identity and career advancement.

Additionally, a person's professional identity may impact their gender identity, particularly in traditionally gendered professions. For example, women may feel pressure to conform to traditional gender roles and expectations in male-dominated fields, which can impact their sense of self and gender identity.

It's important to recognize that each person's gender identity and professional identity are unique to them and should be respected and supported in all aspects of their life. According to Slay & Smith (2011), professional identity is "the constellation of attributes, beliefs, and values people use to define themselves in specialized, skill- and education-based occupations or vocations" (Benveniste, 1987; Ibarra, 1999) (p. 86). They summarize research on professional identity construction and suggest that self-view is shaped in 3 main ways: socialization process and professional rhetoric, adjustments during periods of career transition, and finally life and work experiences. Our experience of the work environment along with cumulative life experiences outside work influence the construction of professional identity since together they lead towards an understanding of the self and one's priorities in life. Gender identity plays a major role in how men and women negotiate their professional identities in their social contexts. For women, the aspects of identity appreciated as part of their gender identity within the gender hegemony are considered unworthy or weak as aspects of one's professional identity. Thereby, conflict arises between one's identity as a woman and as a professional. Katila & Meriläinen (1999) write that.

The only site where women and the feminine are unproblematically seen to belong is within the family, a position that is simultaneously devalued. As a consequence, women are forced to struggle to handle the tension between personal and professional identities at odds with one another.

Women are thus continuously struggling to ensure that gender identity does not threaten the professional identity, evoking gender positioning in such a way that it does not threaten professional identity.

An academic faculty has a professional role with certain meaning; this meaning may change or be challenged when the individual's gender identity as a woman intersects with it. Therefore, what it means to be an academic faculty in India may have different meanings for individuals with different gender identities. While citing Ussher (1992), Thimm et al. (2003) writes that "there are many studies which have shown that knowing the sex of an individual can influence judgments on mental and physical health, on personality traits, achievements, emotional experience, mathematical competence, or power" (p.530). Katila & Merilainen (1999) in their study on resisting patriarchal articulations of women's professional identity reveal that there was a tendency of using stereotypical gender positions of women by categorizing them into 'nice girls,' 'seducers,' and 'beautiful women.' Thus, the study attempts to highlight the 'gendered discursive practices' at the workplace through personal narratives.

2.3 METHODOLOGY

The study uses auto-ethnographic narratives to explore researchers' own subject positions vis-a-vis how they are positioned by others in discourse. While citing Ellis (2004) and Jones (2005), Ellis, Adams & Bochner (2011, p.273) write that "Autoethnography is an approach to research and writing that seeks to describe and systematically analyze (graphy) personal experience (auto) in order to understand cultural experience (ethno)." They suggest that the researchers using the autoethnographic method incorporate "epiphanies" in retrospect which are "remembered moments perceived to have significantly impacted the trajectory of a person's life" (p.280). It is not imperative for the 'epiphanies' to have a "transformative" effect on the individual but their importance lies in the form of feelings the memory of those incidents lead to. These epiphanies are located within specific socio-cultural contexts as well and are part of the larger cultural experience and identity as well. It thus allows the researcher to identify even those issues that are usually ignored or hidden such as "harmful gender norms" (p. 280).

Grant & Zeeman (2012, p.2) assert that autoethnographic storytelling enables the detailed interrogation and critique of potentially or actually oppressive and repressive cultural institutions, norms, values, practices, and logics. Such malign aspects of culture are often otherwise arguably overlooked to the extent that they are frequently represented in benign, magnanimous, or positive terms in rationally nuanced, master narratives. This method also helps in problematizing those experiences that are considered questionably invisible or unworthy of reflective analysis. It allows the authors of narratives a way to understand what happened and make sense of it with reference to overall identity construction as well. In order for something to be subjected to critique, it first needs to be acknowledged. Thus, the use of autoethnographic narratives facilitated the questioning of established assumptions of gender hierarchy in our specific socio-cultural milieu.

Slay & Smith (2011, p. 91) while citing Lieblich et al. (1998) and McAdams (1993) write that "narratives are identities, that is, people come to know who they are through the stories they tell about specific struggles at specific points in time. These historical narratives have less to do with the significance of specific institutions and events than with the ability of certain stories to make sense out of the individual lives." With reference to professional identity, they elaborate that it is "constructed from narratives stemming from a sequence of life events, and while different narratives can be told from the same events, the salience of a given identity depends on which narrative is told (Piore & Stafford, 2006)." Therefore, in narrative research, the participants' stories become the data and it is their experiences that most interest the researcher. Narratives can thus facilitate interpreting social meaning encoded in workplace talk.

The next section presents the narratives by two academicians who are colleagues in the same department at a private university in the Delhi NCR region of India. Although they both have varying experience, one is a mid-career professional while the other is an early career professional in academia. Their gendered experience of the workplace is another point of similarity between them besides the workplace. After attending a guest lecture at the university on 'Subverting Gender Inequities,' they both had a discussion about their own experiences as women in academia who are constantly negotiating the professional sphere to ensure that their gender identity and associated attributes do not overshadow their professional attributes. The narratives were written after the two colleagues decided to have an extended conversation about their shared experiences and document them in order to explore the impact or influence of these experiences on their professional and personal identity construction.

The narratives were written individually and were revised after discussion with each other. It was during the post-writing discussions that the researchers also reflected on the commonalities of their experiences, even though many of the incidents shared in the narratives occurred at least a decade apart, further indicating the insignificant change in the hegemonic gender order and women's role defined within it. These narratives were then read and re-read to identify common themes, which are discussed in the final section of the chapter.

2.3.1 NARRATIVE 1

I am a senior academician with more than 12 years of teaching experience in higher education institutions. Coming from a family of academicians, it was my childhood dream to become a lecturer. I always imagined myself as a respectable academician who is looked up to in the community. To achieve this goal, I worked to the best of my abilities and attained the highest qualifications required for the profession. Even on the job, I consciously made efforts towards continuous professional development in order to update my knowledge, skills, and vision. I strived on constructing my professional identity as a respectable, hardworking academician.

The incident I have discussed below is from one of my later jobs. At this point, I was a seasoned and established academician in my field of expertise. I was quite positive after the interview for the post of Associate Professor in a reputed college in North India. As I had an aptitude for teaching and excelled at my subject, I was always selected in every interview that I appeared for, and the same was true for this one as well. This had strengthened my belief in my academic caliber and professional rigor. But this belief in my ability and skills was challenged by one of my colleagues at this new workplace. On the day I joined the college, I was welcomed by one of the male colleagues with the words *'I knew it must have been a very beautiful woman who got selected as an Associate Professor, bypassing all the eligible male candidates.'* This faculty member was much younger than me as well as a junior in the institutional hierarchy. The comment made me not only uncomfortable but also speechless at that moment.

This was the first time someone had delegated my professional success to my physical attributes as a woman. For a long time, I questioned if my gender identity had overwhelmed my professional identity. I struggled with the suggestion that my eligibility for the position was based on me being considered a beautiful woman as per the beauty standards of hegemonic femininity (Schnurr, Zayts & Hopkins, 2016) in society. Although feminine beauty is considered an advantage in a patriarchal society within the characterization of hegemonic femininity, it was construed negatively in association with my professional identity. This also indicated the preference of a different kind of femininity in relation to professional competence. That person completely sidelined my skills and abilities and attributed my appointment to my socially pleasing physical features. It was the first time that I felt embarrassed about being beautiful and a woman in academia.

This faculty member made similar comments throughout my tenure at this institution that reflected his troubling patriarchal and many times misogynist mindset. In another instance, he commented that *'your class always has the highest attendance because you are a treat for the eyes and students come to your class as they are charmed by your looks.'* Even after pointing out personal and professional boundaries to him on several occasions, he showed little regard for my wishes. He always undermined my position not only as his senior but also as his elder; a hierarchy that is respectfully observed in Indian society. His status as a man in a patriarchal society probably enabled him to disregard professional and age hierarchy.

The overall culture of the organization was also aligned with a patriarchal structure that encouraged a hegemonic gender order within the institutional processes. Time and again, various faculty members would remind women academicians that a woman's main identity is that of a wife/daughter/mother and a professional identity must be treated as secondary to that. In all the events organized by the institution, female faculty were assigned the responsibility of greeting the guests, serving them tea, and acting as hostesses. These roles were very clearly gender-marked. There were no women in the top management of this institution. In various meetings with the senior management, it was explicitly indicated that the institution did not expect professional rigor from women as their respective families would be women's 'natural' priority.

My experience at this organization made me nervous in framing my responses in management meetings. I was always cautious about sharing my views as I did not want to be interpreted in a socially unacceptable way. It changed the way I would normally react in meetings. I gave up many of my favorite dresses so that my perceived identity as a woman would not overpower my identity as an academician. I consciously made efforts to not look good so that others may not interpret my intentions as attempting to attract male attention. I did not want to be labeled as a 'seducer.' Tailoring and monitoring every action and word to fit into an acceptable stereotype was an overwhelming emotional experience. Even today, I am continuously managing my femininity so as not to let my gender identity subsume my professional abilities.

2.3.2 NARRATIVE 2

As a research scholar in one of the premier universities of the country, I believed I was on my way to being a serious professional. I did not think that my identity as a woman in academia intersected significantly with my identity as a research scholar. The realization of my identity as a 'female' scholar was sudden yet passive. In the first year of my doctoral study, I was part of the organizing team of a national conference. For weeks, I worked to the best of my abilities with the team members and participants on the preparation and execution of the event.

On the second or third day of the conference, I was greeted by a senior researcher in the corridor. She told me she was enjoying the conference presentations and that it succinctly brought out the issues of gender in Indian society. She was impressed that the event was well-managed and addressed important issues in the field. She then inquired about my well-being, and we chit-chatted for a couple more minutes. Before we parted, she remarked, *"You are in the wrong profession."* I was confused by this sudden comment and asked her to elaborate. It was then that she elaborated, *"You look like a model, why are you wasting your time in academia!"* I laughed uncomfortably, and we parted ways. She probably assumed that I would take it as a compliment being called a 'model' since a fashion model's body is considered ideal according to the notion of hegemonic femininity (Schippers, 2006).

I thought for a long time about the reasons that made me feel uncomfortable instead of being 'complimented' by my senior's remark. I realized that the institutional context in which the remark was situated made it feel unwelcome. As women, we are taught to feel happy and proud when someone compliments us on our physical appearance as that confirms the woman's identity construction as per the acceptable societal gender stereotypes and expectations. That day I had worn a knee-length black formal dress with a yellow cardigan and black ballerina shoes. Since that day, I felt uncomfortable wearing western formals at the university since Indian wear is considered to indicate seriousness and rigor for women in the academic field. I wanted to be recognized for my intellectual abilities and academic caliber instead of being noticed for my 'acceptable' physical appearance. Thus, every time I got ready for the university, I would consciously make efforts to be 'unnoticeable' or 'less feminine.' I questioned the choice of my clothes and painfully wondered if my lipstick was 'too red' for a female doctoral researcher. I wanted to avoid any chance of being noticed again for my appearance at the university.

It took a few years for me to feel comfortable in my choice of clothes in my academic roles. I experienced an identity crisis in terms of who I was as a person and how I should appear in the academic sphere in order to be taken seriously by my peers and colleagues. Many years later, I do not question my appearance every morning when I get ready for work as an assistant professor at a private university. And that is not because I have stopped receiving similar remarks from colleagues, but because I have now stopped associating my self-worth as an educator and researcher with how others perceive me to a certain extent.

The next significant incident happened while I was looking for a change in the workplace. Over many interviews at different institutions, I found out that it was a commonplace practice to ask a married young female candidate about her plans for pregnancy. At this particular university, the question made me uncomfortable, and I could see the interviewers changing the discourse when they noticed my discomfort. They reasoned that many times women candidates join and as soon as they complete the probation period, they go on maternity leave. And because of that, the institution suffers. Although all public and private universities are legally bound to give maternity leave to all female candidates (Maternity Act, 2017), private universities seem to be evading this by preferring to hire those candidates that have already had children and do not plan to do so in the near future, as reported by almost every female academician acquaintance.

After successfully satisfying my interviewers that I was not planning to have a child in the near future, the next crucial question was that of salary. As I was expecting a hike in salary from my previous employment, I did not accept the offer made by the institution. I received a call from the Human Resource manager of this institution the next day trying to persuade me to join with the given offer. He reasoned that this was a reputable university, and I would receive many chances to grow professionally even if the salary was low. He added that since my husband was making a lot more money than me anyway, I should accept the job offer. The correlation between my husband's high income and me having low salary expectations baffled me. The assumption was clear, that since I was a married woman with a husband with a handsome salary package, I should adjust with the low remuneration in my professional life. He dismissed my professional aspirations, stating that in the patriarchal setup, the man (my husband) was making enough money for the family, and there was no need for me to have expectations of a high salary. My professional identity was disregarded within the patriarchal discourse iterated by the HR Manager for my identity as a married woman. I spoke to my husband about this issue and asked him and some other male friends if they were ever asked about intentions to start a family or were asked to accept a lower salary if their partner was earning well. None of them had ever experienced such a line of questioning in a job interview. It is ironic how starting or having a family is seen as a burden for female employees and is viewed as an impediment to their professional growth and commitment.

2.4 DISCUSSION

Women academicians are constantly faced with difficulties in trying to fit into the dominant gendered discourses at higher education institutions. Both of the above narratives highlight how gender-based treatment has not changed over time, even when the gender identity construction as a woman varies greatly for the two academicians. Similar to what Katila & Meriläinen, (1999, p.15) found in their study, both academicians here "experienced a profound ambivalence in handling the dual experience of being 'feminine' and 'professional' at the same time." (p.15). The three main themes that emerge from the above narratives are: (i) Sexualized Body and Appearance, (ii) Dual Burden of Maternal Aspirations, and (iii) Micro-aggressions at the workplace.

2.4.1 SEXUALIZED BODIES AND APPEARANCE

Policing of gendered bodies by men leads to the maintenance of men's dominant position in the gender order. Both women were perceived in sexual ways by their colleagues in the narratives here and were thereby forced to manage their 'femininity' within a male-dominated sphere. Unfortunately, women at work are often subjected to stereotypes related to their appearance, which can have a negative impact on their career advancement and job satisfaction. Both women are expected to dress in a certain way in order to be taken seriously or be viewed as professional. Dressing up to express one's own femininity in a way one finds interesting, even though decent, is still subjected to negative judgments or assumptions about their character or competence. Both academicians were judged based on their hair or makeup choices.

There is a clear contradiction between the expectations for women's appearance in their private and professional spheres. In their private lives, women are encouraged to express their individuality and personal style through their clothing, makeup, and hairstyles. However, in the professional sphere, the expectations for women to conform to more conservative or traditional standards of dress and appearance in order to be taken seriously. Both the women here struggled with managing their 'appearances' so as to not come across as 'too sexy' or 'too feminine.'

These appearance-based stereotypes are damaging to women's careers and self-esteem. Katila & Meriläinen, (1999, p.15) in their study found that "... after years of hearing how women are lacking in one respect or another, many women start to believe in it as an objective fact while men get support for their often-unconscious assumptions of women as the other sex, the inferior one." This can create a challenging situation for women, who may feel pressure to conform to professional expectations while also wanting to express their personal style and identity. It can also lead to gender-based discrimination and bias, where women who don't conform to traditional standards of appearance may be judged as less competent or professional.

It is important for individuals and organizations to challenge themselves and create a more inclusive and accepting workplace culture. This can include promoting diverse images of beauty and success, providing education and training on implicit bias, and encouraging open dialogue around the impact of appearance-based stereotypes on women at work. Additionally, individuals can challenge gender-based stereotypes and biases by being mindful of their own assumptions and judgments about appearance and advocating for a more accepting and diverse workplace culture. Ultimately, it's important to recognize that appearance should not be the sole determinant of one's seriousness or competence in the workplace, and that individuals should be judged based on their skills, abilities, and contributions to the workplace.

2.4.2 DUAL BURDEN OF MATERNAL ASSUMPTIONS

The personal sphere is constantly interfering with the public sphere of women academicians. Even before getting a job, the woman is expected to explain her position regarding marriage and motherhood. One of the narratives clearly indicates how the chances of getting a job were dependent upon one's plan for motherhood. On the one hand, one's colleagues assume that a woman's main focus should and would be their families since a woman's identity as a 'mother' or 'wife' takes precedence over her professional identity in the workplace within the gender order. Many times, women are expected to show the nurturing behaviors that are expected of them in the personal sphere but are judged less competent for exhibiting those same behaviors.

Women's role as 'wives' who are assumed to be not the breadwinners unlike their husbands are also expected to adjust to lower remuneration. These assumptions negate their professional competence and hard work in favor of gender-based expectations and norms. The narratives indicate that women are constantly struggling to adjust on the one hand to the gendered expectation of childcare and household responsibilities and on the other hand professional role and responsibilities which they are expected to deprioritize because of their roles as wives and mothers.

2.4.3 MICROAGGRESSIONS AT WORKPLACE

Microaggressions are subtle, everyday forms of discrimination that can be experienced by women at work. These can include interrupting or talking over women in meetings or conversations, or dismissing women's ideas or opinions. Both the women academics indicate how their colleagues' made assumptions about their abilities or interests based on their gender. They were often offered feedback on their appearance, clothing, or priorities in life. Microaggressions also include assuming that women are responsible for administrative tasks or emotional labor, regardless of their job responsibilities.

These microaggressions can have a cumulative negative impact on women's self-esteem, job satisfaction, and career advancement. They can also contribute to a toxic and discriminatory workplace culture. To address microaggressions, it's important for organizations to provide education and training to managers and employees on the impact of implicit bias and gender-based stereotypes, and to create clear policies and procedures for addressing discriminatory behavior. Individuals can also challenge microaggressions by speaking up when they occur, seeking support from allies and colleagues, and advocating for a more inclusive and respectful workplace culture.

The role of colleagues in the identity construction of women in the workplace can be significant. Colleagues can contribute positively or negatively to the development of a woman's professional identity, self-esteem, and confidence. A major positive contribution from colleagues can be validation for a woman's professional abilities and accomplishments, which can boost her confidence and help her establish a stronger sense of self-identity. Both the women here instead faced discrimination against them based on gender stereotypes or biases, which led to the undermining of their sense of identity and self-worth. This undermining of professional credibility or accomplishments and attributing success to physical attributes only caused the women to doubt their abilities and feel less confident in their professional identity. Overall, the support and validation of colleagues can play a critical role in the identity construction of women in the workplace. It can help them establish a strong sense of self and contribute to their success and well-being within the organization.

2.5 CONCLUSION

Women constantly feel the pressure to downplay their femininity or suppress aspects of their gender identity in order to fit into the professional environment. This can lead to a conflict between their professional identity and their gender identity. For example, a woman may feel pressure to dress and behave in a more masculine way in order to be perceived as competent and authoritative, even if those behaviors do not align with her true gender identity. These conflicts can be challenging for women, as they may feel like they are forced to choose between being true to their personal identity and fitting in within their professional environment. To address these conflicts, organizations can work to create a more inclusive and supportive workplace culture that recognizes and values diversity, including gender identity. This can include policies and practices that promote gender equity and support the well-being of all employees, regardless of their gender identity or expression. Additionally, individual colleagues can work to be allies to their female colleagues, supporting them in their professional pursuits and recognizing the value they bring to the workplace.

Although glaring expressions of gender-based discrimination have reduced in Indian academia, instead of disappearing, the discrimination has become subtle, disguised as concern (Basford, Offermann & Behrend, 2014). Both narratives also indicate and confirm that over a period of time, women professionals get more attuned to gender-based aggressions and discrimination (Ryan, Haslam, & Postmes, 2007). Both overt and subtle expressions of discrimination must be acknowledged and challenged by the individuals faced with it. By narrating our experiences, we attempted to make them visible and significant. It facilitated the process of breaking the silence over issues otherwise unarticulated. It also allowed us to feel validated and come to terms with ways of coping.

KEYWORDS

- **methodology**
- **microaggressions**
- **stereotypes**
- **subverting gender inequities**
- **transformative**

REFERENCES

Basford, T. E., Offermann, L. R., & Behrend, T. S. (2014). Do you see what I see? Perceptions of gender microaggressions in the workplace. *Psychology of Women Quarterly, 38*(3), 340–349.

Ellis, C., Adams, T. E., & Bochner, A. P. (2011). Autoethnography: An overview. *Historical Social Research / Historische Sozialforschung, 36*(1), 273–290.

Grant, A. J., & Zeeman, L. (2012). Whose story, is it? An autoethnography concerning narrative identity. *Qualitative Report, 17*, Article 72.

Holmes, J. (2008). *Gendered Talk at Work: Constructing Gender Identity Through Workplace Discourse* (Vol. 3). John Wiley & Sons.

Katila, S., & Meriläinen, S. (1999). A serious researcher or just another nice girl? Doing gender in a male-dominated scientific community. *Gender, Work & Organization, 6*(3), 163–173.

Katila, S., & Meriläinen, S. (1999). Getting Out of the Corner—Challenging the Patriarchal Articulations of Professional Identity in Academia. In *CMS International Critical Management Studies Conference, Manchester, UK, 14–16 July, 1999.*

Katila, S., & Meriläinen, S. (2002). Metamorphosis: From 'nice girls' to 'nice bitches': Resisting patriarchal articulations of professional identity. *Gender, Work & Organization, 9*(3), 336–354.

Maheshwari, D. (2019). Discourses of victimhood and agency: A case study of a teenage Indian girl negotiating her identity in a gendered world. *Asian Journal of Women's Studies, 25*(2), 239–257.

Ryan, M. K., Haslam, S. A., & Postmes, T. (2007). Gender differences in the explanations for the precariousness of women's leadership positions. *Journal of Organizational Change Management, 20*, 182–197.

Schippers, M. (2007). Recovering the feminine other: Masculinity, femininity, and gender hegemony. *Theory and Society, 36*(1), 85–102.

Schnurr, S., Zayts, O., & Hopkins, C. (2016). Challenging hegemonic femininities? The discourse of trailing spouses in Hong Kong. *Language in Society, 45*(4), 533–555.

Slay, H. S., & Smith, D. A. (2011). Professional identity construction: Using narrative to understand the negotiation of professional and stigmatized cultural identities. *Human Relations, 64*(1), 85–107.

Thimm, C., Koch, S. C., & Schey, S. (2003). Communicating gendered professional identity: Competence, cooperation, and conflict in the workplace. In J. Holmes & M. Meyerhoff (Eds.), *The Handbook of Language and Gender* (pp. 528–549). Blackwell Publishing.

CHAPTER 3

GENDER-BASED SOCIALIZATION WITHIN FORMAL SYSTEM OF EDUCATION: WITH SPECIAL REFERENCE TO TRANSGENDER AND GENDER DIVERSE (TGD) LEARNERS OCCUPYING THE CLASSROOMS

MANVI ARORA

School of Social Work, University of Montreal, Canada

ABSTRACT

The chapter explicates how education as a system explicitly socializes the learners into a carefully scripted version of gender through the ethos and practices of the educational institutions in multiple ways. These claims are based on first-hand experiences of 100 transgender and gender-diverse persons and their systemic engagement with educational institutions.

3.1 INTRODUCTION

"The individual is not born a member of society. He becomes a member of society. In the life of every individual, there is a temporal sequence, in the course of which he is inducted into participation in the social dialectic" (Berger & Luckmann, 1966, p. 129).

In the modernized world of the digital revolution, globalization, and economic reforms, some basic microstructures of society have managed to retain their traditional status quite well. Entrenched attitudes towards

Subverting Social Inequalities: Gender as a Social Reality.
Akanksha Srivastava, Disha Maheshwari, Chitra Krishnan (Eds.)

traditional family structures, religious values, and community loyalties persist unabatedly, especially in the context of the Indian subcontinent. New members of society are socialized into the carefully played script of gender-based identities. Permissible gender performance and mainstream social constructions of gender tend to demand conformity by adhering to only two kinds of gender identities—male or female, based on a stereotypical understanding of genitals or what is better referred to as sex assigned at birth.

In her influential works (Butler, 1990, 1993), Judith Butler delves into the concept of gender binaries, specifically the notions of masculinity and femininity, and how these prescribed roles and performances create power dynamics in society. According to Butler, the prevailing belief that these gender roles are the only authentic way of existence perpetuates the existing power structures. She refers to gender as a "script" that is seamlessly passed down through generations, entrenched in socially accepted "meanings." Contrary to popular belief, Butler argues that gender is not a radical choice, nor is it forcibly imposed on individuals; rather, it is ingrained through societal norms and practices (Butler, 1988, p. 256). Butler proposes that societal norms have ingrained specific behaviors deemed suitable for men and women, creating a social environment that upholds and justifies a seemingly inherent gender binary. To validate and authenticate gender identities, individuals are expected to perform or conform to what is known as gender essentialism. This perspective dictates that society and culture define certain roles as ideal or fitting for individuals based on their sex. By adhering to these prescribed roles associated with their sex, both men and women perpetuate the notion of gender as a constructed and performed concept (Butler, 1988).

Even though individuals are often influenced by and internalize societal gender norms, many do not conform to the expected and traditional ways of performing gender. Men, women, boys, and girls find themselves in systems where expectations regarding their roles and responsibilities become sources of contention and conflict (Fawcett et al., 2000). Regrettably, throughout human history, gender non-conformity and the diversity of gender identity and expression have faced stigmatization, pathologization, and have been deemed socially undesirable in numerous societies worldwide (Colmen et al., 2022). The more a person deviates from the established norms of gender identity, the more likely they are to face stigma and discrimination. It is crucial to recognize that cultural expectations regarding "appropriate" gender identities can have harmful consequences for those who do not conform to these norms, resulting in discrimination and prejudice. The freedom to express one's gender identity, which is an individual deeply held, internal sense of their own gender as they choose, is essential for their self-confidence and well-being. Consequently, being different, unconventional, or atypical is often viewed as abnormal, burdening the individual or group with the weight of being seen as different and inferior. Such stigma can lead to mistreatment, prejudice, discrimination, and vulnerability. Moreover, these social pressures frequently contribute to a lack of seeking healthcare, lower self-esteem, mental health issues, difficulties in forming interpersonal relationships, and a disillusioned outlook on life.

Transgender[1] and gender diverse learners, that is learners who identify differently from the sex assigned to them at birth, transgress this binary conception of gender by deviating from socially prescribed gender norms associated with assigned sex at birth and thus form peculiar cases for looking into gender-based identity development in general and gendered socialization in particular. It is therefore important that academic discourses engage with different textures of gender performance and with voices of individuals who do not conform to the sex assigned at birth or do not abide by the expected gender roles.

To begin with, it is essential to draw attention to the evolving nature of the language of gender. It is happening at a much faster pace than in most of the other fields of inquiry, to the extent that what might seem appropriate and politically correct today may become questionable tomorrow. This might seem confusing to some, but the key is to keep learning and be up to date with debates around why a certain term came under controversy, eventually became redundant, and then a more sensitive and respectful term took over. This indicates constant refinement of concepts and constructs of diverse ways of expressing and identifying with one's gender.

One must also consciously be open to absorb what others say is comforting for them. Misgendering, calling someone by assumed pronouns, or identifying them with assumed gender markers can be very traumatizing for people with diverse gender identities. Thus, it is vital to ask what identity markers, pronouns, terminologies one is comfortable with, uses for themselves, and use the same for that person both in front and behind them. This chapter intends to foreground that there is no one way of performing a gender and non-conformity is being used in relation to the socio-cultural expectations attributed to their sex assigned at birth.

---

[1]Transgender or trans are umbrella terms used to describe people whose gender identities and/or gender expressions are not what is typically expected for the sex to which they were assigned at birth. These words should always be used as adjectives (as in "trans people") and never as nouns (as in "transgenders") and never as verbs (as in "transgendered") (Colmen et al., 2022).

Amid progressive legislation and political will, with pioneering attempts to address centuries-long discrimination towards the community, the Supreme Court issued its landmark judgment in 2014, popularly known as the NALSA judgment, which clearly grants the right to reservations in educational institutions for the transgender community (National Legal Services Authority v. Union of India, 2014). Additionally, according to the National Education Policy (NEP) 2020, there is a mandate to integrate transgender learners into the formal education system and provide them with an appropriate environment for learning (Government of India, Ministry of Human Resource Development, 2020). However, a shift in rigid social perceptions towards these learners may not be possible unless educators, teacher educators, teachers, and all other professionals involved in education question their inherent biases related to gender conformity, socially desirable/acceptable gender performance, and eventually create inclusive educational spaces for learners with diverse gender identities. This chapter aims to explore how the education system produces and maintains gender norms. It also seeks to gain insight into the developmental and educational experiences of those who are educated within prescribed gender norms and how they navigate this system when their gender identity or performance does not align with what is assumed to be harmoniously compatible.

3.2 EDUCATION: AN ACTIVE AGENT OF GENDER-BASED SOCIALIZATION

The conception of gender in Indian educational discourse is primarily monolithic in nature. Gender identity and assigned sex at birth are assumed to be seamlessly congruent. Educational policies, intellectual inquiry, and allocation of resources have been based on a binary vision. The system of education is predominantly concerned with increasing the number of enrollments of girls and their retention in schools. Attempts to understand the relationship that TGD learners, whose gender identities or expressions differ from the gender socially attributed to them at birth, share with the system of education are rare. The representation of an entire community, who do not conform to hegemonic ways of gender identification, with a few recent exceptions, can hardly be seen in the contemporary educational discourse. Thus, a whole range of educational experiences and identities are made invisible.

The absence is much more than a coincidence or unintentional omission. It is deliberately planned and painstakingly kept in place. It is a well-established fact by now that education is not a neutral enterprise. Socio-economic and political systems cast their effects on education. In return, education not only reproduces norms but also holds the capacity to bring in transformation. The role played by education as an institution with other socio-cultural factors in lending supremacy to a particular ordering of gender, over various other possibilities, will be deconstructed in this chapter.

Education system forms important sites for understanding the institutionalized proceedings of gendering, their enactments and implications in the lives of young people. This chapter is an effort to disturb the 'innocent space' of classrooms, where the transaction of 'pre-designed and valid' knowledge takes place. Educational experiences, concerns, and lived realities of the participants across a spectrum of gender identities in the present-day educational context form the fundamental phenomena under inquiry. This chapter is based on a broader study that looked into the educational, familial, and employment experiences of 100 TGD persons, within the Indian social structures they inhabit, where qualitative research methodology guided the collection of data through semi-structured, in-depth interviews and eventual thematic analysis (Arora, 2020). Participants of the study brought regional and cultural diversity as responses from Northern, North Eastern, Central, Eastern, Western, and Southern Indian zones were recorded. The youngest participant was 16 years old and the oldest was 43. A diverse sample came with heterogeneity in economic class, religion, caste, and gender assigned at birth.

CIS genderism, a situation where gender identity corresponds to the sex one is assigned at birth, is not only assumed to be natural and unchangeable, but also the only legitimate way of being within the Indian education system. The fixing of gender identity such that the whole world has to be identifiably male or female is not an immutable truth. It is more of a process. This process is termed as gender-based socialization. Gender-based socialization comprises some internalized and some violently enforced rules about a deeply felt sense of gender, gender roles, and expected gender performance (dress, speech, body language, and mannerisms), based on the sex assigned at birth. Most contemporary cultures and communities are characterized by gender essentialism that attributes a fixed essence to a particular gender, prescribing rules for what they consider appropriate gender expressions based on the biological sex of a person.

The majority of the respondents, 82%, said that society, family, schooling, and media failed to provide them with the necessary age-appropriate information (biological, anatomical, sexual, and social information) that would have eased their journey of self-discovery and acceptance. An astonishing 70% of the participants initially thought they were the only ones in the whole wide world who were experiencing non-normative gender and sexual feelings. This highlights the cisnormative nature of the society we live in and how any information about non-normative behavior never makes it into classroom-worthy knowledge.

Arpit[2], 38, who identifies as Transman[3], like many other participants, wished for comprehensive sexuality education during young and formative years of his life, and states:

"I always thought I was the only person on this planet who was different and thought I would have to live like this the rest of my life. I had no information that there are options available for sex reassignment or that there were others like me. I had so many questions during my growing up years, which if answered then would have made my life easier. Having been told in school that there are others with various diversities and I am not the only one feeling this way, would have had a big impact. I wish some clarity was offered."

The study recognizes some clearly spelled out structural inadequacies of the formal system of education that justify the normalization of a particular gender ordering, by either maintaining silence on other ways of being or taking proactive steps to keep the dominant order in place. Through covert and overt pedagogical tools, policies, programs, and content taught, students are made to imbibe specified values and beliefs. Gender conformity as a key ideology that runs in the educational environment and practices of the educational institutions could be gazed in the reported instances of interactions among students and teachers, in the content taught, teaching-learning processes, teacher intervention which ranged from occasional support, deliberate silence, omission and 'neutral stance' taken to corrective reprimands.

"There is a boy in my class. He always teases me and calls me a girl. If we have new students in the class or someone from other classes comes to our room, he makes sure he announces to everyone that 'Ye ladka nai hai, ye girl hai. Isse ladka mat samajh lena' (She is a girl and not a boy, do not mistake her as a boy). This is very irritating for me. I just want the world to forget my birth gender and take me for who I am saying I am. Once I was fed put and went to my class teacher, she simply changed his seat and made him sit a little farther away from me" elaborated Shiva, 14, transboy, who

---

[2] All names of participants mentioned in the chapter have been changed in keeping with the principles of confidentiality. As far as possible, all references to geographic location, and other identifiers, have also been generalized or edited out.

[3] Transgender man, Trans man or Trans boy are person who has gender identity as men and who was assigned female at birth. They may or may not have undergone any transition.

was assigned gender female at birth, wishes for Gender Affirming Medical Surgeries after attaining adulthood and has been a part of the same school for years as a girl before socially transitioning[4].

Gender sensitization sessions, discussions around the validity of non-normative forms of gender identities and performances, the right to dignity, respect for diversity, and comprehensive sexuality education are ways to make educational institutions inclusive and fostering spaces for transgender and gender diverse learners. Brushing the issue under the carpet, taking a 'neutral stance' of supporting neither the bully nor the bullied learner, or stepping further by gender policing TGD learners to ensure conformity to gender-based norms is is rooted into transphobia[5] and misogyny and must be questioned. The ideology that lurks behind the absence of an inclusive curriculum, the absence of access to complete and accurate information, in strict gender policing by both elders and peers, in reported anecdotes of on-campus physical, verbal, and sexual harassment, in the lack of freedom of visibility, of making choices of how to behave and what to believe in, is no different. These could be clearly seen in gender-based segregation in sitting arrangements.

Sanch, 16, identifies as genderqueer and thought of themselves to be a good orator; however, regrets that they could never develop this skill fully. After being bullied for feminine body language from the 6th standard onwards, by the time they reached class 9th and got an opportunity for public speaking, they could never take it up completely. They add,

"When you are going on stage and half of your attention is focused on appearing straight, only half of your mind is free to do what you are meant to do. Your efficiency comes down."

---

[4] Transition refers to the process where people generally change the gender expression associated with their assigned sex at birth to desired gender expression that better matches their gender identity in three ways: Socially, medically, and legally. People transition socially by using methods such as changing their name, pronoun, gender performance which includes dress, speech, body language, and mannerisms, medically by gender-affirming medical care which includes medical interventions to affirm one's deeply felt gender through hormone replacement therapy (HRT), puberty blocking, surgeries, and transition legally by changing name and gender markers in identity proofs following a legal procedure. Transition can be used to describe the process of changing one's gender expression from any gender to a different gender. People can transition more than once in their lifetimes.

[5] Transphobia is negative attitudes, beliefs, and actions concerning transgender and gender diverse.

Further, activities permissible to learners of a particular gender, gendered uniform, and discipline policies are not only based on but also promote a cisgender model of gender identity.

Sanya, 20, identifies as trans girl[6], my teachers slapped me for sitting with girls and often said "ladkiyon ki tarha bohot baatain kartay ho (You are talkative like girls). Teacher used to scold me all the time, they made sure I do not behave in a feminine manner in class and was worried, "Dusre baccho pe kya asar padega (they were worried about the effect of my effeminate expressions on other students)."

Clothes are not only an extension of our personality but also have cultural identity. The experiences of those who were not comfortable with the gender assigned at birth were echoed by Vivek. Vivek, 38, who identifies as a trans man, was made to wear frocks before puberty and suits thereafter as his school dress and found them highly uncomfortable.

"I never felt complete in those clothes; it was a very heavy feeling. My confidence level dipped a lot, I had a constant headache, my results dropped because when you are forced to be someone who you are not, confidence level and zeal in your life get lost. Probably if I was left to wear what was comfortable to me, things would have been eased down a lot."

Normative gender is rather explicitly enforced by the ethos and practices of most educational institutions in various ways. Cisgender behavior and practices are integrated and normalized within the educational culture to such a degree that they have become the 'neutral,' natural, and unquestioned environment. This is promoted by both explicit and hidden educational practices and is responsible for systematic othering, repression, and stigmatization of non-conforming ways.

3.3 EXPERIENCING THE FORMAL SYSTEM OF EDUCATION THROUGH THE PERSPECTIVES OF THOSE WHO DO NOT CONFORM TO THE ESTABLISHED GENDER-BASED NORMS

Enquiry into ordinary-looking practices of educational institutions opens up a vast sphere of covert realities of those who are on the fringes of this system, to make sense of what goes on in maintaining what otherwise looks seamless, natural, and thus the only way of being. Despite internalized and socialized gender norms, many fail to comply with the dichotomous ways of being. It is important to acknowledge that prescribed cultural roles and rules for 'appropriate' gender identities can have damaging implications for

[6] Transgender woman, Trans woman or Trans girls are people who have gender identities as women and who were assigned male at birth. They may or may not have undergone any transition.

people who do not conform to these 'natural' norms and therefore often face discrimination and prejudice. The freedom to express one's gender identity, as one chooses, is necessary for an individual's well-being and self-efficacy.

Textbooks in Indian schools are overloaded with stereotypical gender-based tales, images, characters, and examples enforcing conformity. Participants received absolutely no information about the existence and issues faced by a large number of people with non-conforming identities/behaviors. Many participants spelled out how including information about diverse genders in formal education curriculum would not only have helped them move towards acceptance of their identity quickly but also would have made their parents, teachers, peers, and the world around them more informed and humane. Along with lack of information about existence of gender diversity, the pervasive normative gender legitimacy that underlies the text, language, images, examples, all that forms knowledge and the way in which it is transacted and evaluated, confused non-normative young minds further. They could not relate to the knowledge transmitted. This had a direct impact on their academic achievement and the relationships they developed with their bodies. Formal education, which allegedly empowers learners, left the participants of this study confused at best and fearful, ashamed, and vulnerable at worst with the knowledge of the dominant that they received. These learners often feel unsafe, vulnerable, isolated, depressed, with an inability to concentrate on academics, along with lower than potential academic outcomes and suicidal ideations on more than one occasion. The internet serves as the only source of information that a questioning young mind is searching for answers to. In the absence of education and preparedness before entering the vast world of the web, many participants ended up being victims of cyberbullying and online blackmailing. Equipping learners with comprehensive sexuality education to critically consume online content might help in thoughtfully attending to online resources and escaping from fear, confusion, shame, and misconceptions that reportedly come along.

TGD participants of the study were more often bullied, called names, ridiculed, and subjected to transphobic, misogynist, and biased language. Additionally, the social milieu in which these young learners grew up made some of them negate the true sense of their being, to the extent of indulging in self-hatred and self-harm.

Oli, 28, identifies as gender fluid, was assigned male at birth, and was often verbally harassed in school by his 'friends.' He did not know how to fight bullying and how to come out of the pressure to 'act straight.' He underwent isolation and depression and recollects,

"I always wished to be hit by a truck on my way back from school, so that nobody has to answer any question about my suicide and I don't have to live another day."

Krishna, 21, a transman and final year B.A. English literature student, recalls,

"I could not accept myself, as I knew my strict and conservative family won't ever accept me. I tried to commit suicide when I was in 7th grade, then again in 11th grade, by cutting my wrist, and I have these thoughts every day. Throughout these years, I had dark circles, could not sleep for more than 2–3 hours a day, used to stay up late thinking about everything and nothing. My parents and teachers forced me to wear a uniform every morning and did not let me cut my short hair shorter. It was scary."

While the self-assigned task of most social institutions in such situations is to rectify the 'abnormality' and bring the 'deviated' individual back on track, it is high time that this rectification and gender correction, which have a deep impact on the social, mental, and physical well-being of the individual, stops. Internalized transphobia is another consequence of not questioning social norms through educational practices. Normalizing bullying, when participants labeled episodes of verbal bullying, they faced as 'everyday, normal and not out of routine teasing,' 'the usual abuses that gender-diverse people hear, like chakka, faggot,' 'aapko pata hai, bully to karte he hai (you would know, bullying is usual to happen),' 'Yeah! They used to call me names, but in a normal-fun way,' 'I was bullied for obvious reasons like I did not mend my behavior and stayed delicate,' hints at internalized transphobia and normality towards discriminatory treatment for transgressions of gender-based norms.

Formal education explicitly socializes the learners into a carefully scripted form of gender through ethos and practices of the educational institutions in multiple ways. Gender non-conformity is met with repercussions such as regulation, bullying, gender policing, physical and mental harassment, and sexual abuse by peers and staff that eventually gets internalized and turns into self-policing. Intense discussions around instances of bullying and the kind of verbal/physical abuses the participants were subjected to uncovered another rarely talked about affair of educational institutions, that is, Sexual Abuse. 34% of the participants revealed episodes of being sexually abused during growing up years, which was not a one-time affair in most of the cases. Perpetrators in these cases ranged from family members, teachers, principal, senior peers to classmates. Only one out of these cases was ever reported to family or judicial system. Most of the participants continued education attainment in the presence of the perpetrator in the same space.

Ashly, 47, a trans woman, works as a part-time domestic help and part-time sex worker. She was born in a lower-class Christian family in Delhi. She was assigned male at birth but identifies herself as a kothi and is a sexual abuse survivor. While in 4th grade of her primary school, she was sexually abused on the school premises by the school principal himself. It started with the principal noticing her (then a male child) effeminate ways and began calling her frequently to his room with notebooks and class record registers. "Initially, he used to pinch me here and there, which eventually turned into kissing and then penetration. I was too young to understand anything. All I knew was the pain and that I could not go around talking about it. Once the pain was unbearable, I went and told my mother about it." Ashly's mother did not believe her until she saw it for herself. "It was prayer time and everyone was gathered in the backyard. My mother came to the school to pay pending fees for the last 3 months. The principal's room was right at the beginning of the premises. Failing to find any teacher around, my mother came towards the principal's room and saw him undressing me through a broken corner of otherwise dark window panes. She stopped the prayer midway, called all the staff members and the police. Students and teachers reported being aware of the principal's acts. The principal was subsequently suspended from the post and transferred to another town. However, why were teachers and peers quiet for all this while is a question that systemic violence does not let many ask?

After successfully completing her primary education, Ashly was enrolled in a senior secondary school in the neighborhood. She could not forget the episode and turned violent towards classmates who ever made any remarks about her effeminate body performance. Ashly goes on to elaborate how she was brutally raped by a class 10th student in the same year. She was hospitalized for the wounds and did not ever return to formal education since then. She reports working as a domestic help with her mother since then and thinks of her to be more cultured than many of these 'padhay-likay boys jo road pe chalna mushkil kar dete hai (literate boys who tease her on the road).' Most of the sexual abuses reported in the study were either to 'correct the gender deviation' of the participant or to punish them for non-conformity to gender norms. Various other episodes like these stand testimonials to the fact that the consequences of transgressing socially established norms are not mild. The role played by peers/colleagues in essentializing gender and instances of inconsiderate treatment of the non-conforming aspect of the participant's identity are not rare. At the same time, there were specified narratives about the 'friends' who stood by the participants against all odds. These were peers/colleagues, teachers, principals who either instantly or eventually helped participants accept their true selves and provided the necessary congenial educational environment for their overall development.

Sheena, 24, assigned gender male at birth, identifies as girl, recalls:

"I was uncomfortable with the boys' uniform that my parents forced me to wear to school each day. I started skipping school. My teachers noticed my absence and called my parents to school. Upon knowing the reason for my absence, the school principal called me and gave me permission to wear the uniform of my preference. She even sensitized my teachers and helped me throughout my school days whenever I needed any support."

In response to stressors, resilience strategies coined, coping mechanisms relied on, and agency exercised while navigating through intersecting identities could be noted during the study. Participants of the study were voiceless, docile, and vulnerable sets of people who are mute spectators. They possess agency and have self-designed or shared strategies to adapt to the given situations. They were more often seen adapting self-designed or shared resilience strategies to protect themselves from discrimination, to adapt, to withstand shock, to face risk, and to promote acceptance. Some of these strategies include occasional abidance to gender/sexuality norms based on their judgment. For some, occasional commitment to gender norms enabled successful co-existing with those who enforced these norms on them. For many others, becoming part of the larger LGBTQ community, which provides the required medical and social information, support, a sense of belongingness, pride in one's identity, and shared emotions, various strategies to come out to a close acquaintance by judging their openness to gender diversity in advance."

Kreena, 17, who identifies as an androgynous person adds,

"I felt I was being pushed into a box and was made to follow norms that I do not really understand, hence cannot relate to, and ended up deciding not to follow them at all." Dressing up in feminine clothes, walking gently, and talking softly is what they did occasionally to please their teachers, parents, and this worked as a survival technique for them.

Support extended by a few but very strong and accepting classmates, teachers, school staff, family members, and medical practitioners make the tough terrain easier for the TGD learners.

Mivani, 20, is currently questioning her gender identity. She was depressed, undergoing isolation, and was in repression and denial of her same-sex desires until one of her best friends helped her come out of the negativity she had attached to non-normative sexual identity. Her friend, who was better informed when it came to sexual and gender diversity, got her reading material, gave her the required information, and positivity to come to terms with her sexuality.

"She was the first person I told when I didn't even know the exact words to describe it. She accepted me for who I am, even before I had accepted this side of me. Acceptance took time, it did not come in a day, or has not come in completely, but she stood by me throughout."

3.4 FINAL SECTION: QUESTIONING THE IMMUTABLE NATURE OF BINARY MODEL OF GENDER

There are many whose gender identity, gender performance, and gender roles did not fit into the tightly packed gender boxes of male and female. They occupied various positions on the spectrum of lived gender identities and challenge the discrete categorization of gender binaries. By their very existence, they challenge the constructed 'naturalness' of two assumed genders. Public awareness and acceptance of transgender individuals have been gradually increasing in the recent decade. However, there is still a long way to go in ensuring that adequate resources are made available to this population to fight the discrimination, harassment, and social stigmatization that they face (Colmen, et al., 2022). They experience unique barriers when accessing basic human needs such as education, medical care, and making a living for themselves, to name a few.

Lived experiences of these TGD learners within the formal educational system highlighted various themes that are assumably considered natural within the educational setting and are hardly looked through a critical lens. The content taught at the school level is exclusive of gender diversities. The participants clearly highlighted how what forms knowledge and how it is planned, structured, and transacted is normative to the core. Their educational journey failed to provide them with the language to articulate desires and to talk about gender and sexuality. The course of attainment of formal education left these learners feeling unsafe, vulnerable, isolated, and depressed with the inability to concentrate on academics, along with lower than the potential academic outcomes and suicidal ideations on more than one occasion. These learners are more likely to be reprimanded, bullied, corrected, and harassed, even before they have confirmed their gender non-conformity to themselves. People around them in educational institutions assume, judge, and veiled under the garb of bullying and gender policing is the imposition of normativity that has a deep impact on not only their educational journey and achievements but also on their physical and mental well-being.

The success of hegemonic cisgenderism through unquestioned normalization of a particular ordering of gender could be seen in the violent reinforcement of gender norms, policing of educational spaces, 'neutral stances' taken by stakeholders, reluctant acknowledgment of the need for sexuality education by limiting it to sexual and reproductive health rights (SRHR), and not thinking of informal avenues of sexuality education (such as the internet, cuss words, the cultural establishment of masculinity, the spectrum of gender and sexual identities, pleasure) as terrains of education, and in instances of naive, unreflective lack of critical interrogation of structural silences.

Educational institutions are indiscriminately forwarding the social norms through their everyday, natural-looking, and low-energy practices. The research uncovered a social psyche that, in order to stay in correspondence with larger social structuring, deliberately and painstakingly embodied its members into the discursive practice of compulsory gender conformity. However, it is the same institutionalized system of education that holds the power to bring about change. Unlike other social systems such as family, religion, and economy, education largely holds the potential to equip its members with the platform to foster health-seeking behavior, a spirit of inquiry, challenging social norms, informed decision-making, respecting heterogeneity, psycho-physiological integrity, and promoting resilience. It can refrain from rigid and deterministic reproduction of gender-based norms and provide room for resistance, negotiation, contestation, and transformation of these spaces. These are the only ways that education can adopt to mediate social change, cease dehumanizing diversity, be an active agent of disparity, and garner respect for difference.

KEYWORDS

- **Agent of Socialization**
- **gender diverse persons**
- **gender non-conformity**
- **LGBTQ community**
- **National Education Policy**
- **sexual and reproductive health rights**
- **System of Education**
- **transgender and gender diverse**

REFERENCES

Arora, M. (2020). *Beyond the Binary: A Study of Identity Development of Transgenders in the Indian Context* (Unpublished master's dissertation submitted in partial fulfilment of M.A. Psychology degree). Indira Gandhi National Open University (IGNOU), Delhi, India.

Berger, P. L., & Luckmann, T. (1966). *The Social Construction of Reality: A Treatise in the Sociology of Knowledge* (p. 129). Anchor Books.

Butler, J. (1990). *Gender Trouble: Feminism and the Subversion of Identity*. Routledge.

Butler, J. (2017). Bodies that matter. In N. Duncan (Ed.), *Feminist Theory and the Body* (pp. 235–245). Routledge.

Butler, J. (2020). Performative acts and gender constitution: An essay in phenomenology and feminist theory. In L. J. Nicholson (Ed.), *The Feminist Theory Reader* (5th ed., pp. 353–361). Routledge.

Coleman, E., Radix, A. E., Bouman, W. P., Brown, G. R., De Vries, A. L. C., Deutsch, M. B., & Arcelus, J. (2022). Standards of care for the health of transgender and gender diverse people, version 8. *International Journal of Transgender Health, 23*(supp.1), S1–S259.

Fawcett, B., Featherstone, B., Fook, J., & Rossiter, A. (Eds.). (2000). *Practice and Research in Social Work: Postmodern Feminist Perspectives*. Routledge.

Government of India, Ministry of Human Resource Development. (2020). *National Education Policy 2020*. https://www.education.gov.in/sites/upload_files/mhrd/files/NEP_Final_English_0.pdf.

National Legal Services Authority v. Union of India and Others, Writ Petition (Civil) No. 400 of 2012 & Writ Petition (Civil) No. 604 of 2013, 2 S.C.R. 1033 (2014).

Singh, S., Dasgupta, S., Patankar, P., & Sinha, M. (2013). *A People Stronger: The Collectivization of MSM and TG Groups in India*. Sage and United Nations Development Programme.

CHAPTER 4

THE GIRL-CHILD EDUCATION: AN ASSESSMENT OF GENDER-ILLITERACY NEXUS IN NIGERIA

ABEL EBIEGA ENOKELA

Department of Guidance Counselling, Faculty of Education, Ambrose Alli University, Edo State, Nigeria

ABSTRACT

This chapter assesses the gender-illiteracy nexus in Nigeria in relation to girl-child education through the lens of conflict theory. It examines the role gender plays in determining access to education in the country. Gender disparity spreads through the socialization process as individuals come in contact with socialization agents like family, education, peer groups, and mass media. These agents of socialization could impart or reinforce learned gender-based behaviors that could be disadvantageous to the girl child and her educational rights, by and large. This study confirms through secondary data the prevalence of gender inequality or discrimination in access to education in Nigeria as studies reveal higher boys' school enrollment and retention than that of girls. It is observed that gender disparity in education exists because girls are undervalued and are not given the same opportunity to access education as boys. The result of this disparity is a high girls' illiteracy level in the country. Educational gender inequality in the country is hinged on some gender-based factors which include preference for boys, early or forced marriage, early pregnancy leading to abandonment of school, child labor, cultural misconceptions about girls' education, lack of incentives, among others. The study also elucidates how the gender-illiteracy nexus

Subverting Social Inequalities: Gender as a Social Reality.
Akanksha Srivastava, Disha Maheshwari, Chitra Krishnan (Eds.)

could be disrupted or subverted in the country. Some of the measures that could subvert gender disparity in the country include public awareness and sensitization on the importance of girls' education, abolition of early or forced marriage, legislation on child labor and enforcement of existing child labor laws, incentivization, and parental re-orientation, among others.

4.1 INTRODUCTION

Gender as the basis for human differentiation impacts basically all domains of human existence (Bussey & Bandura, 1999). This differentiation phenomenon cuts across time, space, and cultures. Gender differential socialization could lead to the allocation of more privileges of power, autonomy, and independence to male children than their female counterparts. Gender is a term or social construct that dichotomizes humans into masculinity and femininity; and assigns roles, attitudes, and values that are culturally acceptable or deemed appropriate for each sex (Nakpodia & Urien, 2012). Gender socialization processes spread through socialization agents that could, in turn, reinforce and sustain gender-specific behaviors in line with societal culture contents (Conerly, Holmes, & Tamang, 2021). Some of these contents could create gender disparity which is usually unfavorable to girls psychologically, socially, and educationally. A girl child is biologically a female child from 0–18 years of age, covering infancy, childhood, and adolescence (Offor, Anadi, Nwaru, & Chukwuemeka, 2021). Gender differentiation or role has not been fair to the female gender as many cultures in the world are hostile or inimical to feminine growth, leading to discrimination as their potentials could be limited by cultural dictates which could impose passiveness, compulsive obedience, and domestic responsibilities on them (Conerly et al., 2021). Thus, gender inequality as a social process continues to strengthen the gender-illiteracy nexus in many parts of the world to the detriment of girls whose education is being jeopardized as a result of multiple interactions of some sociocultural factors which could strengthen male dominance in our social contexts. For instance, Malala (Malala Fund, n.d. a) recounts that in Pakistan, many consider sending their daughters to secondary school a waste of resources. This situation is similar to what is obtainable in Nigeria as Ikechukwu (2020) reports that gender inequality in educational opportunities and attainment between boys and girls is a consequence of family background, socioeconomic factors, and so on.

There is a call for sustainable education and gender equality in line with the UNO's sustainable development goals 4 and 7, respectively (UNO, 2020). According to UNO (2017), the 2030 sustainable development agenda is hinged on 5 key objectives: People (Eradication of poverty and hunger); Planet (Protection of the planet); Prosperity (Prosperous and fulfilling life for all); Peace (Peaceful, just, and inclusive societies); and Partnership (Mobilization for partnership to achieve sustainable development). Based on the position of the UNO as clearly revealed in the sustainable development goals, educating girls should be prioritized for the promotion of an equitable society for both men and women. However, in spite of this global call for gender equality, the girl-child education, apart from being neglected, is sometimes even directly attacked by religious extremists in Nigeria (Ossai, 2021; UNICEF, n.d. a) and in many other parts of the world. For instance, Malala, an activist, as a schoolgirl, was shot in October 2012 on her way home from school by a masked gunman to stop her from attending school to acquire education (Malala Fund, n.d. b; UNICEF, n.d. b). Education is very important for human development in keeping with Chazan (2022, p.16) who says, "Education is an activity which takes place in many diverse venues and is intended to develop knowledge, understanding, valuing, growing, caring, and behaving." Thus, an attempt to disrupt the girl-child education would have ripple effects on girls and the society as a whole. Basic education is a right of all children and could promote individuals' freedom, empowerment, and development for the purpose of productive and adaptive integration into society (Offor & Orisa, 2017; Okorie, 2017). The process of education could help a young girl to acquire knowledge and also help her to realize useful potentials for self-actualization and for the improvement of society (Offorma, 2009). Hence, gender disparity in education could reduce the potential endowments embedded in girls for their growth and advancement in life. According to UNESCO (2022), "illiteracy is one's inability to read or write which could be measured by one's inability to understand a short simple statement on everyday life." Based on this definition, there are many girls in Nigeria who are illiterates because of a lack of formal basic education that could enable them to read and write. The effect of gender inequality is evident in boys' and girls' school enrollments, as boys dominate based on enrollment statistics. The United Nations Children's Fund report on annual school drop-outs says approximately 1.3 million female children fail to complete their basic education (Tyessi, 2021). Similarly, Ossai (2021) posits that nearly 2 out of 3, representing 6.34 million of 10.19 million out-of-school children in the country are females. In a similar report, Malala Fund (n.d. c) concludes that girls account for 60% of 10 million out-of-school children, with 30% of the girls between ages 9–12 not being able to attend school, citing child marriage, poverty, and discriminatory social norms as barriers. Again, UNICEF (2007) notes that quite a good number of Nigerian girls drop out of primary schools without reaching class six. Studies also show that gender disparity in education is higher in the north, particularly in the northeast region of the country (Lawal, Miachi, & Kalu, 2017; Hot Vibe Media, 2021). Based on these reports, it is obvious that there are primordial socio-cultural patterns that tend to put girls' education at risk, thereby increasing female gender illiteracy in the country. This understanding is in line with the view of Malala Fund (n.d. a), which accuses age-long cultural beliefs as influencers of gender discrimination, limiting girls' potentials. Neglect of the girl child's education would continue to perpetuate gender discrimination with its negative psychosocial effects on society. Moreover, this social phenomenon contradicts the position of the National Policy on Education (NPE) of Nigeria, whose philosophy of education is firmly based on the integration of individuals into the affairs of nation-building, irrespective of gender, in an attempt to raise well-developed, effective, and societally adaptive citizens (FRN, 2004).

The challenges of girl-child education in this chapter are traced back to male dominance, which has kept the female gender in a subordinate position. We argue that the gender-illiteracy nexus is ultimately created and sustained by gender discrimination embedded in cultures against girls and women in Nigeria (Alabi, Bahah, & Alabi, 2014). In addition, Ene-Obong, Onuoha, & Eme (2017) argue that women are often seen as only fit for the kitchen and to assist with farm duties, making them dependent and subservient to men. Education could foster a change in attitudes, thoughts, behaviors, skills, values, and interests in individuals to make them useful to themselves and society. Therefore, it is crucial to emphasize the need for female education. Drawing on the adage that says "educate a man, you educate an individual, but educate a woman, you educate a nation," Offorma (2009) emphasizes the necessity of girls' education, arguing that no nation should underestimate the education of its citizens. The right of the girl-child to quality education is often denied, leading to child labor, loss of childhood potential, dignity, and joy (Okorie, 2017; Alabi et al., 2014). Continued gender inequality in education also denies women the opportunities of securing lucrative jobs, making them reliant on men for survival (Ikechukwu, 2020; Ene-Obong, et al., 2017). Offorma (2009, p. 1) defines education as "the process of providing information to an inexperienced person to help him/her develop physically, mentally, socially, emotionally, spiritually, politically, and economically."

Similarly, Lawrence (1976, p. 27) perceives education as "the deliberate, systematic, and sustained effort to transmit, provoke, or acquire knowledge, values, attitudes, skills, or sensibilities as well as any learning that results from the effort." Going by these definitions, education is needed by all human beings, including all girls. In harmony with the UNO's sustainable development goals, gender equality is the key to sustainable development of all nations of the world.

Considering the preceding, the aim of this chapter is to assess gender inequality as a perpetuator of gender-illiteracy nexus in Nigeria. It also aims to look at ways of disrupting or subverting the gender-illiteracy pipeline to enhance a brighter future for the education of girls in the nation. In an attempt to fulfill the aim of this contribution, the conflict theory is relied upon to provide a theoretical direction. The theory when applied to gender inequality looks at the gender disparities that exist in society as men, being the dominant group, attempt to maintain power and privileges by oppressing women, the subordinate group (Hayes, 2022). Gender disparities or discriminations are embedded within our social behaviors, norms, and belief systems; and they are disadvantageous to the overall development of the female gender.

Furthermore, this chapter adopts a narrative and exploratory style to examine girl-child education in relation to the gender-illiteracy nexus in Nigeria. The study also relies on secondary data downloaded from reliable sources, using the Google search engine. Key phrases like "girl-child education," "gender inequality," "conflict theory," etc., were used independently and paired with other related words to refine the search for specific internet sites with relevant materials that are of interest to this chapter. After downloading many materials, relevant ones that addressed the concerns of this chapter were carefully selected, evaluated, and systematically applied to the study.

4.2 UNDERSTANDING THE CONFLICT THEORY IN RELATION TO GENDER INEQUALITY

The conflict theory provides a theoretical lens for the elucidation of the existence of gender inequality and solutions to girl-child education in society, particularly in Nigeria. Through the lens of this theory, society could be viewed as a place where there is a constant struggle among groups' members to dominate others. Thus, social conflict exists as an outcome of the unequal distribution of scarce resources. Karl Marx, the foremost conflict theorist, focuses on two classes of people: the bourgeoisie, who are the wealthy group, and the proletariat, who are the working class or the poor in society (Hayes, 2022). According to the tenets of the conflict theory, competition prevails among groups because of the inherent scarcity of tangible (e.g., money, property, etc.,) and intangible (e.g., social status, dominance, etc.) resources. The theory rests on four assumptions: competition (struggle for dominance), revolution (change in social order), structural inequality (unequal distribution of resources), and war (Hayes, 2022).

The conflict theory as applicable to gender inequality looks at the struggle that exists between males as the dominating class and females as the oppressed group. The theory postulates that gender could be interpreted as the attempts of men to retain power and privileges while making women a subordinate group. In some societies, the female gender is strongly undervalued, resulting in some young girls not being given the same opportunities as boys in terms of access to nutritious food, healthcare opportunities, and educational access (Conerly, et al., 2021). Thus, education, as a means of power and dominion, is male-dominated in many parts of the world in harmony with the assumptions of the conflict theory which hold that the society is entangled in competition and structural inequality.

Friedrich Engels, in his studies of the familial structure and roles of gender, has observed that the owner-worker relationship as exemplified in the labor force is also replicated in homes, with women being equated with the proletariat (Lumen, n.d.), confirming the existence of gender conflict leading to gender inequality in our society. Conflict does not always mean violence (Okyere, 2018), but its existence in human relations or interactions could create negative outcomes of suffering, pain, and underdevelopment. For instance, as a result of gender inequality at home, girls may grow up with the understanding that they do not deserve equal treatment with boys, and boys may have the understanding that they are superior to girls. This could lead to low self-esteem or an inferiority complex on the part of girls. Gender inequality could result in boys assuming a higher level of freedom to engage in minor deviant acts, even when girls are expected to be highly obedient (Diane, 2001). The sum of gender disparity is a poor quality of life and unfulfilled dreams for the female gender.

A close look at the assumptions of the conflict theory shows that competition and structural inequality components breed conflict, while the revolution and war components may bring about a change in social order and could resolve or minimize an existing conflict. Thus, in this chapter, we attempt to apply the components of revolution and war as a means to disrupt or subvert the gender-illiteracy nexus in the educational system in Nigeria where girl-child education is in a moribund state. However, we endeavor to elucidate and expand the understanding of revolution and war in this chapter to include all attempts made to resist or subvert gender-based educational inequality. Thus, in this chapter, revolution and war could refer to suggestions, recommendations, campaigns, sensitizations, opinions, and criticisms aimed at creating a new social order conducive enough for female education in Nigeria and beyond.

4.3 DISCRIMINATION AGAINST THE GIRL-CHILD EDUCATION IN NIGERIA

Gender discrimination in education continues to thrive in Nigeria despite the government's efforts to curtail it. Previous strategies aimed at entrenching gender equality in the system include: the 1991 National Commission for Mass Literacy and Non-formal Education, 1994 Family Support Basic Education Program, 1999 Universal Basic Education Policy, 2003 Strategy for the Acceleration of Girls Education in Nigeria, and the 2004 Universal Basic Education Act (Lawal, et al., 2017). The prevalence of educational gender inequality in the country has generated a lot of responses from researchers. Hence, a careful review of literature on the subject can avail one the opportunity to harvest some of the factors that could be perceived as perpetuators of gender-illiteracy nexus in the country. These factors are the strength of male dominance and female discrimination in the distribution of education services. They fuel male dominance in the struggle for education as a scarce resource and foster structural inequality to the disadvantage of girls. Research with a focus on this subject has documented quite a number of pieces of evidence to show gender discrimination as the major challenge to gender-friendly education in the country. Thus, a panoramic view of the situation of gender discrimination in relation to the education of girls is necessary.

Offor & colleagues (2021) in their study reveal early marriage and pregnancy as one of the major banes of girl-child education in the country. The researchers also report that an estimated 15 million girls get married before the age of 18 and quit education for life. This development places the girl child at a disadvantage educationally as the male counterpart usually marries much later after acquiring at least basic education. Early marriage or betrothing of children to men as a stumbling block to girls' education could be confirmed in a number of studies (Lawal et al., 2017; Okorie, 2017; Agusiobo, 2018; Akpodiete, 2020; Abdullahi, 2020). Similarly, low value for female children, street hawking, cultural misconceptions are also found in literature as contributory factors to poor girls' access to education (British Council, 2014; Peter, 2021). Thomas-Odia (2021) also presents reactions from a cross-section of women on girls and their education during an event to mark International Day of The Girl Child. The report reveals the withdrawal of female children from school when parents face financial challenges, and fears of sexual harassment as some of the impediments standing against female gender education. From the report, the male child's education could continue even when the family income is low compared to the female child who could be pulled out of school for the same reason. Furthermore, studies reveal that some Nigerians, especially those in rural areas, see women as properties for men's pleasure and machines for producing children (Agahiu, 2016; Ifijeh & Osayande, 2011).

Adding to the list of gender discrimination against the girl child, Eugene, Adline, & Elias (2013) note gender discrimination at home and in the community, negative traditional and cultural practices, and adherence to established cultural norms as challenges to the girl-child education in a study involving 138 males and 1858 females, and covering the six geopolitical zones in Nigeria. It could be observed here that discriminatory cultural practices could limit the girl's access to education in Nigeria. Other studies pinpoint preference for boys over girls, and discriminatory treatments of girls in family, school, and society as obstacles to girl-child education (Alabi et al., 2014; Abdullahi, 2020). Preference for the male child features prominently among the types of gender discrimination affecting female access to education. Usually, the birth of a male child attracts more celebrations than that of a girl child in most African countries, including Nigeria. In addition, Okorie (2017) observes gender-driven violence, cultural attitudes against women's social standing as some of the issues affecting girls' education in the country. In another instance, Offor & colleagues (2021) reveal in a study consisting of 500 parents that parental, traditional, and religious beliefs constitute challenges to girl-child education in Anambra state.

Still on gender discrimination as an impediment to female education, Agusiobo (2018) views hawking and prostitution as causes of female educational underrepresentation. In addition, UNICEF (2007) observes that lesser learning opportunities, among other factors, impede educational equality. Finally, child labor for income generation for families poses a great challenge to female educational advancement in Nigeria (Embwai, Shauri,

Rutto, & Namasaka, 2018; Alabi & Alabi, 2012). Education for the female gender is in jeopardy since many girls in Nigeria are forced into child labor to earn a living. Unfortunately, some of them are even induced or forced into prostitution or sex work to support the family financially (Alabi et al., 2014), while male children continue to go to school to acquire education that would make them more empowered than female children in the long run.

Having gone through studies on gender discrimination against the girl-child education in Nigeria, it is evidently clear that gender discrimination prevails in the educational domain of the country. These discriminations manifest in different forms and could lead to the perpetuation of limited access to education for the girl child. Reflecting on the conflict theory, it is also clear that men's dominance resulting in discrimination against women is central to the problem of the girl-child education in Nigeria. Gender discrimination, as revealed in studies from a cross-section of scholars, reveals a preference for the boy-child as a dominant factor impeding access to girl-child education. Early or forced marriage imposed on the girl-child resulting in early pregnancies and subsequent abandonment of education are built on the dominant nature of men as a social group against the women group. The society, being male dominant, imposes early marriage on girls, but not on boys who are allowed to acquire education before marriage. Trado-religious factors also weaponize gender discrimination. Thus, it is safe to say that gender discrimination against girls creates and sustains a gender-illiteracy nexus, leading to structural inequality and limited females' access to educational services in Nigeria.

4.4 DISRUPTING GENDER-ILLITERACY NEXUS IN NIGERIA

Gender discrimination in education is a social phenomenon that should be adequately addressed with a view to disrupting or subverting its continued existence in society. A reflection on the assumptions of conflict theory shows that conflicts could be resolved through a revolution or war to install a new social order. Leaning on these assumptions, gender inequality could be interrupted through a determination to provoke a change that could curtail the prevalence of gender discrimination in relation to the education of girls. Thus, a revolution or war must be declared against gender discrimination in order to subvert or subdue it in our society, particularly in Nigeria. It is expedient to emphasize that a society should not be static, but be accommodative to positive social change that could bring about human development to improve citizens' quality of life. According to Akujobi & Jack (2017, p. 491), "Social change in society may be as a result of the expediency needed in providing solutions to specific social problems faced in society…" Thus, to disrupt the gender-illiteracy nexus, efforts should be made to alter the current social order which has made women subservient to men to create space for new social norms, values, attitudes, and a gender-friendly atmosphere that could enhance gender-friendly educational access.

Scholars and researchers have offered a number of ways society could wage war against the male-dominated educational system. The will to match words with action and a radical resolve to fight against gender discrimination must be put in place for girl child education to thrive and blossom. According to Peter (2021), sensitization on the essentiality of gender educational equality is the panacea to the escalating cases of out-of-school girls. The researcher suggests person-to-person enlightenment campaigns, government public enlightenment and policy creation, and religious followers' enlightenment through their leaders as ways of overcoming gender disparity in education. UNICEF (n.d. b) reports that Nobel Peace Prize winner and international education activist Malala Yousafzai met and talked to some girls who insisted on continuing their education in Bakassi camp, a home where over 21,000 people affected by Boko Haram insurgents reside in the northeast part of Nigeria. Thus, an enlightenment campaign in support of girl-child education could be a strong weapon in the fight against educational gender inequality. Similarly, Agusiobo (2018) advocates for government funding, creation of a ministry for children's welfare, re-orientation of social and parental values and attitudes, free and compulsory primary education, abolition of early marriage, child abuse, and gender discrimination as solutions to female education. The suggestion of this researcher provides a number of pathways to liberate the girl-child and subvert gender educational inequality in Nigeria. For instance, according to studies, some girls do not go to school or drop out because some parents could not fund all their children's education, leading to sending only boys to school on the basis of the scale of preference. However, if the government adequately funds education and makes it free, girls will stand a good chance of going to school like their male counterparts. Thus, the fight against educational gender discrimination requires the government's political will to confront the challenge and create a favorable atmosphere for both boys and girls to explore their potentials.

Furthermore, Vandima (2020) believes girls' education could improve with the following measures: equal access to education for all, public enlightenment campaigns, community involvement, employment of female teachers, building of more schools, and incentives for girls at the primary school level. Looking at these views, both the government and the community have roles to play in the fight against educational inequality. They should rise with one voice against educational gender inequality. If the government creates equal access to education, girls' education could be guaranteed, and community involvement could arm the general public with the right information on children's education. In addition, Abdullahi (2020) advocates emphasis on girls' education and the establishment of more schools, equal treatment for boys and girls in schools, and parental involvement in children's education without preferential treatment as potent means of kicking out educational gender inequality in Nigeria. The opinion expressed here by this researcher is in harmony with those earlier raised. Importantly, dealing with parental gender discrimination is a major concern. This is because many parents in Nigeria celebrate the boy child more than the girl child, leading to preferential treatment. Thus, the crusade against gender inequality or discrimination in relation to girl-child education cannot be successful without parental cooperation. This means that efforts should be made to help parents realize the importance of the girl child and the need to educate her as they do with the boy child.

In another development, Nakpodia & colleagues (2012) call for more girls' schools, a review of the curriculum to enhance girls' participation in science, bridging the educational gap between males and females, providing incentives for female education, legislation in favor of female education, parental enlightenment, and the provision of formal and non-formal education and training for girls. The points raised by these researchers are quite profound and could empower society against gender educational discrimination. For instance, the point on the provision of non-formal education for the girl-child could be a potent tool for the education of girls, especially for out-of-school girls and school dropouts. This is because non-formal education is a structured education that can be delivered to learners outside a formal school setting. Thus, the arrangement of non-formal education could help out-of-school girls receive education that could enhance their quality of life. Non-formal education could reach out-of-school girls through the radio, television, or any other medium of communication. Similarly, Ishaqi & colleagues (2014) advocate for non-formal education, especially in rural areas for out-of-school girls, mass campaigns on the need for girl-child education, collaboration with community and religious leaders, and incentives for out-of-school girls in literacy centers. Going further, Abolade (2009) suggests equal educational opportunities for all; and sensitization of rural dwellers to see the need for literacy as the way forward. Embwai & colleagues (2018) also emphasize the implementation of existing child labor laws, dealing with early marriages, improving access to education, and the elimination of gender preference. These researchers have raised very important points as we consider ways of subverting gender inequality in the educational system. For instance, as observed by the researchers, the implementation of existing child labor laws will discourage girls' street hawking and other child labor that are imposed on Nigerian girls, which are inimical to their educational progress.

Attempts have been made so far to provide pathways that could subvert or subdue educational gender discrimination in Nigeria. We have argued that a revolutionary approach has to be adopted in order to succeed in this battle. It is encouraging to note that UNICEF (2007) in its project report on girl child education in some states in Nigeria has embarked on national awareness and sensitization of stakeholders in an attempt to curtail educational gender-based disparity.

4.5 CONCLUSION

Female education is an investment whose benefits are unquantifiable to society. This is because nature has endowed women with specific qualities that are absent in men. Thus, excluding women from contributing towards the developmental and growth processes of society is inimical to progress. Education imparts knowledge, skills, attitude, and norms that could build individuals to be maximally profitable, productive, and fruitful in the world of work and society at large. Limited access to education could hinder one from getting lucrative jobs that could make one self-reliant. Unfortunately, the condition of the girl child education in Nigeria is pathetic and worrisome because of an endemic gender inequality that is escalating female illiteracy. The Universal Basic Education (UBE) and other programs embarked upon by the government and NGOs have not yielded tangible results to halt the discrimination against the girl and her quest to acquire education.

This chapter establishes that the girl-child education in Nigeria is stagnant because of the constant gender-based competition that is not favorable to girls. Some of the gender disparities cited in studies include: preference for male child, early marriages or forced marriage, child labor like street hawking, religious and cultural factors among others. Female illiteracy situation in Nigeria unleashes suffering on women as gender inequality continually limits their access to education (Abolade, 2009). As a result of continued gender discrimination, this chapter looks at ways of subverting or disrupting gender inequality or discrimination. We emphasize the need to declare war against educational gender inequality in order to create a new social order or norms that could be congenial to gender-friendly education in Nigeria. Studies reveal a number of potent weapons that could be deployed to deal with this educational quagmire. Some of the pathways suggested by scholars include: enlightenment campaigns on the importance of a girl child, funding of girl child education, incentives for girls to encourage them, legislation in support of girl child education, implementation of child labor laws, and employment of female teachers to serve as role models, among others.

4.6 RECOMMENDATIONS

Actionable plans should be put in place by relevant stakeholders to ensure gender equality in access to education, enrollment, and retention. Thus, we offer the following recommendations to reinforce the need for gender equality to disrupt or interrupt the gender-illiteracy nexus in Nigeria.

We recommend more government involvement in the battle against educational gender discrimination. The Ministry of Education, in conjunction with the Ministry of Information, should embark on national enlightenment and sensitization programs aimed at championing the cause of gender equality in education in society. The legislative arm of government should sponsor and support bills on women's liberation and girl-child education. Punitive measures should be strengthened and enforced to mitigate violence like sexual harassment, rape, and domestic violence against women.

Multinational companies, wealthy individuals in society, and NGOs should support girls' education projects through volunteering. The support could be in the form of funding or renovation of existing schools to make them more functional; building new schools to increase availability and accessibility; and provision of incentives to girls, especially those from poor homes.

Successful women in society should be involved in promoting gender equality and girls' education in particular. They should serve as good role models and organize programs or rallies where they can talk about gender equality and the benefits of girls' education to encourage upcoming girls. Similarly, these successful role models should stand up and defend cases of injustice against women.

Basic education should be made fully free, accessible, and compulsory for both boys and girls. This may require building more basic schools, especially in rural areas, to enhance easy access for girls. The proximity of schools will encourage the girl child to go to school because distant schools may increase threats of insecurity and sexual harassment, especially in rural areas where the girl child may have to walk through bushy roads to school.

Employment of more female teachers in basic schools to serve as role models for the girls should be prioritized. Similarly, girls should be assigned leadership roles like class or school prefects in schools to create equality in the school leadership system. This will make them feel valued and important with a sense of belonging.

School counselors should help girls to discover their academic and vocational strengths without prejudice. This will reduce the tendency to limit girls' vocational choice to certain areas. Generally, girls are not well-represented in technically related areas in schools; and by implication, there are few girls in the engineering fields. This disparity could be corrected through unbiased counseling provided by qualified school counselors who are trained to help individuals discover their potentials.

Religious leaders should avoid religious misinterpretations that are detrimental to the educational needs of girls. Similarly, traditional elders should reject cultural misconceptions that undervalue the girl child and promote gender inequality and discrimination. This is especially necessary in rural areas where cultural misconceptions about the value of girls appear to be prevalent due to the high illiteracy level of parents.

Parents should avoid gender preferential treatment in the family and provide equal educational opportunities to both genders. Likewise, parents should celebrate their daughters in the same way they celebrate their sons. They should also teach their boys to love their sisters without any form of discrimination. The family unit is a very strong agent of socialization and the 'first school' for children. Therefore, the role of parents in the fight against educational disparity is crucial.

Finally, subverting gender inequality and discrimination against girl education in Nigeria requires determination from girls. Therefore, we recommend that girls should rise up to defend their dignity and nobility. They should rid themselves of any misconception imposed on them by the male-dominated society to see themselves as inferior to boys. They should speak up when they are sexually harassed or inflicted with domestic violence. In school, the girl child should report cases of male dominance in the form of bullying or ridiculing to appropriate authorities. By doing so, the girl child could preserve her right to education without considering dropping out of school.

KEYWORDS

- **gender discrimination**
- **gender inequality**
- **girl child education**
- **National Policy on Education**
- **UNICEF**
- **Universal Basic Education**

REFERENCES

Abdullahi, Z. A. (2020). Women/girl-child education as a means of improving women participation in politics. *International Journal of Research and Innovation in Social Science, 4*(3), 296–300.

Abolade, D. P. (2009). A study of females' attitude towards literacy programmes in Southwestern Nigeria. *International Journal of Literacy Education, 6*(1), 185–195.

Agusiobo, B. C. (2018). Education of the girl-child in Nigeria for a just, peaceful, harmonious society and sustainable development. *International Online Journal of Education and Teaching, 5*(4), 768–786.

Akpodiete, H. M. (2020). The synergy between culture and society in the eradication of child molestation in Nigeria. *International Journal of Humanities Social Sciences and Education, 7*(10), 88–93.

Akujobi, T., & Jack, J. (2017). Social change and social problems. In E. M. Abasiekong, E. A. Sibiri, & N. S. Ekpenyong (Eds.), *Major Theories in Sociology: An Introduction Text* (pp. 491–526). Benin City, Mase Perfect Prints.

Alabi, T., & Alabi, O. S. (2012). Child labor amongst urban poor in Lagos and Abuja. *Journal of Peace, Gender and Development, 2*(3), 36–47.

Alabi, T., Bahah, M., & Alabi, S. O. (2014). The girl-child: A sociological view on the problems of girl-child education in Nigeria. *European Scientific Journal, 10*(2), 393–409.

British Council. (2014). Girls' education in Nigeria report 2014: Issues, influencers and actions. Retrieved from: www.britishcouncil.org.ng (accessed on 19 June 2024).

Bussey, K., & Bandura, A. (1999). Social cognitive theory of gender development and differentiation. *Psychological Review, 106*(4), 676–713.

Chazan, B. (2022). What is Education? In: Principles and pedagogies in Jewish education, Palmgrave Macmillan, Cham. https://doi.org/10.1007/978-3-030-83925-3_3.

Conerly, T. J., Holmes, K., & Tamang, A. L. (2021). *Introduction to Sociology 3e*. Houston, TX: OpenStax. https://openstax.org/books/introduction-sociology-3e/pages/1-introduction (accessed on 19 June 2024).

Diane, R. (2001). Spice Girls,' 'nice girls,' 'girlies,' and 'tomboys': Gender discourses, girls' cultures and femininities in the primary classroom. *Gender and Education, 13*(2), 153–167.

Dorcas, K., & Peter, D. K. (2021). Challenges of girl-child education in Nigeria. Retrieved from: https://www.blueprint.ng/challenges-of-girl-child-education-in-nigeria/ (accessed on 19 June 2024).

Egenti, M. N. (2008). Personal and environmental path predictors of girl child retention in Lagos State schools, Nigeria. *International Journal of Educational Research, 4*(1), 127–133.

Embwai, M. A., Shauri, H. S., Rutto, S. K., & Namasaka, F. W. (2018). Impact of socioeconomics on low access to basic education among girls in Bali Local Government Area, Taraba State Nigeria. *European Journal of Education Studies, 4*(10), 227–247.

Ene-Obong, H. N., Onuoha, N. O., & Eme, P. E. (2017). Gender roles, family relationships, and household food and nutrition security in Ohafia matrilineal society in Nigeria. *Maternal and Child Nutrition, 13*(3), 1–13.

Eugene, A. C., Adline, A. C., & Eliassues, A. O. (2013). Challenges and prospects of female education in Nigeria: Implications for sports administration in schools. *Global Journal of Human Social Science Linguistics & Education, 13*(5, 1), 8–16.

Federal Republic of Nigeria. (2004). *National Policy on Education* (4th ed.). Lagos, Nigeria: Nigerian Educational Research and Development Council (NERDC) Press.

Hot Vibe Media. (2021). Girl-child education in Nigeria: Problems and prospects. Retrieved from: https://www.hotvibesmedia.com.ng/2018/02/girl-child-education-in-nigeria-problems-prospects.html (accessed on 19 June 2024).

Ifijeh, G. I., & Osayande, O. (2011). Issues in girl-child education in Nigeria: Implications for library and information support. *Gender & Behavior, 9*(2), 4139–4150.

Ikechukwu, N. C. (2020). Gender inequality in education: Implications for socioeconomic development in Nigeria. *Sapiential Foundation Journal of Education, Sciences and Gender Studies, 2*(3), 257–266.

Ishaqi, A., & Ali, M. (2014). Non-formal education and the girl-child in northern Nigeria: Issues and strategies. *Journal of Education and Practice, 5*(37), 45–50.

Lawal, H. B., Miachi, O. D., & Kalu, U. U. (2017). An examination of girls' education policies in Nigeria with focus on the Northeast. Retrieved from: www.connecteddevelopment.org (accessed on 19 June 2024).

Lawrence, C. (1976). *Public Education*. New York, NY: Basic Books.

Lumen. (n.d.). Introduction to sociology: sociological perspectives on gender stratification. Retrieved from: https://courses.lumenlearning.com/boundless-sociology/chapter/sociological-perspectiveson-genderstratification/#:~:text=According%20to%20conflict%20theory%2C%20society,to%20the%20detriment%20of%20women (accessed on 19 June 2024)..

Malala Fund. (n.d. a). Nigeria: Nigeria accounts for 20% of all out-of-school children in West Africa, with nearly 20 million out-of-school children. Retrieved from: https://malala.org/countries/nigeria (accessed on 19 June 2024).

Malala Fund. (n.d. b). Malala fund: Malala's story. Retrieved from: https://malala.org/malalas-story?sc=header (accessed on 19 June 2024)..

Malala Fund. (n.d. c). Malala fund: Girls' education. Retrieved from: https://malala.org/girlseducation?sc=header (accessed on 19 June 2024).

Nakpodia, E. D., & Urien, J. (2012). Gender discrimination in Nigerian school system. *International Journal of Development and Management Review, 7*, 74–79.

Offor, U. I., Anadi, C. C., & Orisa, A. A. (2017). Political education, an empowerment tool for sustainable political development in Anambra State. *Journal of the Nigerian Academy of Education, 13*(2), 187–197.

Offor, U. I., Anadi, C. C., Nwaru, E. P., & Chukwuemeka, A. O. (2021). Issues in girl-child education in Nigeria: Implications for sustainable development. *Unizik Journal of Educational Research and Policy Studies, 4*, 227–242.

Offorma, G. C. (2009). Girl-child education in Africa. Keynote address presented at The Conference of The Federation of The University Women of Africa, Held in Lagos-Nigeria on 16th – 19th July, 2009. Retrieved from: https://www.researchgate.net/publication/280554452 (accessed on 19 June 2024).

Okorie, M. (2017). An assessment of factors militating against girl child education in Nigeria. *International Journal of Advanced and Multidisciplinary Social Science, 3*(2), 49–54. https://doi.org/10.5923/j.jamss.20170302.

Okyere, J. (2018). Gender and conflict. *Asian Journal of Social Sciences and Management Studies, 5*(3), 82–86.

Omede, A. A., & Agahiu, G. E. (2016). The implications of girl-child education to nation building in the 21st century in Nigeria. *Global Journal of Human-Social Science: Linguistics & Education, 16*(3), 1–4.

Ossai, E. D. (2021). Education in emergency in Nigeria: Creating gender equitable policies so all girls have an uninterrupted right to learn. Retrieved from: https://www.brookings.edu/blog/education-plus-development/2021/07/27/education-in-emergency-in-nigeria-creating-gender-equitable-policies-so-all-girls-have-an-uninterrupted-right-to-learn/ (accessed on 19 June 2024).

Thomas-Odia, I. (2021). Low literacy, early marriage impedes rights, girls' voices. Retrieved from: https://guardian.ng/guardian-woman/low-literacy-early-marriage-impede-rights-girls-voices/.

Tyessi, K. (2021). IDGC: 1.3m girls drop out of school before reaching JS3 in Nigeria, says UNICEF. Retrieved from: https://www.thisdaylive.com/index.php/2021/10/11/idgc-1-3m-girls-drop-out-of-school-before-reaching-js3-in-nigeria-saysunicef.

UNESCO. (2017). Unpacking Sustainable Development Goal 4 Education 2030. Retrieved from: https://www.sdg4education2030.org/unpacking-sustainable-development-goal-4-education-2030-unesco-2017 (accessed on 19 June 2024).

UNESCO. (2018). *Defining literacy: GAML fifth meeting on 17–18 October, 2018,* Hamburg, Germany, UNESCO Institute for Statistics. Retrieved from: https://gaml.uis.unesco.org/wpcontent/uploads/sites/2/2018/12/4.6.1_07_4.6-defining-literacy.pdf.

UNESCO. (2022). Number of illiterates. Retrieved from: http://uis.unesco.org/en/glossary-term/number-illiterates#:~:text=Definition,simple%20statement%20on%20everyday%20 life (accessed on 19 June 2024).

UNICEF. (2007). Information sheet: Girls' education, Nigeria country programme. Retrieved from: https://nairametrics.com (accessed on 19 June 2024).

UNICEF. (n.d.-a). Against all odds girls learn again. Retrieved from: https://www.unicef.org/nigeria/stories/against-all-odds-girls-learn-again (accessed on 19 June 2024).

UNICEF. (n.d.-b). Education is key: Malala visits schoolgirls displaced by the Boko Haram crisis in northeast Nigeria. Retrieved from: https://www.unicef.org/nigeria/stories/

education-key-malala-visits-schoolgirls-displaced-boko-haram-crisis-northeast-nigeria (accessed on 19 June 2024).

United Nations. (2020). Executive summary: COVID-19 and the need for action on mental health. Retrieved from: https://www.un.org/sites/un2.un.org/files/un_policy_brief-covid_and_mental_health.

Vandima, T. M. (2020). Gender inequality among Nigerian students. *International Journal of Research and Scientific Innovation, 7*(1), 173–178.

CHAPTER 5

GENDER DISPARITY IN THE ADOPTION OF ICT

KRITIKA GOSAIN

School of Education, Sharda University, Greater Noida, Uttar Pradesh, India

ABSTRACT

Technological boon in the 21st century has made way for another kind of gender disparity which is digital in nature. Half of the female population of the world lacks access to technology and is thus walled off from the globalized world. Gender disparities are evident in the difference in male and female technological abilities, female participation in the IT industry, and difference in technology utilization by both genders. The present chapter searched the reasons for this digital gender disparity and attempted to provide a rational solution for them.

5.1 INTRODUCTION

The supremacy and transformative possibilities of ICT and access to the Internet are not dispersed evenly. The bulk of the estimated 2.7 billion individuals who are currently disconnected are females. The digital gender gap continues to expand in many developing nations, necessitating a special effort to promote digital gender equality. In 2022, 62% of males will use the Internet globally, compared to 57% of women (Abbiss, 2008). Society benefits when women and girls are empowered to use ICTs. They have opportunities to establish new enterprises, sell items in new markets, and

Subverting Social Inequalities: Gender as a Social Reality.
Akanksha Srivastava, Disha Maheshwari, Chitra Krishnan (Eds.)

obtain better-paying jobs with an Internet connection and digital technology skills. When women gain the right to access the web and the ability to use ICT, it allows them to open businesses, sell products in emerging markets, find better-paid jobs, seek education and access financial and wellness services, share information, and engage more actively in public life. Most countries with a significant gender gap in mobile phone ownership also have a large gender disparity in Internet users. Since mobile phones are the most commonly used method of accessing the web, addressing the gender gap in mobile phone usage may help reduce the gender gap in Internet activity. Digital technologies are a crucial avenue to gender equality and women's empowerment. The global digital gender disparity can be divided into four primary categories: (1) a gap in Internet availability and usage; (2) a gap in digital skills and tool usage; (3) a gap in involvement in STEM subjects; and (4) a deficit in tech sector leadership and entrepreneurship (Abbiss, 2008).

Countries with a comparatively modest gender disparity in Internet and ICT availability might yet have a big gender imbalance in STEM engagement. According to UNESCO, women make up just 30% of the world's researchers on average, and less than a third of female students in higher education take subjects like mathematics and engineering. According to the OECD, female-owned enterprises obtain 23% less capital and are 30% less likely to achieve a good departure than male-owned enterprises. However, between 40 and 160 million females might want to transfer to new jobs by 2030, frequently into more proficient roles requiring more sophisticated ICT competencies.

5.2 GENDER DISPARITY

The research literature on gender and computer science education may be divided into two major discourses: a hegemonic liberal equality narrative and a post-structural critical discourse. The first is largely concerned with issues of equal opportunity, assuming that progressive reforms would solve gender imbalances; the second is concerned with issues of social justice, calling into question the changing, nuanced, and multifaceted nature of society and individuals (Moore, 2004). This critical discourse argues that the 'issue' of gender and computer science education might not be as straightforward as it looks, and that it could be related to how we contemplate about it as much as to particular proof of gender inequalities. The evidence of gender inequality is categorized into the following themes:

5.2.1 UNEQUAL ACCESS TO TECHNOLOGY

a. Computer usage among boys is observed to be quite more frequent than girls at home and in school, to conquer technology and have greater participation rates in information technology classes and more experience with specific activities such as programming (Crombie & Armstrong, 1999; McKinnon & Nolan, 1990; Chen, 1986). There are certain exemptions to the rule of male dominance in programming activity. In an early North American survey, Becker and Sterling (1987) discovered that word processing is the single field in which girls outnumber boys in computer usage. In the British context, Durndell, Glissov & Siann (1995) find exceptions pertaining to computer usage at school and outside of school. At school, the computers are mainly used for gaming and outside of school, the computers are mainly used for information processing. Yet, these outliers reinforce the general claim that gender differences in computer access and use continue. The developed world appears to have expanded its overall level of computer access.
b. Yet, recent data shows considerable gender differences in computer access and usage (Colley & Comber, 2003; Clegg & Trayhurn, 2000). Socioeconomic status and family conditions are taken into account. Pupils from lower socioeconomic origins and ethnic minorities are more likely to be omitted from engaging with computers, and girls are more likely to be marginalized than their male counterparts (Volman et al., 2005).

5.2.2 DIFFERENCE IN COMPUTER USAGE

a. Access and use issues are frequently connected to the notion that men and women prefer distinct computing techniques and have diverse attitudes about computers. Initial research indicates that girls prefer apps that are made for communications and activities centered on presenting and writing new ideas, like word processing, whereas guys prefer computer games and mathematics applications (McKinnon & Nolan, 1990). Recent study has demonstrated persistent gender differences in preferences for a variety of applications. Men, in particular, have been demonstrated to monopolize gaming and have more Internet experience than girls (Wilson, 2002). It also means that as men and women have become more frequent computer users, computers have become a more prevalent component of daily life and trends of use have developed. According to Colley & Comber (2003), ICT is increasingly prevalent in educational institutions, with a diminishing gender gap in students' use of word processing, visuals, programming, and mathematics applications. They also find no broad gender differences in the frequency with newly developed technologies such as emailing, the Internet, and CD-ROMs. Gardyn (2003) observed that both girls and boys routinely access and use computers for entertainment, especially the web, albeit they do so in various ways.

b. Dealing with computers in school appears to motivate students. Yet, as the preceding examples demonstrate, students' experiences with technology in school vary by gender. Gender inequalities in students' perceptions of ICT's educational utility supplement research that shows gender differences in computer attitudes, despite the fact that the gender gap in ICT usage has shrunk (Cooper, 2006). Girls' attitudes on computer confidence are shown to be less positive (Volman et al., 2005).
c. The term "educational tools" refers to the entire spectrum of software and information that may be utilized in educational practice, such as specific educational programs, simulations and games, electronic mail, and the World Wide Web. However, it has become evident in recent years that when discussing gender variations in the use and enjoyment of ICT, we must differentiate between different forms of ICT usage.
d. Males play computer video games more frequently than females, while girls take fewer technology subjects in school than boys (Cassell, 2002). Females use e-mail more regularly than boys. Females are less likely than men to respond positively to questions regarding computer attitudes in general, but they are enthusiastic about word processing and art programs (Volman & Van Eck, 2001). Females appear to like cooperative video games and digital teaching tools more than competitive tools. They choose games that require imagination over those that require dexterity, and they value vivid and colorful pictures in games and instructional technology tools (Fiore, 1999). Also, when using learning tools, girls prefer clear instructions and an intriguing subject over boys, while boys prefer visuals and competitiveness over girls (Heemskerk et al., 2008).

The distinctions indicated above support the hypothesis that using a certain instructional instrument in class may affect males and girls differently. In other words, educational instruments may be less inclusive of either males or girls, resulting in differing learning experiences and outcomes. Yet, the link between the ostensible inclusion of certain instructional technologies and actual student experiences with them has yet to be thoroughly examined.

e. In terms of gender disparities in ICT self-efficacy and ICT interest, meta-analyzes of research conducted spanning decades revealed a recurring result: boys reported greater levels of ICT self-efficacy and ICT interest than girls. According to studies, the gender stereotyping of computers as a "masculine" subject may account for males' relatively positive attitude about computers (Cai, et al., 2017). Computer usage, in particular, has traditionally been regarded as a "masculine" subject that males are better proficient at. This female stereotype of computers has been reinforced by the mass media. According to longitudinal research, the gender difference in ICT self-efficacy is fairly minor in elementary school but expands in secondary school (Volman et al., 2005). The buildup of stereotypes in favor of men might be one of the reasons for worsening the gender gap.

5.2.3 ATTITUDE TOWARDS THE USE OF TECHNOLOGY

a. When it comes to student views about computers, women have less favorable attitudes than males (Mitra, LaFrance & McCullough, 2001). Females are stereotyped as being less confident, timider, and more apprehensive computer users, with lower levels of self-efficacy, notably in programming and computer science (Colley & Comber, 2003). They are also seen to be more cautious in their appraisals of the worth of technical breakthroughs, as well as more skeptical and inclined to question the utility of a computer in comparison to other information sources and ways of information processing (Crombie & Armstrong, 1999).
b. With the advent of information technology into education, a new dimension of "gender disparities" has emerged. This gender difference has arisen along the same lines as earlier societal divides. Gender discrepancies that existed in science-related areas have been generalized into IT. Women and girls may have a more negative attitude

towards technology and technology usage than men and boys, and they may be less actively involved in technology-related activities and behaviors, according to a stereotyped picture of technology use and gender that has formed over time. Technology is viewed by society as highly technical and a male realm, with the usage of IT tools considered a masculine pastime (North & Noyes, 2002).

c. Turkle (1984) proposes that men and women view computer programming in distinct manners. Females, she claims, are 'soft' masters, while males are nearly exclusively 'hard' masters. Hard mastery is the projection of will over using computers via the execution of a well-planned strategy. Soft mastery is more intuitive and participatory than hard mastering. It entails tinkering and is the method used by artists who deal with materials. These two methods are based on Levi-Strauss' conceptions of scientist and bricoleur (Turkle & Papert 1990). Others attribute gender disparities in preferences and methods to learning styles and basic cognitive differences (Culley, 1988).
d. Women are classified as task-oriented users who concentrate on computer utilitarian operations and the final product. Men, on the other hand, are classified as power users who are machine-oriented and regard the computer as a toy to be controlled for the sake of manipulation. Men are said to be more independent and competitive in their computer attitude, whereas females are more sociable. There are widely recognized historical gender variations in computer use and attitudes. Nonetheless, caution should be exercised when extrapolating to new century educational situations (Mitra et al. 2000).
e. Women lag behind males in the ownership of technology and the development of technological abilities in a number of ways. Men, for example, own and use more technology than women, spend more time online, enroll in more technology programs, and are more motivated to gain digital skills (Cooper, 2006). Men have more experience and utilize the Web more than women for a variety of activities, particularly those that involve higher technological abilities, such as job hunting, e-banking, and posting or uploading information (Hargittai & Walejko, 2008).
f. Females have more anxiety than males when it comes to technology use. According to studies, the masculine image of the computer has discouraged girls from utilizing technology, making them less confident or apprehensive (Culley, 1988). The societal image of computer scientists as geeks, nerds, or socially isolated persons, as well as the

impression that computer science is just for men, appear to have an impact on females' unfavorable attitudes about computers.

g. Among all of these factors, a teacher's attitude towards information technology may play a significant influence in its acceptance, successful integration, and usage for good outcomes in education. According to Albirini (2006), the successful use of information technologies in education is dependent on the educators' attitudes, who ultimately decide the manner in which they are employed in the educational process. Not only do attitudes impact initial acceptance, but they also affect future conduct. According to Jencius & Paez (2003) (as cited in Islhani & Nasrin, 2020), knowing attitude is vital because attitudinal hurdles can stymie the adoption of new technologies.
h. The teachers' unfavorable attitude towards technology is a significant element in their resistance to incorporating information technologies into education, despite the resources available in their schools and classrooms (Lloyd & Albion, 2005). They may regard technology as intimidating and overpowering or they may be afraid of appearing ignorant or inept in front of their pupils. This negative attitude may drive instructors to mistrust the efficacy of IT in education and, as a result, be hesitant to employ technology in their classrooms.
i. According to Rogers' (1995) Diffusion of Innovations Theory, people's attitude about a technology is one of the crucial components in its acceptance. Similarly, the Technology Acceptance Model (TAM) (Davis, 1989) provides the same message about having a favorable attitude regarding a technology before accepting it.

5.2.4 CULTURAL DIFFERENCES IN ICT USAGE

a. The prevalence of gender-based preferences and male domination of specific kinds of computers has given rise to the notion that computing is a male realm. A macho computing culture appears to have perpetuated a gendered realm. It has been argued that computer skills are more socially acceptable in the culture of adolescent males than females (Chen, 1986), that computing has become predominantly a male image associated with notions of "boys' toys" (Newton & Beck, 1993) and with male traits or symbols of control, aggression, analytical processes, and technological power. It is said that cultural symbols of computing favor masculinity, which repels girls significantly more than boys, and that this explains the historical lack of females in computer labor and education. Many variables have been identified as contributing to the development and maintenance of a masculine computer culture. Others attribute it to socialization and widespread gender stereotyping in families, social groups, and the media (Dryburgh, 2000).

b. Others point to instructional techniques and school systems that generate and replicate a masculine computing environment. Boys and men have been observed claiming superior expertise, dominating conversation and instructor time, dominating machines, and making ladies feel uncomfortable or inadequate (Culley, 1988).

c. Teachers' attitudes and actions, or lack thereof, are perceived to dissuade females from participating in computing activities and, unknowingly, to support macho computing culture. It has been proposed, for example, that educational techniques that allow pupils to learn on their own are especially harmful for girls. Males are more inclined to have the ability to draw on past experience, whereas girls are blamed for a relative lack of access and lesser usage of computers at home (McKinnon & Nolan, 1990).

d. The computer business is also blamed for fostering a male computer culture, particularly in the sector of computer gaming. It is stated that game software is primarily designed for a male market, and that stereotypical visuals and subject matter are more appealing to men than to women. Furthermore, guys are regarded to be more at ease with the competitive aspect of gaming. It is believed that girls regard computer games as toys for guys and find the computer gaming environment unfriendly, socially inappropriate, rude, or dull (Culley, 1993).

e. The notion that a macho computer culture is repulsive to ladies assumes that the way guys conduct around computers is repulsive to girls. Nonetheless, there are differing perspectives on the nature of this pain. According to cognitive differences learning styles theories, females are put off by a masculine manner of working that is characterized by rational, logical, and systematic approaches to computing (Culley, 1993). Sofia (1998), on the other hand, contends that masculine irrationalities – the competition, desires, and fantasies displayed by guys for technology – rather than rationality and logic, tend to alienate girls and withdraw them from computer usage. Turkle & Papert (1990) argue that computer technology enables epistemic pluralism, or multiple approaches to computing and programming, but that the dominant male computer culture does not. As a result, there is a strong thread in the research literature describing programming as a masculine area backed by a macho computer culture. Different computer habits, by inference, might be understood to establish female domains and feminine culture.

f. Educational technology designers have distinct views of future users and future usage. These "user representations" or "scripts" are inadvertently integrated into technological design. Scripts are assumptions about a presumed user that form an integral element of the overall technical development process. According to one research (Cooper, 2006), teachers who build educational software frequently write with boys in mind, resulting in gender scripts that make the tools more appealing to boys than to girls. Users of technology, on the other hand, are not required to follow the scripts as written by the designers. They can edit the scripts or reject them via "domestication" operations.
g. Van Zoonen (2002) illustrates how gender codes play a significant role in the domestication of the Internet. Teachers and students are active participants in this domestication in the context of educational technology, and they can adjust gender scripts in a variety of ways. According to Heemskerk et al. (2005), there are three parts of educational software that contain such scripts: the content, the visual and acoustic interface, and the instructional structure of the technical tool.
h. Most teachers must agree that instructional tools should not be used purposefully to disfavor certain student groups. As a result, they should provide students with ideal opportunities to identify with the subject matter and the manner in which it is given, and each student should feel both comfortable and challenged when working with an instructional tool. As a result, the content and design of instructional tools should be appealing to both females and males. Furthermore, the program's structure and the types of learning activities it promotes should correspond to the skill levels and learning techniques of distinct student groups.

5.2.5 DISADVANTAGEOUS STATUS OF WOMEN

a. The imperatives of the information age have created a widely held belief that computer skills are a necessity for citizenship and that being digitally illiterate, or less proficient with computers than others, is economically and socially disadvantageous (Spender, 1995).

b. Females are seen to be underrepresented in 'hard' computing fields such as computing and systems analysis, while being disproportionately represented in 'soft' programming areas such as visual design and office applications. Women's lack of engagement in software development and activities, according to the idea of knowledge being power, will weaken and disadvantage them (Selby, 1995).
c. There is a widespread assumption that boys' digital experiences better prepare them for a labor market that requires computer abilities, but ladies are less well-equipped and so economically and socially disadvantaged. A discourse of insufficiency, in which females are blamed for perceived unfairness, coexists alongside the language of disadvantage. Females are criticized for their lack of computer interest and passivity in the face of male control. Girls are regarded to be deficient in self-esteem, bravery, and dedication, preventing them from achieving the same accomplishments as guys.
d. According to Chen (1986), "a major cause of gender disparities is males' higher eagerness to participate in technological activities." By implication, the challenge is the mindset of females, their refusal to engage. Nonetheless, women are not always explicitly accused for this condition. They might be represented as sufferers of socialization procedures which generate distinct gender stereotypes for males and girls. Whatever the source, the remedy is typically framed in initiatives to influence girls' attitudes towards computers.
e. The problematic situation of female disadvantage in computers can be rectified by a range of school-based methods. They aim at modifying the computer instruction and the way it is delivered. Reducing competition for resources by putting computers in traditional classrooms, incorporating IT in a variety of courses, and modifying classroom pedagogy are some suggestions.

5.3 MEASURE TO CONQUER GENDER DISPARITY

The gender disparity could be overcome by providing equal access, building a positive attitude among women to adopt technology, and by providing support to disadvantaged women. The following points will provide solutions to overcome the gender disparity:

5.3.1 PROVIDING EQUAL ACCESS TO TECHNOLOGY

Women must be given access to the Internet as well as the ability to utilize it. This will enable people to start new businesses, obtain better-paying employment, get access to education, health, and financial sectors, and boost their involvement with society and information sharing.

While digital gender disparities have shrunk in many developed countries, they have expanded in many developing countries, demanding a concerted effort to advance digital gender equality in all of those countries. The International Telecommunication Union (ITU) promotes data collection and exchange in order to reduce the gender gap in internet access. It helps nations build the ability to gather, disseminate, and share global and national data, with a focus on individuals who have access to and use ICTs and digital literacy. High-quality, gender-disaggregated data will help in the assessment, evaluation, and development of gender-related policy.

Data reveals that the majority of nations with a big gender disparity in smartphone ownership additionally experience a large gender imbalance in Internet users. Since cellphones are the most often utilized way of accessing the Web, addressing the gender gap in cellphone usage may assist in lessening the gender gap in Web usage. By 2025, the ITU-UNESCO Broadband Commission for Sustainable Development has set a goal of achieving gender equality in all of its aims pertaining to Web access and digital competencies. In 2022, ITU collaborated with the Office of the Secretary-General's Envoy on Technology (OSET) to create a framework that includes an objective for gender parity in Web access by 2030. School is the very first setting where youngsters are exposed to technology while also gaining the reading and arithmetic skills necessary to use digital tools. Hence, school girls must be provided with equal access to acquire appropriate technical skills and digital literacy in school so that they can use digital tools.

5.3.2 BUILDING A POSITIVE ATTITUDE TOWARDS THE USE OF COMPUTERS

The access to the internet will not be of much help unless the perception among women towards the use of computers is made favorable. Women are less prone to using technology compared to their counterparts (Volman et al., 2005). Studies suggest that women are less confident and lack self-efficacy when it comes to computing. The major reason for this is the representation of computers as a "masculine" subject (Cai, et al., 2017). Therefore, technology should not be treated as gender-neutral, so that misconceptions related to the use of computers can be avoided. The school environment should be gender-neutral, and teachers must not regard computers as "masculine," and digital literacy should be considered a right for both girls and boys.

One such study by Bain & Rice (2006), where equal opportunity to access the internet and gender neutrality is practiced, found no difference in attitudes towards using computers based on gender. The majority of women do not find computers challenging, while many men believe they are better computer users than women. Women spend 64% more time on computers than men, with a focus on instant messaging, playing mobile games, and completing homework online. Men, on the other hand, spend more time playing mobile games, using online messaging, and doing homework on the computer. All participants in the study had access to technology at home, which influenced their attitudes towards computers and other technical tools. Participants identified their fathers as the most frequent users of home computers. They were comfortable using computers as they observed their parents and teachers modeling computer use in various activities, including email and work, both at home and in classrooms (Bain & Rice, 2006).

Cooper (2006) mentioned that females also lag behind in the development of technological tools and computational abilities. Additionally, males and females use different technological tools, which lead to different learning experiences. The difference in technological tools also promotes the development of different attitudes and perceptions towards the usage of computers. In order to develop a positive attitude towards technology, developers and designers must create a user-friendly interface that is easy to learn and eliminates the potential for developing any negative attitudes.

Constant encouragement and motivation must be provided by teachers, team leaders, and family members to use technology, which will develop computational abilities. One must refrain from making any negative comments on the errors or shortcomings in the computational abilities of females; instead, technical and moral support needs to be provided to them, which will further boost their confidence.

Training programs and incentives can also be provided to females to empower them for programming and designing several other training programs. To increase the number of girls in technological programs, certain incentives and relaxation can be provided. The policy and curriculum must make appropriate provisions to facilitate the enrollment of girls in computer courses.

5.3.3 OVERCOMING THE DISADVANTAGEOUS STATUS OF WOMEN AND CULTURAL DIFFERENCES

To address the problem of female disadvantage in computers, several strategies can be employed. Focus must be on modifying how computer instruction is organized and delivered in order to reduce resource contention by putting computers in traditional classrooms, incorporating IT in a variety of courses, and modifying classroom pedagogy. Constructionist and group techniques, inquiries, shared problem-solving, debates about social concerns, and peer assessments are particularly suited for females. Selby (1995) proposed using a computer as a tool to foster interest in computation as well as information processing. The goal is to modify the perception of computer education and make it more appealing, consumable, and relevant to a broader spectrum of pupils, particularly girls. Yet, reformist requests for curricular change have the potential to strengthen rather than diminish gendered computer cultures.

5.4 CONCLUSION

Billions of girls and women do not have access to technology and remain disconnected from the global village. Gender disparity is also evident in the gap in digital competencies between males and females, participation of women in the IT sector, and usage of technologies. Many studies have been done to provide evidence of the existence of gender inequality. These studies are categorized into five broad themes: unequal access to technology with respect to gender, differences in computer usage, varying attitudes towards the use of technology, cultural differences, and the disadvantaged status of women. One of the major reasons cited is the unequal distribution of opportunities to access ICT and the web among males and females. The unequal access to ICT also leads to differential usage of technology; males are more frequent users of technology than their female counterparts. Women and girls use ICT mostly for information processing, whereas men use it for playing games and programming. This differential use of technologies leads to the development of different digital temperaments, with males being more frequent and vivid users of ICT developing high technological skills and getting better job opportunities than women. This contributes to another aspect of gender disparity: the disadvantaged status of women. Since women only use computers for utilitarian purposes and not for creating new programs, their role in technology development is regarded as inferior and thus they are usually devoid of opportunities to become digital citizens, which disempowers them. The reason behind the male domination lies in the cultural differences. Most cultures regard computers as 'masculine' and thus consider males to be perfect candidates for mastering the skill of computation rather than females. Also, the attitude of society favors men in terms of using ICT. In schools too, boys were more encouraged to use technology than girls. All these inequalities lead to the development of a negative attitude among females towards ICT and the rate of adoption lessens. Gender disparity can be overcome by formulating policies to provide equal technological access, building a positive attitude among females to use computers, and modifying cultural practices to make them gender-neutral.

KEYWORDS

- **ICT**
- **International Telecommunication Union**
- **Office of the Secretary-Envoy General's on Technology**
- **technology acceptance model**
- **IT industry**
- **STEM**

REFERENCES

Abbiss, J. (2008). Rethinking the 'problem' of gender and IT schooling: Discourses in literature. *Gender and Education, 20*(2), 153–165. https://doi.org/10.1080/09540250701805839.

Albirini, A. (2006). Teachers' attitudes toward information and communication technologies. *Computers & Education, 47*(4), 373–398.

Bain, C. D., & Rice, M. L. (2006). The influence of gender on attitudes, perceptions, and uses of technology. *Journal of Research on Technology in Education, 39*(3), 119–132.

Becker, H. J., & Sterling, C. W. (1987). Equity in school computer use: National data and neglected considerations. *Journal of Educational Computing Research, 3*(3), 289–311. https://doi.org/10.2190/427X-RKEL-QLA5-PUK9.

Cai, Z., Fan, X., & Du, J. (2017). Gender and attitudes toward technology use: A meta-analysis. *Computers and Education, 105*, 1–13. https://doi.org/10.1016/j.compedu.2016.11.003.

Cassell, J. (2002). Genderizing HCI. In J. Jacko & A. Sears (Eds.), *The Handbook of Human-Computer Interaction* (pp. 402–411). Mahwah, NJ: Lawrence Erlbaum. Retrieved from: https://nideffer.net/classes/270-08/week_07_gender_economy/cassell_gendering_hci.pdf .

Chen, M. (1986). Gender and computers: The beneficial effects of experience on attitudes. *Journal of Educational Computing Research, 2*(3), 265–282. https://doi.org/10.2190/WDRY-9K0F-VCP6-JCCD.

Clegg, S., & Trayhurn, D. (2000). Gender and computing: Not the same old problem. *British Educational Research Journal, 26*(1), 75–89. https://doi.org/10.1080/014119200109525.
Colley, A., & Comber, C. (2003). Age and gender differences in computer use and attitudes among secondary students. *Educational Research, 45*(2), 155–165. https://doi.org/10.1080/0013188032000103235.
Cooper, J. (2006). The digital divide: The special case of gender. *Journal of Computer Assisted Learning, 22*(5), 320–334. https://doi.org/10.1111/j.1365-2729.2006.00185.x.
Crombie, G., & Armstrong, P. I. (1999). Effects of classroom gender composition on adolescents' computer-related attitudes and future intentions. *Journal of Educational Computing Research, 20*(4), 317–327. https://doi.org/10.2190/XW2D-THFA-T6RW-Y8H9.
Culley, L. (1988). Option choices and careers guidance: Gender and computing in secondary schools. *British Journal of Counseling and Guidance, 16*(1), 72–82.
Davis, F. D. (1989). Perceived usefulness, perceived ease of use, and user acceptance of information technology. *MIS Quarterly, 13*(3), 319–340. https://doi.org/10.2307/249008.
Dryburgh, H. (2000). Underrepresentation of girls and women in computer science: Classification of the research. *Journal of Educational Computing Research, 23*(2), 181–202. https://doi.org/10.2190/8RYV-9JWH-XQMB-QF41.
Durndell, A., Glissov, P., & Siann, G. (1995). Gender and computing: Persisting differences. *Educational Research, 37*(3), 219–227. https://doi.org/10.1080/0013188950370301.
Fiore, C. (1999). Awakening the tech bug in girls. *Learning and Leading with Technology, 26*(5), 10–17.
Gardyn, R. (2003). Born to be wired. *American Demographics, 25*(3), 14–15.
Hargittai, E., & Walejko, G. (2008). The participation divide: Content creation and sharing in the digital age. *Information, Communication and Society, 11*(2), 239–256. https://doi.org/10.1080/13691180801946150.
Heemskerk, I., Brink, A., Volman, M., & Ten Dam, G. (2005). Inclusiveness and ICT in education: A focus on gender, ethnicity, and social class. *Journal of Computer Assisted Learning, 21*(1), 1–16. https://doi.org/10.1111/j.1365-2729.2005.00106.x.
Heemskerk, I., Volman, M., Ten Dam, G., & Admiraal, W. (2008). Social scripts in educational technology and inclusiveness in classroom practice. Manuscript submitted for publication. *Journal of Research on Technology in Education, 41*(3), 253–276.
Islahi, F., & Nasrin, N. (2019). Exploring teacher attitude towards information technology with a gender perspective. *Contemporary Educational Technology, 10*(1), 37–54. https://doi.org/10.30935/cet.512527.
Lloyd, M. & Albion, P. (2005). Mistaking the Tool for the Outcome: Using Activity System Theory to understand the Complexity of Teacher Technophobia. In C. Crawford, R. Carlsen, I. Gibson, K. McFerrin, J. Price, R. Weber & D. Willis (Eds.), Proceedings of SITE 2005--Society for Information Technology & Teacher Education International Conference (pp. 1480-1487). Phoenix, AZ, USA: Association for the Advancement of Computing in Education (AACE). Retrieved August 29, 2024 from https://www.learntechlib.org/primary/p/19250/.
McKinnon, D., & Nolan, P. (1990). Curriculum innovation with computers: Redressing inequalities of access and use in the Freyberg integrated studies project. In *Computers in Education: Proceedings of the IFIP TC 3 Fifth World Conference in Education: WCCE 90, Sydney, Australia, July 9–13, 1990* (pp. 130–146).

Mitra, A., LaFrance, B., & McCullough, S. (2001). Differences in attitudes between women and men toward computerization. *Journal of Educational Computing Research, 24*(3), 227–244.

Mitra, A., Lenzmeier, S., Steffensmeier, T., Avon, R., Qu, N., & Hazen, M. (2000). Gender and computer use in an academic institution: Report from a longitudinal study. *Journal of Educational Computing Research, 23*(1), 67–84.

Moore, R. (2004). *Education and Society: Issues and Explanations in the Sociology of Education*. Bristol: Polity Press.

Newton, P., & Beck, E. (1993). Computing: An ideal occupation for women? In J. Beynon & H. Mackay (Eds.), *Computers into Classrooms: More Questions Than Answers* (pp. 130–146). Falmer Press.

North, A. S., & Noyes, J. M. (2002). Gender influences on children's computer attitudes and cognitions. *Computers in Human Behavior, 18*(2), 135–150. https://doi.org/10.1016/S0747-5632(01)00043-7.

Rogers, E. M. (1995). *Diffusion of Innovation* (4th ed.). The Free Press.

Selby, L. (1995). Where have all the young women in computing gone? *Computers in New Zealand Schools, 7*(3), 25–27.

Sofia, Z. (1998). The mythic machine: gendered irrationalities and computer culture. In H. Bromley & M. W. Apple (Eds.), *Education/Technology/Power: Educational Computing as a Social Practice* (pp. 307–324). New York: State University of New York Press.

Spender, D. (1995). Nattering on the net. Cocos (Keeling) Islands: Spinifex Press.

Turkle, S. (1986). Book Reviews: The Second Self: Computers and the Human Spirit. *Social Science Microcomputer Review, 4*(2), 269–271. https://doi.org/10.1177/089443938600400229.

Turkle, S., & Papert, S. (1990). Epistemological pluralism: Styles and voices within the computer culture. *Signs: Journal of Women in Culture and Society, 16*(1), 128–157. https://doi.org/10.1086/494648.

Van Zoonen, L. (2002). Gendering the internet: Claims, controversies, and cultures. *European Journal of Communication, 17*(1), 5–23. https://doi.org/10.1177/0267323102017001605.

Volman, M., & van Eck, E. (2001). Gender equity and information technology in education: The second decade. *Review of Educational Research, 71*(4), 613–634. https://doi.org/10.3102/00346543071004613.

Volman, M., Vaneck, E., Heemskerk, I., & Kuiper, E. (2005). New technologies, new differences: Gender and ethnic differences in pupils' use of ICT in primary and secondary education. *Computers and Education, 45*(1), 35–55. https://doi.org/10.1016/S0360-1315(04)00072-7.

Wilson, B. C. (2002). A study of factors promoting success in computer science including gender differences. *Computer Science Education, 12*(1–2), 141–164. https://doi.org/10.1076/csed.12.1.141.8211.

CHAPTER 6

GENDER DIFFERENCE IN MATHEMATICS PERFORMANCE: A GLOBAL PERSPECTIVE

REKHA KAUSHAL

Department of Education, School of Humanities, Social Sciences, and Education, GD Goenka University, Haryana, India

ABSTRACT

There is an assumption that boys outperform girls in the achievement of mathematics because they are biologically different. However, many studies in this field show varied results. Gender differences may be observed among students in the subjects of mathematics and science during early childhood. Gender patterns emerge from the onset of puberty concurrent with the development of gender identities and gender roles in adulthood. One of the main factors that affects math performance is math anxiety, which is more common among female students. European and Western countries such as Canada, the United Kingdom, and the United States are still affected by the gender differences in mathematics and science. To improve outcomes for both genders in the subject of mathematics, the classroom environment, teachers' attitudes, students' learning styles, pedagogical strategies, outside classroom experiences, and activities should be offered to encourage mathematics instruction and need to be addressed wisely.

6.1 INTRODUCTION

Since 1901, 943 Nobel Prizes have been awarded to outstanding researchers in the fields of physics, chemistry, and medicine, but the number of women

Subverting Social Inequalities: Gender as a Social Reality.
Akanksha Srivastava, Disha Maheshwari, Chitra Krishnan (Eds.)

among these researchers is extremely low. To be precise, only 58 of the Nobel Prize winners were women. Of course, the low number of women Nobel laureates can be considered a logical consequence of the already low representation of women in the field of science, but these statistics do not fully explain the difference. Women are still severely underrepresented in mathematics and science, leading to gender inequalities in the workplace and potentially reflecting a loss of skills. Currently, students' abilities cannot account for gender differences in education and career choices. Academic and professional interests develop during this time, leading to a strong attraction and interest in learning mathematics and science, both in and out of school. Further course selection in secondary school then reveals gender-specific differences in mathematics and science class participation.

There are several myths and questions related to mathematics and gender. It is generally said and heard that males outperform in mathematics more than females. (Hyde, Fennema, & Lamon 1990) explored that boys perform better than girls in math tests that involve problem-solving, preferably through high school. Although their counterparts perform better in basic mathematics, when it comes to earning grades in mathematics, girls are better (Kimball 1989). Now the questions arise: can research offer fresh and novel perspectives on the intricate connections between gender and mathematics? Can we assist women in achieving equity in mathematics if we comprehend these complexities? Although the answers to many questions related to gender and mathematics cannot be attained, the answers still lie with research. The level of mathematics instruction in a society's educational system determines its progress and prosperity. Basic mathematical skills in math and life skills are essential for humans to have a better quality of life, and education in mathematics can help to develop these skills. Mathematics is everywhere. Mathematics is being used by illiterate people from morning till evening unintentionally.

Gender socialization is one of the predominant causes of differences in mathematics performance based on gender that favor men, as quoted by Boswell (1980), Brush (1980), Eccles & Jacobs (1986), Linn & Peterson (1986), Parsons, Adler, & Kaczala (1982), Parsons, Kaczala, & Meece (1982), Sherman (1979), Sherman & Fennema (1977), and Stallings (1979). The basis of gender differences in mathematics performance is mainly attributed to gender socialization and the perception of gender differences in mathematics. The common argument is that girls do not have as much aptitude for math (Chipman & Thomas, 1985). These social systems have a negative effect on girls' minds, causing them to lose interest, confidence, and motivation in choosing mathematics as a course for higher education. According to Jones (1984), girls' withdrawal from mathematics courses puts them even further behind because the number of courses taken is considered a major predictor of performance in mathematics. Math anxiety (fear of mathematics) may also be a problem for girls due to how they are treated in society and perceived, making it difficult for them to learn and perform well on tests (Meece, Wigfield, & Eccles 1990; Tobias 1978).

The stereotype belief in mathematics performance is not a new concept. It is age-old but still widespread in society. Several research studies have been conducted to understand the roles of significant stakeholders (teachers, peers, parents, and students themselves). Parsons and others, in a study conducted in 1982, concluded that parents of boys are more likely than parents of girls to believe that their child's proficiency in mathematics is more important than any other subject. Parents of girls, on the other hand, believe that girls cannot perform well in mathematics, which is the opposite scenario for boys' parents. Casserly (1975) explored that the expectations of parents of girls in mathematics performance are lower compared to their sons. Other studies have not found gender differences in parental encouragement for their children in mathematics (Brush 1980; Sherman & Fennema, 1977). Mathematics learning models are still traditional in most classrooms (Becker, 2003; Bevan, 2001; Brodinsky, 1985; Gamoran, 2003). In the mathematics teaching and learning process, memorization and rote recitation are still used more frequently than active concept-based learning. It is not difficult to assume a mathematics class that caters to gender differences while taking into consideration individual learning styles and study habits (Forgasz, Kloosterman, & Leder, 2004; Gavin & Reis, 2003). Mathematical learning may be greatly supported in a classroom that caters to the needs of both genders. The creation of a gender-responsive, progressively appropriate, and individualized curriculum is an essential part of this strategy.

It is observed that gender differences in mathematics performance are less significant at primary and elementary levels globally, where girls outperform boys in mathematics. However, at the high school and college levels, girls tend to drop this subject. The top math performers on college entrance exams differ significantly by gender, with most of them being boys. Up until this point, a few studies have been conducted to learn more about the differences in math achievement abilities between boys and girls. One of the earliest works was done by Stanley & Benbow (1980), which looked at the differences in math scores between male and female test takers and found gender differences on the mathematics SAT exam, a standardized test in the United States for higher education. Fryer & Levitt (2010) found that boys and girls in the United States did not have a gender gap in mathematics achievement in the early years of schooling, conducting another significant study in this domain. Girls, including those whose mothers work in math-related fields, have lower expectations from their parents regarding their math performance. Other low- and middle-income nations also have gender differences in mathematics of the same kind (Bharadwaj et al., 2012). Mathematical anxiety has also been found to be more prevalent among female students of all ages (Devine et al., 2012). This anxiety arises due to the methods of teaching adopted by teachers in school, where teachers might often transcend their math anxiety onto their students (Stuart, 2000). It was also found in the context of mathematics performance and gender gaps that at the end of first grade, girls are more likely than boys to score the same in math, but by fifth grade, their performance is significantly lower (Muralidharan & Seth, 2016). Based on the evidence of research, female students lean more towards art than mathematics when choosing their subjects of study at the higher education level. Mathematics is not considered to be a femininely gendered subject, and from that perspective, it becomes problematic for girls. This gender gap exists across the world for students aged between 7–14 years (Entwisle, Alexander, & Olson, 1994). There is negligible empirical evidence on the subject, despite the fact that the National Curriculum Framework (NCF), which was developed in India by the National Council of Educational Research and Training (NCERT), acknowledges the possibility of differences in learning experiences between male and female students as well as higher levels of mathematical phobia or anxiety among female children (NCERT, 2005). On a global scale, East Asian students have outperformed American students in mathematics. The most recent Trends in International Mathematics and Science Study (TIMSS) found that eighth-graders in Singapore, Taiwan, Hong Kong, South Korea, and Japan did better on the Trends in International Mathematics and Science Study mathematics test on average than eighth-graders in the United States did. Additionally, Asian countries' female eighth-graders scored significantly higher than American students. In addition, these East Asian nations' mean math scores did not differ by gender (Gonzales et al., 2004).

It is generally perceived that mathematics is a field for boys. A meta-analysis study revealed that when it comes to problem-solving, males do better on tests in math (Hyde, Fennema, & Eamon 1990). Fennema & Sherman (1978) investigated males' perceptions of the usefulness of mathematics and their confidence in its understanding. They found that males were confident in their belief that mathematics will always be more useful to boys than to girls. There are several factors contributing to this gap based on gender. In terms of attitudes and participation among students, there is a particularly large gender gap: Males are significantly more enthusiastic about mathematics than females and are more likely to participate. Mathematics Anxiety is a major factor in gender differences in mathematics achievement. In order to function effectively not only in everyday life but also in academic and professional settings, it is essential to improve one's mathematical abilities. It is absolutely necessary to investigate the connection between early childhood math performance and math anxiety because of the significantly higher prevalence of the condition among school students and its long-term effects on math performance. Gender must be taken into consideration when conducting research because math anxiety is frequently more prevalent in women than in men.

In order to clarify gender differences in mathematics, a number of psychologists in the United States have developed the concept of stereotype threat. According to this viewpoint, prevalent opinions that one group of people is better at math performance than another create a risk that directly hampers the achievement of the targeted group. Even for those who do not personally subscribe to such a stereotype, this process of creating stereotypes has a negative impact on the performance of the individuals on the formal test. The existence of the threat of stereotypes and the negative effects it has on test performance among mathematics-proficient individuals who scored well on the "SAT (Scholastic Aptitude Test, USA)," and were confident of their high mathematics ability has been confirmed by numerous US studies. According to a China-based study, both men and women reject the idea that "boys are better than girls at mathematics." However, it appears that girls underestimate their math skills, while boys tend to overestimate them. In this scenario, the high-math-ability girls who are really concerned about their math performance would be more concerned about taking the mathematics section of the College Entrance Examination, as they would be concerned that their anxiety might affect their math performance.

When it comes to mathematics, there are several presumptions about the different abilities of boys and girls. A phenomenon that needs to be considered is the fact that girls only trail boys by about three points on the 2005 NAEP (National Assessment of Educational Progress). Except for the 12th-grade test, girls actually outperformed boys in the 1970s. In addition, a research report which evaluated NAEP data from 1990 to 2003 found that female students still do not think of themselves as "good at math" or "liking math" as much as male students do. There is still work to be done if the goal of equal mathematics outcomes is to be achieved. However, this work needs to attend not only to gender differences but to interactions among race/ethnicity, gender, socio-economic status, and other variables. Furthermore, many researchers think that gender differences affect the entrance to mathematics-related professions and are therefore cause for concern. Others may feel that differences in attitudes toward mathematics play a greater role in determining career choice. A few researchers have also looked into how students feel about mathematics. They found that male students generally have a better outlook on the subject and are more confident than female students. In Ontario, Canada, boys are much more likely than girls to enroll in mathematics classes at the senior secondary level, and this trend continues at the university level.

It was discovered that women strongly opposed this idea, despite the fact that their male classmates did not strongly stereotype mathematics as a male field. Numerous additional studies (Hyde et al., 1990; Leder, 1992) have demonstrated the significance of the previously mentioned variables, including male stereotyping, confidence, and usefulness; their enduring influence; and how they have different effects on men and women. According to a different study that examined the factors that influence the arithmetic accomplishment of 11th graders in math classes with a gender gap (Campbell & Beaudry, 1998), males scored higher than females on the math achievement test for the 11th grade, despite the fact that this disparity decreased from the 10th grade. Some recent research has shown that there are fewer gender inequalities in mathematics education across numerous nations. However, research indicates that as pupils progress through the grades, men tend to demonstrate better levels of mathematics achievement. For instance, the TIMSS data revealed that math achievement scores for each gender group in elementary and middle school were comparable (Beaton et al., 1996; Mullis et al., 1997). American pupils in grades 5 through 8 were evaluated by Hall et al. (1999) for gender variations in math performance. They discovered no significant gender disparities, but there was evidence of differences based on gender in mathematics achievement in the last year of secondary school.

6.2 GENDER DIFFERENCES IN MATHEMATICS

While some researchers have suggested that gender differences in mathematics are caused by genetics, many researchers in the United States have claimed that social and environmental factors are to blame. They argue that these differences are caused by different social conditioning and societal expectations for boys and girls (Ma, 1999; Tobias, 1986). According to a few studies, girls are more likely to view mathematics as a discipline for boys than their counterparts, lack confidence in the ability to perform well in mathematics, and dislike math (Blatchford, 1996; Miller & Bichsel, 2004). Some researchers have linked these beliefs and prejudices against math to gender-specific expectations of parents and teachers who support male students' progress in math more than they do female students. Additionally, they have established connections between these preconceptions and beliefs and math proficiency. According to some theories, girls admire mathematics courses less than males due to lack of self-confidence and interest in the subject, which negatively affects female math ability. Many academically gifted women select other areas to develop their abilities. Additionally, research has demonstrated that personal preferences, rather than intellectual prowess, account for many decisions not to pursue mathematics and the sciences (Richardson, 1980). Recently, the idea of stereotype threat has been actively used by various psychologists in developed countries like the United States to explain gender disparities in mathematics (Newstead, 1998). This point of view holds that widespread notions that a particular group of people is mathematically superior to another pose a threat that directly hinders the performance of members of the targeted group. When the stereotype is emphasized on formal arithmetic tests, even for individuals who do not adhere to such a stereotype, performance suffers significantly (Kellogg et al., 1999). The presence of stereotype threat has been demonstrated in several US studies and its negative effects on test performance are more apparent in individuals who are confident of their high mathematics abilities and have done well in mathematics on the SAT (Ashcraft et al., 2005; Kellogg et al., 1999).

High school seniors in China perform equally well in mathematics on the "College Entrance Examination" regardless of their gender. However, when it comes to math tests, boys perform better than girls do on college entrance exams in both countries. Algebra proficiency is impossible without a foundation in elementary school math, which must be taught. Students of all genders place a high value on rigorous curriculums and superior instruction provided by qualified, well-trained teachers. Most high school teachers in China, along with many female students with high math abilities, are of the opinion that boys perform better in math due to their better visual and spatial abilities. Chinese teachers have also said that intellectually gifted boys' low-test scores are due to their immaturity, which is characterized by being lazy and refusing to use their natural talents before senior high school. When smart boys realize how important education is and start using their math and science skills, they can outperform girls in these subjects (Rubinstein & Tannock, 2010).

There have been a few different explanations offered for why mathematics is different for boys and girls. According to Eccles & Roeser (2011), internal and external factors, such as a perceived lack of opportunities for girls to learn mathematics, were traditionally cited as reasons for girls' lower math performance. According to other studies, the girls' poor math performance was correlated with their perceptions of their classrooms as hostile, rough, and hostile. According to Riegle-Crumb, Farkas, & Muller (2006), girls' mathematics performance was influenced in large part by the teacher and peer support.

Danielsen, Wiium, Wilhelmsen, & Wold (2010) and Eccles & Roeser (2011) explored that academic attitudes, achievement, emotions, learning, motivation, and self-efficacy are positively correlated with teacher and peer support. Orientation impacts factors like accomplishment objectives, homeroom conditions, and science accomplishment among youthful young people uncovered that young lady outflanked young men in arithmetic. According to Ahmad, Minnaert, van der Werf, & Kuyper (2010) and Patrick, Ryan, & Kaplan (2007), teachers' behavior (a) was found to be supportive and receptive, and (b) to be receptive and helpful (Ahmed, Minnaert, van der Werf, & Kuyper, 2010; (Zupancic, Levpuscek, & Puklek, 2009). Jones & Young (1995) investigated still another factor, student attitudes, and discovered that males and girls had different attitudes about math and science. When Frenzel, Pekrun, & Goetz (2007) examined how people felt about mathematics, they discovered that girls felt less pride and happiness than boys did. In contrast, boys felt less dread and pessimism when it came to arithmetic than girls did. They discovered that female students of mathematics felt shame slightly more than their counterparts did (Frenzel et al., 2007).

Women reported higher levels of arithmetic anxiety than men, according to a variety of studies in the related field that looked at differences in adult behavior between the sexes (Hembree, 1990; Miller & Bichsel, 2004; Ferguson et al., 2015; Jansen et al., 2016). Using data from Hembree (1990) and Hopko (2003), Ashcraft & Moore (2009) revealed that on math anxiety assessments, females score about 0.3 standard deviations (SD) higher than males from grade 6 through college, with math anxiety levels reaching their highest points in grades 9 and 10. In the pupils of schools at various levels, there were significant gender differences relating to math anxiety, with girls reporting higher levels than males (ElseQuest et al., 2010; Goetz et al., 2013;

Hill et al., 2016). In a longitudinal study, both boys and girls in grades 7 to 12 participated in order to examine math performance and anxiety levels (Ma & Xu, 2004). According to the authors, girls had significantly stronger stability effects for math anxiety than boys did. This suggests that girls may carry math anxiety from junior high school to senior high school. This suggests that, regardless of math proficiency, girls who experience math anxiety in their early high school years are more likely to experience it for life. Chiu & Henry (1990); Young et al. (2012); Harari et al. (2013); Ramirez et al. (2013); Erturan & Jansen (2015); Schleepen & Van Mier (2016); Kucian et al. (2018) studied that students of primary classes often show no gender variations in scores of mathematics anxiety.

In order to avoid negative long-term repercussions, Mier et al. (2019) has underlined the significance of early detection and treatment of arithmetic anxiety in girls. This study sought to determine whether math anxiety had a different impact on boys and girls in grades two and four. They discovered differences in the relationship between arithmetic anxiety and performance between boys and girls, despite having roughly equal levels of math anxiety and comparable test scores. This association was significant and negative for girls in both grades, but not for boys. Only for girls, a higher level of math anxiety was a poor predictor of math achievement. Hyde and others based on 10 US states' state examinations. Gender disparities in math performance were examined among more than 70 lakh students in grades two through grade 11. They claim that there are no gender differences, even when it comes to difficult tasks that require a great deal of knowledge. In a meta-analysis study that included research published between 1990 and 2007, Lindberg et al. (2010) revealed that gender differences in math ability for elementary- and middle-school-aged pupils were insignificant. Gender inequalities, on the other hand, typically become apparent in high school as revealed by (Hyde et al., 1990; Liu & Co, 2008; Rosselli et al., 2009; Lindberg et al., 2010). Students in junior and senior high schools demonstrated a similar gender gap, in contrast to Hembree's (1990) findings, which found gender differences in math anxiety from elementary school through college (Devine et al., 2012; Goetz et al., 2013; Bieg et al., 2015). Negative attitudes toward math from parents and teachers have been linked to children's poorer arithmetic performance and the emergence of math anxiety. According to recent research (Casad et al., 2015; Maloney et al., 2015), there is a correlation between the math performance of children and parents' arithmetic anxiety. According to a study by Casad et al. (2015), parents' and children's math anxiety affected the outcomes of the children's arithmetic education.

Maloney et al. (2015) discovered that children's performance in mathematics during the school year declined and observed an increase in math anxiety when parents who themselves are anxious about mathematics frequently help their children with math-related problems. It has been demonstrated that anxious teachers, in addition to parents, have a negative impact on their students' attitudes toward math (Beilock et al., 2010). The researchers discovered that girls, but not boys, picked up on the math-anxious attitudes of their female first and second grade teachers. Teachers' attitudes toward mathematics and how they treat their students, such as showing gender bias or shaming students in front of their classmates, may cause math anxiety in children (Jackson & Leffingwell, 1999; Ashcraft, 2002; Furner & Duffy, 2002). According to Park et al. (2014), this may result in a decrease in girls' involvement and perceptions of their mathematical abilities when teachers believe that girls do not understand and are not competent in arithmetic. Moreover, it was discovered that specific math education teaching strategies were linked to math anxiety (Brady & Bowd, 2005).

Teachers are crucial to the implementation of school policies, regardless of the formal structure of the mathematics classroom (Fennema, 1990). Teachers have the potential to assist in the eradication of gender inequalities that currently exist because they are a component of the problem that causes them (Campbell, 1995). Math teachers continue to encourage traditional behaviors and career goals for both sexes, regardless of student interest or aptitude, despite the fact that most teachers agree that education should be a liberating and democratic force (Skolnick, Langbort, & Day, 1982). According to Relich's (1996) study, male and female math teachers have slightly different attitudes and approaches. Even though all of the primary teachers in the sample claimed to be aware of gender issues, only two of them, both female and with low self-esteem, stated that they would reinforce gender stereotypes in the classroom. In contrast, these gender disparities were insignificant and significantly more prevalent at the primary level. According to teachers, their gender does not always influence how they interact with their own students or with male or female students.

Different reasons have been emphasized for the explanations of the gender gap between boys and girls. Girls' inferior arithmetic performance has historically been attributed to both internal and external circumstantial issues, such as lesser considered support for math education (Eccles, 2011). Other research linked the girls' decline in performance to their perceptions of their mathematics classroom infrastructure as ugly, unwelcoming, and unfriendly. Conclusions drawn from the educational literature are generally in line with those drawn from the psychological literature. Before boys and girls entered elementary school or during the early elementary years, there were no significant differences in mathematics achievement, according to Fennema & Sherman (1978). Significant differences were not always apparent in upper elementary and early high school years. When there were significant differences, they were more likely to be in favor of the boys on higher-level cognitive tasks and the girls on lower-level cognitive tasks. Based on research with a variety of achievement tests, the following findings are mostly consistent: I) High school boys perform slightly better than high school girls on tests of mathematical reasoning (primarily word problem solving); II) Boys and girls perform similarly on algebra and basic mathematical knowledge tests; and III) Girls occasionally outperform boys on tests of computational skills. Although the research quoted here was conducted a few decades back, it is still relevant in today's scenario as gender differences in mathematics are prevalent these days as well, and research is being conducted on these issues globally. According to Stanley & Benbow (1980), who used their analysis of some of their studies to refute the hypothesis, if females were encouraged to enroll in advanced mathematics classes at the same rate as men, gender differences would disappear (Sherman & Fennema, 1977). Their work was used as proof that gender differences in mathematics are genetic, according to Stanley & Benbow (1980). By emphasizing problem solving and the mathematical process rather than just the right answer, boys and girls will be able to think in a variety of ways and develop a variety of mathematical behaviors. By understanding that boys and girls approach mathematics in very different ways, there is no difference in aptitude between these differences. Boys and girls both progress at the same rate. We must create experiences and curricula that meet the specific needs of each group in order to encourage boys and girls to excel.

6.3 CONCLUDING REMARKS

A modest shift in the treatment of female students in mathematics education has occurred in part as a result of the research's thorough documentation and awareness of factors connected to gender and mathematics. It is necessary to carry on research that examines the current state of gender inequality. But to be relevant, research as we currently understand it needs to be supplemented by fresh approaches and new kinds of study. Such research will aid in identifying crucial areas for new research and guarantee that women's perspectives are a significant component of all scholarly work in the field of education. Mathematicians, educators, parents, and others have become aware of the issues associated with gender in mathematics. We have come a long way. However, before math education is equitable, there is still a long way to go. Female students continue to believe that they are not as "good at math" or as "like math" as male students. There is still work to be done if we want mathematical outcomes that are equal. However, we must consider not only gender differences but also interactions between race/ethnicity, gender, and other variables if we are to improve our comprehension of the complex relationship between attitudes toward mathematics, achievement, and student-teacher relationships within and across various school contexts.

However, gender differences are not just a topic for school discussions. Gender differences in math ability are minimal even among college students or students entering college to pursue higher education. Therefore, in order to explain the lower% of female students in mathematics courses at higher levels of education and in mathematics-related occupations, we need to look at additional factors, such as internalized belief systems about mathematics, external factors like sex discrimination in education and the workforce (Kimball, 1989), and the mathematics curriculum at the pre-college level. Gender differences and individual preferences should be acknowledged in the classroom. A classroom with this atmosphere would meet the needs of both boys and girls when it comes to math education. Planning a curriculum that is individualized, gender-responsive, and developmentally appropriate is the most crucial aspect of this strategy. This chapter examines the factors that contribute to gender differences in mathematics subject achievement. Motivation, attitude, parental influence, the role of teachers, mathematics anxiety, test anxiety, the classroom environment, and the curriculum of global gender differences in mathematics are among these factors.

KEYWORDS

- **National Assessment of Educational Progress**
- **National Council of Educational Research and Training**
- **National Curriculum Framework**
- **scholastic aptitude test**
- **standard deviations**
- **Trends in International Mathematics and Science Study**

REFERENCES

Ahmed, W., Minnaert, A., van der Werf, G., & Kuyper, H. (2010). Perceived social support and early adolescents' achievement: The meditational roles of motivational beliefs and emotions. *Journal of Youth and Adolescence, 39*, 36–46.

Ashcraft, M. H. (2002). Math anxiety: Personal, educational, and cognitive consequences. *Current Directions in Psychological Science, 11*, 181–185. https://doi.org/10.1111/1467-8721.00196.

Ashcraft, M. H., & Ridley, K. S. (2005). Math anxiety and its cognitive consequences: A tutorial review. In J. I. D. Campbell (Ed.), *The Handbook of Mathematical Cognition* (pp. 315–327). New York: Psychology Press.

Becker, J. R. (2003). Research, reflection, practice: Gender and mathematics: An issue for the twenty-first century. *Teaching Children Mathematics, 9*(8), 470–473.

Beilock, S. L., Gunderson, E. A., Ramirez, G., & Levine, S. C. (2010). Female teachers' math anxiety affects girls' math achievement. *Proceedings of the National Academy of Sciences of the United States of America, 107*, 1860–1863. https://doi.org/10.1073/pnas.0910967107.

Bevan, R. (2001). Boys, girls, and mathematics: Beginning to learn from the gender debate. *Mathematics in School, 30*(4), 2–6.

Bharadwaj, P., De Giorgi, G., Hansen, D. R., & Neilson, C. (2015). The gender gap in mathematics: Evidence from a middle-income country. *Federal Reserve Bank of New York Staff Report* (721).

Bieg, M., Goetz, T., Wolter, I., & Hall, N. C. (2015). Gender stereotype endorsement differentially predicts girls' and boys' trait-state discrepancy in math anxiety. *Frontiers in Psychology, 6*, 1404. https://doi.org/10.3389/fpsyg.2015.01404.

Blatchford, P. (1996). Pupils' views on school work and school from 7 to 16 years. *Research Papers in Education, 11*, 263–288.

Boswell, S. L. (1980). *Women and Mathematics: The Development of Stereotypic Attitudes*. Boulder, CO: Institute for Research on Social Problems.

Brady, P., & Bowd, A. (2005). Mathematics anxiety, prior experience, and confidence to teach mathematics among pre-service education students. *Teaching and Teacher Education, 11*, 37–46. https://doi.org/10.1080/1354060042000337084.

Brodinsky, B. (1985). *Improving Math & Science Education Problems & Solutions*. Arlington, VA: American Association of School Administrators.

Brush, L. R. (1980). *Encouraging Girls in Mathematics: The Problem and the Solution*. Cambridge, MA: Abt Associates.

Campbell, J. R., & Beaudry, J. S. (1998). Gender gap linked to differential socialization for high-achieving senior mathematics students. *Journal of Educational Research, 91*, 140–147.

Campbell, P. B. (1995). Redefining the girl problem in mathematics. In W. Secada, E. Fennema, & L. Adajian (Eds.), *New Directions for Equity in Mathematics Education* (pp. 225–241). Cambridge: Cambridge University Press.

Casad, B. J., Hale, P., & Wachs, F. L. (2015). Parent-child math anxiety and math-gender stereotypes predict adolescents' math education outcomes. *Frontiers in Psychology, 6*, 1597. https://doi.org/10.3389/fpsyg.2015.01597.

Casserly, P. (1980). An assessment of factors affecting female participation in advanced placement programs in mathematics, chemistry, and physics. In L. H. Fox, L. Brody, &

D. Tobin (Eds.), *Women and the Mathematical Mystique* (pp. 138–163). Baltimore : Johns Hopkins University Press.

Chipman, S. F., & Thomas, V. G. (1985). Women's participation in mathematics: Outlining the problem. In S. F. Chipman, L. R. Brush, & D. W. Wilson (Eds.), *Women and Mathematics: Balancing the Equation* (pp. 1–24). Hillsdale, NJ: Erlbaum.

Chiu, L. H., & Henry, L. L. (1990). Development and validation of the mathematics anxiety scale for children. *Measurement and Evaluation in Counseling and Development, 23*, 121–127.

Danielsen, A. G., Wiium, N., Wilhelmsen, B., & Wold, B. (2010). Perceived support provided by teachers and classmates and students' self-reported academic initiative. *Journal of School Psychology, 48*, 247–267.

Devine, A., Fawcett, K., Szűcs, D., & Dowker, A. (2012). Gender differences in mathematics anxiety and the relation to mathematics performance while controlling for test anxiety. *Behavioral and Brain Functions, 8*, 1–9.

Devine, A., Hill, F., Carey, E., & Szűcs, D. (2018). Cognitive and emotional math problems largely dissociate: Prevalence of developmental dyscalculia and mathematics anxiety. *Journal of Educational Psychology, 110*, 431–444. https://doi.org/10.1037/edu0000222.

Eccles, J. S., & Jacobs, J. (1986). Social forces shape math attitudes and performance. *Signs, 11*, 367–380.

Eccles, J. S., & Roeser, R. W. (2011). Schools as developmental contexts during adolescence. *Journal of Research on Adolescence, 21*, 225–241.

Eccles-Parsons, J. (1984). Sex differences in mathematics participation. In R. Ames & C. Ames (Eds.), *Advances in Motivation and Achievement* (Vol. 2, pp. 93–137).

Else-Quest, N. M., Hyde, J. S., & Linn, M. C. (2010). Cross-national patterns of gender differences in mathematics: A meta-analysis. *Psychological Bulletin, 136*, 103–127. https://doi.org/10.1037/a0018053.

Entwisle, D. R., Alexander, K. L., & Olson, L. S. (1994). The gender gap in math: Its possible origins in neighborhood effects. *American Sociological Review, 59*, 822–838.

Erturan, S., & Jansen, B. (2015). An investigation of boys' and girls' emotional experience of math, their math performance, and the relation between these variables. *European Journal of Psychology of Education, 30*, 421–435. https://doi.org/10.1007/s10212-015-0248-7.

Fennema, E. (1974). Mathematics learning and the sexes: A review. *Journal for Research in Mathematics Education, 5*(3), 126–139.

Fennema, E. (1990). Teachers' beliefs and gender differences in mathematics. In E. Fennema & G. C. Leder (Eds.), *Mathematics and Gender* (pp. 169–187). New York: Teachers' College Press.

Fennema, E. H., & Sherman, J. A. (1978). Sex-related differences in mathematics achievement and related factors: A further study. *Journal for Research in Mathematics Education, 9*, 189–203.

Fennema, E., & Sherman, J. (1977). Sex-related differences in mathematics achievement, spatial visualization, and affective factors. *American Educational Research Journal, 14*(1), 51–71.

Forgasz, H. J., Kloosterman, P., & Leder, G. C. (2004). New perspectives on the gender stereotyping of mathematics. *Mathematical Thinking and Learning, 6*(4), 389.

Fox, L. H., Brody, L., & Tobin, D. (1985). The impact of early intervention programs upon course-taking and attitudes in high school. In S. F. Chipman, L. R. Brush, & D. M. Wilson

(Eds.), *Women and Mathematics: Balancing the Equation* (pp. 249–274). Hillsdale, NJ: Lawrence Erlbaum.

Frenzel, A. C., Pekrun, R., & Goetz, T. (2007). Girls and mathematics – A "hopeless" issue? A control-value approach to gender differences in emotions towards mathematics. *European Journal of Psychology of Education, 22*, 497–514.

Fryer, R. G., Jr., & Levitt, S. D. (2010). An empirical analysis of the gender gap in mathematics. *American Economic Journal: Applied Economics, 2*(2), 210–240.

Furner, J. M., & Duffy, M. L. (2002). Equity for all students in the new millennium: Disabling math anxiety. *Intervention in School and Clinic, 38*, 67–74. https://doi.org/10.1177/10534 512020380020101.

Gamoran, A. (Ed.). (2003). *Transforming Teaching in Math and Science: How Schools and Districts Can Support Change*. Teachers College Press.

Gavin, M. K., & Reis, S. M. (2003). Helping teachers to encourage talented girls in mathematics. *Gifted Child Today, 26*(1), 32.

Geist, E. A., & King, M. (2008). Different, not better: Gender differences in mathematics learning and achievement. *Journal of Instructional Psychology, 35*(1), 43–52.

Goetz, T., Bieg, M., Lüdtke, O., Pekrun, R., & Hall, N. C. (2013). Do girls really experience more anxiety in mathematics? *Psychological Science, 24*, 2079–2087. https://doi.org/10.1177/0956797613486989.

Martin, M. O., Mullis, I. V., Gonzalez, E. J., & Chrostowski, S. J. (2004). *Findings from IEA's Trends in International Mathematics and Science Study at the Fourth and Eighth Grades. TIMSS 2003 International Science Report*. International Association for the Evaluation of Educational Achievement. Herengracht 487, Amsterdam, 1017 BT, The Netherlands.

Gonzales, P., Guzman, J. C., Partelow, L., Pahlke, E., Jocelyn, L., Kastberg, D., & Williams, T. (2004). *Highlights From the Trends in International Mathematics and Science Study (TIMSS) 2003*. Washington, D.C.: National Center for Education Statistics.

Harari, R. R., Vukovic, R. K., & Bailey, S. P. (2013). Mathematics anxiety in young children: An exploratory study. *Journal of Experimental Education, 81*, 538–555. https://doi.org/10.1080/00220973.2012.727888.

Hembree, R. (1990). The nature, effects, and relief of mathematics anxiety. *Journal of Research in Mathematics Education, 21*, 33–46. https://doi.org/10.2307/749455.

Hill, F., Mammarella, I. C., Devine, A., Caviola, S., Passolunghi, M. C., & Szucs, D. (2016). Maths anxiety in primary and secondary school students: Gender differences, developmental changes and anxiety specificity. *Learning and Individual Differences, 48*, 45–53. https://doi.org/10.1016/j.lindif.2016.02.006.

Hyde, J. S., Fennema, E., & Lamon, S. J. (1990). Gender differences in mathematics performance: A meta-analysis. *Psychological Bulletin, 107*(2), 139–155. https://doi.org/10.1037/0033-2909.107.2.139.

Hyde, J. S., Lindberg, S. M., Linn, M. C., Ellis, A. B., & Williams, C. C. (2008). Gender similarities characterize math performance. *Science, 321*, 494–495. https://doi.org/10.1126/science.1160364.

Jackson, C. D., & Leffingwell, R. J. (1999). The role of instructors in creating math anxiety in students from kindergarten through college. *The Mathematics Teacher, 92*, 583–586.

Jones, J., & Young, D. J. (1995). Perceptions of the relevance of mathematics and science: An Australian study. *Research in Science Education, 25*, 3–18.

Kellogg, J. S., Hopko, D. R., & Ashcraft, M. H. (1999). The effects of time pressure on arithmetic performance. *Journal of Anxiety Disorders, 13*, 592–600.

Kimball, M. M. (1989). A new perspective on women's math achievement. *Psychological Bulletin, 105*, 198–214.
Kucian, K., Zuber, I., Kohn, J., Poltz, N., Wyschkon, A., Esser, G., et al. (2018). Relation between mathematical performance, math anxiety, and affective priming in children with and without developmental dyscalculia. *Frontiers in Psychology, 9*, 263. https://doi.org/10.3389/fpsyg.2018.00263.
Leder G. C. (1992). Mathematics and gender: Changing perspectives. In Grows D. A. (Ed.), *Handbook of research on mathematics teaching and learning* (pp. 597–622). New York, NY: Macmillan.
Lindberg, S. M., Hyde, J. S., Petersen, J. L., & Linn, M. C. (2010). New trends in gender and mathematics performance: A meta-analysis. *Psychological Bulletin, 136*(6), 1123–1135. https://doi.org/10.1037/a0021276.
Linn, M. C., & Peterson, A. C. (1986). A meta-analysis of gender differences in spatial ability: Implications for mathematics and science achievement. In J. S. Hyde & M. C. Linn (Eds.), *The Psychology of Gender Differences: Advances Through Meta-Analysis* (pp. 67–101). Baltimore: Johns Hopkins Press.
Liu, O. L., Wilson, M., & Paek, I. (2008). A multidimensional Rasch analysis of gender differences in PISA mathematics. *Journal of Applied Measurement, 9*, 18–35.
Ma, X. (1999). A meta-analysis of the relationship between anxiety toward mathematics and achievement in mathematics. *Journal for Research in Mathematics Education, 30*, 520–540.
Ma, X., & Xu, J. (2004). The causal ordering of mathematics anxiety and mathematics achievement: A longitudinal panel analysis. *Journal of Adolescence, 27*, 165–179. https://doi.org/10.1016/j.adolescence.2003.11.003.
Maloney, E. A., Ramirez, G., Gunderson, E. A., Levine, S. C., & Beilock, S. L. (2015). Intergenerational effects of parents' math anxiety on children's math achievement and anxiety. *Psychological Science, 26*(10), 1480–1488. https://doi.org/10.1177/0956797615592630.
Meece, J. L., Wigfield, A., & Eccles, J. S. (1990). Predictors of math anxiety and its influence on young adolescents' course enrollment intentions and performance in mathematics. *Journal of Educational Psychology, 82*, 60–70.
Miller, H., & Bichsel, J. (2004). Anxiety, working memory, gender, and math performance. *Personality and Individual Differences, 37*, 591–606.
Muralidharan, K., & Sheth, K. (2016). Bridging education gender gaps in developing countries: The role of female teachers. *Journal of Human Resources, 51*(2), 269–297.
Newstead, K. (1998). Aspects of children's mathematics anxiety. *Educational Studies in Mathematics, 36*, 53–71.
Park, D., Ramirez, G., & Beilock, S. L. (2014). The role of expressive writing in math anxiety. *Journal of Experimental Psychology: Applied, 20*(2), 103–111. https://doi.org/10.1037/xap0000013.
Parsons, J. E., Adler, T. F., & Kaczala, C. M. (1982). Evaluation of achievement attitudes and beliefs: Parental influences. *Child Development, 53*, 310–321.
Patrick, H., Ryan, A. M., & Kaplan, A. (2007). Early adolescents' perceptions of the classroom social environment, motivational beliefs, and engagement. *Journal of Educational Psychology, 99*, 83–98.
Puklek Levpuscek, M., & Zupancic, M. (2009). Achievement in math in early adolescence: The role of parental involvement, teachers' behavior, and students' motivational beliefs about math. *Journal of Early Adolescence, 29*, 541–570.

Ramirez, G., Gunderson, E. A., Levine, S. C., & Beilock, S. L. (2013). Math anxiety, working memory, and math achievement in early elementary school. *Journal of Cognition and Development, 14*, 187–202. https://doi.org/10.1080/15248372.2012.664593.

Richardson, F. C., & Woolfolk, R. L. (1980). Mathematics anxiety. In I. G. Sarason (Ed.), *Test Anxiety: Theory, Research, and Application* (pp. 275–288). Hillsdale, NJ: Erlbaum.

Riegle-Crumb, C., Farkas, G., & Muller, C. (2006). The role of gender and friendship in advanced course taking. *Sociology of Education, 79*, 206–228.

Rosselli, M., Ardila, A., Matute, E., & Inozemtseva, O. (2009). Gender differences and cognitive correlates of mathematical skills in school-aged children. *Child Neuropsychology, 15*, 216–231. https://doi.org/10.1080/09297040802195205.

Rubinsten, O., & Tannock, R. (2010). Mathematics anxiety in children with developmental dyscalculia. *Behavioral and Brain Functions, 6*, 46. https://doi.org/10.1186/1744-9081-6-46.

Schleepen, T. M., & Van Mier, H. I. (2016). Math anxiety differentially affects boys' and girls' arithmetic, reading and fluid intelligence skills in fifth graders. *Psychology, 7*, 1911–1920. https://doi.org/10.4236/psych.2016.714174.

Sherman, J. (1979). Predicting mathematics performance in high school girls and boys. *Journal of Educational Psychology, 79*, 242–249.

Sherman, J., & Fennema, E. (1977). The study of mathematics by high school girls and boys: Related variables. *American Educational Research Journal, 14*, 159–168.

Skolnick, J., Langbort, C., & Day, L. (1982). *How to Encourage Girls in Mathematics and Science*. Palo Alto, CA: Dale Seymour.

Stanley, J., & Benbow, C. (1980). Sex differences in mathematical ability: Fact or artifact. *Science, 210*, 1262–1264.

Stuart, V. (2000). Math curse or math anxiety? *Teaching Children Mathematics, 6*(5), 330–335.

Tobias, S. (1986). Anxiety and cognitive processing of instruction. In R. Schwarzer (Ed.), *Self-Related Cognitions in Anxiety and Motivation* (pp. 35–54). Hillsdale, NJ: Lawrence Erlbaum Associates.

Van Mier, H. I., Schleepen, T. M., & Van Den Berg, C. G. (2019). Gender differences regarding the impact of math anxiety on arithmetic performance in second and fourth graders. *Frontiers in Psychology, 9*, Article 2690. https://doi.org/10.3389/fpsyg.2018.02690.

Young, C. B., Wu, S. S., & Menon, V. (2012). The neurodevelopmental basis of math anxiety. *Psychological Science, 23*, 492–501. https://doi.org/10.1177/0956797611429134.

CHAPTER 7

INFLUENCE OF 'GENDER SCHOOL CONCEPT' ON GENDER ROLE BEHAVIOR AND GENDER EQUALITY: IN SRI LANKAN CONTEXT

AMILA RUPASINGHE

Senior Lecturer, Faculty of Education, Horizon Campus, Knowledge City, Malabe, Sri Lanka

ABSTRACT

It is very important to understand the roles of one's own and other genders to learn the way of living in society. Children learn gender roles through socialization at a very young age through a variety of sources, and school is seen to be the most significant mechanism through which children learn gender roles. Research studies have empirically shown that school systems affect students' attitudes and values, including attitudes toward gender equality. Gender equality is the state of valuing all activities, behaviors, and needs equally without taking gender into consideration. It also refers to the condition of all people having equal access to resources and opportunities, including economic involvement and decision-making, regardless of their gender. The atmosphere and socialization process of single-gender schools and mixed-gender schools are different; hence gender role behaviors vary depending on the kind of school. According to this idea of a "gender school," the entire institution is built around gender. Male and female characters are positioned in society's economic and political hierarchies, which is illustrated by gendered schools. Along with stereotypical expectations, interpersonal connections, the division of labor along gender lines, images

Subverting Social Inequalities: Gender as a Social Reality.
Akanksha Srivastava, Disha Maheshwari, Chitra Krishnan (Eds.)

and symbols that uphold these divides, and the inclusion of male and female characters in these hierarchies, this pattern of gender relations also contains other aspects (Alfieri, Ruble, & Higgins, 1996). Given these findings, it is clear that gendered schools in Sri Lanka have ingrained certain gender norms within them. Boys and girls exhibit diverse gender role behaviors due to traditions, value systems, mini-cultural backgrounds, and the socialization process in single-gender and mixed-gender schools. As a country that upholds various cultural and traditional values, the influence of the school environment based on gender is a significant factor in shaping society and its qualities, values, and attitudes toward gender equality. The chapter evaluates the advantages and disadvantages of both same-gender and mixed-gender schools and analyzes how socialization in both settings affects the development of gender stereotypes, prejudices, and discrimination. Furthermore, this study hopes to examine the effect on gender equality in single-gender versus mixed-gender (coeducational) schools in Sri Lanka and also to make an effort to suggest the best schooling system that enhances gender equality in the present scenario.

7.1 INTRODUCTION

Gender equality is the lack of discrimination in power, opportunities, the distribution of resources, advantages, and the availability of services based on a person's sex or gender. It is an attitude that believes everyone should be treated equally and shouldn't face discrimination according to their gender. When both genders have equal access to all societal rights and opportunities, including involvement in and power over the economy, gender equality has been attained (Wikipedia, 2023). In a gender-equal environment, everyone's needs are equally regarded and favored. Other names for gender equality include sex equality, gender egalitarianism, sexual equality, and gender equity. Although the term "gender equity" is most similar to "gender equality," gender equity results in gender equality, which is the act of treating both sexes fairly so that they all have access to the same rights and advantages. Gender equity also entails that each sex's particular health requirements will get enough funding (Harker, 2000). Schools have a significant role in socializing children's gender ideas and behaviors. To make most schools gender equal, the culture of power, hierarchy, and social control must be altered (Hilliard & Liben, 2010). In general, it would entail curricular modifications, the dismantling of authority structures that discriminate against females, as well as the breakdown of hierarchies (Kail & Levine, 1976). The causes of bullying, sexism, racism, and homophobia would be better understood by principals and teachers, who could then replace them with more effective interventions (De Silva & Priyashantha, 2014). Students would also participate more directly in the planning and evaluation of their activities, and some emphasis would be placed on their knowledge, experience, and abilities (Kail & Levine, 1976). Schools affect gender differentiation via teachers, peers, and curriculum. Different learning experiences and feedback provided by teachers, peers, and the school community directly influence gender differentiation (Thompson & Ungerleide, 2004). Peers display gender-stereotypic attitudes and conduct, and teachers provide curriculum materials that do the same (Koblinsky, Cruse, & Sugawara, 1978). When kids recognize gender stereotypes, gender roles, and prejudices, their own choices and actions are influenced (McHale, Crouter, & Whiteman, 2003).

Gender inequities are carried into the school environment through society, vice versa schools carry different gender attitudes to society (Taylor & Gelman, 1993). This includes activities that take place across the whole school, such as instruction, teacher-student contact, administration, basic infrastructure design and planning, and the development of teaching-learning resources. As a result, it is crucial to act to promote gender equality in the educational setting (Harker, 2000).

There is systematic gender segregation everywhere, and single-gender schools are the most prevalent example. Since there is a resurgence of interest in gender-specific education around the world, schooling has a huge impact on students' overall development (Spielhofer, Benton, & Schagen, 2004). "When girls or boys attend school exclusively with members of their own gender at school, it is called single-gender or single-sex education" (U.S. Department of Education, 2005). "Mixed-gender or mixed-sex education is an educational system in which students of both sexes attend schools together" (Collins Dictionary, 2023). This school type can be seen as one of the influential factors for the students' attitudes toward gender equality and gender roles. For example, students in same-gender schools may miss out on the chances to positively influence each other and socialize with the other genders. Due to their lack of familiarity with the surroundings, they are unsure of how to respond when they encounter children of other genders. Students in single-gender schools find it hard to adjust to the mixed-gender society outside their schools in the future because they have experienced a safer and more comfortable environment in their single-gender schools (Sullivan, Joshi, & Leonard, 2012). On the other hand, several researchers discovered ample proof that pupils benefit from single-gender learning settings in schools because they are free of gender stereotyping, unconscious bias, and less social pressure (Atherton, 1973). Particularly, single-gender education provides everyone with the unmatched opportunity to hold every leadership position, while mixed-gender educational settings give students the chance to form genuine friendships and lay the groundwork for supportive relationships with students of other genders (Liben, 2015). Furthermore, among single-gender school students, mixed-gender peer relationships that avoid gender salience appeared to have a potential bi-directional meditational friendship with mixed-gender anxiety, which is consistent with a vicious cycle of anxiety that only gets worse and a lack of mixed-gender communication (Halpern et al., 2011). However, it is debatable whether single-gender schools or mixed-gender schools promote or demote gender equality.

7.1.1 KEY QUESTIONS FOR THE GENDER-EQUITY INFLUENCED BY THE SCHOOL ENVIRONMENT

i. What ideas about masculinity and femininity do children have, and what do they demonstrate in the classroom and on the playground?
ii. What are the predominant gender stereotypes that the students are exposed to at school?
iii. Is gender equality a factor in the school's expectations for its teachers?
iv. Is gender equality influenced by the type of school?

7.2 HISTORY OF GENDER SEGREGATION OF SCHOOL SYSTEM IN SRI LANKA

When shedding light on Sri Lankan history, it is clear that the education system was mostly gender-biased in the past. In the pre-historical age, only boys received education for their vocational needs under the 'Gurukula' (residential education at the teacher's home) system (Withanage & Chandrakumara, 2021). Even after the Buddhist education system was established in the historical period, people and administrators of the country believed that only boys should be educated based on 'Piriven' (Buddhist temple-centered) education (Little, 2011). With the development of the country, education opportunities gradually opened up to both genders, although there was a significant disparity. In the colonial period, with the influence of three different empires, the school education system in Sri Lanka changed to a mixed system with both single-gender and mixed-gender setups (Kovinthan, 2019). However, there was a popular trend of single-gender schools where parents chose it as an upper-class choice. Parents believed that studying their daughters in a girls' school was a privilege because they thought they could nurture their child in a safe and special school environment. After independence, the situation changed with the introduction of central colleges due to the specific conditions and facilities provided to the central colleges by the government (Liyanage, 2014). These central colleges were mixed-gender and began to gain popularity among the people. After a golden era of central colleges, the system collapsed, and single-gender schools once again became dominant in society. In the contemporary education system, although the highest number of schools in the country are mixed-gender, a few single-gender schools are again dominant in society (Kalugalagedera & Stefanie, 2018).

7.2.1 THE CURRENT SITUATION IN THE SRI LANKAN SCHOOL SYSTEM

There are government schools and non-government (private or international) schools in Sri Lanka. Government schools are categorized into three different types based on gender segregation (Chamara, 2021). Private schools and international schools are mostly mixed-gender, while only some private schools exist as single-gender schools. Madrasas, Piriven (Buddhist temple-centered educational institutions), and schools for Islamic education are mostly single-gendered (Kalugalagedera, 2018).

TABLE 7.1 Government Schools by Boys, Girls, and Mixed Schools, in Different Districts of Western Province in Sri Lanka in 2020

District	Boys Schools	Girls' Schools	Mixed School	Total Schools
Colombo district	40	56	303	399
Gampaha district	10	20	506	536
Kalutara district	07	15	398	420
Western province	57	91	1207	1355

Source: Statistics Unit, Ministry of Education, Sri Lanka.

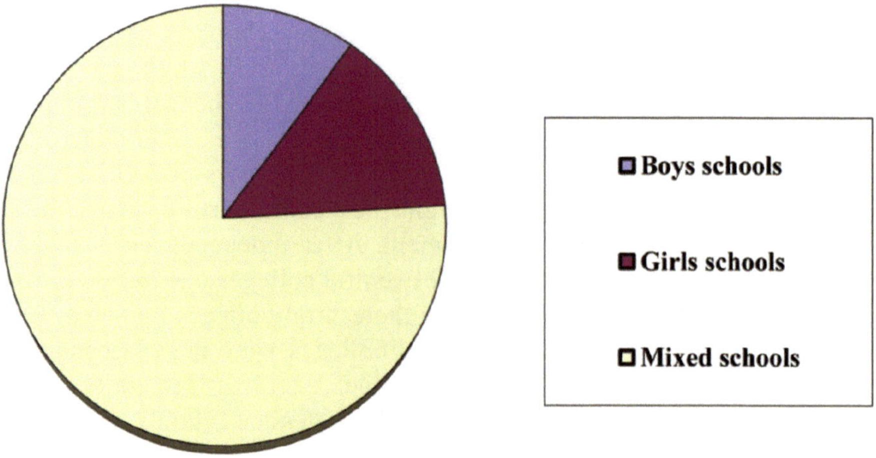

FIGURE 7.1 Government schools by boys, girls, and mixed schools, in western province, Sri Lanka in 2020.

Source: Statistics Unit, Ministry of Education, Sri Lanka.

The Table 7.1 and the chart show the distribution of gender segregation (boys-only, girls-only, or mix-gender) in the Western province of Sri Lanka (Figure 7.1).

7.3 METHODOLOGY

In the argument between single-gender schools and mixed-gender schools, there is a research gap that this study seeks to fill by studying related literature generally and analyzing data collected from real situations in the Sri Lankan school community. Given that education has a significant developmental impact on gender perspectives, extra effort was made to elicit real opinions from the communities connected to schools utilizing a qualitative study methodology, semi-structured interviews, and open-ended questionnaires. Two single-gender schools (a girls' school and a boys' school), and one mixed-gender school were selected from the Colombo district in the Western province of Sri Lanka. Interviews were conducted consisting of 10 senior secondary levels (Advanced level) students, ten teachers, ten parents (mothers or fathers), and ten old girls/boys who were selected under the convenient sampling method from each school. All the collected data were analyzed using thematic analysis. Gender salience, friendships between female and male participants, and mixed-gender anxiety were directly assessed and contrasted. Confounding variables such as family socioeconomic status, cultural and religious differences, and the number of siblings in the family, etc., were considered in selecting participants of the sample for better control.

A variety of factors were found to be indicators (determinants) of participants' gender perspectives, such as economic involvement and opportunity, health and survival, educational accomplishment, overall life satisfaction, gender roles and stereotypes, assets and livelihoods, power, and decision-making, different access to and control over resources, caring behaviors, reproductive health, gender-specific diseases, productive, reproductive, and community roles, cultural beliefs, etc. (Subramanium, 2005; McHale, Crouter, & Whiteman, 2003). Among the above list of determinants, the most significant and measurable five determinants were selected and assumed that the participants will contribute their role in promoting or demoting gender equality based on their gender attitudes and perspectives. The influence of gender segregation on gender equality was analyzed in different settings, by analyzing participants' answers and ideas based on their gender perspectives through the selected determinants. Students and past pupils were questioned about their own perspectives toward the determinants while teachers and parents were questioned about their students' or children's perspectives. Therefore, teachers and parents had to express their students' and children's gender perspectives and behaviors from their point of view to verify the influence of gender-segregated school concept on gender behaviors.

Interviews and questionnaires were designed separately for students, past pupils, teachers, and parents to align with the above intention. After a fine and careful analysis, data was included in an index to simplify the results as positive points and negative points that influence gender equality. If their gender perspective is promoting gender equality, it is considered a positive point, and if it is demoting gender equality, it is considered a negative point. Likewise, all the students' and past pupils' ideas about each determinant were converted to a positive or a negative point (Figures 7.2 and 7.3).

The following determinants were selected to measure the perspectives of participants. Each determinant was analyzed under several questions which were guided to design the questionnaires.

1. **Roles and Responsibilities**
   - What were/are their productive roles in school/home/society?
   - What are/will be their responsibilities for household duties, child care, and the care of the aged and sick?
   - What volunteer work is being done by the community members for the good of the overall community?
   - What part does community politics play in their involvement, decision-making, and representation of the community?
2. **Decision-Making and Power**
   - What decisions do males/females typically engage in making at school, household, and community levels?
   - What decisions do males/females typically control making at the school, household, and community levels?
   - What limitations do they face?
3. **Priorities and Needs**
   - What needs and concerns—genetic, psychological, physiological, legal, societal, and educational—do men and women have?
   - What viewpoints do they hold towards suitable and long-term methods of meeting their needs?
4. **Gender Behaviors**
   - What viewpoints do they hold on social interaction and gender relationships?
   - What perspectives do they have on gender anxiety?
   - What perspectives do they have on gender salience?
   - What perspectives do they have on gender bias?
   - What perspectives do they have on gender discrimination?
5. **Social performance and Contribution to Gender Equality**
   - What are the opportunities they get at school/home/society?
   - To what extent do they perform in different activities and events?
   - To what extent do they contribute to gender equality at school/home/society?
   - How are their relationships and interactions with the opposite genders?

7.4 RESULTS

TABLE 7.2 Perspectives (as Positive/Negative Points) of Pupils Toward Gender Equality Under Selected Determinants

Participants	Pupils in the Girls' School		Pupils in the Boys' School		Pupils in the Mixed School	
Points Determinant	**Positive Points**	**Negative Points**	**Positive Points**	**Negative Points**	**Positive Points**	**Negative Points**
Roles and responsibilities	6	4	5	5	7	3
Power and decision-making	7	3	2	8	8	2
Needs and priorities	8	2	6	4	9	1
Gender behaviors	6	4	6	4	8	2
Social performance	9	1	8	2	5	5
Total points	36	14	27	23	37	13

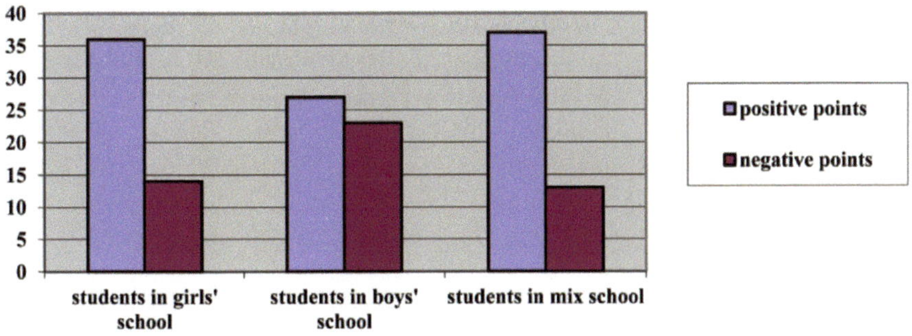

FIGURE 7.2 Positive and negative points toward gender equality of pupils in single-gender and mixed-gender schools.

TABLE 7.3 Perspectives (As Positive/Negative Points) of Past Pupils Toward Gender Equality Under Selected Determinants

Participants	Old Girls of the Girls' School		Old Boys of the Boys' School		Past Pupils of the Mix School	
Points Determinant	**Positive Points**	**Negative Points**	**Positive Points**	**Negative Points**	**Positive Points**	**Negative Points**
Roles and responsibilities	5	5	4	6	9	1
Power and decision-making	6	4	1	9	8	2
Needs and priorities	7	3	5	5	9	1
Gender behaviors	6	4	5	5	8	2
Social performance	8	2	5	5	8	2
Total points	32	18	20	30	42	8

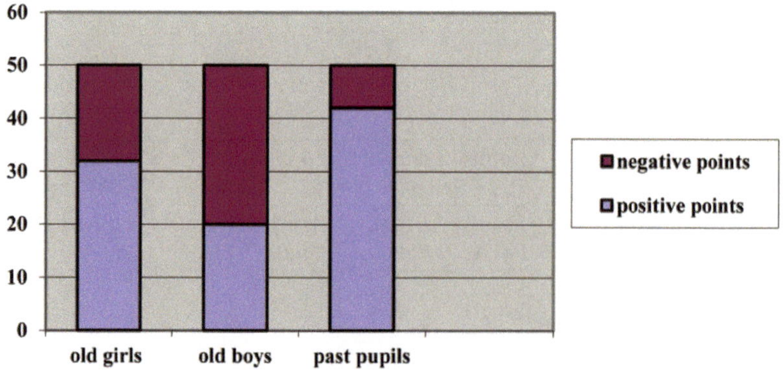

FIGURE 7.3 Positive and negative points toward gender equality of past pupils in single-gender and mixed-gender schools.

TABLE 7.4 Perspectives (as Positive/Negative Points) of Students Toward Gender Equality Under Selected Determinants by Teachers' Point of View

Participants	Teachers of the Girls' School		Teachers of the Boys' School		Teachers of the Mixed-Gender School	
Points Determinant	**Positive points**	**Negative Points**	**Positive Points**	**Negative Points**	**Positive Points**	**Negative Points**
Roles and responsibilities	8	2	4	6	9	1
Power and decision-making	7	3	2	8	8	2
Needs and priorities	7	3	5	5	9	1
Gender behaviors	5	5	5	5	8	2
Social performance	8	2	5	5	8	2
Total points	35	15	21	29	42	8

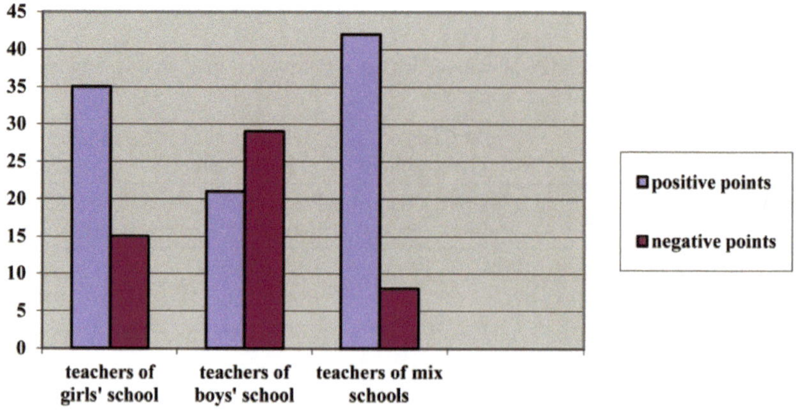

FIGURE 7.4 Positive and negative points toward gender equality of students in same-gender schools and mixed-gender schools in teachers' point of view.

TABLE 7.5 Perspectives (as Positive/Negative Points) of Students Toward Gender Equality Under Selected Determinants by Parents' Point of View

Participants	Parents of the Girls' School		Parents of the Boys' School		Parents of the Mixed-Gender School	
Points Determinant	**Positive Points**	**Negative Points**	**Positive Points**	**Negative Points**	**Positive Points**	**Negative Points**
Roles and responsibilities	2	8	2	8	9	1
Power and decision-making	3	7	3	7	8	2
Needs and priorities	5	5	5	5	9	1
gender behaviors	3	7	2	8	8	2
Social performance	6	4	6	4	8	2
Total points	19	31	18	32	42	8

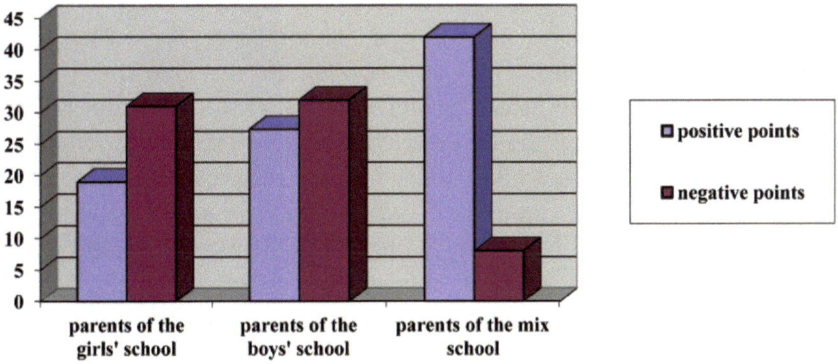

FIGURE 7.5 Positive and negative points toward gender equality of students in same-gender and mixed-gender schools in parents' point of view.

7.5 CONCLUSION AND DISCUSSION

According to the analysis of data collected from the research, the following points can be highlighted:

- Children in mixed-gender schools show more positive behaviors and perspectives towards most of the determinants than the children in same-gender schools.
- Children in mixed-gender schools are more experienced in handling gender problems than children in same-gender schools.
- Children in mixed-gender schools have more positive attitudes towards gender equality than children in same-gender schools.
- Children in same-gender schools promote gender stereotypes more than children in mixed-gender schools.

- Teachers in mixed-gender schools are more experienced in handling problems related to gender than teachers in same-gender schools.
- Boys in same-gender schools show more academic performance than boys in mixed-gender schools.
- Girls in same-gender schools show more academic performance than girls in mixed-gender schools.
- Boys in same-gender schools show higher participation in extracurricular activities than boys in mixed-gender schools.
- Girls in same-gender schools participate more in extracurricular activities than girls in mixed-gender schools.
- In Sri Lanka, boys are more likely than girls to leave school early.
- In Sri Lanka, boys entering tertiary-level education also compare less in most fields, except engineering.

Although there are more positive points in mixed-gender settings toward gender equality promotion, it is still not fair to conclude that a mixed-school setting totally promotes gender equality. Only a few determinants were considered, and all the other external factors that affect participants' perspectives were not controlled in this research. Therefore, considering the facts and information found in the literature and the data collected from the research, the influence of school type on gender equality in Sri Lanka can be explained under the following sub-topics.

7.5.1 BENEFITS OF MIXED-GENDER EDUCATION MORE ACCESS TO A VARIETY

Children's attitudes and progress are shaped when they have access to gender diversity in their learning environments. Students who attend classes with just other students who share their viewpoints produce an echo chamber that exclusively encourages that viewpoint (Chamara, 2021). Exposure to other viewpoints and experiences expands one's options, lessens stereotype mindset, and enhances one's general attitude toward gender equality (Arunatillake, 2017). Furthermore, these deep friendships between people of various genders from a young age in a safe school setting aid in their ability to adjust to changing circumstances as they age. Additionally, it produces advantages for culture and society that are long-lasting (Connect us fund, 2019).

- **Increasing Equality:** Over the past century, gender equality has come a long way in our world. Children learn how to treat each other fairly and with respect at mixed-gender schools, which provide equal chances to all genders. Students are equally treated with no preference for gender in mixed-gender schools that follow the correct philosophy. This promotes opportunities for socialization (Akpakwu & Simon, 2014). Students educated in same-gender schools face difficulties when interacting with people of the opposite sex in society. They have to work hard to establish positive relationships not only in one setting but in every circumstance and setting, including career opportunities that may require regular interactions with individuals of a different gender. By offering children opportunities to practice social interactions in a safe environment and increasing their familiarity with it, they may be better prepared for a society that is moving away from segregation laws rapidly (Chamara, 2021).

- **Educate Children About Real-World Scenarios:** Even though there are benefits to a same-gender school, when taking into account class availability, interpersonal interactions, and respect, mixed-gender schools provide greater preparation for what will happen in everyday life. Understanding the similarities and contrasts between each person while interacting with people of different gender identities throughout the day can assist in creating meaningful and healthy connections. (Bunny, 2022).
- **Develop Better Communication Skills:** When children are not exposed to different genders at a young age, it can create social discomfort. A mixed-gender school may help pupils develop confidence in making a good first impression in important life situations by providing opportunities for communication with the opposite gender in face-to-face scenarios (Bunny, 2022; Mudalige, 2019).
- **Increasing Their Academic Performance to Match That of Their Peers of the Opposite Gender:** Girls and boys can significantly improve their test scores in the classroom compared to the other gender (Connect Us Fund, 2019; Marsh, 1989).
- **Reducing The Overall Cost of School Administration:** The total administrative expenses of schools with mixed-gender settings are reduced. If the administration embraces a mixed-gender approach, they should make the program available to all schools (World Bank, 2018). However, for single-gender schools, there are currently three programs available: one for boys, one for girls, and a mixed-gender option (Amott, 2004).

7.5.2 *DISADVANTAGES OF MIXED-GENDER SCHOOLS CHALLENGE GENDER NORMS*

Due to the traditional and cultural attitudes and viewpoints of different genders in societies, it is challenging to make changes, and this practice and philosophy are difficult to implement (Bigler & Hays, 2013).

- **Create Problems with Sexual Distraction:** Boys and girls at a younger age make friendships and concentrate on their assignments, but as they approach puberty, biological responses to one another might cause variations in gender to become a distraction. Negative reactions to relationship problems can lead to depression in secondary and postsecondary students (Signorella, Hayes, & Li, 2005). Attraction to each other can reduce learning performance as well (Dodge, Heimberg, Nyma & O'Brien, 1987).
- **Forces Pupils to Learn in Inappropriate Environments:** Due to fundamental distinctions in gender, boys and girls have different physiologies. However, both boys and girls in mixed-gender schools follow the same curriculum in an effort to equalize how they learn (Pahlke, Hyde & Allison, 2014). They may become anxious from time to time as a result of being exposed to techniques that are inappropriate for their circumstances. Some kids may not be able to reach their full potential as a result of this problem (Bigler & Hays, 2013).
- **Exacerbate Poor Academic Performance:** Children may feel embarrassed or uncomfortable in mixed-gender settings, and they will not interact in the classroom naturally, especially in their adolescence. Due to this, they would not be able to reach their full potential. (Charles & Bradley, 2002).
- **Risks Associated with Promoting Close Connections in Young People:** Teenagers grow increasingly impulsive, and even violent, with little consideration for the long-term effects of their decisions (Paolini, Harwood & Rubin, 2010). They frequently make choices based more on immediate enjoyment than on creating chances for the future. Students who attend mixed-gender schools have greater opportunities to engage in sexual activity. (Atherton, 1973).
- **Problems with their Confidence or Self-Esteem:** Attending a same-gender school gives students the self-assurance they need

to speak out and give presentations in class. They tend to impress the opposite gender in their teenage years. Especially girls are less confident and shy in mixed-gender schools (Atherton, 1973).

- **Makes Girls Subject to a Double Standard:** In a situation with mixed-gender kids, the administrators will hold boys and girls to different standards since they adhere more to the traditional mindset on gender roles. Even the clothing regulations at schools with mixed-gender environments sometimes favor girls over boys. (Mae, Alonso, Gibson, Rogers, & Smith, 2005).

7.5.3 BENEFITS OF SINGLE-GENDER SCHOOLS

- **Excel in Specific Areas:** It has been discovered that children who learn in an atmosphere without fear of humiliation from the other gender perform better in specific performances such as arts, dramatics, and sports activities (Fabes, Pahlke, Borders, & Galligan, 2015).
- **Improve the Environment for Students and Teachers While Increasing Contact Between Them:** Single-gender schools typically hire teachers who are the same gender as the students; for example, girls' schools typically hire female teachers and boys' schools typically hire male teachers (Priyashantha, De Alwis, & Welmilla, 2021). However, this is not the case in Sri Lanka because teaching is a gender-specific stereotypical profession and there are more women teachers than men in Sri Lanka (Department of Census and Statistics, 2017). However, in general, this improves comfort and fosters more connection between students and teachers (Withanage & Chandrakumara, 2021) (Tables 7.4 and 7.5)
- **Career Opportunities:** In single-gender schools, students have the chance to acquire skills for careers other than gender-specific, stereotyped ones (Mae, Alonso, Gibson, Rogers, & Smith, 2005). Students who are exposed to a variety of professional possibilities in a setting where there is only one gender teaching can freely pick their ideal job without experiencing any hereditary prejudice (Aturupane & Ebenezer, 2017; Ariyawansa, 2013).
- **Soft Skills Development:** There are several leadership and soft talents that are often solely possessed by girls. In single-sex settings,

both genders can develop such skills equally without stereotyping (Withanage & Chandrakumara, 2021).

- **Allow Privacy:** The ability to maintain the amount of privacy and anonymity that kids seek throughout the puberty stage of their life is a really significant benefit of single-gender institutions (Attanapola, 2004). If classes are gender-appropriate, students will find it simpler to handle the demands of their studies (Atherton, 1973).

7.5.4 DISADVANTAGES OF SINGLE-GENDER SCHOOLS

- **Poor Social Performance"** However, as children of different sexes start to enter puberty, there is a general attraction between them, according to the general principles of child psychology (Doughty, Lam, Stanik, & McHale, 2015). Puberty typically begins for females at age 10 and lasts until age 17, whereas it begins for boys at age 12 and lasts until age 18. According to several research studies, children who attend single-gender schools as they get older develop more hostility toward people of the other sex (Hales, 2021; Cota & Dion, 1986).
- **Discomfort for Free Interaction:** Single-gender educational institutions reduce opportunities for the exchange of ideas and learning methods between the sexes (Fabes, Pahlke, Borders, & Galligan, 2015). When in university education, students from single-gender schools find it difficult to study teamwork that is meant to incorporate both genders (Ministry of Higher Education, 2017). Single-gender schools, in a sense, don't assist children in becoming ready for the real world (Withanage & Chandrakumara, 2021).
- **Not Allowing Healthy Academic Competition:** These schools hinder students of both sexes from engaging in healthy academic competition. Students may face distress due to unexpected academic challenges from the other gender when enrolling in a higher education institution (Hales, 2021).
- **Create a Gender Disparity in Minds:** Single-gender classrooms have the potential to instill a gender disparity in pupils' perceptions from an early age (opinionfront.com, 2017).

Positive and negative points of both types of schools demonstrate how the school setting influences gender equality (Koenig & Eagly, 2014). In the present, males and females are becoming integrated; we must provide equal rights and opportunities to all individuals to achieve the highest education and succeed (Charles & Bradley, 2002). The traditions of gendered classroom arrangement and gender classification, according to developmental intergroup theory (Bigler, 2006; Liben, 2007) and gender schema theories (Bem, 1981, 1983; Liben & Bigler, 2002; Martin & Halverson, 1981), enhance gender salience and aid in the formation and maintenance of children's gender bias (Elsevier, 2006). The developmental intergroup theory makes contradictory predictions about single-gender schools because they include elements that both raise and diminish gender salience (Hilliard & Liben, 2010). These results underscore the need for scientifically monitoring gender equality in single-gender and mixed-gender school children to assess the dispute over whether the educational setting emphasizes gender equality more prominently.

7.5.5 THE ROLE THAT SCHOOLS PLAY IN PROMOTING GENDER EQUALITY

Whatever the school type, the school can act its role in reinforcing gender equality using different strategies such as:

- Implementation of gender-based bullying policies
- Putting policies into place and establishing uniform instruction
- Record-keeping and follow-up processes for teachers, other adults, cleaning staff, sports coaches, canteen staff, parents, and volunteers from the community
- Examine classroom equal opportunity policies
- Establish policies mandating separate restrooms for boys and girls, access to adequate sanitary facilities, and a welcoming atmosphere for both boys and girls
- School inspections take gender equality into consideration
- Lessons and textbooks that promote equality between the sexes and are devoid of gender prejudice.
- Examine and change curriculum, textbooks, programs, and teaching techniques to make sure they don't reinforce damaging gender stereotypes
- Updating teacher education curriculum to address gender issues

- Changing teacher attitudes and behaviors through teacher education
- Recognize the pressure on women teachers
- Conduct codes outlining children's rights and obligations as well as fundamental counseling
- Education on sexual harassment in the classroom
- To safeguard students' health and well-being, and encourage teachers to uphold their professional obligations and ethical standards
- Ensure that there is no discrimination, particularly on the grounds of gender
- Adapting the processes of teaching and learning to address the unique requirements of boys and girls
- Developing students' knowledge, skills, and attitudes through school-based comprehensive education programs that place a strong emphasis on human rights, gender equality, sexuality, and skill-building
- Equipping girls with the self-assurance, assertiveness, courage, correct decision-making, and negotiation of their strengths to get through gender-specific barriers
- Promoting boys to be free from gender-sexist behaviors and attitudes like bullying and sexual harassment and to gain the self-assurance they need to embrace gender equality positively
- Encouraging pupils to question stereotypes and biases; envision for them a broad and varied future; and work to make parents, other family members, and community members more sensitive to gender issues
- Providing guidance and counseling for the socio-psychological development of children of both sexes
- Training teachers and students in guidance and counseling skills
- Educating the school community on how to deal with challenges related to both boys' and girls' sexual maturity, focusing on their secondary sexual characteristics and puberty in adolescence (Bigler & Hays, 2013; Blakemore, Berenbaum, & Liben, 2009; Halpern, Eliot, Bigle, Fabes, Hanish, & Hyde,2011; Walker, & Unterhalter, 2007; Zosuls, Miller, Ruble, Martin, & Fabes, 2011)

7.5.6 GENDER SEGREGATION VS GENDER EQUALITY IN THE SRI LANKAN SCHOOL SYSTEM

In terms of the Sri Lankan context for this issue, gender equality has been attained in many facets of schooling. Gender segregation in the school system can be seen largely due to some traditional and cultural norms. Although there is a higher number of mixed-gender schools, most of the leading and popular schools in urban areas are established as either girls-only schools or boys-only schools (Ministry of Education, 2011).

Although it is still debatable about the best type of school for gender equality in the Sri Lankan context, due to the separation of genders in schools, children's attitudes may be affected positively or negatively toward gender equality as they grow (Menike, 2015). However, this study reveals that student enrollment in coeducational schools offers more advantages in terms of gender behavior and gender roles in a positive way (Ministry of Education, 2017).

Furthermore, the findings highlight the need for policy intervention to change the popularity of single-gender schools and implement various programs to change parents' attitudes towards school types in minimizing gender inequality through the single-gender school concept (Ministry of Education, 2020).

A statistical metric known as gender parity is used to characterize the ratios between males and females in a certain group (Wikipedia, 2023). Gender parity is interrelated with gender equality and directly influences gender equality in any community (Dasgupta & Asgari, 2004). Due to the equal enrollment of girls and boys in elementary school, Sri Lanka's educational system has a greater level of gender parity than many other South Asian nations. However, according to statistics, there is a higher number of girls than boys in the secondary education system in Sri Lanka (Athurupane, Shojo, & Ebenezer, 2018).

Although there isn't any issue related to gender disparity, the argument remains about the influence of the gender-segregated school system in the country on gender attitudes, gender roles, gender biases, and the overall concept of gender equality (Withanage & Chandrakumara, 2021). The question that arises from the above points is: 'Is there a significant difference between single-gender schools and mixed-gender schools in opportunities to promote gender equality?' The answer to the question is yes, there are, but the results hardly indicate the limited opportunities for gender equality of students in gender-segregated schools.

Although there is gender parity in enrollment of girls and boys in elementary school, there is a gender disparity in educational access at the primary level due to gender-segregated schools. This issue indirectly creates gender inequality (ADB, 2015).

When students choose their subject streams for the General Certificate of Education, Advanced Level examination, there is a huge difference between opposite-gender students. Boys tend to select the field of Physical Sciences. The number of girls having good results and rates in exams is higher than boys (Akpakwu & Simon, 2014). Possible reasons for this gap cannot be determined with proven evidence, but there can be the influence of gender segregation and unequal treatment in gender-segregated schools, which are connected with social and cultural perceptions. As Sri Lanka prepares for future education development plans, there is a huge need to bridge this gap in the school system as well as the parents' and community's perspectives.

7.6 SUMMARY

From ancient times, we all in different societies shared the attitude of a patriarchal society that feels men are superior to women. But now, we are moving closer to a global community where there is true equality for all gender identities, not only for men and women. The idea of mixed-gender schools has helped to bring about some of this transformation. Students that identify as non-binary, transgender, genderfluid, agender, bigender, intersex, or pangender must now deal with the same prejudice that girls formerly endured in educational systems but nearly conquered. Both same-gender and mixed-gender schools do not welcome these children. According to the dilemma of gender segregation concept, one idea is that single-gender schooling promotes gender equality in education because single-gender schools don't have the chance to differentiate or stratify students based on gender in the learning process. On the other hand, there are shreds of evidence that show the parity in academic achievement in single-gender schooling. Academically, girls are more benefited in single-gender settings because it reduces gender stereotyping and increases girls' participation in specific courses which have been allocated only for boys (Department of Census & Statistics, 2017). Some countries like the USA deliberately create more single-gender schools to create convenient environments for girls' education (US Department of Education, 2006).

This study aimed to investigate how gender segregation in the school system affects gender equality in the Sri Lankan context, by analyzing data obtained from the two types of schools and related literature that exists. There are both advantages and disadvantages of single-gender and mixed-gender school systems, and an unsolved debate among communities regarding this matter. Some of the disadvantages created by mixed-gender settings are due to the traditional attitudes which still remain in our mindsets, and we can overcome them through real effort. If we make a gradual change from a single-gender setting to a mixed-gender setting, allowing the communities to absorb its advantages, it will be accepted in the near future by new generations who have positive attitudes toward gender equality. As educators, we must do a lot to transform society so that it prioritizes gender equality. The journey toward a future where there is gender equality and sustainability begin with our actions now.

However, much like in the worldwide context, the impact of the "Gender School Concept" on gender equality in Sri Lanka is still up for debate.

KEYWORDS

- **gender equality**
- **gender parity**
- **gender roles**
- **gender segregation**
- **gender stereotypes**
- **mix-gender schools**
- **single-gender schools**

REFERENCES

Akpakwu, S. O. (2014). Gender equality in schools: Implications for the curriculum, teaching and classroom interaction. *Journal of Education and Practice, 5*, 154–201.

Alfieri, T., Ruble, D. N., & Higgins, E. T. (1996). Gender stereotypes during adolescence: Developmental changes and the transition to junior high school. *Developmental Psychology, 32*(6), 1129–1137. https://doi.org/10.1037/0012-1649.32.6.1129.

Amott, M. (2004). Gender equality and opportunities in the classroom: Thinking about citizenship, pedagogy and the rights of children. *Beyond Access Seminar, 4(2)*, 131–150.

Ariyawansa, R. (2013). Employability of graduates of Sri Lankan universities. *Sri Lankan Journal of Human Resource Management, 2*(1), 91. https://doi.org/10.4038/sljhrm.v2i1.5107.

Arunatillake, N. (2017). Women in the Sri Lankan workforce: Dissecting education and female labor force participation [Blog]. *IPS Talking Economics* (pp. 1–3). Retrieved from: https://www.ips.lk/wp-content/uploads/2017/03/Island_05August_Women-in-the-Sri-Lankan-workforce.pdf.

Asian Development Bank. (2015). Country gender assessment, Sri Lanka: An update. gender-assessment-update.pdf. 978-92-9257-024-8 (Print)978-92-9257-025-5 (e-ISBN). Retrieved from: https://www.adb.org/documents/country-gender-assessment-sri-lanka-update.

Atherton, B. F. (1973). Coeducational and single-sex schooling and happiness of marriage. *Educational Research, 15*(3), 221–226. https://doi.org/10.1080/0013188730150307.

Athurupane, H., Shojo, M., & Ebenezer, R. (2018). Gender dimensions of educational access and achievement. *Interface Science*, 12–52.

Attanapola, C. T. (2004). Changing gender roles and health impacts among female workers in export-processing industries in Sri Lanka. *Social Science and Medicine, 58*(11), 2301–2312. https://doi.org/10.1016/j.socscimed.2003.08.022.

Aturupane, H., & Ebenezer, R. M. (2017). Sri Lanka: When girls outpace boys in schools. *Education for Global Development*. Retrieved from: https://blogs.worldbank.org/education/sri-lanka-when-girls-outpace-boys-schools (accessed on 19 June 2024).

Bigler, R., & Hays, A. R. (2013). The role of schools in the early socialization of gender differences. University of Texas at Austin, University of California, Santa Cruz. https://www.child-encyclopedia.com/pdf/expert/gender-early-socialization/according-experts/role-schools-early-socialization-gender-differences.

Blakemore, J. E. O., Berenbaum, S. A., & Liben, L. S. (2008). *Gender Development* (1st ed.). Psychology Press. https://doi.org/10.4324/9780203889756. Psychology Press, 2009 by Taylor & Francis Group, LLC. International Standard Book Number-13: 978-0-8058-4170-1. pp. 365–390

Bunny, D. (2022). Ten advantages of sending your child to a mixed school. Evan Williams. Vol. XLI. https://www.cbsl.gov.lk/sites/default/files/cbslweb_documents/statistics/otherpub/ess_2019_e.pdf.

Central Bank of Sri Lanka, & Census and Statistic Department. (2019). *Economic and Social Statistics of Sri Lanka, 2019*. https://www.themorning.lk/articles/114929.

Chamara, S. (2021). Gender-segregated schools and sex education: Is Sri Lanka ready and willing? *TSM WEB Desk*.

Charles, M., & Bradley, K. (2002). Equal but separate? A cross-national study of sex segregation in higher education. *American Sociological Review, 67*(4), 573–600. http://doi.org/10.2307/3088946.

Collins, R., Chafetz, J. S., Blumberg, R. L., Coltrane, S., & Turner, J. H. (1993). Toward an integrated theory of gender stratification. *Sociological Perspectives, 36*(3), 185–216. https://doi.org/10.2307/1389242.

Cota, A. A., & Dion, K. L. (1986). Salience of gender and sex composition of ad hoc groups: An experimental test of distinctiveness theory. *Journal of Personality and Social Psychology, 50*(4), 770–776. https://doi.org/10.1037/0022-3514.50.4.770.

Dasgupta, N., & Asgari, S. (2004). Seeing is believing: Exposure to counter-stereotypic women leaders and its effect on the malleability of automatic gender stereotyping. *Journal of Experimental Social Psychology, 40*(5), 642–658. https://doi.org/10.1016/j.jesp.2004.02.003.

De Silva, M. T. T., & Priyashantha, K. G. (2014). Changing gender stereotypes: the impact of conflicts in dual career families on turnover intention (With special reference to female professionals in Sri Lanka). *International Journal of Arts and Commerce, 3*(5), 1.

Department of Census and Statistics. (2017). Child Activity Survey 2016. Department of Census and Statistics. http://www.statistics.gov.lk/Resource/en/OtherCensusandSurveys/SurveyReports/Child_Activity%20_Survey_2016.pdf.

Department of Census and Statistics. (2017). Sri Lanka labor force statistics bulletin. Retrieved: from: http://www.statistics.gov.lk/Resource/en/LabourForce/Annual_Reports/2017-2ndVersion.pdf.

Dodge, C. S., Heimberg, R. G., Nyman, D., & O'Rien, G. T. (1987). Daily heterosocial interactions of high and low socially anxious college students: A diary study. *Behavior Therapy, 18*(1), 90–96. https://doi.org/10.1016/S0005-7894(87)80054-0.

Doughty, S. E., Lam, C. B., Stanik, C. E., & McHale, S. M. (2015). Links between sibling experiences and romantic competence from adolescence through young adulthood. *Journal of Youth and Adolescence, 44*(11), 2054–2066. https://doi.org/10.1007/s10964-014-0177-9.

Fabes, R. A., Pahlke, E., Galligan, K., & Borders, A. (2015). U.S. Principals' attitudes about and experiences with single-sex schooling. *Educational Studies, 41*(3), 293–311. https://doi.org/10.1080/03055698.2015.1005576.

Hales, C. (2021). Single gender school's vs mixed gender schools. *Aldwick Bury School.* https://www.aldwickbury.org.uk/post/~board/aldwickbury-news/post/single-gender-schools-vs-mixed-gender-schools. 19 May, 2021.

Halpern, D. F., Eliot, L., Bigler, R. S., Fabes, R. A., Hanish, L. D., Hyde, J., Liben, L. S., & Martin, C. L. (2011). Education. The pseudoscience of single-sex schooling. *Science, 333*(6050), 1706–1707. https://doi.org/10.1126/science.1205031.

Harker, R. (2000). Achievement, gender and the single-sex/coed debate. *British Journal of Sociology of Education, 21*(2), 203–218. https://doi.org/10.1080/713655349.

Hilliard, L. J., & Liben, L. S. (2010). Differing levels of gender salience in preschool classrooms: Effects on children's gender attitudes and intergroup bias. *Child Development, 81*(6), 1787–1798. https://doi.org/10.1111/j.1467-8624.2010.01510.x.

Jayatilake, L. V., Kumara, P. S., Withanage, P., & Fernando, P. L. S. (2014). Women managers and their personal barriers for upward mobility in private and public sectors. *Kelaniya Journal of Management, 2*(1), https://kjm.sljol.info/articles/6545/files/submission/proof/6545-1-23237-1-10-20140205.pdf, pp. 2–21.

Kail, R. V., & Levine, L. E. (1976). Encoding processes and sex-role preferences. *Journal of Experimental Child Psychology, 21*(2), 256–263. https://doi.org/10.1016/0022-0965(76)90039-4.

Koblinsky, S. G., Cruse, D. F., & Sugawara, A. I. (1978). Sex role stereotypes and children's memory for story content. *Child Development, 49*(2), 452–458. https://doi.org/10.2307/1128710.

Kovinthan, T. (2019). Teaching gender inequality. *Interface Science Lanka.* Retrieved from: https://www.opendemocracy.net/en/5050/teaching-gender-inequality-textbooks-and-traditions-in-sri-lanka/ (accessed on 19 June 2024).

Liben, L. S. (2015). Probability values and human values in evaluating single-sex education. *Sex Roles, 72*(9–10), 401–426. https://doi.org/10.1007/s11199-014-0438-9.

Little, A. W. (2011). Education policy reform in Sri Lanka: The double-edged sword of political will. *Journal of Education Policy, 26*(4), 499–512. https://doi.org/10.1080/02680939.2011.555005.

Liyanage, K. I. M. (2014). Education system of Sri Lanka: Strengths and weaknesses. Retrieved from: https://www.ide.go.jp/library/Japanese/Publish/Reports/InterimReport/2013/pdf/C02_ch7.pdf (accessed on 19 June 2024).

Mael, F., Alonso, A., Gibson, D., Rogers, K., & Smith, M. (2005). Single-Sex Versus Coeducational Schooling: A Systematic Review. Doc# 2005-01. US Department of

Education. Retrieved from: https://www2.ed.gov/rschstat/eval/other/single-sex/single-sex.pdf (accessed on 19 June 2024).

Marks, J. L., Bun, L. C., & McHale, S. M. (2009). Family patterns of gender role attitudes. *Sex Roles, 61*(3–4), 221–234. https://doi.org/10.1007/s11199-009-9619-3.

Marsh, H. W. (1989). Effects of attending single-sex and coeducational high schools on achievement, attitudes, behaviors, and sex differences. *Journal of Educational Psychology, 81*(1), 70–85. http://doi.org/10.1037/0022-0663.81.1.70.

McHale, S. M., Crouter, A. C., & Whiteman, S. D. (2003). The family contexts of gender development in childhood and adolescence. *Social Development, 12*(1), 125–148. https://doi.org/10.1111/1467-9507.00225.

Menike, A. H. R. (2015). Rural-urban disparity in Sri Lanka. *IPASJ International Journal of Management, 3*(3), 1–11. Retrieved from: https://www.researchgate.net/profile/Hra-Menike/publication/281630412_Rural-Urban_Disparity_in_Sri_Lanka/links/55f1380008aedecb68ffde10/Rural-Urban-Disparity-in-Sri-Lanka.pdf.

Ministry of Education. (2011). Education sector development framework and program (ESDFP) 2012–16. *Ministry of Education*. https://moe.gov.lk/wp-content/uploads/2020/06/Education-Sector-Development-Framework-Program-2012-2016.pdf.

Ministry of Education. (2017). School census. *Ministry of Education, Isurupaya, Bataramulla*. https://moe.gov.lk/wp-content/uploads/2020/06/School-Census-Report-2017.pdf.

Ministry of Education. (2020). *Table 5.4: Boys Schools Girls Schools Mixed Schools*. Retrieved from: https://wp.gov.lk/en/wp-content/uploads/Table-5-4.pdf (accessed on 19 June 2024).

Ministry of Higher Education. (2017). Annual reports. Retrieved from: https://moe.gov.lk/wp-content/uploads/2020/06/Education-Sector-Development-Framework-Program-2012-2016.pdf (accessed on 19 June 2024).

Mudalige, D. (2019). Sri Lanka improves ranking in Human Development Index 2019. *Daily News*. Retrieved from: http://www.dailynews.lk/2019/12/10/local/205301/sri-lanka-improves-ranking-humandevelopment-index-2019.

Opinionfront.com. (2009). Pros-cons-of-single-sex-schools Pros and Cons of Single Sex Schools. *Opinion Front*. Retrieved from: http://www.opinionfront.com/pros-cons-of-single-sex-schools.

Pahlke, E., Hyde, J. S., & Allison, C. M. (2014). The effects of single-sex compared with coeducational schooling on students' performance and attitudes: A meta-analysis. *Psychological Bulletin, 140*(4), 1042–1072. https://doi.org/10.1037/a0035740.

Paolini, S., Harwood, J., & Rubin, M. (2010). Negative intergroup contact makes group memberships salient: Explaining why intergroup conflict endures. *Personality and Social Psychology Bulletin, 36*(12), 1723–1738. https://doi.org/10.1177/0146167210388667.

Priyashantha, K. G., De Alwis, A. C., & Welmilla, I. (2021). Gender stereotypes change outcomes: A systematic literature review. *Journal of Humanities and Applied Social Sciences*. Advance online publication. https://doi.org/10.1108/JHASS-07-2021-0131.

Sarma, V., Licht, S., & Kalugalagedera, T. (2018). Educational inequalities in Sri Lanka: National data and local perspectives on access, quality and learning outcomes. *Center for Poverty Analysis*. ISBN: 978-955-3628-27-5.

Signorella, M. L., Hayes, A. R., & Li, Y. A. (2013). A Meta-Analytic Critique of Mael et al.'s (2005) Review of Single-Sex Schooling. *Sex Roles, 69*(7–8), 423–441. https://doi.org/10.1007/s11199-013-0288-x.

Spielhofer, T., Benton, T., & Schagen, S. (2004). A study of the effects of school size and single-sex education in English schools. *Research Papers in Education, 19*(2), 133–159. https://doi.org/10.1080/0267152041000l695407.

Subrahmanian, R. (2005). Gender equality in education: Definitions and measurements. *International Journal of Educational Development, 25*(4), 395–407. https://doi.org/10.1016/j.ijedudev.2005.04.003.

Sullivan, A., Joshi, H., & Leonard, D. (2012). Single-sex and co-educational secondary schooling: What are the social and family outcomes, in the short and longer term? *Longitudinal and Life Course Studies, 3*(1), 137–156. https://doi.org/10.14301/llcs.v3i1.148.

Taylor, M. G., & Gelman, S. A. (1993). Children's gender- and age-based categorization in similarity and induction tasks. *Social Development, 2*(2), 104–121. https://doi.org/10.1111/j.1467-9507.1993.tb00006.x.

Thompson, T., & Ungerleider, C. (2004). Single-sex schooling: Final report. Canadian Centre for Knowledge Mobilisation: Waterloo, Ontario. Retrieved from: http://www.cmec.ca (accessed on 19 June 2024).

Walker, M., & Unterhalter, E. (2007). Amartya Sen's capability approach and social justice in education. Springer.

Withanage, D. P., & Chandrakumara, D. P. S. (2021). Gender equality in education in Sri Lanka. *Sri Lanka Journal of Economic Research, 9*(1), 29–50. http://doi.org/10.4038/sljer.v9i1.154.

World Bank. (2018). Work or family: Sri Lankan Women shouldn't have to choose. *World Bank.* Retrieved from: http://www.worldbank.org/en/news/feature/2018/06/14/work-or-family-sri-lankanwomen-shouldnt-have-to-choose.

Zosuls, K. M., Miller, C. F., Ruble, D. N., Martin, C. L., & Fabes, R. A. (2011). Gender development research in sex roles: Historical trends and future directions. *Sex Roles, 64*(11–12), 826–842. https://doi.org/10.1007/s11199-010-9902-3.

CHAPTER 8

"THEY'RE ALREADY ON THE MOON WHILE WE'RE STILL STUCK IN STONE AGE": EXPLORING THE LANGUAGE OF GENDER (IN)EQUALITY IN GERMAN WORKPLACES FROM AN EMPLOYEE'S PERSPECTIVE

VIVIAN STEURER and STEPHANIE SCHNURR

Baden-Wuerttemberg Cooperative State University and The University of Warwick, Germany

ABSTRACT

This chapter addresses the topic of subverting social gender inequalities by exploring the language of gender equality in German workplaces. Focusing on an employees' perspective, we bring to the surface some of the gendered and gendering practices that exist in many German workplaces and that employees experience on a daily basis. Compared to gender equality policies and initiatives in other European and Western countries, Germany is often described as lagging behind – not only with regard to the actual implementation of policies and initiatives but also with regard to people's awareness. Taking a socio-constructionist perspective, this chapter provides a snapshot of the current diversity situation in German workplaces and captures employees' perspectives. Conducting qualitative research involving interviews with 20 employees in a range of different workplaces in Germany and using discourse analysis, we identify and describe some of the discursive processes through which those affected by gender equality issues make

Subverting Social Inequalities: Gender as a Social Reality.
Akanksha Srivastava, Disha Maheshwari, Chitra Krishnan (Eds.)

sense of them. Findings illustrate that this sense-making takes place on three interconnected levels: the personal, the organizational, and the societal level. Participants' experiences range from outright denying the existence of gender equality issues to sharing personal experiences and assigning blame to different groups.

8.1 INTRODUCTION

This chapter addresses the topic of subverting social gender inequalities by exploring the language of gender (in)equality in German workplaces. Focusing on an employee's perspective, we bring to the surface some of the gendered and gendering practices that exist in many workplaces and that employees experience on a daily basis. According to a recent PwC Women in Work Index (2020) – which examines women's economic empowerment based on criteria like women's access to employment – Germany was ranked 19th out of the 33 countries studied (Bocksch, 2021). Moreover, previous research established that the progress of increasing gender equality in German workplaces is particularly slow, inconsistent, and insufficient (Kirsch, 2017; Oldemeier, 2017; Krell & Wächter 2006). This dramatically slow progress is brought to the point by one of the participants in our study who, when describing the state of gender equality policies, measures, and initiatives in her own workplace compared to those of others, remarked: "they're already on the moon while we're still stuck in the Stone Age."

It is thus perhaps not surprising that compared to gender equality policies and initiatives in other European and Western countries, Germany is often described as lagging behind – not only with regards to the actual implementation of gender equality policies and initiatives, but also with regards to people's awareness of these policies and the discriminatory practices they target. This paper addresses these issues by exploring the ways in which employees talk about their experiences of gender equality at work. By sharing their everyday workplace experiences, they provide insights into the ways in which gender is produced and reproduced in the work domain – often in ways that allow gendered and discriminatory practices to be normalized and unquestioningly accepted.

However, unlike much previous research on this topic, we are not interested in describing larger patterns, but rather in identifying the specific processes through which those affected by the various gender policies and practices experience and make sense of them. We thereby provide in-depth insights into the complexities of gender (in)equality and give a voice to those directly affected by the current state of gender equality in the organizational landscape in Germany. We hope that this study – with its qualitative research design and discourse analytical approach focusing on employees' lived experiences (Miles, Huberman, & Saldaña, 2014, p. 11) – will contribute to previous – largely quantitative – scholarship (e.g., Kalkum & Otto, 2017; Ipsos, 2019; Antidiskriminierungsstelle des Bundes, 2017).

8.2 BACKGROUND: GENDER EQUALITY IN GERMAN WORKPLACES

Gender equality refers to the "equal rights, responsibilities, and opportunities of women and men, girls and boys" (UN Women, 2021a). As of 2014, "143 out of 195 countries guarantee equality between women and men in their constitutions" (UN Women, 2021b), and according to Article 23 of the EU Charter of Fundamental Rights, "equality between women and men must be ensured in all areas, including employment, work, and pay" (European Parliament, 2021). And yet – in spite of these proclamations – there is little doubt that "[i]n virtually all societies, women are in an inferior position to men" (European Institute for Gender Equality, 2021). Gender equality in the workplace thus remains an important issue – in particular for women.

Although in many countries women make up (more than) half of the workforce, when it comes to managerial or senior positions, women are largely under-represented (e.g., women only held 28% of managerial positions worldwide in 2019 – almost the same proportion as in 1995) (United Nations, 2020), and the pay gap between men and women remains a pressing global issue (OECD, 2017; Appelbaum, Audet, & Miller, 2002; Vial, Napier, & Brescoll, 2016; Fitzsimmons & Callan, 2016; UN Women, 2021b). Moreover, in many workplaces, gendered practices, stereotypes, and prejudices exist which discriminate against women – for example with regards to maternity leave, retirement, and promotion (e.g., Grady, 2015; Pocock, 2005; Huppatz, Sang, & Napier, 2018; see also Mullany & Schnurr, 2022).

Although gender equality and inclusion have been characterized as "mainstream" in public discourse in Germany (Dobusch, 2017, p. 500; Arora-Jonsson & Sijapati, 2018), compared to other European and Western countries, Germany is often described as being "regrettably biased and unnecessarily polarized" (DiversityMine, 2001) and oblivious to the benefits that gender equality can bring to the workplace (Charta der Vielfalt, 2016;

Fehre & Spiegelhalder, 2017). Among the most pressing issues faced by women in the German workforce are the gender pay gap and a lack of women in leadership roles (Ipsos, 2019; Eckertz-Höfer, 2004). For example, a recent study by Oxfam Deutschland (2020) showed that women in Germany earn 21% less than men for their work, equating to 49% less than men in their entire lifetime, resulting in a gender pension gap of 53%.

Among the reasons put forward to explain the lack of gender equality in German workplaces are the relatively low number of open positions at senior management level, the lack of qualified women, as well as negative assumptions, prejudices, and stereotypes about pregnancy and childcare, a relatively widespread resistance to gender quotas and policies, and a tendency to recruit people who are similar to the (often male) recruiters (Wahnbaeck, 2020; Gutmann, 2014; Casdorff, 2018; Peukert, 2018; Maxwell, Connolly, & Ní Laoire, 2018; Hennekam, Syed, Ali, & Dumazert, 2018; Dobusch, 2017; Cahusac & Kanji, 2014; O'Hagan, 2014; Liff & Ward, 2001). Moreover, the success of initiatives to address persisting issues of gender discrimination and inequality – for example, through mentoring programs (e.g., Cranwell-Ward, Bossons, & Gover, 2004) and diversity networking initiatives (Haufe, 2017; Schütze, 2017) – remains relatively limited due to the absence of strict sanctions for organizations not meeting their targets.

8.3 METHODOLOGY

In order to identify and describe some of the discursive processes through which gender is produced and reproduced in the work domain – often in ways that allow gendered and discriminatory practices to be normalized and unquestioningly accepted – we conducted semi-structured interviews with 20 female and male employees in different workplaces in Germany, including public sector and private sector small and medium-sized or large organizations. Semi-structured interviews were conducted as the main data collection method as they constitute "an instrument to probe more deeply into the thoughts, experiences or perceptions of their participants" (Aurini, Heath, & Howells, 2016, p. 80). They allowed for flexibility to "approach different respondents differently, while still covering the same areas of data collection" (Noor, 2008, p. 1604).

The interview questions were largely based on Podsiadlowski, Gröschke, Kogler, Springer and van der Zee's (2013) framework of diversity perspectives. Using discourse analysis, we identify and describe some of the discursive processes through which those affected by gender equality issues make sense of them when sharing their experiences. Most interviews were conducted in German (with only one in English) by the first author and lasted between 18 to 45 minutes. Overall, the interviews made up more than 10 hours of recording time. All interviews were fully transcribed using the Jefferson system of transcription notation (Jefferson, 2004, p. 13).

8.4 ANALYSIS

Our analysis of the interviews consisted of two stages. In the first stage, we coded the interviews using thematic analysis to identify key emerging themes (Braun & Clarke, 2006, p. 6). In this initial phase of analysis, we noticed that contradictory themes emerged with regard to participants' experiences of the gender equality initiatives in their organizations. More specifically, while some participants denied that the lack of gender equality was problematic in their workplace, others admitted that this was indeed an issue which they had experienced themselves. Among the latter, we identified three types of different responses: i) claiming that the lack of gender equality and resulting discrimination is "just the way things are" and nobody was to blame; ii) arguing that the lack of gender equality is (at least partly) the fault of those who are being discriminated against; and iii) maintaining that the existence of gender inequality is due to societal gender ideologies.

In the second stage of the analysis, we conducted an in-depth analysis of selected excerpts that best represent the different types of responses identified in the thematic analysis. More specifically, we employed discourse analytical tools and processes to identify and describe the discursive strategies used by participants when sharing their experiences of gender equality at their workplaces, thereby creating and negotiating the meaning of their lived experiences (Miles, Huberman, & Saldaña, 2014, p. 11). Taking such an approach enabled us to illustrate "how people understand and experience their world at a particular point in time and in a particular context" (Merriam & Grenier, 2019, p. 4; see also Schnurr, Zayts, Schroeder, & Le Coyte-Hopkins, 2019).

- **Denying That Gender Equality is an Issue:** Many of the people we interviewed stated that gender equality was not an issue in their workplace and that "there is no need, no need to explicate specific [gender equality] rules," or devise policies, as one of our participants (a male professor in higher education) declared. The overwhelming tenor among interviewees was that the organization's productivity and profit would steer practices and processes (such as hiring and promotion) irrespective of candidates' gender. This attitude is exemplified by remarks such as "we need employees with whom we can make a profit and preserve our organization" (male executive board member of a small and medium-sized organization in the mechanical engineering industry) and "I would not care at all who gets the task done, the most important thing is that the profit is right" (male professor in higher education). This gender-blind view was adopted by all our male participants, but only by a small minority of female participants. There is ample evidence in our data that most of the male participants appear to be oblivious to the relevance of gender equality and the problematic existence of gender bias (e.g., "I would only pin it down on, can someone do the job, is he [sic!] suitable for it and then it does not matter at all, who does it" – as a male professor in higher education remarked). We also found that the lack of gender equality policies at participants' organizations was regularly justified and normalized by deflecting the responsibility from the organization and shifting the blame onto the hypothetical job applicants themselves with statements such as "men and women would be hired equally, but there are rarely women who have the qualifications to be business management or economics professors" (male professor in higher education). These explanations heavily rely on mainstream discourses denying or rejecting the need for gender equality measures (e.g., Utzeri, Nagy, & Ilie, 2020; Broadbridge & Simpson, 2011; Rhode, 1997). However, in addition to those participants who denied the existence of issues around gender equality in their workplaces, others acknowledged that they have experienced such issues. In what follows, we analyze three different types of responses that our interviewees provided when acknowledging a lack of gender equality at their workplace.

- **Acknowledging that a Lack of Gender Equality is an Issue But Providing Different Responses:** While some stated that this lack of gender equality was "nobody's fault," others claimed that it was (at least partly) the women's own fault or that it was due to underlying societal gender ideologies. We discuss each of these responses below in more detail.

- **Nobody's Fault:** Many of our interviewees acknowledged a lack of gender equality in their organization but were quick to assert that nobody was to blame for this. To justify this situation, participants often referred to the generally low number of female employees and applicants in certain traditionally male-dominated occupations and industries, such as informatics, mechanical engineering, and the technology industry. Similar to the line of argument that denies that gender equality is an issue, participants often argued that the relatively small number of qualified women in the application pool was the main reason for a lack of gender equality in management positions, and in specific industries.

Example 1 is taken from an interview with a male participant, who is a member of the executive board and who is also the director of multiple subsidiaries in a private organization in the mechanical engineering industry.

Example 1

At this point in the interview, we asked about any efforts the interviewee's company may undertake to support gender diversity and inclusion. I = interviewer; MP = male participant

1. MP: Also wir haben seit vielen, vielen Jahren m/w
   Well, for many, many years, we have had the m/f
2. in Stellenausschreibungen und jetzt
   option in job advertisements and now
3. seit vielleicht ein, zwei Jahren
   since maybe one, two years
4. auch noch /d ausgeschrieben.
   we have also used the /d option.
5. Wir hatten vor Jahren eine Personalleiterin eingestellt,
   We have hired a female head of HR a few years ago,
6. die aber innerhalb der Probezeit gekündigt hatte, weil sie
   who quit during her probation period, because she
7. weil sie aus [Name der Stadt] kam, ist täglich gefahren und
   came from [name of city], she drove in every day and
8. hatte dann 'nen Job in ihrer heimatlichen Nähe gefunden innerhalb ihrer
   found a job closer to home during her
9. Probezeit und äh, wir hatten auch mal ne
   probation period and erm we have also had a

10. Geschäftsführerin in [Land] bei
female managing director in [country] at
11. unserer Tochtergesellschaft, die vor zwei Jahren in Rente gegangen ist,
our subsidiary who retired two years ago,
12. also soll heißen, an diesen zwei kleinen Beispielen
so that means, based on these two small examples
13. sind wir durchaus für weibliche Führungskräfte
that we are definitely for female senior managers and directors
14. in der (Name der Organization),
at [name of organization],
15. nur um ehrlich zu bleiben, in den Bewerbungen tauchen kaum Frauen auf,
but to be honest, hardly any women hand in applications
16. und schon gar nicht auf
and certainly not for
17. die technischen Positionen, die wir ausschreiben,
the technical positions that we advertise,
18. und äh, wir benachteiligen keine Frauen,
and erm we do not disadvantage women,
19. jedenfalls nicht bewusst,
at least not consciously,
20. aber wir bevorzugen auch keine Frauen bewusst.
but we do not actively favor women either.
21. Ist ein privatwirtschaftliches Unternehmen und da
It is a privately-owned company and thus
22. sind wir unseren Gesellschaftern verpflichtet,
we are obliged to our shareholders
23. dass wir die Positionen bestmöglich besetzen.
to fill job positions with the most suitable candidate.
24. Und, wir hatten zum Beispiel eine Mitarbeiterin gefragt,
And, for example, we have asked a female employee,
25. ob sie sich vorstellen könnte, im Vertrieb zu arbeiten,
whether she could imagine working in sales and
26. im Außendienst und das hat sie abgelehnt,
distribution, in the field and she declined,
27. weil ihr das zu technisch war.
because it was too technical for her.
28. I: Okay (.).
Okay(.).

29. MP: = und so kann man es dann nicht erzwingen,
= and so, one cannot force it,
30. aber wir sind da offen, äh und es wird sich sicherlich
but we are open, erm and something will certainly
31. auch in den nächsten Jahren was verändern, aber es ist eine sehr
change during the next years, but it is a very
32. konservative Branche und wie ich berichtet habe,
conservative industry and as I have said,
33. aus der Erfahrung aus meinem Studium,
based on my experience during my academic studies,
34. und das ist heute auch nicht viel anders, was ich so höre,
and that has not changed much today from what I hear,
35. zumindest an Ingenieuren kommen halt hauptsächlich
at least regarding engineers, there are mainly
36. männliche Bewerber auf den Arbeitsmarkt male applicants entering the job market.

When asked about organizational efforts to support gender equality and inclusion, this participant outlines some of his organization's efforts of making job advertisements more gender inclusive (by adding the additional information "m/f" and "/d") (lines 1–4). He then moves on to a short narrative about a former female head of HR to provide evidence of his organization's efforts to support gender equality (lines 5–9). This short narrative is followed by the disagreement token "but" (line 15) which introduces his next argument, namely that the lack of gender equality is at least partly due to the lack of female candidates. He strengthens this claim by stating that "we do not disadvantage women" (line 18), which is immediately mitigated by the insertion "at least not consciously" (line 19) and the admission that "we do not actively favor women either" (line 20). His choice of pronouns here is noteworthy in that he identifies with this organization as reflected in his use of the inclusive first-person plural pronoun "we" (lines 1, 5, 9, 13, 17, 18, 20, 22, 24, 30) throughout his answer. This explanation is followed by another brief narrative about a female employee who declined to work in "sales and distribution" (lines 25–26) maintaining that she considered it to be "too technical for her" (lines 27). This line of argument is thus built on and reinforces the gender stereotype about women's aversion against technology and their reported preference for an office (rather than a field) job (e.g., Atal, Berenguer, & Borwankar, 2019; McGuire et al., 2020; European Commission, 2020).

After some minimal feedback from the interviewer ("okay") and a small pause (line 28), the participant sums up the organization's (and by implication his own) stance as "we are open" (line 30), while at the same time rejecting any responsibility: "one cannot force it" (line 29). He further states that although there are not many women who apply for certain positions, the ones who do are neither favored nor discriminated against (lines 15–20). The fact that he adds "at least not consciously" (line 19) suggests that he is aware that there may be an unconscious bias in the recruitment process. This topic was also picked up by several of our other participants, who often referred to an unconscious bias among recruiters to look for applicants who are similar to themselves. One of our participants described this as a "clone vote." According to this line of argument, the predominantly male recruiters tend to recruit male applicants who resemble themselves in gender, education, ethnicity, and other social aspects. The implications of this "clone vote" on gender in recruitment are also highlighted in an All Bright (2017) report, which called it "a perpetual Thomas-cycle," as it found that the number of women on the boards of directors in German stock exchange organizations roughly corresponded to the simultaneous increase in the number of men on these boards named Thomas.

In Example 1, our participant emphasizes that recruitment is primarily concerned with finding "the most suitable candidate" (line 23). His reference to a "very conservative industry" (lines 31, 32) and "mainly male applicants entering the job market" (lines 35, 36) further emphasizes his stance that the lack of gender equality in his organization is "nobody's fault." Thus, while he partly acknowledges that the lack of gender equality is an issue in his workplace and is indeed "something [that] will certainly change during the next years" (lines 30, 31), he portrays this in a rather factual way and without acknowledging the problematics behind it. In the next section, we illustrate another, albeit related, response strategy, namely claiming that the lack of gender diversity is (at least partly) women's own fault.

(At least partly) women's own fault

There seems to be consensus among our participants that the current lack of gender diversity – in particular the lack of women in leadership positions – can (at least partly) be ascribed to women's lack of self-confidence and self-marketing, being less demanding regarding wages and promotions, adhering to traditional gender roles, and taking fewer risks. Many of our participants commented that they thought men more regularly requested higher wages and applied more readily for promotions. Several women also stated that the lack of a women's network negatively impacted their own performance as they would like to "inform, empower, and connect with each other" (female senior product manager of a large organization in the research and publishing industry), and find a "place for their views [and] opinions" (female senior product manager of a large organization in the research and publishing industry) to be shared.

The next example illustrates several of these issues. It occurred during an interview with a female participant who worked as an assistant branch manager at a bank.

Example 2

At this point during the interview, we talked about the introduction of a quota for women, and we specifically asked about the interviewee's opinion on why so few women reach leadership positions in her company. FP = female participant

1 FP: Es gibt zwei Themen, die ich beide auch
There are two issues, that I have both
2 selber schon erlebt habe, aus meiner Zeit als
personally experienced during my time as
3 Frauenbeauftragte. (.) Das eine ist eben die Boys-Group,
women's representative. (.) One is that boys group that
4 die sich dann abends noch mal auf ein Bier trifft,
meet up again in the evening for a beer,
5 wo man als Frau dann halt einfach eben auch nicht mitgehen kann,
whereas a woman, you cannot just come along,
6 weil das einen komischen Eindruck bieten würde (.),
because it would give a weird impression (.),
7 ja, (.) dass man einfach diese
well, (.) that one simply
8 außerberuflichen, sozialen Kontakte mit Männern eben nicht so wahrnehmen kann,
cannot use these social contacts with men outside one's job,
9 dann ist man schon da gleich mal außen vor (.),
so that one is excluded there straight away (.),
10 aber auf der anderen Seite sind es auch die Frauen
but on the other hand, it is also the women
11 selber (.), die sagen, „nein, ich traue mir das nicht zu "(.).
themselves (.), who say 'no, I do not trust myself to do this.'
12 Ganz spannend ist gewesen, wenn ich
It was really interesting when I

13 diese Bewerbergespräche miterlebt habe (.).
participated in these interviews (.).
14 Eine Frau, (.) also erstmal eine Frau bewirbt sich auf eine Stelle nur,
A woman (.) so firstly, a woman only applies for a job only
15 wenn sie eigentlich nahezu 100% der
if she actually almost fulfills 100% of
16 Anforderungen erfüllt, sitzt dann aber im Gespräch
the job requirements; however, in the interview
17 und sagt „hmm, ich kann aber das nicht und kann das nicht
she then says 'hmm, I can't do this and I can't do that
18 und das nicht zu 100% "und ein Mann bewirbt sich mit 70%
and this I can't do 100%' and a man applies with 70% of
19 der Qualifikation und sagt „ich kann das alles
the qualification and says 'I can do everything,
20 und was ich nicht kann, das habe ich ganz schnell gelernt." (.)
and what I can't do, I'll learn very quickly.' (.)
21 ja (.) und das ist wirklich tatsächlich so.
yes (.) and it is actually like that.
22 Also, ich hätte das nicht für möglich gehalten,
Well, I wouldn't have thought it possible,
23 aber das ist wirklich ein unterschiedliches Einschätzen
but it really is a different way of assessing
24 und Verkaufen der eigenen Fähigkeiten und dann
and selling one's own skills and then
25 noch das andere Thema: Frauen nageln sich selbst gerne
the other topic: Women tend to pin themselves down
26 auf diese Mutterrolle fest (.) und haben diese
on the role of the mother (.) and have this
27 Anforderung an sich, sich hauptsächlich um die
expectation of themselves, to mainly
28 Kinder zu kümmern und dann nur am Rande andere
care for the children and to only to a small extent involve other
29 Personen, auch den Vater nur am Rande mit einzubinden (.). Ich erlebe das von
people, also the father (.). I experience this from
30 den jungen Vätern so, dass sie sich gerne
young fathers in such a way, that they would like to
31 mehr einbringen würden, dass die Frauen das aber nicht so
be more involved, but that the women do not really

32 zulassen. Das ist sehr, sehr spannend,
allow it. That is very, very interesting,
33 sehr spannend (.) Deswegen stehen sich Frauen
very interesting (.) Therefore, women stand in their
34 in diesen beiden Punkten, glaube ich, selber im Weg
own way regarding these two points, I think.

This participant's narrative highlights two specific issues which she considers are preventing women from reaching senior leadership positions in her company. She firstly states that it is more difficult for women to foster social contacts with men, due to difficulties of joining an existing "boys' group that meets up again in the evening for a beer" (lines 3, 4). There is a lot of research supporting such claims that informal networks in workplace contexts usually exist for men but hardly for women (e.g., Durbin, 2011). Women are largely excluded from such informal networks, and as our participant comments, if they were to attend, this "would give a weird impression" (lines 5–6).

This lamenting of the exclusivity of these all-male networks is followed up by another line of argument in which she blames women for not moving into senior leadership positions. Giving women a voice and using the first-person singular pronoun when speaking on their behalf ("no, I don't trust myself to do this") (line 11) makes her claim stronger and more vivid. She then introduces a short narrative of personal experience (Clifton, Schnurr, & Van De Mieroop, 2019) in which she recounts her experiences during "these interviews" (line 13) that she attended as a recruiter in the past (lines 12, 13). However, unlike what is typical for these types of narratives (Labov & Waletzky, 1966), the participant uses quotative verbs in the present – rather than past – tense, rendering her story more vivid and general. This last effect is further intensified by her use of relatively generic terminology when referring to "these interviews" (line 13) (rather than a specific one) and "a woman" (line 14) (rather than a specific one). However, the resulting generalizability is to some extent counterbalanced when she voices what "a woman" (line 14) said during the job interviews, namely outlining all the tasks that she cannot perform and all the skills that she does not possess (lines 14–18). Repeating the negation "I can't" (lines 17–18) three times makes this claim particularly strong.

This reported behavior of "a woman" (line 14) is set in opposition to the reported behavior of a less qualified man who is also given a voice in our participant's narrative to state exactly the opposite of what the woman previously said – thereby juxtaposing "I can't do this" (lines 17–18) with "I can do everything" (line 19). Due to the positive connotations of the phrases "I can do everything" (line 19) and "learn very quickly" (line 20), the hypothetical male job applicant is portrayed in a more positive light than the female candidate. This opposition of female and male interview candidates is followed up by the agreement marker "yes" (line 21) and the affirmative and assertive formulation "it is actually like that" (line 21). With this formulation in addition to the subsequent admission "I wouldn't have thought it possible" (line 22), our participant addresses potential challenges and queries regarding the accuracy of her claims.

The utterance initial pragmatic particle "well" (line 22) and the disagreement marker "but" (line 23) give further weight to this part of her account. They also introduce the subsequent generalizations about "women" (line 25) and their tendency to "pin themselves down on the role of the mother" (lines 25–26). By using the term "women" (line 25) rather than "we," the participant at the same time distances herself from this group and puts herself in a position to evaluate and criticize them. Her criticism is directed at another stereotype generally associated with women at work, namely the double-bind they face as working mothers. However, rather than talking about the difficulties that these women may experience in their everyday workplace encounters, our participant accuses them of being overly focused on the "care for the children" (lines 27–28) and for wrongly excluding the father from childcare responsibilities, thereby assigning the blame for this gender imbalance and lack of gender equality to the women (lines 25–32).

We briefly discuss one more response strategy that we observed in our data, namely where participants argued that a lack of gender equality was due to societal gender ideologies.

- **Due to Societal Gender Ideologies**

There was a strong consensus among our participants that societal gender ideologies have an impact on the (lack of) gender equality in their own workplaces. Many of our participants provided examples in support of this claim. For instance, one female participant recounted how – since she was the only woman in a meeting – it was automatically assumed that she would take the minutes. Another one told us how her (male) customers requested to be advised by her (male) colleagues because they felt a woman would not have the technical knowledge relevant to solve their problems. Many participants also lamented the existence of gender stereotypes that expect women to stay at home (looking after children and housework), while men are considered to be the main or, in some cases, sole income earners. These gender stereotypes manifested themselves, for example, in female participants being asked about their plans of having children during job interviews.

The next example illustrates some of these gender ideologies. It is taken from an interview with a female participant who works as a senior revenue controller in the research and publishing industry.

Example 3

We asked her what gender diversity means for her and whether she considers it "personally important." FP = female participant

1 FP: […] besonders als Frau und auch Mutter hat man
Especially as a woman and also as a mother, one
2 halt wirklich einfach andere Hürden als
simply really encounters other obstacles than
3 Männer, also zum Beispiel, wenn ich meinen Mann wähle
men, so for example, if I choose my husband,
4 als Beispiel, der muss sich nicht überlegen,
as an example, he does not need to think about
5 wer die Kinder versorgt, wer die Kinder abholt,
who takes care of the children, who picks up the children,
6 sondern das liegt halt ganz alleine bei mir und diese Aufteilung
it is entirely up to me and this role distribution
7 ist halt wahrscheinlich noch so eine Aufteilung
is probably, well a distribution
8 wie aus den 60ern, also wir müssten eigentlich auch zu Hause anfangen
like it was in the 60s, so we actually have to start
9 und dort über Gender Diversity sprechen, aber
talking about gender diversity at home, but it is
10 Fakt ist, dass in vielen, vielen Familien es zurzeit
a fact, that in many, many families it is currently
11 wirklich noch so ist, dass der Mann der Hauptverdiener ist
really still the case that the man is the main breadwinner
12 und selbst wenn die Frau gleich
and that even if the woman earns the
13 verdient, trotzdem ist die Frau
same wage, nevertheless the woman is,
14 trotzdem halt die Mutter und der Ansprechpartner
nevertheless, the mother and the main contact person

15 für die Kinder und um das quasi in Einklang zu bringen
for the children and to actually balance
16 mit der Arbeit und auch Führungsposition einnehmen zu können,
that with work and to be able to take on leadership positions,
17 finde ich ist das nicht möglich mit einem
I think that this is not possible with a
18 Teilzeitjob zum Beispiel (.). Also, ich finde
part-time job for example (.). So, I believe that
19 solche Sachen wie Jobsharing in Leadership-Positionen
things like job-sharing in leadership positions
20 wäre eine wichtige Sache, die man hier
would be an important thing that one could
21 auch einführen könnte. Aber was ich mir eher
introduce here as well. But what I would rather
22 wünschen würde wären so Marketingmaßnahmen (.)
welcome would be marketing initiatives (.)
23 ja (.), dass man eigentlich auch
yes (.), that one actually also explains,
24 auch in der Gesellschaft und in den Köpfen das erklärt warum man das
in society and [people's] minds, why there is a
25 wirklich braucht, weil hier in
need for it [gender diversity], because here in
26 Deutschland herrscht oft so dieses Rabenmutter (.)
Germany, we have this "Rabenmutter[1]*" (.)*
27 ich weiß gar nicht (.) dieses Rabenmutter-Phänomen
I don't know (.) this "Rabenmutter"-phenomenon
28 oder was man (.). Also, wenn man als Mutter arbeitet
or what (.). So, if you as a mother are working,
29 und dann auch noch 100% arbeitet und dann mit anderen
and then even working 100%, and then talking
30 Müttern aus dem Kindergarten oder aus der Schule spricht die eben
with other mothers at the nursery or school who are
31 nur Teilzeit-Mamis sind, hat man ganz schnell so
just part-time mums, then one is very quickly
32 so dieses Rabenmutter-Emblem und ich wünschte
regarded as a "Rabenmutter" and I would welcome

---

[1] The German idiom "Rabenmutter" ("raven mother") is often used as a harsh, unjustified verdict to describe hard-working, career-oriented mothers who, as a result, are assumed to neglect their children). It comes from "the bird's reputation for being neglectful of its young" (Rutherford, 2011, p. 104).

33 mir mehr Informationen dahingehend (.),
more information regarding this issue (.),
34 warum es eigentlich so wichtig ist (.),
why it is actually so important (.),
35 also so mehr Marketing (.), Social-Marketing (.),
so, more marketing (.), social marketing (.),
36 warum es so wichtig ist, eigentlich diese Gender-Diversity herbeizuführen
why it is so important to introduce gender diversity
37 oder warum es wichtig ist auch
or why it is also so important to have
38 Frauen oder auch das dritte Geschlecht eigentlich auch in
women or also the third gender actually in
39 Führungspositionen zu haben (.), um einfach dieses
leadership positions (.), to simply get
40 Rabenmutter-Image loszuwerden.
rid of this "Rabenmutter"-image.

Using her own familial situation as an illustration, the participant in this excerpt exemplifies how professional women generally (as reflected in her choice of the generic pronoun "one" rather than "I") (lines 1, 20, 23, 28, 31) are often discriminated against by others. Although we specifically asked about the participant's personal opinion, right from the start she makes it clear that she does not only speak for herself but that her answer applies more widely to women and mothers. She then uses her own husband and his position in the family as an example (lines 3–9). Outlining how they (do not) share the childcare responsibilities in the family, she makes it clear that this is not balanced at all: her husband does not need to worry about "who takes care of the children...it is entirely up to me" (lines 4–6). Although she acknowledges that such a gender-specific role distribution is reminiscent of the 1960s, she explicitly states the need to "start talking about gender diversity at home" (lines 8–9). Her use of the inclusive first-person plural pronoun "we" (line 8) is noteworthy here as this ambiguous pronoun could either refer to herself and her husband, or it could refer to the German society more widely where such a traditional and discriminatory role distribution is considered to be the norm.

By using her own familial situation as an example, the interviewee thus problematizes prevailing gender ideologies and argues that they exist on a societal – rather than only organizational – level. Categorically stating that "it is a fact" (lines 9–10) and repeating "many" (line 10), she further emphasizes the widespread nature of the issue. Against this background, she then begins to outline some measures, such as introducing part-time work and job-sharing opportunities (lines 14–21). Initially, her suggestions refer to concrete activities that need to be implemented on the organizational level. However, these measures are then complemented by a call for ideological changes.

The use of the utterance initial disagreement marker "but" (line 21) signals right from the start that her subsequent argument is particularly important. With the syntactic "but … rather" (line 21) construction, the participant sets this part of her argument up in contrast to her previous remarks. In this part of her answer, she again uses generic pronouns ("one") (line 23), thereby emphasizing the general applicability of what she says. Here, she laments the existence of what she calls "this Rabenmutter-phenomenon" (line 27), which she explains as the pressure and negative judgments regularly experienced by working mothers for allegedly neglecting their children (lines 25–33). This is a widespread issue in Germany, as motherhood is seen as strongly child-oriented, propagating that mothers should only work part-time or not at all (Schneider, Diabaté, & Ruckdeschel, 2015; Waffenschmidt, 2015; Reichwein, 2012).

Just like in her previous argument, our participant here again uses her own (negative) experience (of "talking with other mothers at the nursery or school") (lines 29–30) as a call for ideological changes – this time in the concrete form of "marketing initiatives" (line 22) and "social marketing" (line 35). These initiatives, she argues, would help foster an understanding of "why it is so important to introduce gender diversity or why it is also so important to have women or also the third gender actually in leadership positions" (lines 36–39) and "to simply get rid of this 'Rabenmutter'-image" (lines 39–40).

8.5 DISCUSSION

In line with the aim of this edited volume to bring to the surface some of the gendered practices and gender discrimination that occur in various fields of social life, this chapter has identified and described employees' experiences of some of the gender inequalities that still exist in many German workplaces. Analyzing the ways in which employees recount and make sense of their everyday work lives provided insights into some of the processes through which gender is produced and reproduced in the work domain. As we have shown, this often involves being faced with and having to maneuver gendered and discriminatory practices which are often normalized and unquestioningly accepted.

Perhaps not surprisingly, we observed considerable variation in the ways in which professionals talk about their experiences of gender equality policies and practices in their own workplaces. While some of our participants demonstrated an awareness of gender equality issues – sometimes sharing their own experience of prejudices and discrimination – others appeared to be surprisingly oblivious about and sometimes even dismissive of gender equality. Our findings thus largely reflect and provide further empirical evidence for some of the issues identified in previous research. For example, there was a noticeable lack of awareness of gender equality being an issue in participants' own organization (see also Utzeri, 2020; Kormanik, 2009; Rhode, 1997). Moreover, our participants' experiences provided more evidence for the widespread existence of gender stereotypes and prejudices regarding pregnancy and childcare (Examples 2 and 3; see also e.g., Bergmann, Scheele, & Sorger, 2018; Kangas, Lämsä, & Jyrkinen, 2019; Huppatz, Sang, & Napier, 2018), as well as negative views on gender quotas and policies (e.g., Example 1; see also Mölders, Brosi, Bekk, Spörrle, & Welpe, 2018).

As we have shown, the sense-making processes around these experiences of gender (in)equality in the workplace take place on three interconnected levels: the personal, the organizational, and the societal level. On the personal level, many of our (often female) participants shared stories about their own experiences of gender issues – often in the form of discrimination (Example 3). On the organizational level, participants described policies and practices – for example, regarding promotion and hiring – where the lack of gender equality was apparent (Examples 2 and 3). On the societal level, ideological questions about gender equality and diversity were made relevant and sometimes explicitly oriented to (Example 3), and participants often mobilized stereotypical assumptions about the roles of men (as bread-winners) and women (as main caregivers).

Taking a discourse analytical approach in this study enabled us to capture the sense-making processes employed by participants on each of these levels. As our analyzes have shown, such an approach does not only provide further empirical evidence to support findings from previous – largely quantitative – research, but also re-evaluates the current situation of gender (in)equality at German workplaces, thereby identifying gaps in gender equality policies and initiatives which have not yet been addressed (sufficiently) and which should influence future actions. Focusing on the micro-level of individual experiences rather than aiming to describe general patterns on the macro-level enabled us to gain a better understanding of how gender equality is actually experienced and responded to by employees, which, we believe, is an important step in an endeavor to address these issues and change the current situation.

Clearly, more qualitative research is necessary to further understand the specific processes through which those affected by a lack of gender equality make sense of their experiences to gain further insights into the specific sense-making strategies involved in the management of gender equality to help address, challenge, and ultimately change the current situation. For example, a general awareness of gender equality could be increased by debunking some of the reasons provided to explain the lack of gender equality as "lame excuses" and "empty arguments" – such as the claims that there are simply not enough female applicants for a specific position rather than acknowledging underlying issues of inclusion and diversity in the recruitment process. At the same time, the comments from many of our participants highlighted the need to explore alternative channels to more effectively and more widely communicate economic arguments for gender equality in German workplaces, and the benefits of quotas for women and other affirmative actions (Fine, Sojo, & Lawford-Smith, 2020; Utoft, 2020; Coe, Wiley, & Bekker, 2019; Kirsch, 2017). The importance of engaging men in such campaigns and other efforts to increase gender equality has previously been established (e.g., Healey, 2014), and the responses from some of our male participants provide further support for this.

We hope that future research will continue to explore some of the issues outlined here and provide additional empirical insights into the numerous facets of gender (in)equality in German workplaces. Our research is meant as a step in this direction with the ultimate aim of facilitating the move out of "Stone Age" as lamented by one of our participants.

- **Transcription Conventions (Based on the Jefferson Transcription System)**

(.)	A full stop inside brackets denotes a micro pause, a notable pause but of no significant length.
(0.2)	A number inside brackets denotes a timed pause. This is a pause long enough to time and subsequently show in transcription.

[·	Square brackets denote a point where overlapping speech occurs.
(·)	Where there is space between brackets denotes that the words spoken here were too unclear to transcribe
((·))	Where double brackets appear with a description inserted denotes some contextual information where no symbol of representation was available.
Under	When a word or part of a word is underlines it denotes a raise in volume or emphasis
↑	When an upward arrow appears, it means there is a rise in intonation
↓	When a downward arrow appears, it means there is a drop in intonation
CAPITALS	Where capital letters appear it denotes that something was said loudly or even shouted
Hum(h)our	When a bracketed 'h' appears it means that there was laughter within the talk
=	The equal sign represents latched speech, a continuation of talk
::	Colons appear to represent elongated speech, a stretched sound

KEYWORDS

- **analysis**
- **gender equality**
- **methodology**
- **perpetual Thomas-cycle**
- **PwC**

REFERENCES

AllBright. (2017). Ein Ewiger Thomas-Kreislauf? Wie deutsche Börsenunternehmen ihre Vorstände rekrutieren. Retrieved from: https://static1.squarespace.com/static/5c7e8528f4755a0bedc3f8f1/t/5cda985836d36b00013b5cfa/1557829765572/Allbright-Bericht-2017-Thomas.pdf (accessed on 19 June 2024).

Antidiskriminierungsstelle des Bundes. (n.d.). Zentrale Ergebnisse der Studie "Out im Office?!" Retrieved from: https://www.antidiskriminierungsstelle.de/SharedDocs/Downloads/DE/publikationen/Umfragen/20170719_Umfrageergebnisse_Out_im_Office.html (accessed on 19 June 2024).

Appelbaum, S., Audet, L., & Miller, J. (2002). Gender and Leadership? Leadership and Gender? A Journey Through the Landscape of Theories. *Leadership & Organization Development Journal, 24*(1/2), 43–51. https://doi.org/10.1108/01437730310457320.

Arora-Jonsson, S., & Sijapati, B. B. (2018). Disciplining Gender in Environmental Organizations: The Texts and Practices of Gender Mainstreaming. *Gender, Work & Organization, 25*(3), 309–325.

Atal, N., Berenguer, G., & Borwankar, S. (2019). Gender equality issues in the IT industry: How can your sourcing group help? *Business Horizons, 62*(5), 595–602. https://doi.org/10.1016/j.bushor.2019.04.004.

Aurini, J. D., Heath, M., & Howells, S. (2016). *The How to Of Qualitative Research.* London: SAGE Publications Ltd.

Bergmann, N., Scheele, A., & Sorger, C. (2018). Variations of the same? A sectoral analysis of the gender pay gap in Germany and Austria. *Gender, Work & Organization, 26*(5), 668–687. https://doi.org/10.1111/gwao.12299.

Bocksch, R. (2021). So steht es um Arbeitsbedingungen für Frauen. Retrieved from: https://de.statista.com/infografik/17284/laender-mit-den-besten-arbeitsbedingungen-fuer-frauen/ (accessed on 19 June 2024).

Braun, V., & Clarke, V. (2006). Using thematic analysis in psychology. *Qualitative Research in Psychology, 3*(2), 77–101. https://doi.org/10.1191/1478088706qp063oa.

Broadbridge, A., & Simpson, R. (2011). 25 Years On: Reflecting on the Past and Looking to the Future in Gender and Management Research. *British Journal of Management, 22*(3), 470–483. https://doi.org/10.1111/j.1467-8551.2011.00758.x.

Cahusac, E., & Kanji, S. (2014). How Gendered Organizational Cultures Push Mothers Out. *Gender, Work & Organization, 21*(1), 57–70. https://doi.org/10.1111/gwao.12011.

Casdorff, S. A. (2018). Frauen in Vorständen? Deutsche Unternehmen tun sich schwer. Retrieved from: https://www.tagesspiegel.de/wirtschaft/gleichstellung-von-maennern-und-frauen-frauen-in-vorstaenden-deutsche-unternehmen-tun-sich-schwer/23138974.html (accessed on 19 June 2024).

Charta der Vielfalt. (2016). Diversity in Germany. Retrieved from: https://www.charta-der-vielfalt.de/fileadmin/user_upload/Studien_Publikationen_Charta/Diversity_in_Germany_2016_en.pdf (accessed on 19 June 2024).

Clifton, J., Schnurr, S., & Van De Mieroop, D. (2019). *The Language of Leadership Narratives: A Social Practice Perspective*. Abingdon: Routledge.

Coe, I. R., Wiley, R., & Bekker, L. G. (2019). Organisational best practices towards gender equality in science and medicine. *The Lancet, 393*(10171), 587–593. https://doi.org/10.1016/S0140-6736(18)33188-X.

Cranwell-Ward, J., Bossons, P., & Gover, S. (2004). *Mentoring*. Basingstoke: Palgrave Macmillan.

DiversityMine. (2001). Geschlechter–Vielfalt als Erfolgsfaktor. Retrieved from: http://de.diversitymine.eu/geschlechter-vielfalt-als-erfolgsfaktor/ (accessed on 19 June 2024).

Dobusch, L. (2017). Gender, Dis-/ability and Diversity Management: Unequal Dynamics of Inclusion? *Gender, Work & Organization, 24*(5), 487–505. https://doi.org/10.1111/gwao.12159.

Durbin, S. (2011). Creating Knowledge through Networks: a Gender Perspective. *Gender, Work & Organization, 18*(1), 90–112. https://doi.org/10.1111/j.1468-0432.2010.00536.x.

Eckertz-Höfer, M. (2004). Frauenförderung im öffentlichen Dienst – Wirksamkeitsfragen. In M. Koreuber & U. Mager (Eds.), *Recht und Geschlecht. Zwischen Gleichberechtigung, Gleichstellung und Differenz* (pp. 171–189). Baden-Baden: Nomos.

European Commission. (2020). Women's situation in the labor market. Retrieved from: https://ec.europa.eu/info/policies/justice-and-fundamental-rights/gender-equality/women-labour-market-work-life-balance/womens-situation-labour-market_en (accessed on 19 June 2024).

European Institute for Gender Equality. (2021). Gender inequality. Retrieved from: https://eige.europa.eu/thesaurus/terms/1182 (accessed on 19 June 2024).

European Parliament. (2021). Timeline: milestones in the EU's fight for women's rights. Retrieved from: https://www.europarl.europa.eu/news/en/headlines/society/20210225STO98706/timeline-milestones-in-the-eu-s-fight-for-women-s-rights-video (accessed on 19 June 2024).

Fehre, K., & Spiegelhalder, R. (2017). Same same, but different: Eine Analyse des Humankapitals weiblicher und männlicher Aufsichtsräte in Deutschland. *Schmalenbachs Zeitschrift betriebswirtschaftliche Forschung, 69*(3), 311–343. https://doi.org/10.1007/s41471-017-0031-3.

Fine, C., Sojo, V., & Lawford-Smith, H. (2020). Why Does Workplace Gender equality Matter? Justice, Organizational Benefits, and Policy. *Social Issues and Policy Review, 14*(1), 36–72. https://doi.org/10.1111/sipr.12064.

Fitzsimmons, T. W., & Callan, V. J. (2016). Applying a capital perspective to explain continued gender equality in the C-suite. *The Leadership Quarterly, 27*(2), 354–370. https://doi.org/10.1016/j.leaqua.2015.11.003.

Grady, J. (2015). Gendering Pensions: Making Women Visible. *Gender, Work and Organization, 22*(5), 445–458. https://doi.org/10.1111/gwao.12096.

Gutmann, A. (2014). In Frankreich ist die Glucke die Rabenmutter. Retrieved from: https://www.handelsblatt.com/meinung/gastbeitraege/frauen-und-berufsleben-in-frankreich-ist-die-glucke-die-rabenmutter/10620488.html?ticket=ST-429923-1YEDBT4MCABavr4j3Tgr-ap6 (accessed on 19 June 2024).

Haufe. (2017). So werden interne Frauennetzwerke zum Erfolg. Retrieved from: https://www.haufe.de/personal/hr-management/frauennetzwerke-in-unternehmen_80_426374.html (accessed on 19 June 2024).

Healey, J. (2014). *Sexual Orientation and Gender Identity*. Thirroul: The Spinney Press.

Hennekam, S., Syed, J., Ali, F., & Dumazert, J. P. (2018). A multilevel perspective of the identity transition to motherhood. *Gender, Work & Organization, 26*(7), 915–933. https://doi.org/10.1111/gwao.12334.

Huppatz, K., Sang, K., & Napier, J. (2018). 'If you put pressure on yourself to produce then that's your responsibility': Mothers' experiences of maternity leave and flexible work in the neoliberal university. *Gender, Work & Organization, 26*(6), 772–788. https://doi.org/10.1111/gwao.12314.

Ipsos. (2019). Studie zum Weltfrauentag: Deutsche sehen Männer immer noch im Vorteil. Retrieved from: https://www.ipsos.com/de-de/studie-zum-weltfrauentag-gender-pay-gap-deutsche-sehen-manner-immer-noch-im-vorteil (accessed on 19 June 2024).

Jefferson, G. (2004). Glossary of transcript symbols with an introduction. In G. H. Lerner (Ed.), *Conversation Analysis Studies from the First Generation* (pp. 13–32). Amsterdam: John Benjamins. https://doi.org/10.1075/pbns.125.

Kalkum, D., & Otto, M. (2017). Diskriminierungserfahrungen in Deutschland anhand der sexuellen Identität. Retrieved from: https://www.diversity-institut.info/downloads/Expertise_Diskrimerfahrungen_in_DE_anhand_der_sex_Identitaet.pdf (accessed on 19 June 2024).

Kangas, E., Lämsä, A. M., & Jyrkinen, M. (2019). Is fatherhood allowed? Media discourses of fatherhood in organizational life. *Gender, Work & Organization, 26*(11), 1433–1450. https://doi.org/10.1111/gwao.12352.

Kirsch, A. (2017). Women's Access to Boards in Germany— Regulation and Symbolic Change. In C. Seierstad, P. Gabaldon, & H. Mensi-Klarbach (Eds.), *Gender Equality in the Boardroom* (pp. 205–232). Cham, CH: Palgrave Macmillan. https://doi.org/10.1007/978-3-319-56142-4.

Kormanik, M. B. (2009). Sexuality as a Diversity Factor: An Examination of Awareness. *Advances in Developing Human Resources, 11*(1), 24–36. https://doi.org/10.1177/1523422308329369.

Krell, G., & Wächter, H. (2006). *Diversity Management Impulse Aus der Personalforschung*. München: Rainer Hampp Verlag.

Labov, W., & Waletzky, J. (1966). Narrative analysis: Oral versions of personal experience. In J. Helm (Ed.), *Essays on the Verbal and Visual Arts* (pp. 12–44). Seattle: University of Washington Press.

Liff, S., & Ward, K. (2001). Distorted Views Through the Glass Ceiling: The Construction of Women's Understandings of Promotion and Senior Management Positions. *Gender, Work & Organization, 8*(1), 19–36. https://doi.org/10.1111/1468-0432.00120.

Maxwell, N., Connolly, L., & Ní Laoire, C. (2018). Informality, emotion and gendered career paths: The hidden toll of maternity leave on female academics and researchers. *Gender, Work & Organization, 26*(2), 140–157. https://doi.org/10.1111/gwao.12306.

McGuire, L., Mulvey, K. L., Goff, E., Irvin, M. J., Winterbottom, M., Fields, G. E., Hartstone-Rose, A., & Rutland, A. (2020). STEM gender stereotypes from early childhood through adolescence at informal science centers. *Journal of Applied Developmental Psychology, 67*, 101–109. https://doi.org/10.1016/j.appdev.2020.101109.

Merriam, S. B., & Grenier, R. S. (2019). *Qualitative Research in Practice: Examples for Discussion and Analysis*. San Francisco: Jossey-Bass.

Miles, M. B., Huberman, M. A., & Saldaña, J. (2014). *Qualitative Data Analysis*. Thousand Oaks: SAGE Publications Inc.

Mölders, S., Brosi, P., Bekk, M., Spörrle, M., & Welpe, I. M. (2018). Support for quotas for women in leadership: The influence of gender stereotypes. *Human Resource Management, 57*(4), 869–882. https://doi.org/10.1002/hrm.21882.

Mullany, L., & Schnurr, S. (Eds.). (n.d.). *Globalization, Geopolitics and Gender: Professional Communication at Work*. Abingdon: Routledge.

Noor, K. B. M. (2008). Case Study: A Strategic Research Methodology. *American Journal of Applied Sciences, 5*(11), 1602–1604.

O'Hagan, C. (2014). Broadening the Intersectional Path: Revealing Organizational Practices through 'Working Mothers' Narratives about Time. *Gender, Work & Organization, 25*(5), 443–458. https://doi.org/10.1111/gwao.12056.

OECD. (2017). Gender wage gap. Retrieved from: https://data.oecd.org/earnwage/gender-wage-gap.htm (accessed on 19 June 2024).

Oldemeier, K. (2017). Sexuelle und geschlechtliche Diversität aus salutogenetischer Perspektive: Erfahrungen von jungen LSBTQ*-Menschen in Deutschland. *Journal of*

Childhood and Adolescence Research, 12, 145–159. https://doi.org/10.3224/diskurs.v12i2.02.
Oxfam Deutschland. (2020). Im Schatten der Profite – Wie die systematische Abwertung von Hausarbeit, Pflege und Fürsorge Ungleichheit schafft und vertieft. Retrieved from: https://www.oxfam.de/system/files/2020_oxfam_ungleichheit_studie_deutsch_schatten-der-profite.pdf (accessed on 19 June 2024).
Peukert, A. (2018). 'Little children are not for dads?' Challenging and undoing hegemonic masculinity. *Gender, Work & Organization, 26*(10), 1451–1466. https://doi.org/10.1111/gwao.12312.
Pocock, B. (2005). Work/Care Regimes: Institutions, Culture and Behavior and the Australian Case. *Gender, Work & Organization, 12*(1), 32–49. https://doi.org/10.1111/j.1468-0432.2005.00261.x.
Podsiadlowski, A., Gröschke, D., Kogler, M., Springer, C., & van der Zee, K. (2013). Managing a culturally diverse workforce: Diversity perspectives in organizations. *International Journal of Intercultural Relations, 37*, 159–175. https://doi.org/10.1016/j.ijintrel.2012.09.001.
PwC. (2021). Women in Work 2021. Retrieved from: https://www.pwc.co.uk/economic-services/WIWI/women-in-work-2021-executive-summary.pdf (accessed on 19 June 2024).
Reichwein, E. (2012). *Kinderarmut in der Bundesrepublik Deutschland: Lebenslagen, gesellschaftliche Wahrnehmung und Sozialpolitik.* Wiesbaden: Springer Fachmedien Wiesbaden GmbH.
Rhode, D. L. (1997). *Speaking of Sex the Denial of Gender Equality*. Cambridge: Harvard University Press.
Rutherford, S. (2011). *Women's Work Men's Cultures Overcoming Resistance and Changing Organizational Cultures*. London: Palgrave Macmillan.
Schneider, N. F., Diabaté, S., & Ruckdeschel, K. (2015). Familienleitbilder in Deutschland: Kulturelle Vorstellungen zu Partnerschaft, Elternschaft und Familienleben. Berlin: Barbara Budrich.
Schnurr, S., Zayts, O., Schroeder, A., & Le Coyte-Hopkins, C. (2019). 'It's not acceptable for the husband to stay at home': Taking a discourse analytical approach to capture the gendering of work. *Gender, Work & Organization, 27*(4), 414–434. https://doi.org/10.1111/gwao.12408.
Schütze, M. (2017). Karriere-booster netzwerk, mit Vitamin B zum Erfolg. Retrieved from: https://www.stellenanzeigen.de/arbeitgeber/vorteile/studien/netzwerkstudie-2017/ (accessed on 19 June 2024).
UN Women. (2021a). Gender Mainstreaming concepts and definitions. Retrieved from: https://www.un.org/womenwatch/osagi/conceptsandefinitions.htm (accessed on 19 June 2024).
UN Women. (2021b). 12 critical areas. Retrieved from: https://www.unwomen.org/en/news/in-focus/csw59/feature-stories#media (accessed on 19 June 2024).
United Nations. (2020). Sustainable development goals – Goal 5: Achieve gender equality and empower all women and girls. Retrieved from: https://www.un.org/sustainabledevelopment/gender-equality/ (accessed on 19 June 2024).
Utoft, E. H. (2020). Exploring linkages between organizational culture and gender equality work—An ethnography of a multinational engineering company. *Evaluation and Program Planning, 79*, 1–8. https://doi.org/10.1016/j.evalprogplan.2020.101791.

Utzeri, M., Nagy, B., & Ilie, I. A. (2020). Gender Initiatives Between Support and Denial a Cross-Cultural Study of Two Automotive Companies in Germany and France. In J. Mahadevan, P. Henriett, & L. Romani (Eds.), *Cases in Critical Cross-Cultural Management: An Intersectional Approach to Culture* (pp. 163–173). New York: Routledge.

Vial, A. C., Napier, J. L., & Brescoll, V. L. (2016). A bed of thorns: Female leaders and the self-reinforcing cycle of illegitimacy. *The Leadership Quarterly, 27*(3), 400–414. http://dx.doi.org/10.1016/j.leaqua.2015.12.004.

Waffenschmidt, B. (2015). *Familienleben und Erwerbsarbeit bei Doppelkarrierepaaren: Auswirkungen betrieblicher und staatlicher Maßnahmen.* Wiesbaden: Springer Fachmedien Wiesbaden GmbH.

Wahnbaeck, C. (2020). Raus aus der Komfortzone. Retrieved from: https://www.spiegel.de/karriere/frauen-in-fuehrungspositionen-studie-zeigt-wege-zum-erfolg-a-a812713e-8678-4ddf-80ec-706d38d438f1 (accessed on 19 June 2024).

CHAPTER 9

FEMINIZATION OF LABOR-FORCE IN WASTE SECTOR: A CASE STUDY OF KERALA, INDIA

S. RAKENDU, NEELAM RANA, and N. C. NARAYANAN

Indian Institute of Technology–Bombay, Mumbai, Maharashtra, India

ABSTRACT

The informal waste sector in India predominantly sees a large number of women working, while the formal waste management system run by the urban local bodies is dominated by men. Kerala, being one of the first states in the country to shift to a state-wide decentralized model of waste management, has managed to create livelihood opportunities for around 30,000 women in the formal waste management sector. The feminization process replaced municipal sweepers (who are predominantly men) and engaged Haritha Karma Sena women to carry out the collection, segregation, and processing of waste. With this, waste management in the state improved many folds, receiving awards and accolades from across the world, along with large cost savings for urban local bodies. Associated with the feminization process is the issue of precariousness, especially low and unstable income, lack of social security benefits, decent working conditions and bargaining power, high health risks, social stigma, and discrimination. These are typical traits of informal work. Yet women undertake and continue to be part of such jobs. We studied such differentiated and complex realities to identify and explain what facilitates such processes through an empirical study of Haritha Karama Sena in the solid waste sector in Kerala. The study also adds to the literature on the gendered division of labor in the waste sector.

Subverting Social Inequalities: Gender as a Social Reality.
Akanksha Srivastava, Disha Maheshwari, Chitra Krishnan (Eds.)

9.1 INTRODUCTION

The gap in labor supply and employment opportunities in the formal sectors has forced many into the informal and unorganized sectors in India (Mehrotra, 2019). The workforce, especially women, plays a critical role in infrastructure-deficient sectors in countries like India. According to the United Nations India Business Forum, more than 50% of the work done by women in India is unpaid, and almost all of it is informal (Ferguson, 2021). The solid waste management (SWM) sector is no different (World Bank, 2018).

High poverty rates coupled with increasing waste generation have already created abundant informal labor near the waste landfills (Madson, 2005), with a large proportion of women working in appalling conditions (Rogerson, 2001; Horn, 2010; Harshey & Sharma, 2016). But the formal waste management system, primarily dominated by men, in most cities has not created many employment opportunities due to their continued dependence on centralized solutions and technologies like landfills and waste incinerators (Oates et al., 2018). However, in Kerala – a small South Indian state – the failure of centralized solutions led to a 'waste crisis' causing public health and environmental concerns that forced the state government to shift to a decentralized[1] mode of waste governance and management (Isaac & Gopakumar, 2014; Ganesan, 2017) generating a demand for labor both at the household and commercial level.

While the household-level waste management demands have been catered to by women as an extension of their domestic chores for ages, a new kind of formalization of labor has evolved to cater to waste management at the commercial level. This led to the formation of Haritha Karma Sena (HKS) (literal meaning, Green Task Force), a group of women replacing municipal sweepers (mostly men) and becoming the frontline workforce for waste management. This process can be identified as the 'feminization' of the solid waste sector in the state.

The term 'feminization of labor' was first coined by Guy Standing (1989) to define the trend of increasing participation of women in the workforce by replacing men and the nature of work getting geared towards jobs traditionally handled by women. This happened as a result of globalization and

[1] A decentralized SWM model involves segregation and treatment of wet waste at source and segregation of dry waste and further streamlining them to recycling centers. In centralized mode, usually mixed waste is collected and either taken to the centralized processing plant or dumped in the landfills.

neoliberal policies (post-1980s) that accompanied labor market deregulations (Standing, 1989).

The impact of the feminization of labor is understood both as women's emancipation and empowerment and as an issue of their social and economic exploitation (Kabeer et al., 2013; Kabeer et al., 2018; Elgin et al., 2021). Research, particularly that from low-income countries, indicates that women are pushed into precarious jobs with low income and no social security benefits. The new jobs created are characterized by informality i.e., unregulated and unprotected work which is part time and contractual in nature, lack of fixed income, and employment benefits (Chen, 2007; Benería et al., 2015; Pattnaik et al., 2018; Prasad, 2018; Elgin et al., 2021)[2]. Thus, workers in informal jobs have a higher risk of losing jobs and earning. They have no or limited authority and autonomy over the establishment, and decision-making processes (Chen, 2005). Consequently, workers have no or limited bargaining power to bargain for their right to a decent place, working hours, better wages, and leaves (ibid).

To explain these differentiated effects and complex realities, the literature on the 'feminization of labor' (Shah, 2017; Elgin et al., 2021) points to the need to look at both demand and supply-side factors. While the study of demand-side factors can point to the structural inequalities and discrimination against women and the nature of demand created for women's labor, the study of supply-side factors discusses the circumstances or individual choices that led women to take up precarious jobs (*see* Elgin et al., 2021). This is a major gap in the existing literature that apply a gender lens to waste management as they are mostly limited to the segregated nature of work and capital (*see* Muller & Scheinberg, 1998; Samson, 2008) and the impacts on lives and livelihoods of women (*see* Muller et al., 2002; Foster et al., 2012).

This chapter is an attempt to understand the feminization of labor in the SWM sector (in Kerala) from demand and supply side factors, and what facilitates such processes through an empirical study. It also adds to the literature on the gendered division of labor in the sector. The next (second) section details the methods. The third section is divided into three subsections. The first subsection describes how and why paid labor in the waste sector was feminized in Kerala – the demand side factors. The second subsection discusses the attributes of informality steered by feminization and its consequences on women workers. The third subsection discusses the supply side factors of feminization that led women to take up work in the waste sector. The fourth section talks about the influence of patriarchal

[2] In low-income countries, 92.1% of the employed women are in the informal sector (Bonnet et al., 2019).

society that propagates certain narratives around gender roles in facilitating feminization. The fifth section concludes the chapter.

9.2 MATERIALS AND METHODS

The study was conducted over a period of one year starting August 2021 to August 2022. Secondary data sources include academic literature, government reports, HKS working guidelines, and webinars conducted by the state government departments. Socio-economic data of HKS workers were collected from the municipalities. Data on SWM service coverage and service fee collection of HKS (for Jan-June 2022 period) were collected from Integrated Rural Technology Centre (IRTC)[3], Kerala.

The fieldwork for primary data collection was conducted in Alappuzha municipality, Kerala. Alappuzha municipality has been one of the pioneering municipalities to implement decentralized SWM and form HKS. HKS was formed in 2018 in Alappuzha Municipality as per the government order 2420/2017 with around 30 workers; the strength of which gradually increased and currently constituted 91 workers. Non-participant observations and interviews of HKS workers, political representatives, ward councilors, officials at the state and local level were conducted to understand the demand and supply-side factors of feminization and the gendered nature of work in SWM. A participant-specific semi-structured key was used for conducting interviews. A total of 35 interviews were conducted. Interviews were recorded as handwritten notes. The qualitative data thus obtained was thematically analyzed to address the study objectives.

9.3 FEMINIZATION OF WASTE SECTOR: INSIGHTS FROM KERALA

In India, feminization of the workforce happened only in certain sectors where there was demand for cheap and intense labor (Das, 2018) like agriculture (Kalamkar & Shende, 2011; Pattnaik et al., 2018), garment industry (Mezzadri, 2017; Prasad, 2018), export processing zones (Ghosh, 2004), waste management (Madson, 2005; Harshey & Sharma, 2016; Wittmer, 2020).

[3] IRTC -an autonomous research and development organization- that provides consultancy to many LSGs in handholding HKS until they become self-sustaining. See more at https://www.irtc.org.in/about-us/.

Among Indian states, Kerala performs rather poorly in female labor force participation rate (LFPR) (Eapen & Kodoth, 2002)[4], despite having a higher ranking in various gender indicators (female literacy rate, sex ratio, maternity mortality rate, etc.) (Dreze & Sen, 2002). This indicates that gains in demography, health, and education have not reflected much in employment and economic gains for women.

To address the economic empowerment of women, the state government formed the *Kudumbashree* program in 1997 as part of the State Poverty Eradication Mission. This, along with the Kerala Panchayati Raj Act-1994, encouraged women's participation in decentralized governance. The convergence of *Kudumbashree* with local self-governments (LSGs) through the Community Development Society (CDS)[5] has been playing a major role in feminizing various government programs (Narayan, 2022). *Kudumbashree* women form a major labor force of the LSGs in implementing various developmental activities, including SWM. The *Kudumbashree* women were mobilized to form Haritha Karama Sena (HKS) during the solid waste governance regime change. The current section, focusing on the HKS, discusses demand-side factors that induced increased women participation in the waste sector in Kerala and their consequences for the HKS women.

9.3.1 DEMAND SIDE FACTORS

The *Kudumbashree* program, which started as a women's empowerment initiative, became especially relevant during the state-wide 'waste crisis' that lasted for almost a decade starting from the early 2000s. This period witnessed almost all the cities protesting against the local and state governments. The sheer scale of these protests forced governments to initiate a change in the regime of waste governance from centralized to decentralized SWM.

The alternative model, based on the principles of reduce, reuse, and recycle, mandates: i) segregation and treatment of kitchen/wet waste at the source, ii) reduction in waste generation at household and community levels, iii) collection and segregation of dry waste, and iv) streamlining segregated

---

[4] With 28.5% female LFPR and 73.5% male LFPR, the state ranks third from bottom in female LFPR. (Ministry of Health and Family Welfare, 2020).

[5] CDSs as community wings of LSGs represent a vast network of neighbourhood groups in Panchayat/Municipal area, and serve as dissemination organs for government programs and as an annunciator of community needs on governance issues. See more at: https://www.kudumbashree.org/pages/9 (accessed on 22 June 2024).

waste to recycling centers (Isaac & Gopakumar, 2014). The scale at which the changes were required highlighted the huge gap in the demand and supply of skilled workforce, but at a much cheaper cost.

The government turned to the well-established network of *Kudumbashree* to mobilize the workforce for HKS. Around 30,000 women were mobilized for SWM activities (Ratheesh, 2019), making HKS an integral part of the SWM over a short period.

The HKS provides waste management services to households and commercial establishments (door-to-door collection), runs waste processing units, streamlines waste to recycling centers after segregation (See Figure 9.1), does awareness creation on scientific waste management practices, and promotes organic farming. They are also encouraged to find business opportunities from waste like running eco-friendly enterprises that help in attaining 'Garbage free Kerala.' They function as frontline workers in implementing various programs of state and local governments that facilitate waste reduction and recycling (Haritha Karma Sena Working Guidelines, 2018).

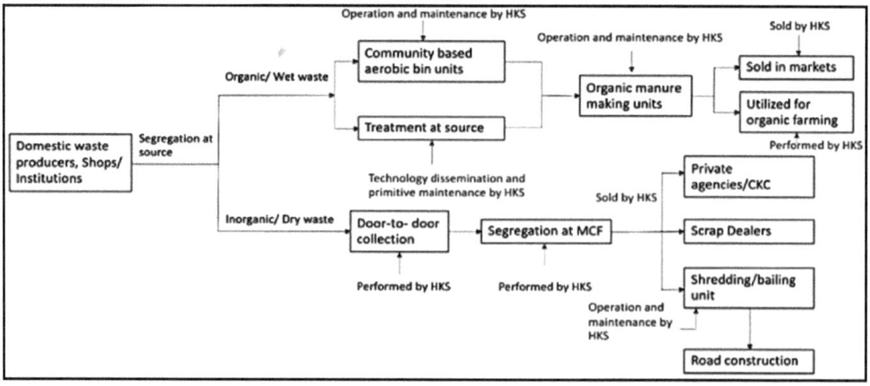

FIGURE 9.1 Role of HKS in solid waste chain.

Source: Authors.

As per recent estimates of the state government, HKS workers provide service to 47% of the households across the state and 53% of the institutions across the municipal corporations (LSGD, 2021). The involvement of HKS in SWM, especially their massive awareness campaigns and daily conversations with people, has led to drastic changes in the way waste is handled, managed, treated, and disposed at the household level (Kerala Institute of Local Administration, 2020). For example, the percentage of households segregating their waste rose from 22% in 2017 to 59.5% in 2020, utilizing at-source treatment facilities increased from 23% in 2017 to 59% in 2020, handing over their dry waste to HKS improved from 23.4% in 2017 to 47% in 2020 (Haritha Kerala Mission, 2020). In October 2020, 589 out of 941 LSGs in the state were given the title of 'Suchitwa Padavi'[6] and HKS was declared as the central pillar of SWM in the state by the state government (Ibid).

Involvement of HKS has also led to larger economic benefits for the government.

Promoted as micro-enterprises, the HKS workers have user fees (collected from the service users), sale of recyclables, and profit from other income-generating activities (if any) as primary income sources. As of 2020, 85% of the LSGs have registered HKS as micro-enterprises (*Kudumbashree*, 2020a). In few municipalities and gram panchayats where it is not feasible to run HKS as micro-enterprises (Consultant, Haritha Kerala Mission, personal communication, August 10, 2022), HKS workers are appointed as daily wage workers. These are non-enterprise models of HKS (*Kudumbashree*, 2020b). However, only 15% of the LSGs have such non-enterprise models.

Formulation of HKS as micro-enterprise models does not mandate the LSGs to ensure a stable and fixed minimum income to the HKS workers. This makes 'feminizing labor' economically beneficial for the LSGs. The daily wage rate of a full-time sanitation worker in Kerala is INR 675[7]. The expected yearly labor cost of employing HKS workers for minimum wages would be around INR 1.8 Crores (91 workers*25 days* minimum wage*12 months) in the case of Alappuzha municipality. There are 87 such municipalities in Kerala, apart from municipal corporations and Gram Panchayats[8]. This amounts to a huge saving for the government.

9.3.2 FEMINIZATION STEERING INFORMALITY AND CONSEQUENCES FOR WOMEN LABOR

Our study hints towards informality in the labor practices in the waste sector which are steered by the demand side factors of feminization. The current section highlights such labor practices and consequences thereof on women laborers.

---

[6] Sanitation award by the state government to LSGs based on status of SWM.

[7] Government order dated 11.02.2021

[8] Municipal Corporation is the type of urban local government that works for the development of a city with more than 1 million population. Municipalities also known as municipal councils, oversee the administration of towns and smaller cities. Under Panchayati- Raj Act 1994, Gram panchayats are governing bodies at the local village level.

9.3.2.1 LOW AND UNSTABLE INCOME

On a regular basis, the HKS workers face low income, delays in income, and zero income security. This is largely due to shifting the burden of financial sustenance of micro-enterprise units to HKS. Table 9.1 shows that HKS workers working in municipalities have the highest income (up to INR 10,000), followed by corporations (INR 8,000) and lowest in Gram Panchayats (INR 3,000). Their average daily earning is much below (81% to 49%) the minimum wage rate (INR 675) of full-time sweeper-cum-sanitation workers in Kerala.

TABLE 9.1 Average Monthly Income of HKS in Kerala

Level of LSGs	Number of LSGs	Average Per Capita Monthly Income of HKS Workers (INR)	Average Daily Per Capita Income of HKS Workers (INR)
Corporations	6	8,543	285
Municipalities	87	10,343	345
Gram Panchayats	941	3,766	126

Source: LSGD (2021).

They are particularly economically vulnerable in times of unexpected crises such as COVID. In Kerala, when there was no collection of waste during the COVID lockdown, the income of HKS workers in most units suddenly dropped to zero. On top of that, the HKS workers incur enormous financial losses due to refusals or delays in the payment of user fees. Our analysis of Alappuzha municipality shows that only 33% of households and 20% of shops that received HKS services between January and June 2022 paid the user fee. The volatile nature of user fee payment, which forms a major portion of their income, further adds to their economic vulnerability.

9.3.2.2 LACK OF SKILLED JOBS

Although HKS is originally envisioned to perform multiple roles like entrepreneurship and operating machinery, our analysis shows that much of it is limited to labor- and time-intensive work like waste collection and segregation. Our study in Alappuzha municipality shows that even though HKS workers are skilled laborers, they are utilized only for low-grade unskilled activities in the municipal area. There is no access to composting technologies like aerobic bin units, which are currently provided to the municipal sweepers. Only 19% of HKS micro-enterprises in the state have formed additional income-generating activities other than waste collection and segregation (Kudumbashree, 2020a).

9.3.2.3 LACK OF DECENT WORKING CONDITIONS

Our study in Alappuzha reveals that the HKS workers work in unsafe and unhygienic working conditions. This goes against the state HKS Working Guidelines (2018). As per these guidelines, LSGs are the responsible bodies to ensure safe and hygienic working conditions for HKS workers.

For example, the Material Collection Facility (MCF)[9] where HKS workers spend most of their time segregating the waste is an abandoned public building without sufficient storage facilities, without electricity, safe sanitation and drinking water, and office facilities (*See* Figure 9.2). The unkempt surroundings overgrown with bushes risks them to accidental cuts and wounds and attack from rodents, reptiles, and street dogs. The space is also notorious for 'inappropriate' activities by local men at night.

"Men use this space for drinking and smoking purposes at night they leave their broken bottles around…stamping on it, I recently got eight stitches in my foot when we started using this space, people were worried they said it is not safe for women to use this space. But we didn't have any other option. Where else do we keep the collected waste…" (HKS worker, personal communication, 25 December 2022).

Furthermore, the failure of LSG in establishing intermediate storage spaces between MCFs is making it difficult for HKS workers to carry heavy loads for a long distance. Transportation facilities are not available to meet the requirements, which not only affects their functioning but also makes their work unnecessarily laborious.

9.3.2.4 HIGH HEALTH RISKS AND NO SOCIAL SECURITY BENEFITS

Engaged in the tedious tasks of collection and segregation of waste, walking long distances (8–10 km per day), many HKS workers in personal interactions reported skin and eye irritation and body pain. They are daily exposed to health risks like accidental cuts and wounds, bites from animals, rodents, and insects, mental and physical stress due to increased workload. Moreover, 17% of the LSGs have not provided personal protection equipment and safety gear to HKS workers, exposing them further to such health risks

[9] MCFs are centers where waste is segregated and stored.

FIGURE 9.2 Material collection facility provided to the HKS workers.

(LSGD, 2021). HKS workers in Alappuzha find the provided gloves ineffective for speedy segregation, inhibiting their usage. With no safety gear, many reported slipping and falling during the monsoon. They are also prone to various kinds of verbal and physical abuse and violence from the users of the service. Their gender identity as women has made them specifically vulnerable to such risks.

Despite being involved in a risky job that facilitates better management of waste, workers are not provided with any social security benefits.

9.3.2.5 SOCIAL STIGMA AND DISCRIMINATION

Beyond the gender disparities, 'working with waste' is often accompanied by social discrimination and stigma. In India, waste is seen as something inauspicious, which is a reflection of still prevalent socio-cultural concepts of purity and pollution beyond the intrinsic composition (Cornea et al., 2017). This makes it complicated to ensure dignity in the livelihoods created. Being front-end waste handlers, people usually perceive HKS workers as mere waste collectors and often get abused with derogatory racial slurs/terms like *chavaruperukkikal, kannasum kadalasum, annachikal, thottipanikkar*.

A Haritha Karma Sena (HKS) worker said;

"They just shut the door or lock the gate when they see us coming. One time one of the households left their dog to bite us and one among us got seriously injured and bitten by a dog" (HKS worker, personal communication, August 20, 2022).

Another HKS worker said;

"One day there was a function going on at one house and the house owner asked us to take away the wet waste generated. We said we don't have the provision to take it away like that. He got very angry at us and threw the waste over our heads" (HKS worker, personal communication, December 21, 2022).

One major reason for the frequent dropout of HKS workers is also the notion that they are doing 'dirty work.'

"...The ward councilors mobilize women saying that they will be well-paid and do not detail about the conditions in which we are working... once they recognize it, they leave the job. Who will come for this dirty work... only us who do not have much choice..." (HKS worker, personal communication, December 21, 2022).

Though HKS working guidelines (2018) holds LSGs responsibly to ensure dignified livelihoods; and efforts have been made from the state government through public recognitions to HKS workers, it remains an ambitious task in the existing socio-cultural scenario, where it is considered as the duty of few people based on their birth or their nature of work or class (Doron & Jeffrey, 2018; Harshey & Sharma, 2016).

9.3.2.6 LACK OF BARGAINING POWER

The bargaining power of HKS workers in Alappuzha municipality is found limited due to conflicts among the workers. Moreover, since their income is dependent on the user fees and sale of recyclables, it requires them to engage in tedious work, limiting their time for organizational activities.

"If we do not provide timely service, we do not get user fees... we have to segregate around 40 kgs of waste every day to get a minimal income...in between all this where is the time to meet everyone... meetings with health inspector happens every month where the President and Secretary may sometimes express few grievances but not many actions are taken to address them..." (HKS worker, personal communication, August 20, 2022)

9.3.3 SUPPLY SIDE FACTORS

The above section explained demand-side factors that create demand for cheap labor force and discussed its implications for the women workforce.

The current section discusses supply-side factors that question (a) why do women choose to work as HKS, and (b) why do women continue to work as HKS despite much evident indecent working conditions, health risks, and low incomes.

9.3.3.1 POOR SOCIO-ECONOMIC BACKGROUND

Our study shows that structural inequalities related to poor socio-economic background and lower educational status have pushed many of the HKS women to work in the SWM sector. 14% of HKS workers attribute the reasons for them joining HKS to choiceless circumstances like their husband's death, separation, or illness. 62% of them joined because they consider it as a safety net for their households[10]. It is to be noted that 60% of HKS workers hold Below Poverty Line (BPL) cards[11]. The average monthly household income of HKS workers is only INR 3,200. 96% of HKS workers have attained a maximum of up to secondary education (till class 10), limiting their job opportunities mostly to casual, temporary, and home-based work.

9.3.3.2 RELATIVELY POOR INCOME AND WORKING CONDITIONS IN OTHER SECTORS

The job opportunities created in other sectors are found to be worse in terms of income and working conditions. Though the incomes of HKS workers are found to be marginal among sanitation workers who receive daily wages, our survey in Alappuzha shows that for 71% of HKS workers income has relatively increased in comparison to their previous jobs. Most of them were either not working or working in further lower income jobs or relied on MGNREGA (which has a limited number of guaranteed working days). Besides, lower income 25% of HKS workers also mentioned that their previous jobs had worse working conditions. These are mainly women who were working as saleswomen in textile shops, tailors, and domestic workers. An HKS worker who was a former domestic worker responded: "While working in HKS, absence due to any personal reasons results only in reduced income. Working as a domestic help, I had to face abusive treatment from the employers too" (HKS worker, personal communication, August 28, 2022).

---

[10] Primary survey of HKS workers in Alappuzha municipality, n=30

[11] Socio-economic data of 91 HKS workers collected from municipality

- **A Former Saleswoman in Textile Shop Responded:**

"They didn't even give us a chair to sit on, thinking that we would be plowing. In this job, there are no such harassments" (HKS worker, personal communication, August 28, 2022).

This indicates that the nature of employment opportunities available for these women is limited to sectors that have even lesser income and working conditions. It can be noted that other sectors in Kerala, including MGNREGA, are already being feminized. Hence, we can say that the feminization of labor in the SWM sector is found to be better in comparison to certain other sectors. Moreover, working in association with the LSGs and *Kudumbashree* is giving them a sense of dignity and security, compared to jobs in other private sectors (HKS worker, personal communication, July 21, 2022).

9.3.3.3 FLEXIBLE JOB TO BALANCE HOUSEHOLD WORK

Many respondents mentioned the flexibility in SWM work that helps them to balance their household chores. Flexibility for HKS workers is characterized by a shorter distance to their home, time-bound nature of the work, and the ability to take leaves even though they are unpaid.

9.3.3.4 INCREASED SOCIAL AND POLITICAL CAPITAL

While 32% of HKS workers mentioned that being employed financially empowers them and helps them be independent, a similar proportion of workers (29%) also mentioned their enhanced social capital. The *Kudumbashree* network in Kerala is already known for being an accessible gateway to enhancing the social capital of the poorest women and their increased participation in public life (Williams et al., 2011; Prathap, 2019). The characteristics of enhanced social capital as felt distinctively by different HKS women include an increase in self-confidence and communication skills, sharing and bonding with fellow workers, increased social networks, and the ability to organize group activities. A few quotes from the interviews are listed below to illustrate this.

"Earlier, I had a huge inferiority complex was afraid to talk to people never had good friends working as a collective in HKS helped me gain communication skills attained friends whom I could share my sorrows with because of which I prefer working here" (HKS worker, personal communication, July 21, 2022)

"Alappuzha, being a large town, it was very difficult to manage door to door collection, segregation and transportation of waste simultaneously... gradually all of us gained skills to work in groups and thus effectively deliver a better waste management service" (HKS worker, personal communication, July 21, 2022).

"Here we get a lot of opportunities to interact with different types of people from health officials and ward councilors in municipalities, to police officers, bank managers, school teachers.in case of any needs in our daily life we know people to approach." (HKS worker, personal communication, July 21, 2022).

The enhanced social capital has translated into political capital for many HKS women. The LSG elections in the state (in December 2022) witnessed many HKS leaders contesting and winning. Interviews with them revealed that they could utilize their active engagement in SWM, working closely with both LSG and people in enhancing their political capital too.

A former HKS worker elected as ward councilor said,

"Visiting households every day for collection of waste, awareness generation, petty talks, and guidance regarding waste management helped me strengthen relationships with people. People had started treating me like a family member. Winning elections thus became easy." (HKS worker, personal communication, July 21, 2022).

Another former HKS worker also attributed her winning LSG elections to her role in SWM.

"My work in managing waste helped me gain popularity and acceptance among people due to which I was identified as a perfect candidate for the election even by the opposition." (HKS worker, personal communication, July 21, 2022).

9.4 PATRIARCHY FACILITATING FEMINIZATION AND INFORMALITY

The study findings must be understood within the larger context of patriarchal societies. Prominent in a patriarchal society is the narrative that 'cleaning and removal of wastes are part of women's domestic roles. The waste management done by women in the households remains unpaid and often unrecognized, which gets 'naturally' extended to roles of low-paid 'community caregivers' (Muller & Scienberg, 2003). Croft (1986) has highlighted how establishing women as ‘caring’ leads to their social and economic exploitation.

Our study shows that the narrative is facilitating both demand and supply side factors of feminization. The interviews with the HKS workers corroborated the literature findings. The ‘caring and protective’ nature of the work, high public health risk involved in improper waste management, and consequential societal compulsions have persuaded HKS women to work for low wages.

For example, when we asked an educated HKS worker who is a Bachelor of Arts about the reason for her to continue working in HKS, she replied,

“… more than a job, I consider it as a service to society, waste management is very much needed and I believe that someone should be there to do this job..” (HKS worker, personal communication, August 28, 2022).

Another worker said;

“I took this job, because I believe that, because of people like us there will be a decline in the number of cancer patients in the state…” (HKS worker, personal communication, August 28, 2022).

A government officer had replied when asked about women being frontline workers in HKS,

“Women have an innate nature of doing better in keeping the surroundings clean compared to men” (Government official, personal communication, August 29, 2022).

Meanwhile, we can see the contradiction in the job of municipal sweepers, which is a better paid job[12]. 80% of the municipal sweepers in Alappuzha municipality are men even though the task to be performed is cleaning[13].

This indicates that the gender narrative around ‘cleaning jobs’ is persistent only in sectors that are low paid. Moreover, it must be noted that men in the state are not available to work for such low wages (Government Official, personal communication, 14 August 2022). The availability of women to work for lower wages has resulted in attaining developmental objectives at much lower costs.

Such narratives further glorify and justify the poorly paid work of HKS workers as a ‘voluntary service’ to society. Even though HKS workers are both service providers (door-to-door collection and segregation) and entrepreneurs at the same time, their role as service providers is increasingly getting glorified.

[12] Monthly income of temporary workers is INR 18,225 and that of permanent workers is minimum INR 28,000 (as basic income).

[13] Data obtained from municipal records.

"...They are angels who make sacrifices for the countries' betterment..." (HKS coordinator, personal communication, August 20, 2022).

Though such narratives help in attaining a greater acceptance among the public, it perpetuates the 'idea of women' as 'caring citizens' who do 'voluntary jobs.' This reinforces traditional gender roles and certain elements of Kerala's conservative gender norms along with their economic exploitation.

9.5 DISCUSSION AND CONCLUSION

The chapter was an attempt to understand the feminization of labor in the solid waste sector in Kerala both from the demand side and supply side factors. The demand for the formation of a cheap but trained and efficient workforce was created due to the change in the waste governance regime from centralized to decentralized model which was/is an attempt to address the state-wide waste crisis that lasted over a decade. The sheer scale of envisaged changes in SWM governance needed trained workforce in large numbers (proportional to the population in LSGs) for their daily engagement with people in awareness generation, collection, segregation, and processing of solid waste. This demand led to the formation of HKS, employing women across the state. Despite being touted as 'women entrepreneurs,' the formulation of HKS as micro-enterprises seems to be a cost-cutting strategy.

While feminization of the waste sector has provided employment opportunities for women in Kerala, the quality of work remains poor in terms of low income, high economic vulnerability, poor working conditions, high health risks, social stigma, discrimination, and limited bargaining power. However, relatively better income, working conditions and social status compared to their previous jobs, flexible working conditions, and HKS as a platform to attain social and political capital are key motivations for women to continue as HKS workers. Further, women agree to work under these conditions because there are no better opportunities made available for them, within and in other sectors.

This can also be attributed to the structural constraints at the intersections of caste, class, and gender. HKS women's higher economic vulnerability (due to husband's illness or poor household income) presses them to take up any job available in the market than nothing. Caste further normalizes women working in the waste sector for poor wages. These structural constraints not only have limited their educational qualifications but also employment choices and opportunities.

The patriarchal gender narratives that view women as 'caretakers' and managing waste as a 'voluntary service' to society further facilitate both demand and supply-side factors. While this helps the government in cost-cutting, it persuades more women to work in the waste sector for low wages. Moreover, such culturally determined gender roles persist only for low-paid jobs. 'Cleaning' jobs are undertaken by men when it is better paid, as we discussed in the case of municipal sweepers in Alappuzha municipality.

The study concludes that the supply side factors are only an effect of the demand side, that along with structural inequalities generates only a certain kind of work for women. Even though women do benefit in terms of social, political, and financial capital when compared to a state of unemployment or poor employment, the ultimate beneficiary is the employer in terms of cost savings and improved waste management. All in all, the feminization of labor in the waste sector in Kerala is more exploitative and women's continued involvement is a response to their lack of choice rather than being a choice.

ACKNOWLEDGMENT

The study was conducted as part of the r4d program of the Swiss National Science Foundation and Swiss Agency for Development and Cooperation project 'Challenges of Municipal Waste Management: Learning from Post-Crisis Initiatives in South Asia.'

KEYWORDS

- **Community Development Society**
- **feminization of labor**
- **Haritha Karma Sena**
- **Kerala**
- **labor force participation rate**
- **local self-governments**
- **solid waste management**
- **waste management**

REFERENCES

Benería, L., Berik, G., & Floro, M. (2015). *Gender, Development, And Globalization: Economics as if all people mattered.* Second edition. Routledge. Pp. 135–175. https://doi.org/10.4324/9780203107935.

Bonnet, F., Vanek, J., & Chen, M. (2019). *Women and men in the informal economy: A statistical brief.* Manchester, UK: WIEGO. pp. 1–25. https://www.wiego.org/sites/default/files/migrated/publications/files/Women%20and%20Men%20in%20the%20Informal%20Economy%20-%20A%20Statistical%20Brief%20-%20for%20web.pdf.

Chen, M. (2007, April). *Rethinking the Informal Economy. Linkages with the Formal Economy and the Formal Regulatory Environment.* Working Paper No. 2005/10. The United Nations University World Institute for Development Economics Research (UNU-WIDER), Helsinki. pp. 1–28. https://www.econstor.eu/bitstream/10419/63329/1/488006546.pdf.

Chen, M., Vanek, J., Lund, F., Heintz, J., Jhabvala, R., & Bonner, C. (2005). *Women Work and Poverty. Progress of the World's Women.* United Nations Development Fund for Women. pp. 1–112. https://www.unwomen.org/sites/default/files/Headquarters/Media/Publications/UNIFEM/PoWW2005_eng.pdf.

Cornea, N., Véron, R., & Zimmer, A. (2017). Clean city politics: An urban political ecology of solid waste in West Bengal, India. *Environment and Planning A, 49*(4), 728–744.

Croft, S. (1986). Women, caring and the recasting of need — A feminist reappraisal. *Critical Social Policy, 6*(16), 23–39. doi:10.1177/02610183860060160.

Doron, A., & Jeffrey, R. (2018). *Waste of a Nation: Garbage and Growth in India.* Harvard University Press. pp. 95–126.

Dreze, J., & Sen, A. (2002). Gender inequality and women's agency. In Jean Dreze & Amartya Sen (Eds.). *India: Development and participation.* Oxford University Press. pp. 1–49. doi: 10.1093/acprof:oso/9780199257492.003.0003.

Eapen, M., & Kodoth, P. (2002). Family structure, women's education and work: Re-examining the high status of women in Kerala. *Centre for Development Studies, Trivandrum Working Papers 341*, Centre for Development Studies, Trivandrum, India.

Elgin, C., & Elveren, A. Y. (2021). Informality, inequality, and feminization of labor. *Women's Studies International Forum, 88*, 102505. Pergamon.

Ferguson, Susan. (2021, June 1). *Expert's take: Investing in the lives and livelihoods of India's women is crucial to the nation's full recovery.* UN Women. Retrieved from: https://www.unwomen.org/en/news/stories/2021/6/experts-take-investing-in-women-crucial-to-india-recovery (accessed on: 31 August 2024).

Foster, S., Dixey, R., Oberlin, A., & Nkhama, E. (2012). 'Sweeping is women's work': Employment and empowerment opportunities for women through engagement in solid waste management in Tanzania and Zambia. *International Journal of Health Promotion and Education, 50*(4), 203–217. doi:10.1080/14635240.2012.703392.

Ganesan, P. (2017). Landfill sites, solid waste management and people's resistance: a study of two municipal corporations in Kerala. *International Journal of Environmental Studies, 74*(6), 958–978.

Ghosh, J. (2004). Globalization, export-oriented employment for women and social policy: A case study of India. In Globalization, Export-oriented Employment and Social Policy (pp. 91–125). doi:10.1057/9780230524217_4.

Haritha Karma Sena working guidelines, Pub. L. No. 10394-D-2017/KSHO, 1 (2018). https://www.kudumbashree.org/storage/files/4kpdx_kudumbashree-haritha karmasena guidelines.pdf (accessed on 19 June 2024).

Haritha Kerala Mission. (2020). Announcement of Suchitwa Padavi (an achievement in the sanitation sector) achieved by Local Self Governments in Kerala [Webinar]. *Youtube.* https://www.youtube.com/watch?v=eW9fozV8ihY (accessed on 19 June 2024).

Harshey, S., & Sharma, P. (2016). Making waste matter: Reimagining urban renewal and advocating for women waste-pickers' right to a dignified livelihood. In *Land, Labor and Livelihoods* (pp. 263–283). doi:10.1007/978-3-319-40865-1_13.

Horn, Z. E. (2010). The effects of the global economic crisis on women in the informal economy: Research findings from WIEGO and the Inclusive Cities partners. *Gender and Development, 18*(2), 263–276. doi:10.1080/13552074.2010.491339.

Isaac, T. T., & Gopakumar, M. (2014). *Changing Minds and waste free streets: When Alappuzha is Cleaned.* Chintha Publishers. Thiruvananthapuram. pp. 51-89.

Kabeer, N., Assaad, R., Darkwah, A., Mahmud, S., Sholkamy, H., Tasneem, S., & Sulaiman, M. (2013). *Paid work, women's empowerment and inclusive growth: Transforming the structures of constraint.* UN Women. pp. 1–22. https://www.unwomen.org/sites/default/files/Headquarters/Attachments/Sections/Library/Publications/2013/1/Paid-work-womens-empowerment-and-inclusive-growth-I%20pdf.pdf.

Kabeer, N., Mahmud, S., & Tasneem, S. (2018). The contested relationship between paid work and women's empowerment: Empirical analysis from Bangladesh. *The European Journal of Development Research, 30*(2), 235–251.

Kalamkar, S. S., & Shende, N. V. (2011). Feminization of Agricultural Labour in India. *Agricultural Economics Research Review, 24*(conf). pp. 554–554.

Kerala Institute of Local Administration. (2020). *National webinar series on non-biodegradable waste management and local self-governments* [Webinar]. Kerala Institute of Local Administration. https://www.youtube.com/watch?v=anUuCgpAw5k.

Kudumbashree. (2020a). 100 days programme announced by Government of Kerala. Retrieved from https://kudumbashree.org/pages/876. (accessed on 31 August 2024).

Kudumbashree. (2020b). 1000 Green Enterprises in association with Haritha Karma Sena Project. pp. 1–4. Retrieved from: https://kudumbashree.org/storage/files/riylv_hks.pdf (accessed on 19 June 2024).

Local Self Government Department (LSGD). (2021). *The State of Decentralised Solid Waste Management in Kerala Report 2021.* Local Self Government Department, Government of Kerala. pp. 1–67. https://www.kila.ac.in/wp-content/uploads/2022/04/Report.pdf.

Madsen, C. A. (2005). Feminizing waste: waste-picking as an empowerment opportunity for women and children in impoverished communities. *Colorado Journal of International Environmental Law & Policy, 17*, 165.

Mehrotra, S. (2019). *Informal Employment Trends in the Indian Economy. Persistent Informality, but growing positive development. Employment.* Working Paper No. 254. Employment Policy Department, International Labour Organization, Geneva. pp. 1–23.

Mezzadri, A. (2017). *Sweatshop Regimes in the Indian Garment Industry. Labouring bodies, exploitation and garments made in India.* Cambridge University Press. pp. 1–13.

Muller, M. (2002). Differing interpretations of community management in Bamako and Bangalore: some methodological considerations. *Environment and Urbanization, 14*(2), 241–258.

Muller, M., & Scheinberg, A. (1998). *Gender and waste: integrating gender into community waste management.* UWEP working document. Vol 2, pp. 1–41.

Muller, M., & Scienberg, A. (2003). Gender-linked livelihoods from modernizing the waste management and recycling sector: A framework for analysis and decision making. In V.

Maclaren & N. T. A. Thu (Eds.), *Waste-Econ Program* (pp. 1–144). National political publisher Waste-econ program. Retrieved from: http://sites.utoronto.ca/waste-econ/GenderBook.pdf# (accessed on 19 June 2024).

Narayan, S. (2022). Breaking new ground: women's employment in India's NREGA, the pandemic lifeline. *Gender and Development, 30*(1–2), 217–246. doi:10.1080/13552074.2022.2071978.

Oates, L., Sudmant, A., Gouldson, A., & Gillard, R. (2018). *Reduced waste and improved livelihoods for all: Lessons on waste management from Ahmedabad, India.* Coalition For Urban Transitions. pp. 1–15.

Pattnaik, I., Lahiri-Dutt, K., Lockie, S., & Pritchard, B. (2018). The feminization of agriculture or the feminization of agrarian distress? Tracking the trajectory of women in agriculture in India. *Journal of the Asia Pacific Economy, 23*(1), 138–155. doi:10.1080/13547860.2017.1394569.

Prasad, A. (2018). De-feminization and (dis)empowerment of women workers in garment factories. *Antyajaa Indian Journal of Women and Social Change, 3*(1), 12–23. doi:10.1177/2455632718778355.

Prathap, S. K. (2019). Social Capital as a Driver of Entrepreneurship Behavior among Low Income Population: A Study among Kudumbashree Micro Enterprises in Kerala. In Sasi Misra, Suni Shukla, Ganapathi Batthini (Eds.). *Thirteenth Biennial Conference on Entrepreneurship.* Bookwell. pp. 869–878. http://library.ediindia.ac.in:8181/jspui/handle/123456789/8071.

Ratheesh. (2019). *Haritha Karma Sena –The Green Force of Kudumbashree in Action for Green Kerala Mission.* Kudumbasree, Kerala. Retrieved from: http://kudumbashree.org/storage//files/zdnxb_ratheesh%202.pdf (accessed on 19 June 2024).

Rogerson, C. M. (2001). The waste sector and informal entrepreneurship in developing world cities. *Urban Forum, 12*, 247–259.

Samson, M. (2008). Mopping up the labour shortage: the privatisation of waste management and gendered work reorganisation. *Work Organisation, Labour and Globalisation, 2*(2). pp: 85-100. https://doi.org/10.13169/workorgalaboglob.2.2.0085.

Shah, T. (2017). Question of feminization and marginalization. In Women and Globalization. IGNOU. pp. 475-492. Retrieved from: http://hdl.handle.net/123456789/6215 (accessed on 19 June 2024).

Standing, G. (1989). Global Feminization through Flexible Labor. *World Development, 17*(7), 1077–1095. International Labor Organization, Geneva.

Williams, G., Thampi, B. V., Narayana, D., Nandigama, S., & Bhattacharyya, D. (2011). Performing participatory citizenship – Politics and power in Kerala's Kudumbashree Programme. *The Journal of Development Studies, 47*(8), 1261–1280. doi:10.1080/00220388.2010.527949.

Wittmer, J. (2020). *Women's work in the 'clean city': Perspectives on wellbeing, waste governance, and inclusion from the urban margins in Ahmedabad, India* (Doctoral dissertation, University of Guelph). DOI: 10.1016/j.worlddev.2020.105253.

World Bank. (2018). *What a Waste 2.0. A Global Snapshot of Solid Waste Management to 2050.* World Bank. pp. 129–133. https://hdl.handle.net/10986/30317.

CHAPTER 10

THE PARADOX OF GENDER EQUALITY IN THE CORPORATE WORLD

SUPRIYA LAMBA SAHDEV,[1] CHITRA KRISHNAN,[2] KIRAN NAIR,[3] and ASHUTOSH SHARAD[4]

[1]*Department–Management, ISBR Business School, Bangalore, Karnataka, India*

[2]*Symbiosis Center for Management Studies, Noida, Symbiosis International Deemed University, Pune, Maharashtra, India*

[3]*Abu Dhabi University, Abu Dhabi*

[4]*ISBR Business School, Bangalore, Karnataka, India*

ABSTRACT

The paradox of gender equality in the corporate world is a complex and multifaceted issue. At the outset, we would call the phrases "gender" and "equality" a paradox or an observably contradictory phenomenon. Despite progress towards achieving gender diversity in the workplace, women still face significant challenges in advancing to senior leadership positions and in receiving equal pay for equal work. Similarly, while many companies have made strides to create more inclusive workplaces for LGBTQIA$^+$ employees, there is still a significant gap between the rhetoric of corporate inclusion and the reality experienced by many LGBTQIA$^+$ individuals. Addressing these paradoxes requires a comprehensive approach that goes beyond simply implementing policies and initiatives. Companies must create a culture of inclusivity and actively work to dismantle systemic discrimination and bias, providing training on gender issues for all employees, and holding

Subverting Social Inequalities: Gender as a Social Reality.
Akanksha Srivastava, Disha Maheshwari, Chitra Krishnan (Eds.)

leadership accountable for creating and maintaining an inclusive workplace. It is imperative that companies take meaningful steps toward creating more inclusive workplaces to ensure that all employees have equal opportunities for advancement and success. In this chapter, let us try to understand the issue at hand and also try coming up with practical solutions. By providing a deeper understanding of the paradox of gender equality in the corporate world, this paper aims to encourage and support efforts toward creating more diverse and inclusive workplaces. Through an examination of best practices and successful strategies, this paper aims to provide actionable recommendations that can help companies create a culture of respect and inclusivity for all employees, regardless of their gender.

10.1 INTRODUCTION

The chapter analyzes and presents a proposition that states for there to exist equality, equity must be created. Parity is an effect and not the cause. It is important to understand the cause-effect relationship and solve the problem at the root cause, rather than wasting time or resources on the symptoms (Darby & Mathew, 2021). For example, if a person is infected with COVID and is suffering from fever and a cold, taking a tablet for a cold will not solve COVID as a cold is just a symptom. The root cause of the problem is COVID. It involves a detailed root cause analysis, sticking with the problem, and analyzing it in depth, as understanding specific problems is crucial in delivering niche and customized solutions. The chapter details the approaches that individuals, governments, and corporations can take to bridge the gap in gender and create parity for an equitable, long-term sustainable future. Therefore, instead of adopting an avoidance approach and opting for short-term solutions with incentives, we should pursue long-term sustainable solutions (Susan & Ida, 2015) by creating the right conditions for equity. This will be the central argument presented in this chapter.

The sub-themes are going to revolve around the measure of progress – differential levels of progress (The World's Women, 2015) in different parts of the world, different problems, different viewpoints (Hooks, 2000), and lenses to view the problems, customization of solutions, and so on. The gap that we aim to bridge is that research and literature in this area is either carried out in terms of a sociological perspective, historical perspective, or in terms of correlation with culture. Even if there is literature to talk about the structural and post-modern issues, only individual aspects are considered and there is no consolidation of the individual pieces to complete the jigsaw. We have consolidated most aspects that integrate the sum total of all variables put in an organized and structured manner. That is, we have considered both the breadth of perspective and the depth of knowledge. The reason that makes this chapter very relevant is that we have focused on delivering customized solutions to a complex and diverse set of problems.

Throughout the chapter, we analyze the modern-day discourse around gender equality. We analyze the various views, perspectives, prospective solutions proposed, positions taken, and so on. In today's day and age, this topic has become very ideologically driven, with people taking positions based on the political and social ideologies that they identify with. Therefore, the discourse has been highly polarized, and the scope for independent and critical thought is fading by the day. Through our work, we look critically into arguments from all sides and take a non-ideological stand. That is, the lens with which we apply to validate our views is not based on ideology but on facts, research, practicality, and influence on all stakeholders. We also advise readers to examine this piece of literature critically, analytically, and non-ideologically. This is because, through this chapter, we aim to break the shackles of polarization and initiate a genuine fact-based, non-ideological, critical, and analytical conversation with citizens across ideological lines.

The study that we undertake here is an inclusive manifestation. Most studies that touch upon this topic do so in the light of the disparity between men and women, but we not only discuss these genders but also the other 72+ genders that individuals identify themselves with. The LGBTQIA+ community is one of the most underrepresented and neglected communities in the world, so much so that if we think about gender parity, we consider only men and women, ignoring the fact that they even exist. The progress in terms of awareness and empowerment is still in a very immature phase, apart from a few countries which are negligible exceptions. There is a need for a consolidated effort from all wings of society – i.e., members of the community, the general public, social justice groups, governments, corporates, influencers, and pop culture (multiplier effect). We systematically state that recognition, awareness, education, gathering societal consensus, and research are the integrated steps that need to be taken by all stakeholders as a strategic and integrated solution to the above problem. We also argue that until there is a mass social movement that captures the imagination of society, the situation can change only in gear-1. Again, favorable conditions need to be created for making these communities feel included as a part of the corporate world and society at large.

This is the premise or the backdrop against which the whole chapter is centered around. To summarize the major objectives of our work, we aim to create a roadmap for sustainable gender progress, explain the importance of compartmentalizing problems and delivering customized solutions for various degrees of the problem, to analyze the importance of creating equity as opposed to demanding equality and to mainstream the LGBTQIA+ community in the discourse on gender disparity.

10.1.1 OBJECTIVES

- To create a roadmap for sustainable gender progress
- To explain the importance of compartmentalizing problems and delivering customized solutions for various degrees of the problem
- To analyze the importance of creating equity as opposed to demanding equality for sustainability (Investment on creating an ambience for gender progress)

10.2 METHODOLOGY

The chapter is written revolving around contemporary debates on gender equality – problems, solutions, narratives, progress, and ideological positions. It examines various positions taken by modern-day scholars on polarizing issues – the lens through which they view various problems and the validity/practicality of the solutions. It is also a critical piece of literature on various ideological positions and how they have contributed to the polarization of the debate, sometimes resulting in no common ground. It acknowledges the progress made by communities across the world with references to specific countries and their progress stories. To support our positions with practicality, we have used secondary data from several credible research sources to add credibility to the arguments. An important point to note is that there is an element of opinion, but it is supported by solid, credible data and research sources. The style of organization, structure, and writing is kept simple for easy understanding by all readers. There is no prior knowledge or reference required for readers to understand the content provided in this chapter. The style of writing is explanatory, critical, comparative, and argumentative in nature. That is, it aims to explain certain phenomena in depth of knowledge and breadth of perspective (Dam & Siang, 2021). It gives a critical account and analysis of various positions and proposed solutions, acts as a compilation of several scholarly and informal sources, and aims to present an argument for the placed proposition with the lens of evidence, practicality, research, and past track record. We rely primarily on secondary qualitative sources like interviews of scholars, activists, the general public, government representatives, etc., and quantitative sources such as surveys on a mass scale.

10.3 EXPANDING ON THE CENTRAL THEME: CREATING EQUITY VS. DEMANDING EQUALITY

Let us assume a hypothetical situation: The Prime Minister of India comes on TV with an announcement saying that from this moment on, all avenues of work will have a workforce ratio of 50:50 male and female ratio, there will be official recognition of all 72+ genders, and the pay scale of all these genders will be the same for the same post. It sounds really great and ideal, but can it actually happen? To understand this, let us analyze the repercussions. The labor participation rate in India as of 2019 is 20% female and 80% male (Maniprabha, 2022). To make the workforce ratio equal, we would have to fire 50% of all the men who are employed. To replace all these men, for example in the field of engineering (Consulting Editor, 2023), considering the graduate rate of women, is not mathematically possible. In other fields where the ratio of females is greater but nowhere close to a majority, you might find candidates, but due to the narrow pool to choose from, we would not be able to replace the male employees with female employees of the same professional standards, affecting the economic growth of an organization and the country as a whole. In areas involving physical labor like construction work, the ratio of male to female is 7:1 (Consulting Editor,(2023). This is due to the nature of work and lack of desirability. If the government passes laws for the social security of the LGBTQIA+ community, how far can it be implemented given the fact that the overwhelming majority of the community is not comfortable coming out with their identity? Finally, for the aspect of equal pay, let us analyze cricket as an example. Men's cricket in India has a following of hundreds of millions of loyal fans who will view matches regularly on TV and other digital platforms. All matches are played in packed stadiums, merchandise sales are extremely high, and due to their popularity, they get paid hefty amounts to perform in ads. Therefore, they rake in sponsorships, generate ad revenue for streaming channels, and sell merchandise and products under their name, raking in massive sums in revenue. Whereas, on the other hand, women's cricket doesn't even have a fraction of the same traction. From a business perspective, why would a sponsor or a brand invest the same amount of money? These are the reasons why demanding for equality without laying the right groundwork is impractical. It is important for us to analyze, as stated earlier, that equality will be the effect, but creating equity will be the process to achieve equality. For example, encouraging more female enrollment in education is one way to create equity. The in-depth roadmap to create equity is detailed in further parts of the study. The primary aim of this section is to draw your attention to the fact that inorganically altering social structures is very disruptive and impractical in nature. Whereas, if there is a genuine intent towards the solution, long-term sustained action needs to be taken to create the right conditions for the same (Women, 2018).

10.4 ANALYZING CONTEMPORARY DISCOURSE

Recently in an interview, Ronda Rousey, who was the World heavyweight champion in the UFC (Ultimate Fighting Championship), was asked a question about unequal pay grades between men and women athletes. She replied saying that this is going to be the case until matches of female wrestlers rake in the same viewership and revenue as that of their male counterparts, which are greater, drawing investments and sponsorships on a larger scale, as the ultimate aim of any employer would be to maximize profits. She also mentioned that the efforts of society should be in the direction of creating such an environment rather than inorganically screaming for equality. Although this statement might not be wholly representative of the situation across industries and cultures, it still holds some water.

Activism and social movements have played a major role in breaking stereotypes and prejudices against women across the globe. Most cultures have started viewing women as social equals and also started understanding the importance of a vibrant women workforce leading to a vibrant economy (Eastin & Prakash, 2013). There has been ample amount of knowledge in the form of great study material and pop culture that have come out with great explanation of how women were mistreated in the past and how there was a breakthrough and the situation has been reversed for the better due to social movements. (Note: The above-mentioned phenomena have exceptions in parts of the world like Afghanistan due to a radical belief system, in parts of Africa due to extreme poverty and so on). But is better enough?

Let us consider a country like India, which has made tremendous progress in terms of economic and technological growth. Is there a change in perception for the better in terms of gender equality? Yes. Does there exist equality? No. Are there still prejudicial customs, traditions, and beliefs? Yes. The solution to the third question would be to spread awareness and educate, as was successfully done in the past for different segments. But what is the answer to the contradictory phenomena in the first two questions? Let us examine this.

The female workforce fell by around 40% in the decade between 2010–2020, from 32% in 2010 to 19% in 2020 (Lauren & Raksha, 2023). This is a period in which awareness and social movements grew. Therefore, the first lesson is that social movements and activism are only relevant in the initial phases of awakening a society, but the multiplier effect must be created through other means and more needs to be done (Naina, 2022).

Let us move on to the argument of reservation for equal representation in the workplace. Yes, equal representation in the workplace sounds great, but is the groundwork set to make it happen? Let us take a developed country like the U.S.A. Out of all engineering graduates, 86.03% are male and 13.97% are female. Out of all science graduates, 75% are male and 25% are female. The numbers are in the same line in technology with better numbers in management (40% women) and a majority in humanities. If an employer has to choose 100 engineers – 50 male and 50 female, the pool of available resources to choose from is way higher for men and proportionally the employer can find more skilled employees in the pool of 86% rather than the 14%. Therefore, a 1:1 reservation would choke business productivity. Now, let us analyze a few phenomena in the corporate world that act as modern-day choke points preventing women from going to work:

Maternity is the time when most working women lose touch with work and employment. They are not allowed paid or sometimes even unpaid maternity leave. Most of them lose touch with the relevancies and developments thereafter. It becomes very difficult for them mentally and competency-wise to cope. Even if they do find a breakthrough and get back to work, they find themselves demoted in the corporate ladder and underpaid for the human resource that they bring in. There was research conducted by Ashoka University titled "Predicament of Returning Mothers" (Prakash, Rammohan & Swamy, 2022) sampling Indian women employed in the corporate, media, and entertainment industries. The results were revealing and quite mind-boggling. It stated that 73% of women leave work upon giving birth and only 50% of these women return. Of those who return, 48% of them end up leaving their jobs within 4 months. Only 27% of them advance in their careers and 16% of them go on to hold positions of power. An important fact to note is that along with corporate policies on maternity, social stigma around the sole purpose of women's existence – nurturing and upbringing of the child along with taking up all household responsibilities is also a factor contributing to the same. Therefore, we can say that corporate maternity policies are one of the biggest barriers to the goal of achieving a 50:50 male-female workforce ratio by 2030. The UN predicts that this will not happen before 2077.

Furthermore, there is significant evidence to show that women in positions of power empower the growth and development of other women. They are more empathetic to women-specific problems, don't hold general gender stereotypes, and encourage their female counterparts to strive and move ahead in their careers. Moreover, these are women who have strived hard and achieved great heights in their careers, breaking stereotypes such as women can't make tough decisions, women are not very analytical but only fit for creative work, they cannot handle pressure, and so on. Most importantly, they act as inspirational figures to show other women that it can be done.

Moving on to the LGBTQIA+ community, except for a few developed Western countries, the rest of the world is still in phase 1, i.e., lack of awareness, knowledge, and education. There have been social movements, but very few have captured mass consensus. Society is either not aware of or divided on such an issue. It must be a convergent effort from governments, corporates, and citizens to reverse this (Caroline, 2019).

Governments must start with education (Rafa, Atchison, Diffey & Sarubbi, 2017) as the bedrock to change. More money and political will must be invested in mainstreaming these concepts through research and introducing concepts in the curriculum, making a full generation of aware citizens. They can also roll out a set of schemes to empower the suppressed communities. Before all of this, it must begin by recognizing the existence of these genders.

Corporates can play a vital role in recognizing genders and encouraging open manifestations and conversations about the same. Not only are they solving a societal problem, but they also gain goodwill and can market diversity in the workforce. They must be made to feel confident that opening up about their genders would not affect their employment. CSR initiatives can be taken up to empower suppressed communities via employment and support in education.

The role of society is the most essential and crucial one, societal effort must be a combination of acceptance, self-education, activism, encouragement and empathy.

10.5 PROBLEMS IN GENERAL

The major issue in the contemporary discourse is that we haven't been able to define the problem statement accurately and we haven't been able to segment the problem. This becomes essential, as the root causes are different in different parts of the world and progress is different in different parts of the world. For example, in the U.S., the issue may be to get recognition for newer gender identities in the workplace and government, whereas, in Afghanistan, the fight is for women to be allowed to go to school. We can't apply a one-size-fits-all approach to understand problems. With this context, let us define a few general problems derived from the analysis of contemporary discourse:

10.5.1 PROBLEMS FACED BY WOMEN

1. **Social Structures Preventing Women from Going to Work:** Social structures that prevent women from going to work include gender stereotypes and biases, unequal pay, lack of affordable childcare, and a lack of workplace policies that support working mothers. These structures are often deeply ingrained in society and can limit women's opportunities and choices, making it difficult for them to enter and succeed in the workforce. This can lead to a gender pay gap, as well as a concentration of women in lower-paying occupations. Addressing these structures requires a multi-faceted approach, including education and awareness campaigns, promoting gender diversity in the workplace, and enacting policies that support working mothers and promote equal pay for equal work.
2. **Regressive Belief Systems:** Regressive belief systems can prevent women from going to work by perpetuating gender stereotypes and limiting their opportunities. For example, traditional gender roles that view women as caretakers and men as breadwinners can discourage women from pursuing careers and limit their economic opportunities. Additionally, beliefs about the capabilities of women

can lead to gender discrimination in the workplace, making it difficult for women to succeed and advance. These belief systems can also lead to a lack of support for working mothers, as well as a lack of workplace policies that accommodate their needs.

3. **Lack of Education Among Women:** Deferred education among women is a common issue that can result from a variety of factors, including poverty, cultural attitudes, and a lack of access to educational opportunities. Women who defer their education may face difficulties entering and succeeding in the workforce, as well as a potential wage gap compared to their male peers. This can also have a negative impact on their overall well-being and financial stability. To address this issue, it is important to provide women with equal access to education and support their academic and professional goals. This can be achieved through policies that promote gender equity in education, as well as programs that provide financial support and resources for women seeking higher education. Additionally, challenging cultural attitudes and promoting education for women can help to break down gender stereotypes and create a more equal society.
4. **Maternity Policy of Corporates:** Maternity policies can have a significant impact on women going to work. These policies can influence the choices women make about starting a family and continuing their careers. Here are some ways in which maternity policies can affect women going to work:
   i. **Length of Leave:** A lengthy maternity leave can discourage women from returning to work after having a baby. If they have been out of the workforce for an extended period, they may find it difficult to get back into the swing of things and re-establish their careers.

   ii. **Pay During Leave:** If women are not paid during their maternity leave, they may be hesitant to take time off work. This can lead to women returning to work earlier than they would like or working while still recovering from childbirth.

   iii. **Lack of Job Security:** Women may be reluctant to take time off work if they fear that their job may not be available when they return. This can result in women staying in the workforce longer than they would like, or taking on fewer demanding roles.

v. **Support for Breastfeeding:** If a workplace does not offer adequate support for breastfeeding mothers, women may be discouraged from returning to work after having a baby. This can include providing a private space for breastfeeding or expressing milk, or offering flexible working hours.

Overall, maternity policies can play a major role in the decisions women make about starting a family and continuing their careers. It is important for employers to offer supportive and inclusive policies that allow women to take time off work when they need it, while still being able to progress in their careers and provide for their families.

5. **Fewer Women in Positions of Power:** Fewer women in positions of power can have a negative impact on working women. Here are some ways in which this can happen:

   i. **Lack of Role Models:** If there are few women in senior positions, it can be difficult for working women to see themselves in these roles. This can make it harder for them to envision themselves advancing in their careers and reaching their professional goals.

   ii. **Glass Ceiling:** With fewer women in leadership positions, it can be more difficult for women to break through the "glass ceiling" and advance to the highest levels of an organization. This can result in a lack of representation and voice for women in decision-making processes.

   iii. **Bias and Discrimination:** Research has shown that women in male-dominated industries often face gender bias and discrimination in the workplace. With fewer women in positions of power, it can be harder for working women to address these issues and receive support in overcoming them.

   iv. **Work-Life Balance:** Women in leadership positions can play an important role in advocating for policies that support work-life balance, such as flexible working hours and paid parental leave. Without these advocates, such policies may not be implemented or may be less comprehensive.

   v. **Pay Equity:** Women in positions of power can play a role in promoting pay equity, ensuring that women are paid the same as their male counterparts for the same work. With fewer women in leadership, this issue may not receive the attention it deserves.

In conclusion, fewer women in positions of power can have a significant impact on working women, affecting their career progression, pay, and overall experience in the workplace. It is important to increase the representation of women in leadership positions to help address these issues and create a more inclusive and supportive work environment for all.

6. **Lack of Emphasis of Governments on Creating Equitable Solutions:** The lack of emphasis by governments to create an equitable future in terms of gender can have negative consequences for women and society as a whole. Governments play a crucial role in setting the tone for equality and creating policies that support women in the workplace and in their personal lives. Without adequate focus and resources dedicated to this issue, progress towards gender equality can stall. This can result in persistent disparities in pay, representation in leadership positions, and access to education and healthcare. Furthermore, a lack of government emphasis on gender equity can send a message that this issue is not a priority, which can discourage progress and action at all levels of society. In order to create a truly equitable future, it is important for governments to prioritize gender equality and take concrete steps to support and empower women.

10.5.2 PROBLEMS FOR THE LGBTQIA+ COMMUNITY

1. **Lack of Awareness:** As mentioned earlier, in most parts of the world, the knowledge pertaining to the LGBTQIA+ community is very dismal (with only rare exceptions that come from the West). Therefore, knowledge and awareness are not mainstreamed through education, recognition, research, popular discourse, and so on. There are individuals with belief systems that it is a disease, disorder, or mental health issue and not a natural orientation.

2. **Polarization of Discourse:** In several countries, the discourse on LGBTQIA+ rights have become highly polarized and has been hijacked by political and social ideologies. Therefore, more than individuals who empathize and wish well for the community, the members of this community become tools who are supported or dismissed because of the leaning of an individual/community

towards an ideology. This causes polarization of the discourse, not allowing for a nuanced understanding and establishes a bias for or against the community which is not based on facts.

3. **Regressive Attitudes to Acceptance:** This is the cultural component that comes into play. In several cultures and belief systems, homosexuality, bisexuality, and so on have been considered taboo, and these beliefs have their origins from scriptures, practices, and so on. There are various schools of thought which have prescribed punishment for the same. These structures have been in place for many generations and have shaped societal consciousness.
4. **No Social Movement Which Captured Mass Societal Consciousness:** For there to be a social change, a genuine and rigorous social churn is essential. For example, the American movement for democracy, the European movement for secularism, and so on. There have been movements that have shaped social opinion toward the LGBTQIA+ issue but none so far that has been able to arrive at a mass societal consensus.
5. **Govt Failure**
   a. no recognition of gender
   b. no formal education on the concept
   c. no govt policies for empowerment
   d. very fewer research budgets for the issue
   e. lack of political will and so on…
6. **Corporate Support:** There are many things that corporates do but they don't. For example, transgenders are one of the most mistreated, underrepresented, and under-employed communities in India. There is a CSR initiative called transcend which focuses on social inclusion through employment and also focuses on ending gender-based violence. But this is a one-off case and there are very few corporates working on these initiatives whereas, they can act as catalysts towards solving them.

10.6 SOLUTIONS

As the problems must be compartmentalized, so should the solutions. The solution also must be drawn based on the identified root cause. In the case of premature societies in terms of understanding, the course of action should revolve around awareness, education, evangelism, social movements, and so on, all directed towards achieving societal consensus. It is when this stage is crossed that the nature of the creature becomes complex. It becomes essential to customize solutions based on specific problems. If the problem is in government policy, the solution will come from societal pressure and political will. If there is a problem in cultural aspects, the solution will come from social movements, awareness, education, and the influence of pop culture. If it is the problem with corporate policy, it can change by consolidated employee consensus and consumer consensus, and so on. But the major aspect to note for sustainable and irreversible change is creating equitable conditions which will act as a catalyst to equality. That is, improve the literacy rate, progressive maternity policy by Corporates, merit freebies by governments which will encourage women and the LGBTQIA+ communities to come out and go to work, taking leaping steps towards the safety and security of women in the workplace and elsewhere, aspirational upbringing rather than submissive (Research by The Indian Express shows that 79% of Indian women are brought up with the premise that they and their aspirations are subservient to men), reducing barriers of entry, more women in positions of power, and so on. A few of the other common solutions are also discussed in the analysis of contemporary discourse. Let us analyze the solutions discussed here in a structured manner:

a. **Education and Awareness:** One of the crucial ways to promote gender equity is through education and awareness. Education is the foundation for breaking down gender stereotypes and promoting equal opportunities for all individuals. It is essential to educate individuals, particularly young people, about gender equality and the impacts of gender-based discrimination. This can be done through schools, universities, community organizations, and media. In addition, awareness campaigns can help to challenge gender-based stereotypes and promote gender equity in different areas of society (Souto-Manning, et al., 2019).

b. **Encouraging Gender Diversity in Workplaces:** Workplaces play a significant role in promoting gender equity. It is essential for organizations to promote gender diversity by providing equal pay for equal work, offering equal opportunities for career advancement, and creating a work environment that is free from gender-based discrimination and harassment. Organizations can also promote gender equity by encouraging and supporting women to take on leadership positions and creating mentorship programs that connect women with experienced leaders.

c. **Promoting Gender-Inclusive Policies:** Governments have a crucial role to play in promoting gender equity. This includes enacting policies that address the gender pay gap, provide equal opportunities for education and employment, and offer support for working mothers. In addition, governments can promote gender equity by enacting laws and policies that protect individuals from gender-based violence and harassment.

d. **Addressing Gender-Based Violence:** Gender-based violence is a major barrier to gender equity and needs to be addressed. Governments and organizations can work together to prevent and respond to gender-based violence by providing support services for survivors, educating individuals about the impacts of violence, and enacting laws and policies that protect individuals from violence.

e. **Encouraging Gender Equity in All Spheres of Life:** Gender equity needs to be promoted in all spheres of life, including education, employment, politics, and culture. This requires breaking down gender-based biases and stereotypes and creating equal opportunities for individuals regardless of their gender. This can be achieved through education and awareness campaigns, encouraging gender diversity in workplaces, and promoting gender-inclusive policies.

f. **Encouraging Gender-Inclusive Language:** The language that we use can also play a role in promoting or hindering gender equity. Encouraging the use of gender-inclusive languages, such as using "they" instead of "he" or "she," can help to break down gender-based biases and stereotypes.

g. **Challenging Gender Stereotypes:** Gender stereotypes have a profound impact on gender equity, as they limit individuals' opportunities and shape their expectations and behaviors. It is essential to challenge these stereotypes by promoting education and awareness, encouraging gender diversity in workplaces, and supporting women in leadership roles.

h. **Supporting Gender Equity in Education:** Education plays a crucial role in promoting gender equity, as it provides individuals with the knowledge and skills to succeed in different areas of life.

Governments and organizations can support gender equity in education by providing equal opportunities for education, addressing gender-based violence in schools, and promoting gender-inclusive policies and curricula.

i. **Encouraging Gender-Inclusive Sports:** Sports are a major part of many cultures, and they can play a role in promoting gender equity. Governments and organizations can promote gender equity in sports by providing equal opportunities for women and girls to participate in sports, addressing gender-based violence in sports, and promoting gender-inclusive policies and programs.

By taking a comprehensive approach to achieving LGBTQIA + equality in the corporate world, companies can create a more supportive and inclusive workplace for all employees. This not only benefits LGBTQIA + individuals but also helps to create a more diverse and innovative workforce that can drive business success.

10.7 CONCLUSION

Creating equitable conditions is the organic path to creating a future of parity, i.e., Don't feed a hungry person a fish, teach her/him how to fish. The environment creates the person, so we must put our efforts, will, and resources to create the environment. Equality cannot be achieved overnight; it requires sustained efforts from all stakeholders. Last, but not least, we would like to reiterate the fact that we must look at specific problems and root causes in a compartmentalized fashion to design effective and customized solutions. In conclusion, we would like to reiterate the fact that gender progress has been a significantly progressive phenomenon in the last few decades, but the destination is far from near. Higher women workforce participation is one of the most significant economic and social phenomena since the 20th century, according to data from the World Bank. But a complementary report also clearly mentions that this development is highly skewed and differential in different parts of the world, with early industrialized countries being far ahead than the developing and underdeveloped world. Sub-Saharan Africa has a woman labor participation rate of 21.3%, and countries like Iceland, New Zealand, and Norway are the most gender-equal countries according to the World Economic Forum's Global Gender Gap report of 2021, with labor participation rates almost equal to men. We can clearly note differential levels of progress in different parts of the world. Therefore, we must adopt an approach of nuanced understanding of the problems and social context and tailor solutions accordingly.

For example, let us take Tamil Nadu, which has a female workforce participation (Urban) rate of 35.1% according to the Hindustan Times, much greater than that of India, whose national average stands at 15.4%. The government of Tamil Nadu identified that the reason why women were not going to work was that most of the income that they generated was shelled out by way of long-distance travel. Therefore, they brought in a policy wherein bus travel was made free for women. There are several correlational studies, one carried out by the State Government of Tamil Nadu themselves, which shows a high degree of positive correlation between this policy and the female workforce participation rate. Therefore, understanding the root cause and tailoring solutions accordingly becomes very essential.

Another important aspect to summarize as part of the conclusion is that the goal post needs to shift in terms of the demand proposition from demanding equality to demanding equity. Creating equitable conditions is the organic path to create a future of parity. i.e.: Don't feed a hungry person a fish, teach her/him how to fish. The environment creates the person so we must put our efforts, will, and resources to create the environment. The above case is a fine example of the same. Conditions were created such that equality becomes a reality.

Finally, the mission of an equitable future should be taken up with equal vigor and direction by all stakeholders, only then can we see an equitable future which is only a talk of idealism in today's reality.

KEYWORDS

- **customization of solutions**
- **gender equality**
- **number of genders**
- **segmented understanding of the problem**
- **sustainable gender progress**
- **ultimate fighting championship**

REFERENCES

Caroline, K. (2019). 5 things women can do to empower other women. Empower Ambitious Women. https://www.empoweringambitiouswomen.com/5-things-women-can-do-to-empower-other-women/ (accessed on 19 June 2024).

Consulting Editor. (2023). Female construction workers earn 30–40% less than male workers, says report by Primus Partners & World Trade Center. Business Insider. https://www.businessinsider.in/india/news/female-construction-workers-earn-30-40-less-than-male-workers-says-report-by-primus-partners-world-trade-center/amp_articleshow/96855421.cms (accessed on 19 June 2024).

Darby, S., & Mathew, T. (2021). The difference between equity and equality and why both matters. Trinet Publication. https://www.trinet.com/insights/the-difference-between-equity-and-equality-and-why-both-matter (accessed on 19 June 2024).

Eastin, J., & Prakash, A. (2013). Economic development and gender equality: Is there a gender Kuznets curve? *World Politics, 65*(1), 156–186.

Esquivel, V., & Sweetman, C. (2016). Gender and the sustainable development goals. *Gender & Development, 24*(1), 1–8.

Hooks, B. (2000). *Feminism is for everybody: Passionate politics*. Pluto Press.

Interaction Design Foundation, Dam, R. F., & Siang, T. Y. (2021). What is design thinking and why is it so popular? https://www.interaction-design.org/literature/article/what-is-design-thinking-and-why-is-it-so-popular (accessed on 19 June 2024).

Lauren, F., & Raksha, A. (2023). It's a mystery: Women in India drop out of the workforce even as the economy grows. NPR. https://www.npr.org/sections/goatsandsoda/2023/01/04/1146953384/why-women-in-india-are-dropping-out-the-workforce-even-as-the-economy-grows (accessed on 19 June 2024).

Maniprabha, K. (2022). 10 successful women engineers of India. Alma Matters. https://www.almamatters.io/article/10-successful-women-engineers-india/ (accessed on 19 June 2024).

Naina, B. (2022). Women and work in India: Trends and analysis. India Briefing. https://www.india-briefing.com/news/women-and-work-in-india-trends-and-analysis-24758.html/ (accessed on 19 June 2024).

Prakash, S., Rammohan, R., & Swamy, D. (2022). Workplace flexibility: Helping talented women professionals return to work and businesses grow in an agile manner. *NHRD Network Journal, 15*(1), 41–55.

Rafa, A., Atchison, B., Diffey, L., & Sarubbi, M. (2017). Equity in Education: Key Questions to Consider. http://hdl.handle.net/10919/90707.

Souto-Manning, M., Rabadi-Raol, A., Robinson, D., & Perez, A. (2019). What stories do my classroom and its materials tell? Preparing early childhood teachers to engage in equitable and inclusive teaching. *Young Exceptional Children, 22*(2), 62–73.

Women, U. N. (2015). Monitoring gender equality and the empowerment of women and girls in the 2030 agenda for sustainable development: opportunities and challenges. *UN Women.*

Women, U. N. (2018). Gender Equality and the Sustainable Development Goals in Asia and the Pacific Baseline and pathways for transformative change by 2030.

CHAPTER 11

"WHEN PEOPLE HEARD I WAS GOING INSTEAD OF MY HUSBAND, EVERYONE WAS SHOCKED AND DISCRIMINATED AGAINST US": EXPLORING THE GENDERING OF PROFESSIONAL MOBILITY FROM THE PERSPECTIVE OF A NON-ELITE MIGRANT

YESIM KAKALIC, MARIANNA SLUTSKAYA, and STEPHANIE SCHNURR

The University of Warwick, England

ABSTRACT

This chapter explores the gendering of professional mobility by focusing on the reported experiences of a non-elite migrant. More specifically, we explore the life story of a Turkish woman who immigrated to Germany in the early 1970s as part of the "Gastarbeiter" programme, which largely attracted men. Although the programme was targeted at both men and women, the migration of women was generally frowned upon and viewed as highly problematic and immoral by large parts of Turkish society (Mattes, 2019). Consequently, women who joined this scheme and moved to Germany to find work challenged hegemonic gendered expectations and practices, including the gender order and its underlying ideologies. This chapter gives a voice to one of these women as it captures her experiences of professional mobility and

Subverting Social Inequalities: Gender as a Social Reality.
Akanksha Srivastava, Disha Maheshwari, Chitra Krishnan (Eds.)

discrimination at a time when this was rather uncommon and frowned upon. Drawing on two semi-structured in-depth interviews as well as previous research, which has established that the notions of mobility and professional work are heavily gendered—often in ways that disadvantage women—the chapter highlights ways in which gender is produced and reproduced in the context of mobility and provides insights about various ways in which gendered practices are normalized unquestioningly on the one hand and challenged and rejected on the other hand. Utilizing discourse analysis, we explore the gendering of mobility from the perspective of a non-elite migrant and critically discuss her experiences against the background of gender(ed) practices and ideologies in elite professional mobility outlined in previous research. By unpacking the discursive processes through which the notions of mobility and work are gendered in and through these stories, we provide insights into the complex ways in which gender is produced, reproduced, and either naturalized or challenged in the increasingly important context of mobility and ultimately bring forth issues of subversion and internalization.

11.1 INTRODUCTION

This chapter explores the gendering of professional mobility by focusing on the reported experiences of a non-elite immigrant. Drawing on previous research which has established that the notions of mobility and professional work are heavily gendered-often in ways that disadvantage women (e.g., Uteng & Creswell, 2008; Schnurr, Zayts, Schroeder & Le Coyte-Hopkins, 2020)-we analyze the life story of a Turkish woman who immigrated to Germany in the early 1970s as part of the "Gastarbeiter" program which largely attracted men.

The "Gastarbeiter" program (or labor migration program), which was signed between Turkey and Germany in the early 1960s with the aim of addressing the shortage of labor in Germany resulting from World War II (Çelik, 2015, Thelen, 2017), led to the recruitment and-at least initially-temporary migration of around 750,000 Turkish laborers, most of whom were male, and largely uneducated, farmworkers (Yurdakul, 2016). Although the program was targeted at both men and women, the migration of women was generally frowned upon and viewed as highly problematic and immoral by large parts of Turkish society (Mattes, 2019). As a consequence, women who joined this scheme and moved to Germany to find work challenged hegemonic gendered expectations and practices, including the gender order (Connell, 1987) and its underlying ideologies.

According to Connell (1987, p. 168), the gender order is "a historically constructed pattern of power relations between men and women and definitions of masculinity and femininity" which inform all aspects of social life. For example, the gender order-and the male dominance that it propagates in many Western societies-is reflected in the roles that men and women are traditionally expected to take on, with men being the main breadwinner and women taking on caring responsibilities in the domestic domain (e.g., Kamp Dush, Yavorsky & Schoppe-Sullivan, 2018; Pocock, 2005; Wheatley, 2013). As a consequence of this gender order, the man's job and career rather than the women would influence decisions on professional mobility (Schnurr et al., 2020).

However, in this chapter, we focus on a woman who challenged the gender order and the gendered assumptions, practices, and expectations by migrating to Germany and leaving her family behind. By capturing her experiences of professional mobility and discrimination, this chapter gives a voice to the largely overlooked group of women who also joined the Gastarbeiter program in the 1970s. We thereby look beyond elite migrants who, with their social and political capital grants, live in "exclusive zones and corridors of connectivity" (Hannam, Sheller, & Urry, 2006) and who are often well-traveled, highly educated, and assumed to possess all the necessary competencies to make smooth transitions across borders (Faist, 2013). These constructions of an ideal "mobile subject" are not only upheld through political and media discourses but also through theorizations in the academic field (Endres, 2016, p. 118). By contrast, here we explore the gendering of mobility from the perspective of a non-elite migrant and critically discuss her experiences against the background of gender(ed) practices and ideologies in elite professional mobility outlined in previous research (e.g., Cohen et al., 2020).

11.2 GENDER AND (PROFESSIONAL) MOBILITY

Gender and mobility influence and shape each other in a myriad of ways (Hanson, 2010, p. 5), yet early scholarship in international migration has been criticized for its gender blindness (Pessar & Mahler, 2006). That is, up until the 1980s much of the research in the field did not explicitly focus on the relationship between gender and migration, resting on the idea that "it was men who migrated and women who remained behind or who moved as dependents of men" (Datta et al., 2009, p. 855). At the same time, across the social sciences, scholars were already starting to pay attention to female experiences of migration (e.g., Ets, 1970; Morokvasic, 1984). However, while migration studies were not far behind in starting to hone in on the significance of gender, much of this earlier research focused primarily on classifying and comparing the mobility patterns between the two sexes (Hanson, 2010, pp. 11–14).

More recently, however, research on mobility has started to address the interdependence of gender and mobility and how the two are mutually co-constructive across social, political, and historical contexts (e.g., Bonfanti, 2016; Cresswell & Uteng, 2016; Donato, Gabaccia, Holdaway, Manalansan & Pessar, 2018; Pessar & Mahler, 2006; Porter, 2011). Drawing on postcolonial, feminist, and social constructionist thinking (e.g., Appadurai, 2005; Butler, 2011; Kaplan, 2000), recent mobility research has begun to account for immobile infrastructures, social exclusion and fixity, as well as the "meanings given to mobility through representation" (Cresswell, 2006, p. 4)-all of which traditionally disadvantage women. For example, since mobility is often equated with status and power, it is a resource that is not equally accessible to all (Skeggs, 2004, p. 49); and since the public sphere in(to) which mobility takes place is traditionally associated with masculinity (e.g., Creswell, 1999), women who (attempt to) move are often faced with and excluded by a range of rigid "gendered expectations about who moves, how they move and where they move" (Cresswell & Uteng, 2016, p. 5).

Moreover, a large body of literature on gender and mobility focuses on privileged women, often in the field of academia. For example, Cohen et al. (2020) explore the gendering of home and childcare expectations and the impact of this on academic mobility decisions. While their findings demonstrate that women's engagement in academic mobility is largely disturbed and fragmented through heteronormative discourses, some fathers in their study are also shown to resist these discourses, articulating "emotional strain associated with academic mobility" (p. 149). Similar observations were made by Gray, Ciolfi & Pinatti de Carvalho's (2020) study on mobile knowledge workers in academia, digital creative work, and technology management. The authors demonstrate how gendered expectations about childcare can contribute to devaluing the place of home as a workplace and contribute to constructing a mother's digital mobility as insufficient in demonstrating her commitment to work (p. 68).

When it comes to the experiences of women from less privileged socio-economic and social-cultural backgrounds, research has mostly focused on fields of domestic work (Moya, 2007; Ladegaard, 2017), childcare (Colen, 1995), and sex work (Peano, 2012). Much of the existing research has been criticized for representing female labor migrants as victims (Kambori, 2008). However, within this field of research on gendered labor migration, there has been a shift to examining the roles of women as political subjects with influence on the social and economic fields, and the reproduction and challenging of cultural norms in their home and host countries (e.g., Coles, Gray & Momsen, 2015; Floya Anthias & Gabriella Lazaridis, 2000; Kambori, 2008).

Furthermore, almost two decades ago, Cresswell (2006) argued that in accounts of mobility the issue of meaning is largely absent, making it hard to draw out the interconnection between physical movement, meaning, and embodiments that constitute mobility (p. 7). While some advances have been made in this direction (e.g., Doughty & Murray, 2014; Endres, Manderscheid, & Mincke, 2016; Frello, 2008; Porter, 2011), contributions from the field of sociolinguistics have been relatively small, especially studies focusing on both gender and mobility (e.g., Baynham, 2005; De Fina & King, 2011; Schnurr et al., 2020).

11.3 METHODOLOGY, DATA, AND ANALYTICAL FRAMEWORK

Firmly located within the "new mobilities paradigm" (Sheller & Urry, 2006), we conceptualize mobility not simply as physical movement, but rather acknowledge that it involves "a set of highly meaningful social practices that make up social, cultural, and political life" (Adey et al., 2014, p. 3). One of these meaningful social practices that interact with and are mutually constitutive of mobility is gender-which is the focus of this chapter.

This chapter draws on three in-depth semi-structured interviews conducted with a non-elite migrant-who we have given the pseudonym Sabiha-and over 50 WhatsApp voice messages that were sent as a follow-up to the interviews. The focus of our analysis is stories of personal experience, some of which are co-constructed between Sabiha and her husband, Ayhan. Semi-structured interviews were chosen as the data collection method as they constitute a social practice in which meanings are situationally co-constructed among participants (Talmy, 2010, p. 129). Conceptualized as social events in their own right, these kinds of interviews allow the researcher to focus the discussion on the topics relevant to their study, while at the same time creating a space where participants are empowered to bring up issues relevant to them (Brinkmann, 2013, p. 27), for example by elaborating, transforming, and shaping specific aspects of their accounts (Holstein & Gubrium, 2011, p. 3).

11.3.1 OUR PARTICIPANTS

Sabiha was 35 years old when she applied for and was accepted to take part in the "Gastarbeiter" program in the early 1970s. She had four children between the ages of two and 17. One year after she left for Germany, her husband Ayhan brought their second youngest daughter to Germany, who was 11 years old at that time. Ayhan returned to Turkey soon afterwards to take care of the rest of their children in Turkey. Four years later, in 1977, their second oldest son was sent to Germany on his own to join his mother and sister upon a reunion request that Sabiha applied for in Germany. Eventually, seven years after Sabiha's departure to Germany, Ayhan joined the rest of the family in Germany with their youngest son to stay permanently. Their oldest daughter decided to stay in Turkey and got married soon after.

Sabiha & Ayhan were born and grew up in rural North-East Turkey in a city by the Black Sea. When they heard that their neighbors had applied for and been accepted to move to Austria as guest workers, they decided to apply as well. In the early 1970s, Germany was actively recruiting. They both applied together-Sabiha as a tailor and Ayhan as a glassmaker. But while Ayhan was rejected because he was illiterate, Sabiha's application was successful. However, although Sabiha applied to go to Germany as a tailor, she was not allowed to join the program in this capacity, as she did not meet the requirement of having worked with a motorized tailoring machine for a minimum of 15 years. As a result, she was allocated to a cleaning company in Northern Germany where she would spend more than 40 years as cleaning staff before retiring and moving back to Turkey with her husband. After Ayhan moved to Germany to join his family, he worked for the same company as his wife until his retirement. To date, three of their children still live in the same place where Sabiha began her life as a "Gastarbeiter," and most of their grandchildren live nearby.

Using discourse analysis and conceptualizing narratives as social practice (e.g., Clifton, Schnurr & Van De Mieroop, 2019), our analysis identifies and describes some of the discursive processes through which our participants make gender relevant by orienting to gender stereotypes and gendered expectations, which they often challenge and reject.

11.4 ANALYSIS

We have chosen two stories that occurred in one of the face-to-face interviews and one story that was told in a WhatsApp voice message to illustrate some of the ways in which participants make gender relevant in the context of professional mobility-thereby often challenging the gender order and traditional expectations about the roles of men and women in Turkey in the 1970s.

11.4.1 MAKING GENDER RELEVANT IN THE CONTEXT OF PROFESSIONAL MOBILITY

Throughout the interviews, Sabiha repeatedly makes gender relevant and more or less explicitly compares and evaluates her own behavior (and that of her husband) in relation to what she describes as expected and appropriate behavior for men and women at the time when she moved to Germany as part of the "Gastarbeiter program" described above.

Example 1

Context: At this point in the interview, Sabiha was asked how she felt before moving to Germany all by herself without her family.

Millet [kocamın] yerine benim gideceğimi duyunca
1 *When people heard I was going instead of [my husband]*
herkes şaşırdı ve bize karşı ayrımcılık yaptılar.
2 *everyone was shocked and discriminated against us.*
Giderken ben kendi babama haber vermedim ki benim babam
3 *I did not tell my own father when I left because my father*
öyle yerlere bizi göndermez.
4 *would not send us to places like that.*
Okumuş kafalı insan
5 *[He is] an educated wise person (.)*
öyle şeye razı olmaz babam, rahmetlik.
6 *he would not agree to this kind of thing, God rest his soul.*
Bizim adetimizde bir genç kadın
7 *For our customs a young woman*
kocasız Almanya'ya gitmek (.)
8 *going to Germany without a husband (.)*
çok ayıp gelirdi bizim millete.

9 *it was considered as a big shame for our people.*
Bir genç kadına yakışmazdı.
10 *It was beneath a young woman's dignity.*

In this excerpt, Sabiha explicitly orients to gendered expectations and practices, thereby making gender relevant in the context of professional mobility. Recounting the discrimination that she and her husband experienced and using the strong and derogatory terms and phrases "shocked" (line 2), "big shame" (line 9), and "beneath a young woman's dignity" (line 10), she portrays her move as problematic and against societal expectations and norms. This effect is further strengthened through positioning herself (and her husband) in opposition to the relatively generic and broad groups of "people" (line 1) and "everyone" (line 2). Through these discursive strategies, the exceptionality and unconventionality of Sabiha's move is emphasized, and the gender order (in the form of expected, normative, and appropriate behavior for women at this point in time) is oriented to.

This positioning against others (and the gender order) is further reflected in Sabiha's use of the first-person plural pronoun "us." This collective "us" is here and elsewhere during the interview used to refer to the storyteller and her husband, and often occurs in combination with the first-person singular "I." While at the beginning of the excerpt, Sabiha explains how her decisions and actions (as reflected in her use of singular "I") impacted both her and her husband (as reflected in her use of the collective "us"), a layer of additional meaning is added when she refers to "our customs" and "our people" (lines 7 and 9). Using the inclusive pronoun "our" (rather than the exclusive and distancing "their"), she positions herself as part of this collective and as sharing (at least some of the) customs and ideologies about the expected and appropriate behavior of men and women. Thus, although this story recounts Sabiha's experience as a mobile woman in Turkey in the 1970s, it at the same time also makes some universality claims, for example when she repeatedly refers to herself as "a young woman" (lines 7 and 10). Through this labeling, she distances herself from the protagonist of her story and transforms this story from a personal experience to a more general story.

Another aspect in which gender is made relevant in this excerpt is by referring to the patriarchal structures that characterized Turkey in the 1970s, in which men had the authority to make decisions for the family (Sati, 2021). These patriarchal structures are shown, for example, by the exclusively male reference points in Sabiha's story. While she mentions explicitly her "father" (line 3) and her "husband" (line 6), her mother, female relatives, friends, and other reference persons remain noticeably absent in her story. Moreover, her father is described very positively as "educated and wise" (line 5) and agentive, while she portrays herself-and by reference young women in general-as innocent, naive, and reliant on a husband (lines 7 and 8). This reliance on a husband is particularly relevant for mobility as it seems to be a crucial factor in determining whether an act of mobility is judged negatively as "a big shame" and "beneath a young woman's dignity" (lines 9 and 10). The cultural, historical, and geographical context is relevant in understanding this quote, of course. In the 1970s in Turkey, particularly in the rural areas in the North-East, women had a lower position in terms of privilege and agency (Sati, 2021). Although Turkey was officially a secular country, Islam played an important role in society and in shaping cultural practices and ideologies. In this context, women were not traditionally involved in the decision-making processes in the family but were expected to follow and adhere to decisions that were rather taken for them (Baumgartner-Karabak & Landesberger, 1978; Rita, 2011).

Thus, although Sabiha makes gender relevant in this excerpt, she does not challenge the gender order and its underlying ideologies as such. Rather, she portrays herself as being aware of (and regretting) the fact that her move to Germany would go against societal norms and expectations, which she seems to take for granted and hence naturalizes in this excerpt. However, at other points during the interviews, Sabiha-often relatively explicitly-challenges the gender order.

11.4.2 CHALLENGING THE GENDER ORDER

We have chosen two examples to illustrate how, in and through her stories of personal experience, Sabiha sometimes challenges the gender order and underlying gender ideologies.

Example 2

Context: At this point in the interview, we asked Sabiha about the selection process that she underwent before her move to Germany. She explains how she and Ayhan went to the recruitment center in Istanbul.

Bak Yesim bide içeriye girdik e eben olduk muayenne olduk,
1 Look Yesim we went in, were controlled, and checked out.
Ben kazandım (.) kazandım
2 I won ((sad tone of voice and slow pace of speaking)) I won

ağlayarak dişarı çıktım ama nasıl ağlıyorum böyle hüngür hüngür
3 went outside crying but THE WAY I am crying like "hüngür hüngür"[1]
yaşlarım önüme dökülüyor. [Kocam] kızıyor
4 my tears drop down in front of me. [My husband] is angry
"ağlama kızım, kazandın!" Orda bir (.) köfteciye girdik,
5 "don't cry my girl you WON!" We went (.) into a meatball shop,
nasil ben böyle ağlıyorum ağlıyorum(.)
6 how I am crying and crying (.)
Cem'de yanımızda (.)
7 Cem[2] is also with us (.)
ehh "teyzeciğim kazanamadın da ağlıyorsun galiba (.)
8 ehh "my aunt[3] you are probably crying because you didn't win (.)
NIYE! Ağlıyorsun (.) boşver bidahaki sefer kazanırsın (.)
9 WHY are you crying? ((consolidating tone of voice)) (.) forget about it
10 (.) you will win next time"
[kocam]'da dediki yok oğlum yok, kazandıda ağliyor (.)
11 and [my husband] said "no my son no, she is crying because she won (.)
'Çocuklarımdan, kocamdan nasıl ayrılıp gitcem' diye ağlıyor (.)
12 'How can I be separated from my children, my husband?'
13 ((imitating Sabiha in this reported speech)) that's why she is crying" (.) ((she takes a deep breath))
Çocuk dediki "Aman teyzse dedi e eben ne istiyorsun?
14 The boy ((meatball shop owner)) then said "Oh aunt what else do you want?
Sen dünyanın ne iyi insanisinki (.)
15 You are the world's most amazing person (.)
çocukların hayatını kurtarmaya taa:: dünyanın
16 to rescue the life of your children you are going the:re
diğer ucuna gidiyorsun (.)insan ağlarmı?
17 to the other side of the world. Why would you cry?
Valla helal olsun senin gibi bir Anneye bir aileye (.)
18 Honestly bless you (.) a mother, a family like you (.)
ben (.) e eben yani senden bir Annem olarak iftihar duydum
19 I ((deep breath)) I am proud of you as my [a] mother
+ B- Bu ne biçim Annelik kazandın Almanyaya gidiyorsunn diye

---

[1] Translated as "crying her heart out"

[2] Cem is her youngest son. Pseudonyms are used for interviewees as well all names they mentioned in their narratives.

[3] This term is used in Turkey to address female stranger women who are older.

20 + Wh- WHAT kind of motherhood is this? You won, and
21 you cry because you are going to Germany
çocuklarından ayrıldın diye ağlıyorsun (.)
22 because you are separated from your children" ((deep breath))
Sana helal! Olsun, bana ilham veriyorsun (.)
23 God bless! You. You inspire me (.)
gittiğin yerde Allah sana rahatlık versin (.) huzur versin "
24 Wherever you go may God give you peace (.) give you happiness."

This example is a very good illustration of the dilemma that many women who move and leave their families behind experience (e.g., Abrego, 2014; Parreñas, 2001; Veazey, 2022). Although there is a lot to be said about this excerpt, we focus here primarily on how in and through their stories our participants make gender relevant by orienting to gender stereotypes and gendered expectations, which they often challenge and reject.

The story starts with a very brief introduction ("we went in, were controlled, and checked out") which is closely followed by the climax, i.e., the result of the examination, namely "I won" (line 1). However, the way in which this achievement is recounted (as reflected, for example, in the short sentence, the absence of any adjectives and evaluative expressions, as well as Sabiha's sad and slow way of speaking) portrays this win not as a cause for celebration but rather as a tragedy. This sentiment continues throughout almost the entire story (see e.g., Sabiha's frequent use of the verb "crying" (lines 3, 5, 6, 8, 9, 11, 13, 17, and 21), tears (line 4), and the metaphorical expression "crying my heart out" (line 3)). Even her husband's reported attempt to console her (lines 4 and 5) by reinterpreting the experience as a win (e.g., the emphasis on "WON") remains unsuccessful.

In line 5, the story takes a turn as Sabiha and her husband reportedly went "into a meatball shop" in which they engage in an interaction with the shop owner. In the reported dialogue that follows (line 5ff) between the male shop owner and Sabiha's husband, these men are given a voice and a key role in meaning-making as their interaction explains to the listener (the first author) the dilemma that the storyteller is facing, namely having to leave her family behind when moving to Germany. Interestingly, in line 12, Sabiha incorporates her own voice, which is followed by an explanatory summary provided by her husband in reported speech ("that's why she's crying" (line 13)).

This explanation and complicating action of the story is followed by the resolution (Labov & Waletzky, 1966) which is presented by the meatball shop owner who Sabiha refers to as "the boy" (line 14). Using the affectionate address term “aunt” (line 14)-which is traditionally used to address older women-he asks several rhetorical questions (lines 14, 17, and 20) which are interwoven with compliments (e.g., he describes Sabiha as “the world’s most amazing person” (line 15)) and expressions of admiration and support (e.g., “I am proud of you” and “bless you” (lines 19, 18, and 23)).

By describing the situation and Sabiha’s achievements in such positive terms, he produces a counter-narrative (Bamberg & Andrews, 2004) emphasizing the positive aspects of her upcoming move while downplaying the negative. In doing this, he portrays Sabiha as a hero and perhaps even a saint who is selflessly embarking on the move to “rescue the life of your children” (line 16). Thus, while he explicitly uses the identity category “mother”-even metaphorically calling her “my mother” (line 19)-he, at least partly, challenges traditional views of a mother as someone who needs to physically be with her children and family. This challenge becomes particularly obvious when he asks: “what kind of motherhood is this?” (line 20). In what follows, he then constructs an alternative version of a good mother as someone who “won” (line 20) and who “inspires” him (line 23), which he puts in opposition to the traditional mother image which he rejects. This emphasis on winning and the positive accomplishment this entails could also be understood as a challenging of the prevailing and deep-rooted patriarchal structures and unequal power relations that characterized Turkish society in the 1970s (Kambori, 2008). The story ends with the shop owner giving Sabiha his blessings for the move (line 24).

Unlike in example 1, Sabiha does not explicitly make gender relevant in this excerpt. Rather, this story rests on the idea that women should not leave their families behind, which supports the gender order and its underlying ideological assumptions about the roles of men and women and the idea that women “belong” in the domestic domain and men in the public (Cresswell, 1999). However, in her story, Sabiha challenges these gendered assumptions and ideologies-especially when questioning traditional roles of mothers and the concept of motherhood itself (lines 14–24). It is interesting to note that this challenging take place through the reported speech of the shop owner-a third party and (male!) outsider to Sabiha’s family. This observation contrasts the findings of other studies (e.g., Schnurr et al, 2016) which reported that many women who moved orient to traditional gender norms and often uphold the gender order. We look at one more example-a story told collaboratively by Sabiha and Ayhan in which they challenge societal expectations towards mobility and migration in the context of traditional gender roles and the gender order in Turkey in the 1970s. This excerpt, which follows shortly after example 1, zooms in on the derogatory experiences that Ayhan was facing after Sabiha had left for Germany.

Example 3

Context: This story was told by Sabiha right after she talked about the issues of discrimination that she and her husband faced due to the fact that she left for Germany instead of Ayhan (example 1).

Sabiha: Kocam çok azarlar çekti kızım. Ama ne fayda
1 [My husband] had to listen to many demeaning words
2 my child{f}, but what can you do
he deyip geçcek kızım
3 he has to get over his pride my child
(.) gurur murur yapamaz (.) başka caremız yoktu.
4 (.) he can't have pride (.) we had no other choice.
Çocuklarımız aç. Biz aç. Fakirlikten MECBUR kaldık kizim
5 Our children starve. We starve. We were FORCED due to
6 famine my child{f}
[...]
"Kötü yolla gircek" diyenler vardı. "Orospu olcak"
7 "She will go down the bad route" some said.
8 "She will become a whore"
"Nasıl bir kadın ailesini, çocuklarını geride bırakır"?
9 "What kind of woman would leave her family; her kids behind?"
"Nasıl bir adam eşini tek başına bırakır,
10 "What kind of man would leave his wife alone,
tek başına gavur ülkesine gönderir?"
11 sent her all by herself to a "gavur country[4]"
Korkuyorduk yavrum (.) Ama ben yinede gittim.
12 We were scared my child. I still went (.)
Çocuklarım için gittim. Beyim kabul etti.
13 I went for my children. My husband accepted.
Sağolsun çoluğa çocuğa baktı, yaptı pişirdi kurtardı.
14 Thankfully he took care of the children, he did and
15 cooked and rescued ((in this context used to express household
16 accomplishments/chores))
[...]
Kimse gitmemi istemedi, ayıptı. Ama kocam dediki:

---

[4] "Gavur" is a derogatory term addressing everything/anyone that is not Muslim

17 No one wanted me to go, it was shameful. But my husband said:
"Hanım, benim sana güvenim sonsuz!
18 "Wife, my trust towards you is endless.
Biliyorumki sana hiç birşey olmayacak."
19 I know nothing will happen to you.
Ayhan: Dedimki başına bişey GELSE BILE, sen benim bir parçamsın.
20 I said EVEN IF something would happen to you, you are a part of me.
Ne olursa olsun sen benim kabulumsun. Bunu dedim.
21 I accept you no matter what. But I trust you and I know nothing will
22 happen. That's what I said.

When describing the negative judgment and abuse that Ayhan had to endure after Sabiha's move to Germany, she initially uses the third person singular pronouns "he" and "his" (lines 3 and 4) before making it clear that the decision that led to these experiences was a joint one and was borne out of necessity ("we had no other choice" (line 4) and "we were FORCED" (line 3)). Sabiha's short and factual sentences (without any adjectives) contribute to portraying the situation they found themselves in as very dire, leaving Sabiha with no other options but to move to Germany (e.g., the emphasis on "FORCED" in line 5). After the short introduction and background to the story, Sabiha begins to quote some of the discriminatory comments she and Ayhan received (line 7ff). Using reported speech and referring to herself in the third person singular ("she" and "her") makes this part of the story particularly lively and renders the criticisms implied in the comments stronger. The reported speech largely takes the form of predictions about Sabiha's future (e.g., "she will go down the bad route" (line 7)) and rhetorical questions (e.g., "What kind of man would leave his wife alone?" (line 10)). Through these voices that she assigns to "some" unspecified people (line 8), Sabiha is portrayed negatively as "a whore," a bad mother, and a bad wife. Equally, Ayhan is portrayed as a bad husband for allowing (and supporting!) his wife to move.

These subjection positions to which Sabiha refers closely reflect and orient traditional roles available to women. Moreover, using rhetorical questions and formulating these questions about men and women in general terms (rather than making them specifically about Sabiha and Ayhan) creates associations with the gender order and mobilizes expectations and norms of what was considered acceptable for men and women. According to the gender order of Turkey in the 1970s, women were expected to be good wives and mothers by staying at home, looking after their children, and obeying their husbands, while men had the authority and control in their family and were expected to take care of their financial and material needs (Cindoglu & Toktas, 2002). Sabiha's move and Ayhan's support pose challenges to these assumptions and the underlying power structures and ideologies that informed this gender order. They also challenge the close link between mobility and migration of a woman and experiences of shame and a loss of dignity as established at the beginning of the story (lines 1–4). In particular, by describing her move as an indisputable necessity to save her children's lives (lines 5–6), she abrogates and overrides the applicability of the gender order and its underlying ideologies in this specific context.

These challenges to the gender order are also, to some extent, reflected in the noticeable shift that takes place throughout the story in terms of agency for the decision to move. Initially, this decision is portrayed as joint (as reflected, for example, in Sabiha's choice of pronouns as described above), but in line 13 these changes: Sabiha shifts her perspective and now focuses on her actions, assigning herself agency and decision-making power as reflected in her use of the first-person singular pronoun "I" (e.g., "I still went (.) I went for my children" (lines 12 and 13)). The adverb "still" implies a conscious decision which is set in opposition to societal expectations and norms, and while she takes ownership of the decision to move, she assigns Ayhan a passive role, which he "accepted" (line 14) together with the implications this would have for his own role which changed from being the breadwinner to the caregiver and household organizer (lines 14–16).

However, while Sabiha challenges the gender order here, in other parts of this story she seems to accept and reinforce it. For example, when she describes her husband as accepting her move and supporting it, she makes it clear that she would not have been able to undertake the move if he had withheld his approval and support. At this point in the story, Ayhan-who up to this point remained rather quiet-joins the interview and clarifies his role. He supports and ratifies Sabiha's story and further emphasizes how much he trusted her (lines 20). This interplay between both challenging and reinforcing the gender order is also shown at other points throughout the interviews. For example, when talking about her experiences of working in Germany she commented that "I worked hard like a man (…)" thereby acknowledging that (physical) labor is traditionally a male domain, which she entered out of necessity rather than because of a belief in gender equality. Like the domestic workers who participated in Kambori's (2008) study, Sabiha thereby-at least partly-redefined and challenged the gender norms that associate paid physical labor in the public sphere with male roles.

Thus, like in the previous example, this challenging of the gender order remains on the personal level, and rather than arguing that the gender order and its underlying ideologies are limiting, prohibitive, and discriminatory against women more broadly (who may equally well take on the role of breadwinners as Sabiha's stories show), the story and its implications are presented as applying to this specific case without making any claims for wider applicability or relevance. In other words, it remains a story of personal experience and any wider implications are left to be drawn out by the audience but are not made explicit by the storyteller.

11.5 DISCUSSION AND CONCLUSION

It was the aim of this chapter to explore the gendering of professional mobility by focusing on the reported experiences of a non-elite migrant, thereby giving a voice to this often-overlooked group of women. By unpacking the discursive processes through which the notion of mobility and the activity of moving are gendered in and through these stories, we have provided insights into the complex ways in which gender is produced, reproduced, and sometimes naturalized (Example 1) or challenged (Examples 2 and 3) in the increasingly important context of professional mobility.

Our analysis of three stories told by Sabiha, a woman who migrated from Turkey to Germany as part of the Gastarbeiter program in the 1970s, illustrates that when recounting her experiences of mobility and migration, she often makes gender relevant-sometimes reproducing and naturalizing gendered expectations, roles, and stereotypes, and sometimes challenging them and the gender order that informs them. This is achieved, for example, by using someone else's voice, as in Example 2, where Sabiha uses the male meatball shop owner to challenge traditional expectations associated with the mother role (and the concept of motherhood) and to question the prevailing and deep-rooted patriarchal structures and unequal power relations of Turkey in the 1970s. Referring to motherhood and the mother role in this and other stories is particularly noteworthy as previous research has established that negative perceptions of women's mobility are often closely associated with women leaving their families behind and being unable to perform the responsibilities and duties associated with traditional understandings of the roles of mother (e.g., Abrego, 2014; Parreñas, 2001; Williams Veazey, 2022) and wife (e.g., Platt, 2018; Silvey, 2000), which are heavily based on "idealized gender norms which posit a male breadwinner and a female housewife" (Silvey, 2000, p. 152).

However, as we have shown, many of Sabiha's stories that challenge the gender order do not explicitly question or criticize the underlying gender ideologies and assumptions that inform it. Rather, like the stories told by other non-privileged women about their migration experience captured in previous research (e.g., Ladegaard 2017; Platt 2018), Sabiha portrays her move as problematic and violating societal expectations and norms (see also Silvey, 2000; Williams, 2008). She (together with her husband, with whom she co-tells some of the stories) repeatedly makes it clear that her move was triggered by despair and material necessity—she simply had "no other choice" (as she repeatedly emphasizes in Example 3)—rather than ideological reasons. She thus justifies her move in terms of meeting the needs of her husband and children or the family more generally; and she emphasizes her husband's support and approval of her move. This is in line with previous research which also found that mobile women often seek permission from their husbands before moving, thereby explicitly orienting and adhering to gendered expectations and norms which set up men as the primary decision-makers in the family (e.g., Silvey, 2006; Platt, 2018).

Thus, unlike the Turkish women researched by Cindoglu & Toktas (2002, p. 16) who "were seeking a better future through the critique of the gendered division of labor in the family"-according to which the husband was the main breadwinner and the wife the sole caregiver and household worker-Sabiha does not explicitly engage in such a critique. Nor does she portray her movement and her new economic role as a strategy to gain more social and "economic independence" from her husband as previous research has observed (e.g., Cindoglu & Toktas 2002, p. 7; Silvey, 2000; Silvey, 2006). Rather, Sabiha's stories partly challenge and partly reinforce the gender order in complex ways, as we have demonstrated in our analysis above. It is precisely this apparent contradiction that makes her stories such an interesting and relevant case study.

As previous research has established (e.g., Schnurr 2022), stories are a powerful tool to challenge and subvert existing gender inequalities, and we hope that future research will pay more attention to the complexities with which this is achieved by exploring the multi-layered ways in which the storytellers orient to the underlying gender order-sometimes reinforcing and sometimes challenging it. We also hope that this research illustrates the importance of giving a voice to those largely overlooked professional, non-elite migrants who more than a decade ago were trailblazers who subverted the gender order. Their stories-although often framed as narratives of personal experiences-transcend the personal level and effectively demonstrate how limiting, prohibitive, and discriminatory the gender order and its underlying ideologies are. These stories are thus important resources for future generations as they ultimately contribute to transforming the gendered realities of mobile women.

TRANSCRIPTION CONVENTIONS

[laughs]	Paralinguistic features in square brackets
(.)	Short pause (under 1 s)
+	Long pause (3 to 5 s)
.../...\.../...\\	Simultaneous speech
((snips fingers))	Researcher's comment
(hello)	Transcriber's best guess at unclear utterance
VERY	Capitals indicate emphatic stress
[...]	Section of transcript omitted
-	Cut off sentences

KEYWORDS

- **gender**
- **labor migration program**
- **methodology**
- **mobilities paradigm**
- **mobility**
- **non-elite immigrant**
- **professional mobility**

REFERENCES

Abrego, L. J. (2014). *Sacrificing Families: Navigating Laws, Labor, and Love Across Borders*. Stanford, CA: Stanford University Press.

Adey, P., Bissell, D., Hannam, K., Merriman, P., & Sheller, M. (2014). Introduction. In P. Adey, D. Bissell, K. Hannam, P. Merriman, & M. Sheller (Eds.), *The Routledge Handbook of Mobilities* (pp. 1–20). London: Routledge.

Andrijasevic, R. (2003). The difference borders make: (Il)legality, migration and trafficking in Italy among Eastern European women in prostitution. In S. Ahmed, C. Castaneda, A. Fortier, & M. Sheller (Eds.), *Uprooting's/Regrinding's: Questions of Home and Migration* (pp. 251–272). Oxford: Berg.

Appadurai, A. (2005). *Modernity at Large: Cultural Dimensions of Globalization* (7th ed.). Volume 1 of Public Worlds. Minneapolis: University of Minnesota Press.

Augustin, L. M. (2003). Forget victimization: Granting agency to migrants. *Development, 46*(3), 30–36. https://doi.org/10.1177/10116370030463005.

Bamberg, M. (1997). Positioning between structure and performance. *Journal of Narrative and Life History, 7*(1–4), 335–342.

Baumgartner-Karabak, & Landesberger, G. (1978). *Die verkauften Bräute: Türkische Frauen zwischen Kreuzberg und Anatolien* (Vol. 4268). Rowohlt.

Baynham, M. (2005). Network and agency in the migration stories of Moroccan women. In M. Baynham & A. De Fina (Eds.), *Dislocations/Relocations: Narratives of Displacement* (pp. 15–35). Manchester: St Jerome.

Baynham, M. (2006). Performing self, family and community in Moroccan narratives of migration and settlement. In A. De Fina, D. Schiffrin, & M. Bamberg (Eds.), *Discourse and Identity* (pp. 376–397). Cambridge: Cambridge University Press.

Blackstone, A. (2003). *Gender Roles and Society* (p. 2). https://digitalcommons.library.umaine.edu/cgi/viewcontent.cgi?article=1000&context=soc_facpub (accessed on 19 June 2024).

Bonfanti, S. (2016). Dislocating Punjabiyat: Gendered mobilities among Indian diasporas in Italy. In M. Gutekunst, A. Hackl, S. Leoncini, J. S. Schwarz, & I. Götz (Eds.), *Bounded Mobilities: Ethnographic Perspectives on Social Hierarchies and global Inequalities* (pp. 183–206). Bielefeld: transcript Verlag.

Butler, J. (2011). *Bodies That Matter*. On the Discursive Limits of Sex. London: Routledge.

CHAPTER 12

INEQUALITY IN THE LAND OF OPPORTUNITY: A CASE STUDY ON THE GENDER DIFFERENCES IN PURSUING THE AMERICAN DREAM FOR INDIAN IMMIGRANTS

ASHIKA SRIVASTAVA

Georgia Institute of Technology, Georgia

ABSTRACT

This chapter delves into the gendered dimensions of the American Dream among Indian immigrants in the U.S., examining how traditional gender roles shape their aspirations and experiences. Through a case study involving semi-structured interviews with an Indian immigrant couple residing in the U.S. for nearly two decades, the chapter reveals how gender influences the pursuit of the American Dream. The findings show that while Raj, the male participant, navigates the American Dream primarily through career advancement and financial success, Simran, the female participant, aligns her aspirations with traditional familial responsibilities. This divergence emphasizes the impact of gender norms on the fulfillment of the American Dream, demonstrating that gender significantly impacts how Indian immigrants experience and strive for success in their adopted homeland.

12.1 INTRODUCTION

This chapter analyzes the role of gender on Indian immigrants' perspectives on what is known in the United States as the "American Dream" (Churchwell,

Subverting Social Inequalities: Gender as a Social Reality.
Akanksha Srivastava, Disha Maheshwari, Chitra Krishnan (Eds.)

2022). While mainly associated with wealth and success, the American Dream is said to be different for each person who chooses to pursue it. However, this chapter intends to look more closely at the underlying differences in what this pursuit entails when gender roles and norms come into play specifically for Indian immigrants. Through a series of in-depth semi-structured interviews, this research aims to draw upon the real-life experiences of an Indian couple that immigrated to the United States and has lived there for almost 20 years.

The concept of the American Dream was first created by James Truslow Adams, a historian, in 1931 during the Great Depression period in the United States (Diamond, 2018). During this period of economic, social, and political suffering (Romer, 2003), Adams referred to the American Dream as attaining more of a moral success rather than a material success. For him, it was a "dream of social order" that promoted democracy and equality in a nation (Churchwell, 2022). He described it to be an opportunity given to all to live a better life, where "better" was not always correlated with greater wealth or material possessions. No single person was entitled or guaranteed the American Dream (Damon, n.d.). It was something one had to achieve or earn on account of their own merit and accomplishments.

This definition of the American Dream was further supported by prominent figures such as Dr. Martin Luther King Jr. and Walter Lippmann, author of the 1914 book Drift and Mastery, until it evolved to its current definition. Today, the American Dream is known as a vision for a better quality of life regardless of one's social class or position (Wolak & Peterson, 2020). Immigrants from all parts of the world come to settle in America in hopes of achieving this American Dream and enjoying an improved standard of living. In their eyes, the American Dream symbolizes the opportunity and prosperity that can be achieved by any hardworking individual.

12.2 INDIAN IMMIGRANTS AND THE AMERICAN DREAM

"Indian immigrants make up about 6% of the U.S. foreign-born population and are the third-largest immigrant group in the U.S., after immigrants from Mexico" (Hanna & Batalova, 2022). Indian immigration goes back to the 19th century where immigrants mainly lived on the West Coast and worked in the agriculture and railroad industries. The population size fluctuated with the passing of several quotas and bans on the number of Indian immigrants allowed to enter the United States. Eventually, the Immigration and Nationality Act of 1965 (Chin & Rose Cuison Villazor, 2015) allowed for non-European immigrants to enter the United States and developed work programs and visas for skilled immigrants, many of whom were of Indian origin. As a result, "from 1980 to 2019, the Indian immigrant population in the United States increased 13-fold" (Hanna & Batalova, 2022).

In terms of the current definition of the American Dream, Indian immigrants, for the most part, wished to pursue the American Dream to improve their standard of living and take advantage of the economic and social opportunities available in the United States (Hanna & Batalova, 2022). For many, it was a chance to provide themselves and their families with a better quality of life along with engaging in greater career-related and personal ventures.

Indian immigrants have greater incomes than those of U.S. natives and other foreign immigrants combined. In 2021, households headed by an Indian immigrant had a median annual income of $150,000, while other immigrant and native-led households had a median annual income of $70,000. Additionally, "in 2021, Indian immigrants were less likely to be in poverty than immigrants overall or those born in the U.S." (Hoffman & Batalova, 2022). Therefore, Indian immigrants are often recognized as one of the more successful immigrant groups living out their versions of the American Dream.

Two main characteristics of Indian immigrants were determined as crucial to their successful journeys: their emphasis on education and family. "82% of Indian American adults ages 25–55 is college educated, compared to 42% of Americans who have a degree, while 78% of Indian Americans ages 25–55 is married compared to 58% of Americans" (Jilani et al., 2021). Indian immigrants place great emphasis on education for themselves and their children, which translates to greater financial success in the future.

According to MassMutual's 2017 study conducted on the educational and financial priorities of Indian families living in America, "90% of Asian Indian parents rate a college education as important, and by the time a child has reached the age of ten, 79% of Asian Indian parents, more than any other ethnic group in the study, are saving for college" (MassMutual, 2017). These parents ensure that their children have access to all educational opportunities available without there being any sort of financial obstacles.

Additionally, Indian immigrants place a certain importance on preserving traditional family values. This includes the concepts of marriage, extended family, respecting one's elders, and traditional gender roles (Patel et al., 1996). Therefore, Indian immigrant families have very high family stability as "94% of Indian immigrants with children are stably married, compared to 66% of native-born Americans and 87% of native-born Indian Americans"

(Jilani et al., 2021). Having such strong familism-based core values creates a support system for each member of the family to pursue their own ambitions.

It can also serve as motivation for such ambitions as was discussed in the education aspect of Indian immigrant families. The driving force behind many Indian immigrants' pursuit of the American Dream is being able to support their family, whether immediate or extended back home. Marriage and Family Therapist Pooja Mamidanna puts it best: "You want to give back to your elders. You want to honor your family's name, and you take care of your elders. … It's not I vs. you. (It is a) collectivistic family dynamics that exists, it's we come together first. So, it's not even about putting yourself first. It's putting your family first" (Jilani et al., 2021).

12.3 TRADITIONAL GENDER ROLES AND THE AMERICAN DREAM

The term "gender" can be defined as "the meanings, values, and characteristics that people ascribe to different sexes" (Patel, 2021). Traditional gender roles originate from the societies in which they are established. It is the interactions between individuals within societies that create the foundation for how these gender roles define how different genders in a society are expected to act (Patel, 2021).

In the early 20th century, traditional gender roles heavily influenced the American Dream (Patel, 2021). Men were seen as the main providers, expected to build careers and ensure financial stability for their families. Women, on the other hand, were mostly expected to focus on managing the household and raising children. This division not only defined their roles but also shaped the idea of success in a way that favored men. Men's achievements were celebrated as the true measure of the American Dream, while women's contributions were often ignored or undervalued (Patel, 2021).

By the 1960s and 70s, feminist movements began challenging these traditional roles, pushing for a more inclusive view of the American Dream (Deshpande, 2018). They argued that success and opportunities should not be limited by gender. Although significant progress was made, the old gender roles still influence how people view success and fulfillment. The ongoing discussion about the American Dream continues to wrestle with these historical expectations and the push for greater equality (Deshpande, 2018).

For Indian immigrants emigrating to the U.S., traditional gender roles often carried over, especially those pertaining to women. "72% of the female migration in India can be attributed to marriage, with marriage migration being most prominent among women 25 years and younger" (Chatterjee & Desai, 2020). This can also be seen with women emigrating to foreign countries, like the U.S., as many of them are doing so as part of their marriage or in support of their spouses (Deshpande, 2018).

Therefore, the American Dream for Indian women is oftentimes related to being a support system for their spouses and ensuring a good environment for raising their families. This demonstrates a contrast from the original definition of the American Dream and what it represents for many of the Indian women incorporating the principle into their new lives. They are expected to have similar responsibilities and priorities when living in the U.S., so the concept of moving to America for greater opportunities or a "better life" is not always applied in the same sense as for men. Some women are not even given the chance to pursue these opportunities as they must abide by their respective gender roles. In contrast, the standard definition of the American Dream applies more for Indian men, according to traditional gender roles. Growing up, young men are taught to aim for a strong, stable career that can support their families in the future (Sivakumar & Manimekalai, 2021). As a result, they are more inclined to pursue the American Dream for the opportunities it claims to provide. Doing so will help them fulfill their role as the "man of the house."

In this chapter, the focus will be on a case study of an Indian immigrant couple living in the United States and the specific gender differences in the reasoning behind their quest for the American Dream.

12.4 METHODOLOGY

By definition, a semi-structured interview is "a qualitative data collection strategy in which the researcher asks informants a series of predetermined but open-ended questions." It mimics a discussion more than a serious interview, making it an optimal method of data collection from human participants who are sharing personal details and stories in a discussion-like manner (Mueller & Segal, n.d.; Nordgaard et al., n.d.). The first step in the process of conducting the study was to identify the primary couple on which the case study would be conducted. The couple had to have grown up and completed schooling in India and have lived in the U.S for at least 10 years. Also, both participants had to have been familiar with the idea of the

American Dream for them to be able to have a clear discussion on the matter and how it affected their lives.

The couple selected met the criteria listed and consented to participate. The male participant was of age 48 and held a bachelor's equivalent level of education, while the female participant was of age 44 and held a master's equivalent level of education. It is important to note that their specific ages were not participant criteria as the only criteria within this category was the ten-year minimum residence in the U.S. However, it was required that the participants have at least a bachelor's equivalent of education to be considered for the study. They were located in a suburb of metro-Atlanta in the state of Georgia, United States as it was more convenient for contact and relevant to the study's focus demographic.

Next, the semi-structured interviews were conducted over the video-conferencing platform Zoom. The topics for discussion were separated into three categories: personal reasons for pursuing the American Dream, financial reasons for pursuing the American Dream, and familial reasons for pursuing the American Dream. After the interviews were concluded, they were fully transcribed using the online transcription software Otter.ai in which recordings of the interviews, taken with permission, were uploaded. This software produced word-for-word transcriptions that were coded using a simple content analysis coding method (Columbia Public Health, 2019). Five nonconsecutive one-hour long interviews were conducted with the two participants together for a total of 300 minutes of interviews.

For the thematic analysis portion, the themes from the interviews were generated through initial categories with similar themes in the accounts of each member's experiences. This was done by coding the information from the interviews, categorizing ideas, removing irrelevant information (long pauses, small talk), and summarizing the main points of all the interviews. The central themes that could be observed from the narrative groupings were recorded and supported with quoted evidence.

12.5 RESULTS AND DISCUSSION

For the sake of anonymity, the female member of the couple is referred to as "Simran" and the male member as "Raj."

Through the semi-structured interview that was conducted, transcribed, and analyzed for common themes, three final main themes emerged to describe the Indian immigrants' experiences with and reasoning behind the American Dream. The themes were as follows:

1. Professional and career-related development
2. Personal and familial expectations
3. The idea of "America"

12.6 PROFESSIONAL AND CAREER-RELATED DEVELOPMENT

When comparing Raj and Simran's professional motives for emigrating and pursuing the American Dream, they both seemed to agree that the United States had better job prospects for them overall. Raj had a degree in computer engineering and wanted to work in a similar field, while Simran was more rooted in the field of education. However, the main reason for their shift to the U.S. was specifically Raj's new job.

"I had received an offer in the U.S., so [my family] said I should go. For us, going to the U.S. was a very big thing. Everyone wanted to go there because they knew that there were very good opportunities for advancement and good pay. So, we decided to go as well because we also wanted a good job to have a good life for us and our future kids" [Raj].

This was significantly different for Simran as she had been uncertain about her career prospects post-marriage. She was not familiar with the career opportunities in the new country she was moving to and considered shifting her focus to better support her husband.

"We were moving for Raj's job, so I was not thinking about my job. I was thinking that I have to go and support my husband, and I will move wherever he has to move because we are married. Maybe over there I will not even continue my job because of our family and the kids and all. So, this was not something I was thinking of at the time" [Simran].

Emphasis on family can be seen here as Simran contemplated leaving her job to help raise her family in the U.S. She eventually follows through with this decision.

"I had done my college in India, even my master's degree, but when we came to America, my new job became [taking] care of the house and the family. And that is something that I actually wanted to do. I wanted to come to America with my husband so we can have a nice family and give them all the things that we could not get in our childhood. This was important for me" [Simran].

Traditionally, the woman's role in a family is to support her husband and put her family first, and this can be seen in Simran's experience with moving to the U.S with Raj to further support her family. She stresses how this was not something she was forced to do, but rather was expected to do.

While both Raj and Simran were motivated to pursue the American Dream for career advancement opportunities, Raj's pursuit of the American Dream seems to be more conventionally career-focused compared to Simran.

"This job gave me better pay, connections, and reputation than what I had before in India. I would be able to do so many more things with my life, so I could not pass up on this wonderful opportunity. Looking back, I think I made the correct choice because I could have never imagined my life to be the way it is now" [Raj].

12.7 PERSONAL AND FAMILIAL EXPECTATIONS

On the personal side, differences between Raj and Simran were more clearly shown according to the traditional gender roles in India. Nearly two-thirds of Indians (64%) – including 61% of women – fully agree with the idea that a wife is always obligated to obey her husband (Mitchell, 2023). In this context, "Indians" refers to the ideologies of native-born Indians living on the subcontinent of India.

For Simran, the expectation was to join her husband in his decision to move due to this unspoken rule that women are expected to obey and rely on their spouses. Furthermore, 43% of Indians believe that men should be the primary earners (Mitchell, 2023). Therefore, Raj had this personal expectation that he was the family's assumed breadwinner, furthering his motives for choosing to pursue the American Dream by moving to the U.S.

"After marriage, there was this kind of unspoken understanding that I would be going to the U.S. with my husband to start a new life. I was his wife, so there were never any questions asked about how it would affect me and my life since that did not really matter. It was not about my life anymore, but more about our life together and how I could best support that" [Simran].

Simran explicitly saying, "It was not about my life anymore, but more about our life together," implies that she had put her individual priorities on hold to prioritize her husband and her family, conforming to the traditional gender role of an Indian woman. Raj too had taken on his respective gender role when assuming the breadwinner position.

"My wife actually had more education than me and could have gotten some good job prospects in the U.S as well. But it was our family's expectation that I should be the one to earn for the family, and I decided that a better job in the U.S was the best way to do that" [Raj].

In this case, Simran is given less of an individual choice on whether she should choose to pursue the American Dream, while Raj finds the American Dream as a solution to fulfill the expectation placed on him as the family's sole provider.

12.8 THE IDEA OF "AMERICA"

The final theme that emerged was marginally distinct from the others in that it pertained to Raj and Simran's perceptions of the U.S. as a country and how that affected their decision to emigrate there. Nearly 6 in 10 Indians have a positive view of American people (Mitchell, 2023), and both Raj and Simran discussed the impact of their views of America on their respective gender roles. Once again, Raj had more of a career-based view of the U.S. in that he saw it as a place of intense growth, especially within his field of work.

"Microsoft, Google, Facebook, and all these big companies had their headquarters and working locations in the U.S., so I always saw the country as a place of great opportunity and advancement. My field is computer engineering, and there are so many good jobs for that in the U.S. Also, all of us where I was from just dreamed of going to the U.S. one day because it was the country of big companies, big brands, big names. It was drilled in my head basically that if I wanted to be big and successful, I would have to go to the U.S." [Raj]

Simran had a similar mindset, but more family and personal life-oriented rather than being associated with her career. She saw the opportunity as a way to start a new life where she would not have to conform to the more traditional gender roles in her home state. It was a way of breaking from the patriarchal lifestyle of her past to what she viewed to be a more "modern" lifestyle of the future.

"Of course, I was happy at home in India being with all my family and friends, but it was also like being trapped within a cage. I always had to be taking care of everyone and making sure everything was okay at the home. So, when I heard there was the opportunity to move to the U.S, some part of me was excited to try something new. My friends and I always used to talk about how housewives in U.S did not have to stay at home all the time and could have some freedom. They lived in big houses, wore beautiful dresses, and had a great living standard. That was our perception of how America was" [Simran].

However, this is not quite what occurred as it connects back to the notion of the "altered" definition of the American Dream for many Indian women. Simran finds herself living a similarly domestic American Dream in the U.S., showing that life does not change for her as it is supposed to. She is still confined to the same gender roles, but in a different environment with different social norms.

Raj shared a similar viewpoint based on outside influences from the media. These influences had portrayed the U.S. in a specific light that attracted many young men of the generation, and even continue to do so today.

"I had always watched Western movies and TV with these young guys going to work in huge office buildings with all the latest technology. They were driving such nice cars and all, and I thought to myself, 'Hey, I want a life like that one day as well.' And I think that is something that still happens now with how the U.S. is seen by people living in other countries" [Raj].

12.9 CONCLUSION

The case study discussed in this chapter aimed to investigate the impact of traditional gender roles on Indian immigrants' pursuit of the American Dream. By delving deep into one couple's immigration journey and experiences, this research has uncovered some of the relationships that exist for Indian immigrants regarding the traditional gender roles that they abide by and their decision to emigrate to the United States for a better standard of living.

In this case study of Raj and Simran, both individuals had their reasons for choosing to pursue the American Dream, and these reasons were categorized into professional and career-related development reasons, personal and familial expectation-based reasons, and Raj and Simran's ideas of America. The traditional male gender roles include the expectations of providing for one's family in the best way possible, focusing on one's career, and being in control when it comes to making decisions (Patel et al., 1996). This was apparent for Raj who discussed his experiences with his motives for choosing the American Dream to be mostly based on his future career choices and how that aligned with expectations from his role in the family. The reason Raj was given an opportunity to move to the U.S was his job, and his greatest motive for taking this opportunity was the plethora of resources and incentives that he would be given. As the man of the family is expected to work and provide for the family, Raj felt a certain pressure to take this new opportunity. Similarly, the expectation on Raj to be the only source of income for his family, regardless of his wife's educational status, influences him greatly in his decision as well. Finally, Raj's perception of America as a nation teeming with powerful companies and a higher standard of living can relate to his need to provide all of this for his family. He is attracted to the power and status that he has seen in the U.S through the media, as he has been taught that it is the man that should hold all the power in the family.

The traditional gender roles for women in India were clearly reflected in Simran's discussion of her reasons for choosing the American Dream. Women in India are often held to the expectations of putting their families before themselves, staying at home to care for the family, and serving as a loyal support system to their spouses (Deshpande, 2018). These expectations are exhibited in Simran's motives as she discusses giving up her job and her own professional development to come to the U.S with her husband. She does not discuss having any hesitations over this decision as it was important for her to be there for her family and husband. This further supports the naturalization of gender roles and how that pushes for the difference in Raj and Simran's reasons for pursuing the American Dream. In addition, Simran's main reason for emigrating to the U.S. was her relationship with her husband. At one point, she states, "I will move wherever he has to move because we are married," and this shows how her role as his wife greatly affects her choice, or lack thereof, of emigrating. The other side of this is shown in Simran's discussion of how her life as an Indian housewife differed from that in the U.S. Although she truly believes in supporting her family and her husband at all times, she explains how this can become slightly suffocating at times, like being "trapped within a cage." Her perception of America as a place where even housewives are free to live great modern lives relates to her occasional disliking of how she must act in accordance with her gender role back home. And while she is not given much of a choice regarding the move, this perception of the same gender roles in the U.S. as compared to in India encourages her to accept the decision with open arms.

In a study conducted by Deepa Patel of Antioch University, the effect of traditional gender roles was studied in Indian immigrant couples with a different set of results (Blackstone, 2003). The following series of quotes from the interviewees (edited for readability, comprehension, and connection to this study) of this study describes many changes in observing these gender roles as the interviewees adjusted to their new lives living the American Dream.

"What I grew up seeing was my dad tending to the finances of the house. He took care of things at home, and my mom cooked, cleaned, and worked on maintaining the house. There are no traditional gender roles in our marriage currently, but this was not the case when we were just entering into the marriage. In the first couple of years, expectations were created based on what we saw in our respective households. However, we quickly realized that probably wasn't going to work for us."

"I saw that it sheltered my mom since she was very confined in what her day-to-day life was like. My dad was always trying to get us involved in everyday things that would be useful to us later, like managing the different bills in a household and how to fix things that would break around the house. So, I grew up doing it, knowing it, and seeing how my mom did not have that experience in doing these things, and how she did not really trust herself to know and take care of things, which kind of handicapped her. So, I did not want to start my own marriage in a similar manner."

The interviewees here explain how the traditional gender roles passed down in their families did not completely translate for them, especially due to the change in environment from living in the U.S.

"Mom would do all the cooking. But then, she would feel very guilty if my dad helped with the cooking, so she would not let him help in any way. Also, in a sense, it's kind of like she feels the duty to always be in the kitchen, but sometimes she would appreciate his help when he insisted on providing it, but she kind of felt like she was assigned to the kitchen, and then so my dad never really cooked. He did do a variety of other things to help keep the house running. For example, paying the bills, taking out the trash, household chores. He pretty much did all that. All the handy jobs around the house. So, he also used to take care of all those phone bills or utilities, you know, all those things."

"My mom didn't have a professional job. She was a stay-at-home mom. She did everything in the house, cooked for us, and took us to all our different activities. My dad had a job that was like two jobs in one. He was mostly at work, doing his job. Since he was the main earner, he managed all the finances of the house. This was similar for my mom, but more focused on household matters since she didn't work. As for why my mom quit her previous job, my dad suggested she stay home with the kids. Many women around me, including my friends, also end up leaving their jobs because they don't earn enough to contribute significantly to the family. They prefer to contribute in ways they find more helpful."

Both interviewees highlight the gender roles where women typically handled tasks like cooking, cleaning, and house care, while men worked to support the family and engaged in more technical or "masculine" activities.

"In my marriage, the way we split up work for running our house is very different than how it was done with my parents. We mostly do all tasks evenly amongst ourselves. If he is busy, I will take on a role and vice versa. We don't follow any gender roles. We mainly look at our schedules and see when we are busy and when we are free to get tasks done. Then, we split the tasks accordingly so that one person is not doing too much work.

In our marriage, I do not think that there is even the concept of gender roles in that he does something because he is the guy in the family, and I do something because I am the girl. At this point in our marriage, we understand what we each have to offer to the marriage as a whole and to the family in that there is no need to rely on gender roles. Therefore, we barely have any conflicts related to gender roles or who should be doing what based on if they are a girl or guy.

For traditional gender roles, the reason they were what they were was because the man in the family was going to work while the woman did not go to work because women were not allowed to. That's how it worked back then. In current times, women have jobs and lives outside the house, so they cannot do all the household work as well. It will be too much for them.

The men need to contribute by helping to take care of the kids and assist with the many household chores that need to be done. They need to also contribute to the marriage to help keep up that sense of equality that women fought for in the first place. The main theme within the different couples shown through these excerpts is that the Indian immigrant couples are veering away from the concept of traditional gender roles as they pursue their own versions of the American Dream and are compelled to adapt to a different way of living. They also adopt a change in mindset from their parents and those before them. This difference in these couples from the couple in this study could be due to many different factors including age, as the couples in the study were about 10–15 years younger and may have had a different outlook as a result, personal upbringing, and length of marriage along with the number of children (significantly fewer for the interviewees of the comparison study).

Overall, it is apparent that for Indian immigrants coming to the U.S., there are several gender-based differences that affect their personal choices when choosing to pursue the American Dream. Traditional gender roles for men and women were ingrained in these choices for many in the past, and still are today. However, it is important to acknowledge that these findings are only based on a single case study and should not be used to generalize the choices of all Indian immigrants or how traditional gender roles come into play, as there are several families around the world that may not take gender and gender roles into account. Rather, this chapter should be used as a starting point for further analysis on the gender-based differences that arise for many Indian immigrants living in the U.S. Doing so is important to working to eliminate instances of gender discrimination and inequality, since understanding the ideas and thoughts behind these differences can provide insight into the root from which gender inequality stems.

KEYWORDS

- **agriculture and railroad industries**
- **American Dream for Indian**
- **Indian immigrants**
- **methodology**
- **thematic analysis**

REFERENCES

Chatterjee, E., & Desai, S. (2020). Physical versus imagined communities: Migration and women's autonomy in India. *Journal of Ethnic and Migration Studies, 46*(14), 2977–2996. https://doi.org/10.1080/1369183X.2019.1585016.

Chin, G. J., & Villazor, R. C. (2018). *The Immigration and Nationality Act of 1965: Legislating a New America.* (pp. 20–25). Cambridge University Press.

Chin, R. (2011). Türkische Frauen und westdeutsche Feministinnen. *Springerin, 1*(2), 26–33.

Churchwell, S. (2022). A brief history of the American dream. *The Catalyst,* 2(1), 100–120. Retrieved from https://www.bushcenter.org/catalyst/state-of-the-american-dream/churchwell-history-of-theamerican-dream (accessed on 19 June 2024).

Cindoglu, D., & Toktaş, Ş. (2002). Empowerment and resistance strategies of working women in Turkey: The case of 1960—70 graduates of the girls' institutes. *European Journal of Women's Studies, 9*(1), 31–48. https://doi.org/10.1177/1350506802009001380.

Clifton, J., Schnurr, S., & Van De Mieroop, D. (2019). *The Language of Leadership Narratives: A Social Practice Perspective.* (pp. 41–50). Routledge. https://doi.org/10.4324/9781351041829.

Cohen, S., Hanna, P., Higham, J., Hopkins, D., & Orchiston, C. (2020). Gender discourses in academic mobility. *Gender, Work & Organization, 27*(2), 149–165. https://doi.org/10.1111/gwao.12413.

Colen, S. (1995). 'Like a mother to them': Stratified reproduction and West Indian childcare workers and employers in New York. In F. Ginsburg & R. Rapp (Eds.), *Conceiving the New World Order: The Global Politics of Reproduction* (pp. 78–102). Berkeley: University of California Press.

Coles, A., Gray, L., & Momsen, J. (Eds.). (2015). *The Routledge Handbook of Gender and Development* (1st ed.). (pp. 115–132). London: Routledge.

Columbia Public Health. (2019). Content analysis. *Columbia Public Health.* 1(1), 85–96. Retrieved from https://www.publichealth.columbia.edu/research/population-health-methods/content-analysis (accessed on 19 June 2024).

Connell, R. W. (1987). *Gender and Power: Society, The Person and Sexual Politics.* (pp. 21−32). Sydney: Allen & Unwin.

Cresswell, T. (1999). Embodiment, power and the politics of mobility: The case of female tramps and hobos. *Transactions of the Institute of British Geographers, 24*(2), 175–192. https://doi.org/10.1111/j.0020-2754.1999.00175.x.

Cresswell, T. (2006). *On the Move: Mobility in the Modern Western World.* (pp. 13−18). New York: Routledge.

Cresswell, T., & Uteng, T. P. (2016). Gendered mobilities: Towards a holistic understanding. In T. Cresswell & T. P. Uteng (Eds.), *Gendered Mobilities* (pp. 1–12). Oxon: Routledge.

Damon, W. (n.d.). The American dream is alive in the minds of young Americans. *Hoover.* 1(1), 10–16. Retrieved from: https://www.hoover.org/sites/default/files/research/docs/amerex_ch13.pdf (accessed on 19 June 2024).

Datta, K., McIlwaine, C., Herbert, J., Evans, Y., May, J., & Wills, J. (2009). Men on the move: Narratives of migration and work among low-paid migrant men in London. *Social and Cultural Geography, 10*(8), 853–873. https://doi.org/10.1080/14649360903305809.

De Fina, A., & King, K. A. (2011). Language problem or language conflict? Narratives of immigrant women's experiences in the US. *Discourse Studies, 13*(2), 163–188. https://doi.org/10.1177/1461445610392135.

Deshpande, A. A. (2018). *The Immigration Journey: Asian Indian Immigrant Women's Experiences of Gender and Acculturation.* (pp. 54−57). Boston College Libraries.

Diamond, A. (2018, October 19). The original meanings of the "American Dream" and "America first" were starkly different from how we use them today. *Smithsonian Magazine.* https://www.smithsonianmag.com/history/behold-america-american-dream-slogan-booksarah-churchwell-180970311/.

Donato, K. M., Gabaccia, D., Holdaway, J., Manalansan IV, M., & Pessar, P. R. (2018). A glass half full? Gender in migration studies. *International Migration Review, 40*(1), 3–26. https://doi.org/10.1111/j.1747-7379.2006.00001.x.

Doughty, K., & Murray, L. (2014). Discourses of mobility: Institutions, everyday lives and embodiment. *Mobilities, 11*(2), 303–322. https://doi.org/10.1080/17450101.2014.941257.

El Mafaalani, A. (2017). Sphärendiskrepanz und Erwartungsdilemma. Migrationsspezifische Ambivalenzen sozialer Mobilität. *Zeitschrift für Pädagogik, 63*(6), 708–725. https://doi.org/10.25656/01:18823.

Endres, M. (2016). Passengers without havens? Discourses on the hypermobile subject and self-conceptions of frequent travelers. In M. Endres, K. Manderscheid, & C. Mincke (Eds.), *The Mobilities Paradigm: Discourses and Ideologies* (pp. 114–143). London: Routledge.

Endres, M., Manderscheid, K., & Mincke, C. (Eds.). (2016). *The Mobilities Paradigm: Discourses and Ideologies*. (pp. 29-37). London: Routledge.

ESL Conversation Questions – Gender Roles (I-TESL-J). (n.d.). *iteslj.org*. http://iteslj.org/questions/gender.html.

Ets, M. H. (1970). Rosa: *The Life of An Italian Immigrant*. (pp. 30–42). Madison: University of Wisconsin Press.

Floya Anthias, & Gabriella Lazaridis (Eds.). (2000). *Gender and Migration in Southern Europe: Women of the Move* (1st ed.). (pp. 10–12). London: Routledge.

Frello, B. (2008). Towards discursive analytics of movement: On the making and unmaking of movement as an object of knowledge. *Mobilities, 3*(1), 25–50. https://doi.org/10.1080/17450100701797299.

Given, L. M. (2008). Semi-structured interview. *In The SAGE Encyclopedia of Qualitative Research Methods*. 1(1), 22–31. https://doi.org/10.4135/9781412963909.n420.

Gray, B., Ciolfi, L., & Pinatti de Carvalho, A. F. (2020). *Made to Work: Mobilizing Contemporary Work Lives*. (pp. 87–89). Oxon: Routledge.

Hanna, M., & Batalova, J. (2022). Indian immigrants in the United States. *Migrationpolicy.org. 1*(1), 05–12. Retrieved from: https://www.migrationpolicy.org/article/indian-immigrants-united-states- 2019 (accessed on 19 June 2024).

Hannam, K., Sheller, M., & Urry, J. (2006). Editorial: Mobilities, immobility's and moorings. *Mobilities, 1*(1), 1–22. https://doi.org/10.1080/17450100500489189.

Hanson, S. (2010). Gender and mobility: New approaches for informing sustainability. *Gender, Place and Culture, 17*(1), 5–23. https://doi.org/10.1080/09663690903498225.

Hoffman, A., & Batalova, J. (2022). *Indian immigrants in the United States*. Migrationpolicy.org. *2*(1), 30–31. Retrieved from https://www.migrationpolicy.org/article/indian-immigrants-unitedstates#income_poverty (accessed on 19 June 2024).

Jilani, Z., Wilcox, B., & Wang, W. (2021, June 19). The Indian American dream: By putting family and education first, Indian Americans rise. *Institute for Family Studies*. 1(1), 01–05. https://ifstudies.org/blog/the-indian-american-dream-by-putting-family-and-education-first-indian-americans-rise.

Kambouri, H. (2008). Feminine jobs/masculine becoming: Gender and identity in the discourse of Albanian domestic workers in Greece. *European Journal of Women's Studies, 15*(1), 7–22. https://doi.org/10.1177/1350506807084853.

Kamp Dush, C. M., Yavorsky, J. E., & Schoppe-Sullivan, S. J. (2018). What are men doing while women perform extra unpaid labor? Leisure and specialization at the transitions to parenthood. *Sex Roles, 78*(11), 715–730.

Kandiyoti, D. (2016). Locating the politics of gender: Patriarchy, neo-liberal governance and violence in Turkey. *Research and Policy on Turkey, 1*(2), 103–111. https://doi.org/10.1080/23760818.2016.1201242.

Kaplan, C. (2000). *Questions of Travel: Postmodern Discourses of Displacement* (3rd ed.). (pp. 67—71). Durham, NC: Duke University Press.

Labov, W., & Waletzky, J. (1966). Narrative analysis: Oral versions of personal experience. In J. Helm (Ed.), *Essays on the Verbal and Visual Arts* (pp. 12–44). Seattle, WA: University of Washington Press.

Ladegaard, H. (2017). *The Discourse of Powerlessness and Repression: Life Stories of Domestic Migrant Workers In Hong Kong* (Routledge Studies in Sociolinguistics). (pp. 115—124). London: Routledge.

MassMutual. (2017). Asian Indians: Educational and financial priorities. *MassMutual. 1*(1), 01–02. Retrieved from: https://www.massmutual.com/static/path/media/files/asian-indian-americans.pdf (accessed on 19 June 2024).

Mitchell, T. (2023, January 26). How Indians view gender roles in families and society. *Pew Research Center's Religion & Public Life Project.* Retrieved from: https://www.pewresearch.org/religion/2022/03/02/how-indians-view-gender-roles-in-families-and-society/ (accessed on 19 June 2024).

Morokvasic, M. (1984). Birds of passage are also women. *International Migration Review, 18*(4), 886–907. https://doi.org/10.2307/2546066.

Moya, J. C. (2007). Domestic service in a global perspective: Gender, migration, and ethnic niches. *Journal of Ethnic and Migration Studies, 33*(4), 559–579. https://doi.org/10.1080/13691830701265420.

Mueller, A. E., & Segal, D. L. (2013). Structured versus semistructured versus unstructured interviews. In J. C. Norcross & G. R. VandenBos (Eds.), *The encyclopedia of clinical psychology* (pp. 1–7). Wiley. https://doi.org/10.1002/9781118625392.wbecp127.

Nordgaard, J., Sass, L. A., & Parnas, J. (2013). The psychiatric interview: Validity, structure, and subjectivity. *European Archives of Psychiatry and Clinical Neuroscience, 263*(5), 353–364.

OHCHR. (n.d.). Working Group on discrimination against women and girls. *OHCHR.* 1(1), 02–03. Retrieved from: https://www.ohchr.org/en/special-procedures/wg-women-and-girls (accessed on 19 June 2024).

Osella, F., & Osella, C. (2000). Migration, money and masculinity in Kerala. *Journal of the Royal Anthropological Institute, 6*(1), 117–133. https://doi.org/10.1111/1467-9655.T01-1-00007.

Parreñas, R. S. (2001). Mothering from a distance: Emotions, gender, and intergenerational relations in Filipino transnational families. *Feminist Studies, 27*(2), 361–390. https://doi.org/10.2307/3178765.

Patel, D. (2021). Experience of gender role expectations and negotiation in second generation Desi couples. https://aura.antioch.edu/cgi/viewcontent.cgi?article=1765&context=etds (accessed on 19 June 2024).

Patel, N., Power, T. G., & Bhavnagri, N. P. (1996). Socialization values and practices of Indian immigrant parents: Correlates of modernity and acculturation. *Child Development, 67*(2), 302–313. https://doi.org/10.2307/1131815.

Peano, I. (2012). Excesses and double standards: Migrant prostitutes, sovereignty and exceptions in contemporary Italy. *Modern Italy, 17*(4), 419–432. https://doi.org/10.1080/13532944.2012.706994.

Pessar, P. R., & Mahler, S. J. (2006). Transnational migration: Bringing gender in. *International Migration Review, 37*(3), 812–846. https://doi.org/10.4324/9781315447599-8.

Porter, G. (2011). 'I think a woman who travels a lot is befriending other men and that's why she travels': Mobility constraints and their implications for rural women and girls in sub-Saharan Africa. *Gender, Place and Culture, 18*(1), 65–81. https://doi.org/10.1080/0966369X.2011.535304.

Romer, C. D. (2003). *Great Depression.* Nowandfutures. Retrieved from: https://www.nowandfutures.com/d2/great_depression_romer.pdf (accessed on 19 June 2024).

Satı, B. (2021). Working-Class Women, Gender, and Union Politics in Turkey, 1965–1980. *International Labor and Working-Class History, 100,* 87–108. https://doi.org/10.1017/S0147547921000119.

Sayan, S. (2004). Guest workers' remittances and output fluctuations in host and home countries: The case of remittances from Turkish workers in Germany. *Emerging Markets Finance and Trade, 40*(6), 68–81.

Schnurr, S., Zayts, O., & Hopkins, C. (2016). Challenging hegemonic femininities? The discourse of trailing spouses in Hong Kong. *Language in Society, 45*(4), 533–555. https://doi.org/10.1017/S0047404516000415.

Schnurr, S., Zayts, O., Schroeder, A., & Le Coyte-Hopkins, C. (2020). 'It's not acceptable for the husband to stay at home': Taking a discourse analytical approach to capture the gendering of work. *Gender, Work and Organization, 27*(3), 414–434. https://doi.org/10.1111/gwao.12408.

Sheller, M., & Urry, J. (2006). The new mobilities paradigm. *Environment and Planning A: Economy and Space, 38*(2), 207–226. https://doi.org/10.1068/a37268.

Silvey, R. (2006). Consuming the transnational family: Indonesian migrant domestic workers to Saudi Arabia. *Global Networks, 6*(1), 23–40. https://doi.org/10.1111/j.1471-0374.2006.00131.x.

Silvey, R. M. (2000). Stigmatized spaces: Gender and mobility under crisis in South Sulawesi, Indonesia. *Gender, Place and Culture, 7*(2), 143–161. https://doi.org/10.1080/713668869.

Sivakumar, I., & Manimekalai, K. (2021). Masculinity and challenges for women in Indian culture. *Journal of International Women's Studies, 22*(5), 427–436. https://vc.bridgew.edu/cgi/viewcontent.cgi?article=2461&context=jiws (accessed on 19 June 2024).

Skeggs, B. (2004). *Class, Self, Culture* (1st ed.). (pp. 33—42). London: Routledge.

Veazey, W. L. (2022). Mothers in the middle: Rethinking middling migration as relational. In S. Robertson & R. Roberts (Eds.), *Rethinking Privilege and Social Mobility in Middle-Class Migration* (pp. 191–212). London: Routledge.

Wang, W. (2021, June 19). Immigrant families are more stable. *Institute for Family Studies. 1*(1), 1–5. https://ifstudies.org/blog/immigrant-families-are-more-stable.

Williams, C. P. (2008). Female transnational migration, religion and subjectivity: The case of Indonesian domestic workers. *Asia Pacific Viewpoint, 49*(3), 344–353. https://doi.org/10.1111/j.1467-8373.2008.00382.x.

Wolak, J., & Peterson, D. A. M. (2020). The dynamic American dream. *American Journal of Political Science, 64*(4), 968–981. http://www.jstor.org/stable/45295360 (accessed on 19 June 2024).

APPENDIX A

This list of questions was asked to both participants to gain insight into their reasons for pursuing the American Dream and how it related back to their current lives

What is your full name?
Where was the place you were born and originally grew up?
What was the main reason for your emigration to the U.S?
Which factors influenced that decision?
How did you personally feel about that decision?
How did others in your environment around you feel about that decision?
How did your spouse feel about that decision?
What is your current job?
What was your job at the time you decided to move?
How did your career affect your decision?
How did your spouse and/or marriage affect your decision?
How did you perceive the U.S as a country before moving?
Did anything in particular influence your perception of the U.S?
Do you believe that your gender played a role in how your life is today?

The following list of questions was adapted from The Internet TESL Journal (ESL Conversation Questions – Gender Roles (I-TESL-J), n.d.) and the UN Working Group on the issue of Discrimination against Women in Law and Practice (OHCHR | Working Group on Discrimination against Women and Girls, n.d.) and asked to both participants to gain insight and some background on their basis for traditional gender roles as to not make any assumptions throughout the interviews.

*Home country refers to country of origin

- Do you believe that the responsibilities of a mother can be the same as the responsibilities of a father for their families?
- What are a father's responsibilities for his family?
- What are a mother's responsibilities for her family?
- Do you believe that a mother and father can exchange duties?
- Do sons and daughters have different expectations for their respective roles in a family?

- Which habits do you think are appropriate for men, but not appropriate for women?
- Which behaviors do you think are appropriate for men, but not appropriate for women?
- Which jobs do you think are appropriate for men, but not appropriate for women?
- In your home country, do you have more male or female doctors?
- In your home country, do you have more male or female nurses?
- In your home country, do you have more male or female professional musicians?
- In your home country, do you have more male or female teachers?
- Do you think that men and women equal in terms of ability and intelligence? Why/Why not?
- What do you believe, in society today, that men can do that women cannot and vice versa?
- In today's society, what type of clothing do men wear?
- In today's society, what type of clothing do women wear?
- Do you think that men can wear women's clothing, or that women can wear men's clothing? Why/Why not?
- Do you think it is appropriate for men to wear pink clothes?
- Do you think it is appropriate for men to cry?
- Do you think it is appropriate for women to cry?
- In today's society, what do people think of men and/or women crying?
- In today's society, what do people think of a man who backs down from a fight?
- In today's society, what do people think of two women involved in a fist fight?
- Do you think that it is okay for men to appear sad?
- Do you think that it is okay for women to appear sad?
- Do you think that it is okay for men to appear weak?
- In today's society, is it common for women and men to participate in sports? Do they participate in the same type of sports?
- Who does the cooking, cleaning, and household chores in your household?
- In your home country, is it possible for women to join the army?
- In your home country, is it required for men and women to join the army?
- In your home country, do women swear a lot?
- Do you think there are more male or female managers and executives? Why do you think so?
- In your home country, what jobs do men do and women not do?
- In your household, who is regarded as the head of the family?
- Do you think that boys and girls should be raised differently?

- Do you think that boys and girls should be treated differently by their parents?
- What would you do if your parents switched family roles for one day?
- How do you think the world would look like without men?
- How do you think the world would look like without women?
- In your society, when a woman and a man are seen with each other, who does more talking? Why is it like this?
- Do you think a man and a woman can be only friends?
- Do you think that male friendships differ from female and male or female friendships? How so?
- In your society, what are the responsibilities of a father for his family?
- In your society, what are the responsibilities of a mother to her family?
- Do you think that fathers can conduct the duties done by a mother and vice versa?
- In your household, who do the children go to for emotional support, and who do they go to for financial support?
- In your household, are there different expectations for sons and daughters?
- Do you think that boys and girls should be brought up differently?
- In your home country, what social behaviors are appropriate for women, but not for men?
- In your home country, what social behaviors are appropriate for men, but not for women?
- In your home country, what cultural mannerisms are appropriate for women, but not for men?
- In your household, is there a legal designation of head of household?
- If yes, is the head of household for you a male member of your family?
- In your household, what types of rights or characteristics are correlated with the head of household?
- In your home country, is dowry a common practice in marriage contracts or in traditional social situations?
- In your home country, do both spouses have the same rights in terms of choosing a family name, choosing a profession, choosing a place of residence, retaining one's nationality, and the freedom of movement including traveling abroad?
- In your home country, do both spouses have the same rights in terms of property and land ownership, land and property management, and land and property usage and enjoyment?
- Do you think that women who get married are subjected to male guardianship? If yes, are there any conditions, and what type of restrictions do these conditions create for women?

CHAPTER 13

A STUDY ON BARRIERS FOR WOMEN TO SUSTAIN IN EDUCATIONAL LEADERSHIP POSITIONS IN SRI LANKA: HOW SRI LANKA EDUCATIONAL ADMINISTRATIVE SERVICE FEMALE OFFICERS COPE WITH THE BARRIERS?

THANUJA MAITHRIE WITHARANA

Deputy Commissioner of Educational Publications, Educational Publications Department, Ministry of Education, Sri Lanka

ABSTRACT

The last several decades have seen a rise in interest in the topic of gender equality. Women's leadership is likewise fully committed to supporting global gender equality. However, because of the prevalent prejudices and standards in society, women face numerous obstacles when it comes to leadership. In this chapter, the obstacles faced by women leaders in the Sri Lankan education field will be discussed in detail. The inquiry encompasses the areas of institutional mindset, individual mindset, and lifestyle. A sample of women leaders was chosen randomly from the Sri Lanka Educational Administrative Service (SLEAS) for this study. The study used a qualitative approach to investigate the social foundations of gender barriers in leadership among women in Sri Lanka.

Subverting Social Inequalities: Gender as a Social Reality.
Akanksha Srivastava, Disha Maheshwari, Chitra Krishnan (Eds.)

13.1 INTRODUCTION

In the 21st century, we can observe an advancement of women's leadership in many sectors. It is a positive fact that facilitates gender equality in any society. Over the past 50 years, there has been substantial progress for women in the workplace (Sule et al., 2017). On the other hand, it is well recognized that women are severely underrepresented in senior leadership roles in industry and politics (The World Economic Forum, 2015; Sui Chu Ho, 2015; Sule et al., 2017). This can happen due to many reasons, such as pre-established stereotypes and norms in society. Bias and prejudice against professional women may result from social constructs such as stereotypes that contradict the actual characteristics of these women. Because of the social expectations they must fulfill, these prejudices can inhibit women from reaching their goals.

This chapter aims to address the barriers that Sri Lankan women in educational leadership roles are currently experiencing, including those caused by preconceptions, cultural norms, and the need to choose between jobs and family. Accordingly, the chapter would narrow its focus on the possible barriers that women leaders in the Sri Lanka Educational Administrative Service (SLEAS) are currently facing.

Accordingly, a brief description of the background of women's workforce in the Sri Lankan context would be given for readers to understand the women's working position in the Sri Lankan context. Also, a description of the Sri Lanka Administrative Service would be given for readers to understand the nature and scope of the positions that the leaders have to occupy. Moreover, through the literature review, the chapter presents the barriers faced by women leaders in the global context. Then it converges on the Sri Lankan context, describing the barriers Sri Lankan women in the education sector face. Then a sample of SLEAS officers currently holding leadership positions is randomly selected and interviewed to see if they face the same barriers in their leadership positions in the education sector within the Sri Lankan context. Further, the chapter will discuss the information gathered from interviews. Moreover, the chapter will give examples of real cases at present.

13.1.1 BACKGROUND OF WOMAN CONTRIBUTION TO THE WORKFORCE IN THE SRI LANKAN CONTEXT

Sri Lanka, a South Asian country, has displayed many instances of significant female leadership in the past. For example, the world's first female Prime Minister, Mrs. Sirimavo Bandaranaike, is from Sri Lanka. Mrs. Chandrika Kumaratunga, the world's first female president, was also from Sri Lanka.

Furthermore, women have served in the Sri Lankan parliament since 1960. Accordingly, Sri Lanka has a favorable history of female leadership.

Women in Sri Lanka make up 57% of the country's population, which is estimated at 21 million, according to a survey conducted by the Department of Labor in 2017. However, only 35.9% of the 8 million economically engaged people in the country are women. Withanage & Chandrakumara, (2021) state that gender disparities are rapidly disappearing in Sri Lanka through the formal education system in the country. Moreover, the percentage of women who work increases with education, according to calculations made by the Institute of Policy Changes in Sri Lanka (IPS) in 2015. According to the calculations, the rate of female labor force participation with a bachelor's degree is high, at 83.9%, at 49.9% for the advanced level, and at 29.2% for the ordinary level. However, the number of women ascending to higher positions within an organization is significantly low. However, 63.8% of Sri Lanka's professionals are women, making up the majority of the workforce (Labor Force Survey, 2017). According to the report, women made up 35.2% of the overall workforce in middle-level jobs across a variety of industries, including management, senior officials, and legislative posts, as stated in the Labor Force Survey 2017. That is, more and more women are joining the workforce, yet there are still few top leadership roles available (Eagly & Carli, 2003).

13.1.2 WOMEN LEADERS IN SRI LANKA

The administrative positions in Sri Lanka's government sector are filled through competitive examinations that are published in the gazette. As a result, leaders for government administration positions are appointed to managerial-level positions depending on their educational qualifications, knowledge, and skills without the gender factor being a barrier. Accordingly, the Sri Lankan government ensures equal opportunity for female leaders in the education industry to some extent. In such a background, the administration of the education sector is done by the Sri Lanka Educational Administration Service (SLEAS). Sri Lanka Educational Administrative Service (SLEAS) is a well-reputed and privileged service spread island-wide.

13.1.3 SRI LANKA EDUCATIONAL ADMINISTRATION SERVICE (SLEAS)

The Sri Lanka Educational Administrative Service is considered a highly recognized service in Sri Lanka. It serves the education sector of Sri Lanka. The leadership positions covered by this service are permanent and pensionable. Moreover, the officers in the service are liable to work in any part of the country. The recruitment process for the service is done in three different ways. That is through

1. Open competitive exam
2. Limited competitive exam
3. Merit-based

1. **Open Competitive Exam:** Applicants need to be not less than 22 years old and not more than 30 years old to fall into this category. Another main eligibility criterion is possessing a legitimate degree from a university that the University Grants Commission recognizes (UGC). Further, all applicants must be in good enough physical and mental health to serve and carry out the duties of the position wherever in the nation.
2. **Limited Competitive Exam:** Applicants need to be less than 45 years of age to fall into this category. At least 5 years of experience as a public-school teacher is also required. Accordingly, only government sector teachers are absorbed into SLEAS positions.
3. **Merit-Based:** Applicants need to be less than 60 years old. Need to work as a teacher in the government sector and need to prove certain skills as requested in the gazette.

Anyone fulfilling the requirements and falling into any one of the above categories has the chance of enrolling as a SLEAS officer. The newly appointed officers will be appointed as class 3 officers and need to work for 6 years in the respective position to be promoted to the class 2 level. Meanwhile, they have to acquire certain entry qualifications to be promoted to class 2 positions. For example, officers need to complete a postgraduate diploma in education as well as a language bar. Moreover, the officers need to pass the efficiency bar, which contains many subjects. To be promoted to the Class 1 position, the officers need to complete a Master's in Education degree and a capacity-building program. Further, officers need to have a combined experience of 10 years in class 2 and 3 positions to be promoted to a class 1 position. Furthermore, only a few positions are assigned to the "super grade," which is the higher grade for positions considered superior.

13.1.4 SLEAS POSITIONS OCCUPIED BY WOMAN OFFICERS AT PRESENT

The SLEAS cadre has nine super-grade positions, and two of them are occupied by women. That is, women leaders hold approximately 22% of super-grade positions.

Among the 331 officers who are in class 1 positions currently, 158 are women (MOE, 2022). That is, approximately 48% are occupied by women. However, even if you get a leadership position, sustaining it is challenging for many females as well as male officers. This research is done to inquire about the challenges faced by female leaders in leadership positions.

13.2 LITERATURE REVIEW

There have been many studies done to identify the barriers to women's leadership. Many factors influence the barriers that women leaders face, including culture, social attitudes, political reasons, geographical reasons, religious beliefs, and so on. Whatever the factor, these barriers hold back women's leadership journeys. Accordingly, it is very important to identify the barriers in each context so that they can take the necessary precautions.

13.2.1 WOMAN LEADERSHIP BARRIERS IN A GLOBAL CONTEXT

As stated by the social-role theory of Eagly (1987), the social roles that govern adult conduct are what cause gender differences. According to this view, the behavioral disparities between men and women are caused by the various roles that each gender fulfills in accordance with societal norms (Eagly & Sczesny, 2009). The social-role hypothesis describes the widespread stereotypes of gender defining roles of men and women in society. Accordingly, females as well as men are expected to behave accordingly. When it comes to leadership roles, it appears to be an obstacle for women leaders, restricting their capacity for empowerment by aiming for and obtaining leadership positions. According to Alqahtani (2019), gender stereotypes result in inequalities between men and women in leadership roles: more often than not, accepted stereotypes establish men's superior positions in society over women. Furthermore & Heilman (2001) contends that gender stereotypes and gender bias devalue the performance of female leaders. Moreover, he claims, even if a woman leader is capable, she may not advance to the same organizational level as a man who does just as well.

Schein, Mueller, Lituchy, & Liu (1996), on the other hand, state that their research has confirmed the "think manager, think male" phenomenon, which is unfavorable for female leadership. Social stereotypes and gender bias are visible in society, creating barriers to women's leadership; additionally, female leaders encounter opposition and unfavorable responses when they try to use their influence in a way that deviates from gender stereotypes (St. Catherine University, 2022). Andrews (2016), also claims that the notion of role congruity contends that it is challenging for both men and women to be successful as leaders if their behavior is not interpreted as being consistent with their genders. In other words, incongruity takes place when someone harbors stereotypes, prejudices, or biases about men or women that go against the conduct deemed necessary to thrive in a certain role. People contend that men are less effective when the leadership role is gendered than when it is masculinized, and vice versa (Kessler, 2014). For example, as Andrew (2016) describes, a woman leader can be an efficacious military leader, but her team may not cooperate with her because the assigned role for her in this instance is incongruent with feminism. Accordingly, he reveals the institutional mindset as well as the individual mindset, which is that gender bias or stereotyping is a barrier for women leaders.

The American Council on Education (2007) suggests that institutions of higher learning have been hesitant to increase opportunities for women to hold senior leadership positions. It is asserted that attitudes on an individual and institutional level contribute to excluding women from higher-level leadership roles in higher education. Ballenger, (2010) – Woman leadership barriers-Sri Lankan context.

In the Sri Lankan context too, males and females are not equally represented in managerial career possibilities (Department of Census and Statistics, 2017). According to Kuruppuarachchi & Surangi (2020), there are three main barriers for Sri Lankan women. Individual barriers, institutional barriers, and social barriers are the three types. Morley & Crossouard (2016) indicate that in the Sri Lankan context, women's desire for leadership was not always present. Women who disobeyed patriarchal socio-cultural conventions and disrupted the symbolic hierarchy of men leading women typically carried a heavy emotional burden because it was associated with specific forms of masculinity.

As argued by Morley & Crossouard (2015), among the obstacles to female job advancement were the difficulties of juggling family and work and the demands of women in the home. Women have described being stuck in unpromoted, non-research roles as a result of the gendered division of labor in higher education, such as that which surrounds teaching and research and different types of management and administration. Prejudice against women, favoritism of men in hiring and promotion decisions, and the gendering of time, space, and course material generally muted retrogressive views of women in management—essentialized conceptions that women bring different or more nurturing qualities to this, more democratic/participatory leadership approaches to such work. Further, in the studies of higher education leadership conducted today, gender problems are still marginalized. Gunawardena & Lekamge (2002). Recent articles highlight how the number of courses teaching about women's issues is declining. A major concern about gender-based violence on college campuses is reported by Gunawardena (2013) and Goonesekere (2013). Concerns are raised by the high unemployment rates among recent female graduates (Gunawardena 2013).

The country gender evaluation conducted by the Asian Development Bank (ADB 2008) identified harmful gender stereotypes, the ineffectiveness of new school curricula in addressing them, and the manner in which this has deterred women from entering politics.

13.3 METHODOLOGY

The qualitative methodology was chosen for this study. The sample for the study was chosen randomly from the Sri Lanka Educational Administrative Service. The participants were drawn from super-grade and class-grade positions, and the study focused on super-grade and class-grade positions. In this study, 20 members of SLEAS were interviewed to get information.

13.4 RESULTS

The chart below shows the population distribution in Sri Lanka. Approximately 57% of the population is female (Figure 13.1).

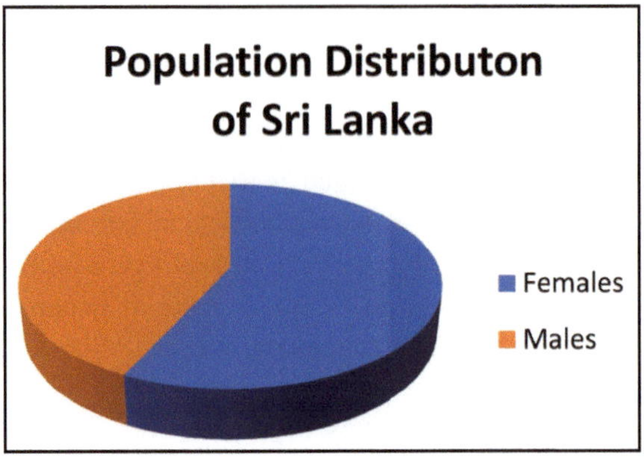

FIGURE 13.1 The woman workforce in Sri Lanka.

The economically engaged population of Sri Lanka is approximately 8 million. Among them, approximately 34% are female (Figure 13.2).

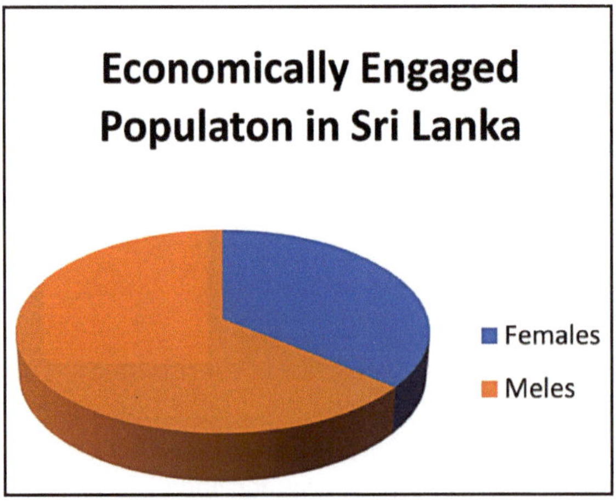

FIGURE 13.2 Economically engaged female and male percentage in Sri Lanka.

The below chart shows how the top positions are distributed among female and male officers In Educational sector (Table 13.1).

TABLE 13.1 Distribution of SLEAS Positions

Position	Total	Male	Female
Super Grade	9	7	2
Class 1	331	173	158

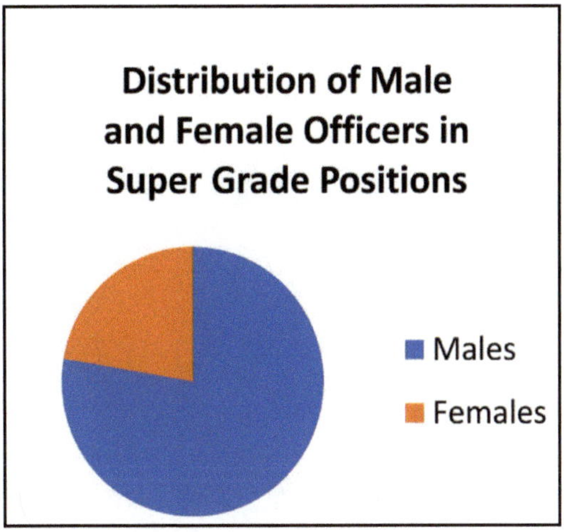

FIGURE 13.3 Distribution of super grade positions in SLEAS.

According to the above chart only 22% of the super grade positions are obtained by female officers (Figure 13.3).

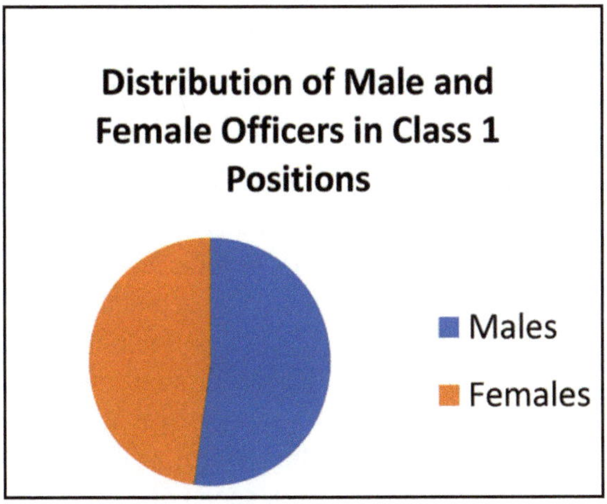

FIGURE 13.4 Distribution of class 1 positions in SLEAS.

The above charts show how class 1 positions are obtained by female officers. It shows that almost half the positions are obtained by females, unlike super-grade positions. The reason for this significant information will be discussed in the discussion section (Figure 13.4).

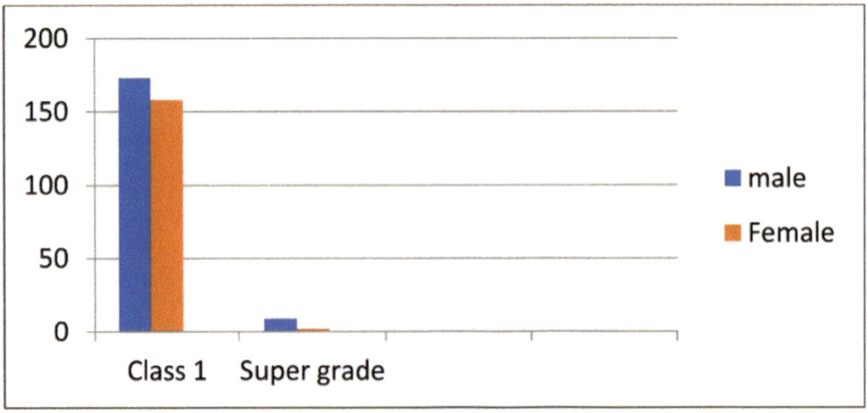

FIGURE 13.5 Distribution of leadership positions in SLEAS.

13.5 DISCUSSION AND SUGGESTIONS

13.5.1 INSTITUTIONAL MINDSET

Institutional mindset refers to numerous gender biases and stereotypes within organizations (St. Catherine University, 2022). That is, many people believe that because of variations in gender, men and women perform better in particular roles. In the Sri Lankan context, stereotyped mindsets in society as well as in educational institutions can be observed. Organizations, based on their conventional roles in society, assume certain things about women in the workplace and as leaders. As a result, certain positions are masculinized and certain positions are feminized in educational institutions.

According to the sample, 100% of female leaders in this organization face conflict in the Sri Lankan context. Consequently, if given the opportunity to choose the highest-level position, all female leaders would accept a feminized position. Through further discussion, the reason for this was revealed. The majority of the sample expressed that getting appointed to a top position is very competitive, and they didn't want to miss the opportunity due to stereotypes in the organization or society.

However, changing the institutional mindset is a significant barrier for Sri Lankan women, and it is a major obstacle to getting appointed as well as sustaining themselves in top leadership positions. In the Sri Lankan educational context, top-level positions are limited for women due to masculinized institutional mindsets in educational organizations. This affects the success as well as the leadership journey of female leaders. For example, in the topmost position of the Education Ministry in Sri Lanka, the Secretary of

Education post is most frequently given to men. The position was only given once to a woman, namely Dr. Tara De Mel (Figure 13.5).

Furthermore, certain leadership positions, such as “principal of a boys’ school,” are always given to male officers. The leadership position of “principal of a boys’ school” is masculinized in the Sri Lankan context. It is believed that a principal of a boys’ school must be male to be successful as a leader. However, the deputy principal positions in boys’ schools are given to women. According to the data gathered, the role congruity theory is also to blame. The recruiters for this position expect the deputy principal, who is a woman, to do the paperwork, as it is believed women are more effective at handling paperwork than handling human resources in a boys’ school.

According to the data collected, another instance where an institutional mindset affects a woman is when societies combine agented conduct, which is linked to stereotypically masculine attributes like assertiveness, aggression, competition, dominance, independence, and self-resilience, with leadership behavior, etc., 100% of the women leaders in the sample say this relationship puts women leaders in conflict in the Sri Lankan context. When they attain a leadership position in Sri Lanka, they must behave in a leadership capacity, which means society as well as the institution expects them to be assertive, aggressive, etc. (“male” traits) as the leadership position is bonded with male traits. But at the same time, the institution expects them to act like women too, which means being soft, flexible, etc. (“female” traits). This type of institutional mindset is highly challenging for women leaders when working in a leadership position. This situation challenges the behavior as well as the decisions of the female leader in a given situation. Accordingly, to be accepted as a successful leader in the Sri Lankan context, women frequently have to straddle two conflicting demands.

13.5.2 THE INDIVIDUAL MINDSET IN SRI LANKAN CONTEXT

This is also a very common barrier that prevents the success of women’s leadership in the Sri Lankan context. According to Andrew, (2016), “individual mindset” refers to the beliefs and actions that women could have that limit and impede their advancement in leadership. Further, he explains how the majority of women reach a particular level and remain there. They do not intend to reach higher positions such as vice president or president. The reasons for this are revealed by Andrew A. as socialization pressure, lack of confidence, risk aversion, preference for work-life balance, or a desire to stay away from politics. He explains that this type of negative individual mindset is a barrier for female leaders because it limits their leadership journey.

According to the data collected, the individual mindsets of women leaders hold them back. Most Sri Lankan women resist being appointed to the highest position due to various reasons. For example, nine super-grade positions for SLEAS are available. Among them, 7 are male, while 2 are held by women. Only 22% of women's representation is displayed in super-grade positions so far. After obtaining the class 1 position, most women hold themselves back from applying for super-grade positions. They are satisfied with what they have obtained. 80% of those polled say they have no desire to be appointed as a super-grade officer. Further, 78% of the sample said they resist being appointed as top-level leaders due to family commitments. Another 19% resist appointments to the top level to avoid political influencing, while 2% are not willing to handle the social pressure. Also, 1% expressed an absence of faith in their capacity to manage such high-level roles.

On the other hand, the few women leaders in higher positions also display negative behaviors such as resistance to taking risks, resistance to public speaking, and lack of confidence. The SLEAS position, which is held by women, exhibits delay in decision-making, lack of coordination, low efficiency, etc. Moreover, Mathipa & Tsoka (2001) state that poor self-image is a barrier mainly identified among education professionals. This can also be seen in the Sri Lankan context. Women leaders underestimate themselves, and this attitude holds them back in decision-making. As a result, they try to maintain their position without intending to step forward and make a change. Only a low percentage of women leaders intend to succeed in the position of a successful leader. I see appointing women to higher positions as a positive factor in terms of gender equality in Sri Lanka. However, attitudes need to be urgently changed for women to succeed as leaders.

13.5.3 LIFESTYLE AS A BARRIER TO LEADERSHIP IN SRI LANKAN CONTEXT

Work-life balance, family priorities, and personal preferences are all part of the lifestyle. Despite the fact that these are not poor decisions, they do act as hurdles since these women close the gender gap in leadership. They are held back, and their leadership journey is limited due to lifestyle priorities such as family choices. Accordingly, it is considered a barrier in terms of women's leadership.

Almost all the sample members agreed that the lifestyle is a barrier to women's leadership. All of them give priority to family choices. On the other hand, by society's standards, it is expected that women do household work such as cooking, cleaning, laundry, etc. Also, most women think it is their duty. 84% of the sample wants to do household work such as cooking themselves, though they can afford to have a helper. Most Sri Lankan women work and earn money. Most women try to achieve higher goals in education. Parents urge their children to study hard and earn a good job for a living. As a result, most women in Sri Lanka have a good education. However, when it comes to family, most women choose the caregiver role in the family, supporting the males. At this point, they mostly focus on children's education and bringing them up. As a result of prioritizing family over occupation, they intend to restrict themselves and have time for family. This becomes a barrier in the Sri Lankan context from the point of view of women's leadership.

13.5.4 REAL CASES CURRENTLY TAKING PLACE IN SRI LANKAN CONTEXT

There are many barriers that women face when sustaining leadership positions. However, it is encouraging to see some female leaders who overcame adversity and established themselves as successful leaders in their respective fields. There are many legends in Sri Lanka about people who successfully overcame obstacles. For example, a female SLEAS officer was appointed as a principal in a leading girls' school. However, she was transferred to another school in favor of another person. But she sued against the transfer and was able to sustain herself in the position because she had relevant qualifications. Moreover, she was able to sustain herself as the principal of the school from 2009 to 2022, until she retired. Further, another SLEAS lady officer whom I know has worked as a deputy principal, assistant director, deputy director, and director. Finally, she was able to reach the additional secretary position and served for many years until she retired as the additional secretary of the Ministry of Education in 2022.

Currently, a female officer is successfully serving in the additional secretary post. It is encouraging to see women advancing in the education sector, even though they face many obstacles in real life due to cultural stereotypes and mindsets in society. However, one female officer was accused of being immersed in gossip about a disciplinary situation, which was informally reported. The stereotypical thinking of society made things worse for her. But she fought against it for more than a year. However, it was very unfortunate that she had to give up the job due to this personal matter, which was not related to work. Similar disciplinary situations for male officers were handled very differently. In such personal matters, society does not hold male officers accountable. This type of stereotypical thinking affects both female officers and those serving in any position.

On the other hand, there may be unrecognized effective female leaders who could have achieved legendary status but were hidden or disappeared as a result of feminist barriers. Also, though we generalize the barriers, the barriers will be customized for each individual. Therefore, it is very important to identify their customized barriers and find solutions to overcome them. I would like to suggest the following models for identifying your own barriers as leaders.

13.5.5 SUGGESTIONS TO OVERCOME BARRIERS TO WOMAN LEADERSHIP

Sri Lanka needs to work more on reducing gender bias as well as stereotyping in leadership. Sri Lanka needs an attitudinal change in society regarding women's leadership. This has to be done at the school level in a more organized and practical manner. This could be done through awareness programs, mentoring, and introducing and presenting more female role models. More motivational programs would help achieve the target. Discussion sessions and experience-sharing sessions could do a lot to advance the effectiveness of women's leadership.

Additionally, by providing leadership support to help women advance, it is also important to educate them on leadership styles and theories. However, proper leadership education must be provided virtually so that female leaders can develop their own style rather than simply following a theory in a book. I suggest incorporating leadership studies into the school curriculum as well. Also, females must be given chances to handle leadership positions at the school level.

I believe it is critical to identify the obstacles you face. You need to deeply analyze your background and working conditions to identify your barriers. Following that, you can take precautions on both a personal and official level to overcome the barriers. As SLEAS officers, women can work together to overcome problems regarding feminism as a union.

13.5.5.1 SUGGESTED STEPS TO IDENTIFY YOUR OWN LEADERSHIP BARRIERS

1. Decide your target in work life (final destination)

2. Write the steps to reach the target
3. List the barriers you feel and think which prevent you or holding back from achieving your targets. Identify the barriers (SWOT analysis)
4. Ask a colleague to list the barriers you might be experience based on his/her opinion
5. Ask your immediate boss to list the barriers for you as he/she sees
6. Discuss with your boss about these barriers and colleagues
7. Prepare a final list of barriers for next five years
8. Prepare a mind map
9. List what precautions that you can take to prevent each barrier.

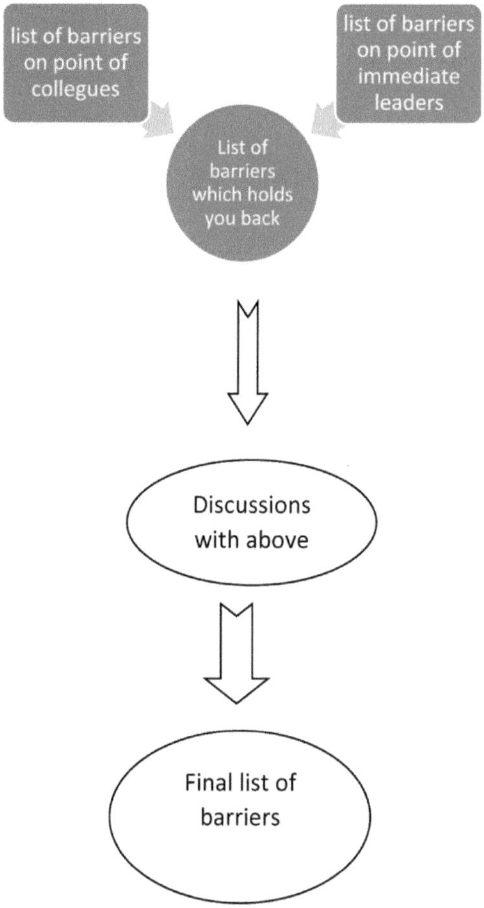

FIGURE 13.6 A model to identify your own barriers

KEYWORDS

- **Institute of Policy Changes in Sri Lanka**
- **literature review**
- **methodology**
- **Sri Lanka Educational Administrative Service**
- **University Grants Commission**

REFERENCES

Alqahtani, T. (2019). Barriers to women's leadership. *Granite Journal: A Postgraduate Interdisciplinary Journal, 3*(2), 34–41.

Andrews, S. D. (2016). Gender barriers by Dr. Shawn Andrews and solutions to leadership. Retrieved from: http://www.nxtbook.com/nxtbooks/trainingindustry/tiq_2016summer/index.php?startid=36 (accessed on 19 June 2024).

Asian Development Bank. Southeast Asia Department, Asian Development Bank. Regional, & Sustainable Development Department. (2006). *Indonesia: Country Gender Assessment.* Southeast Asia Regional Department.

Ballenger, J. (2010). Women's access to higher education leadership: Cultural and structural barriers. *Forum on Public Policy Online, 2010*(5), 1. https://www.forumonpublicpolicy.co.uk/_files/ugd/553e83_a9ecf3e4be43424ebf66c4bdf8b645b7.pdf.

Department of Census and Statistics (DCS). (2017). *Census of Population and Labor Force Survey.* Colombo. http://statistics.gov.lk/LabourForce/StaticalInformation/AnnualReports/2017-2ndVersion.

Eagly, A. H., & Sczesny, S. (2009). Stereotypes about women, men, and leaders: Have times changed? *American Psychological Association.* Stereotypes about women, men, and leaders: Have times changed? (apa.org).

Gunawardena, C. (2013b). University statistics 2011 gender and category. Paper presented at the Promoting Gender Equity/Equality in Sri Lankan Universities. National Workshop organized by the Centre for Gender Studies, University of Kelaniya (CGSUK) in collaboration with the Association of Commonwealth Universities (ACU) and the International Labor Organization (ILO), Colombo, Sri Lanka, 29-31 July 2013.

Gunawardena, C., & Lekamge, D. (2002). Men and women in leadership roles: A study of the Open University of Sri Lanka. In *8th National Convention on Women's Studies*, 4, 801–814. Colombo.

Heilman, M. E. (2001). Description and prescription: How gender stereotypes prevent women's ascent up the organizational ladder. *Journal of Social Issues, 57*(4), 657–674.

Kessler, M. (2008). Macht Macht erotisch. *Authentisch leben-eine Herausforderung in der christlichen Mission. Am Beispiel sexueller Versuchlichkeit weiblicher, lediger, hetrosexueller Führungskräfte in Deutschland. MTh Dissertation. University of South Africa. Pretoria.*

Kesslner, M. (2014). Female leaders in the 21st century in a masculine world. *82*. Retrieved from: http://www.scielo.org.za/scielo.php?script=sci_arttext&pid=S2304-85572014000200007 (accessed on 19 June 2024).

Kuruppuarachchi, K. A. P. S. T., & Surangi, H. A. K. N. S. (2020). The glass ceiling and women career advancement: A study based on ready-made garment industry in Sri Lanka. *Kelaniya Journal of Management, 8*(2), 18–39.

Mathipa, E. R., & Tsoka, E. M. (2001). Possible barriers to the advancement of women leadership positions in the education profession. *South African Journal of Education, 21*(4), 324–330.

Ministry of Education (MOE). (2022). Service minute of Sri Lanka educational administration service. Battaramula, Sri Lanka. Retrieved from: https://moe.gov.lk/ (accessed on 19 June 2024).

Morley, L., & Crossouard, B. (2015). Women in higher education leadership in South Asia: Rejection, refusal, reluctance, revisioning. *British Council Report*. Chapter 7, pp. 45–55, morley_crossouard_final_report_22_dec2014.pdf (britishcouncil.org).

Morley, L., & Crossouard, B. (2016). Women's leadership in the Asian century: Does expansion mean inclusion? *Studies in Higher Education, 41*(5), 801–814.

Schein, V. E., Mueller, R., Lituchy, T., & Liu, J. (1996). Think manager—think male: A global phenomenon? *Journal of Organizational Behavior, 17*(1), 33–41.

St. Catherine University. (2022). Overcome barriers to female leadership. St. Catherine University, Battaramula, Sri Lanka. Retrieved from: https://www.stkate.edu/academics/women-in-leadership-degrees/barriers-to-female-leadership (accessed on 19 June 2024).

Sui Chu Ho, E. (2015). Overview: Confronting the barriers of women leaders around the world. In E. C. Reilly & Q. Bauer (Eds.), *Women Leading Education Across the Continents: Overcoming the Barriers* (pp. 85–90). Lanham: Rowman and Littlefield.

Sule, A., Seda, E., Elif, K., & Gyongyi, L. (2017). Understanding gender differences in leadership. Retrieved from: http://mysite.ku.edu.tr/ekubilay/wpcontent/uploads/sites/90/2017/01/Manuscript_AlanErtacKubilayLoranth.pdf (accessed on 19 June 2024).

Svensson, G. (2006). Sustainable components of leadership effectiveness in organizational performance. *Journal of Management Development, 25*, 522–534, https://doi.org/10.1108/02621710610670100.

The World Economic Forum. (2015). *The Global Gender Gap Report 2015*. Retrieved from: http://reports.weforum.org/global-gender-gap-report-2015/ (accessed on 19 June 2024).

Withanage, D. P., & Chandrakumara, D. P. S. (2021). Gender equality in education in Sri Lanka. *Economic Research, 9*, 1.

CHAPTER 14

NAVIGATING UNCERTAINTY: ADVANCING GENDER EQUALITY IN CHALLENGING TIMES

JASMINE MARIAPPAN, ABDULLA THANSEER, MOHAMED RIYAS, and JOSHI RAGHAVAN EDASSERY

UTAS, IBRA, Oman

ABSTRACT

Gender equality is a critical issue that continues to be relevant in today's world, despite significant progress in recent years. Gender equality has been a pressing issue for decades, with numerous international agreements and efforts made to address it. The pandemic has had a disproportionate impact on women, exacerbating existing gender inequalities and creating new challenges. Women have been more likely to lose their jobs, face increased caregiving responsibilities, and experience a rise in domestic violence. The pandemic has also highlighted the systemic undervaluing of women's work, particularly in the care sector, and the need for a more equitable and sustainable economy that values care and other forms of unpaid work. Therefore, gender equality has become a crucial need in times of uncertainty, and concerted efforts are necessary to create a more just and equitable society for all.

This paper explores the concept of gender equality, its root causes, and its impact on various aspects of society, including education, employment, entrepreneurship, and politics. The chapter explores the significance of unpaid care work in the examination of gender differences in labor outcomes and emphasizes the necessity for governments, civil society organizations,

Subverting Social Inequalities: Gender as a Social Reality.
Akanksha Srivastava, Disha Maheshwari, Chitra Krishnan (Eds.)

and people to engage together in addressing gender inequality. The paper also presents a literature review on the topic of gender equality, covering various studies and reports on the subject. Ultimately, the paper argues that achieving gender equality is essential for creating a more just and prosperous society and that it requires a sustained and collaborative effort from all stakeholders.

14.1 INTRODUCTION

Gender equality is a critical issue that needs to be addressed in times of uncertainty, as it affects not just individuals but also communities and societies as a whole. Gender equality is a fundamental human right that has been recognized by international organizations, governments, and civil society. It is the state of equal access to resources and opportunities regardless of gender. The concept of gender equality has evolved over time, and significant progress has been made in many countries. However, gender inequality remains a pervasive issue in various areas, such as education, employment, health, and political participation. The COVID-19 pandemic has further exposed and amplified pre-existing gender inequalities, particularly in the labor market and unpaid care work (Kabeer & Natali, 2013).

Gender equality has suffered a great deal as a result of the COVID-19 pandemic. Women have been disproportionately affected by job losses, reduced working hours, and increased caregiving responsibilities, all of which have exacerbated pre-existing gender inequalities. In this context, it is essential that we act to prevent the pandemic from setting back gender equality gains that have been made in recent decades. To address these challenges, we need a range of interventions that target both the immediate effects of the pandemic and the underlying structural factors that contribute to gender inequality. Such interventions might include providing direct support to women who have lost their jobs or seen a reduction in working hours, increasing access to affordable childcare and eldercare services, and implementing policies that promote flexible work arrangements (Mahajan et al., 2020).

Women have been disproportionately affected in a number of areas, including health, education, and employment, making the need for gender equality more apparent in light of the COVID-19 epidemic. One of the major challenges for women during the epidemic has been the burden of unpaid caregiving. In order to reconcile work and home life and run their own enterprises, women have traditionally been expected to take on additional duties like childcare and housework. This has significantly decreased women's economic engagement as well as increased stress and burnout among them.

The gender disparity in access to healthcare has also been exposed by the pandemic. Women have faced barriers to accessing healthcare services due to various factors, including their caregiving responsibilities, limited mobility, and lack of financial resources. This has further exacerbated existing health disparities, particularly for marginalized communities.

Furthermore, women have been disproportionately affected by the pandemic's economic instability and job losses. Women, particularly those in low-wage jobs, have been more likely to lose their jobs or experience reduced working hours, making it more difficult for them to support themselves and their families. To address these challenges, it is essential to prioritize gender equality in policy responses to the pandemic. This entails ensuring that women have access to inexpensive, high-quality healthcare, supporting women who provide unpaid care, and putting policies in place to close the gender gap in employment and entrepreneurship. Addressing the underlying factors that contribute to gender inequality is also essential, including patriarchal attitudes and behaviors that support discrimination against women. To question and alter harmful gender norms and advance equality in all spheres of life, this calls for a concerted effort from governments, civil society organizations, and individuals.

Gender inequality has significant economic, social, and political implications, including reduced economic growth, limited social progress, and weakened democratic institutions. In addition to being important for social justice, achieving gender equality is also crucial for the Sustainable Development Goals (SDGs) of the United Nations (Errami, et al., 2021). Understanding the underlying causes of gender disparity is therefore crucial in order to create solutions. In this context, this paper aims to analyze the need for gender equality, particularly in times of uncertainty, and the various challenges in achieving it. This paper draws on existing literature on gender equality and the impacts of the COVID-19 pandemic on gender inequality. Furthermore, this paper examines the role of various actors, including governments, civil society organizations, and individuals, in addressing gender inequality and promoting gender equality.

14.2 LITERATURE REVIEW

Kabeer & Natali's (2013) study explores the relationship between gender equality and economic growth. The authors argue that gender equality is not only a matter of social justice but also a key driver of economic growth and development. They discuss the ways in which gender inequality can undermine economic growth, including through limited access to education and employment opportunities for women. The study also examines the impact of various policy interventions on promoting gender equality and economic growth. The authors argue that policies that specifically target gender inequality, such as affirmative action and gender budgeting, can be effective in promoting gender equality and economic growth. They also note that policies that promote women's education and employment can have significant positive impacts on economic growth.

Welter & Smallbone's (2011) article explore the role of institutions in shaping entrepreneurial behavior in challenging environments. The authors argue that institutional factors, including formal and informal rules, regulations, and cultural norms, can significantly impact the success or failure of entrepreneurial ventures. The study draws on institutional theory to examine the impact of institutional factors on entrepreneurial behavior in challenging environments, including post-conflict and post-socialist economies. The authors highlight the importance of understanding the institutional context in which entrepreneurship takes place, including the regulatory environment, cultural attitudes towards entrepreneurship, and access to resources and support networks. The study also looks at how policy changes could be made to change institutional settings in ways that encourage entrepreneurship. The authors contend that entrepreneurship-friendly policies, such as tax breaks, easier access to credit, and entrepreneurship training, can be successful in encouraging entrepreneurial behavior in adverse conditions.

According to a paper from the OECD Development Centre (2014), women's disproportionate responsibility for unpaid care work, which includes activities such as household chores and caring for children and elderly family members, limits their opportunities for paid work and career advancement. The data from several nations presented in the research demonstrates that women spend a disproportionate amount of time providing unpaid care compared to men. For women, especially those living in low-income homes, this creates a time poverty trap since they are unable to invest the necessary time and energy in pursuing paid employment or developing their skills, which keeps them in a low-income situation. The paper emphasizes the requirement for legislative actions that acknowledge and appreciate unpaid caregiving and support its equitable distribution among men and women. The authors contend that measures like paid time off for parents, accessible, high-quality childcare, and flexible work schedules can lessen the burden of unpaid care work on women and boost their involvement in the labor sector (Ferrant, et al., 2014).

The paper by Rania Antonopoulos (2009) highlights the crucial role of unpaid care work in shaping gender inequality and the need to recognize and value its economic contributions. It also underscores the interconnectedness of unpaid care work with paid work and the impact on women's ability to make choices and exercise voice over decision-making. The undervaluing of unpaid care work not only assigns paid social reproduction jobs to women but also imposes a time tax on them, affecting their ability to accumulate savings and assets. This, in turn, reinforces power relations between men and women and connects the private and public spheres of households and the economy in exploitative ways. The paper calls for increased attention to these interconnections and the need for policies that reduce the burden of unpaid care work and address the undervaluing of care jobs.

Carranza et al. (2018) analyze the differences between male and female entrepreneurs and identify the factors that contribute to those differences. The report uses data from the World Bank Enterprise Survey, which covers more than 130,000 enterprises in 139 countries. The report finds that female-owned businesses tend to be smaller, have lower sales and profits, and are less likely to have access to credit than male-owned businesses. Women entrepreneurs are also more likely to be in retail, personal services, and other low-growth sectors, and less likely to be in manufacturing or high-growth sectors. The report identifies several factors that contribute to these differences, including social and cultural barriers, legal and regulatory barriers, and access to finance. It also highlights the importance of education and training, access to networks and mentors, and supportive policies and programs in promoting women's entrepreneurship and addressing the gender gap in business ownership. Overall, the report emphasizes the need for targeted interventions that address the specific challenges faced by women entrepreneurs and the importance of collecting and analyzing sex-disaggregated data to inform policy and programming in this area.

The COVID-19 pandemic has had a significant impact on the global economy, with women and marginalized groups being disproportionately affected. The author highlighted the gendered impacts of the pandemic, including the fact that women are overrepresented in sectors such as healthcare and retail that have been hit hard by the crisis. They also note that women are more likely to work in informal or precarious employment, making it difficult for them to access social protections and economic relief measures (Kabeer et al., 2021).

The COVID-19 pandemic's effects on marginalized employees in precarious working settings are discussed by Cubrich, Tengesdal, Ugueto-Rey,

Stahl, and Crow Brauer. The authors contend that the pandemic has increased labor market disparities and brought attention to the need for legislative adjustments to address the particular difficulties encountered by employees in precarious employment conditions. The article discusses the impact of the COVID-19 pandemic on precarious, low-wage, and non-traditional workers around the world. These workers were already facing challenges such as low wages, lack of access to benefits and resources, and job insecurity before the pandemic, and the pandemic has exacerbated these issues while also creating new challenges. According to the article, research in the domains of organizational behavior and industrial-organizational psychology has typically concentrated on white-collar employees, underrepresenting hourly wage workers, contract employees, and gig workers. The paper underlines how members of marginalized groups are overrepresented in insecure employment and are disproportionately affected by crises like the COVID-19 outbreak. In order to comprehend the experiences of minority employees during the epidemic, it is crucial to use an intersectional lens (Cubrich, et al., 2022).

Gender disparity is a significant issue in Indian culture. Despite the nation's constitution, which guarantees equal rights for men and women, and decades of laws, gender discrimination still has a severe impact on women's lives in India. Despite tremendous economic advancement, there are still gender inequities, and every day 1,000 girls under the age of five die from abuse. India has been ranked poorly on numerous indices that measure gender equality, including economic participation and opportunity, educational attainment, health and survival, political empowerment, and legal protection, due to a variety of factors, including the high levels of discrimination against women in India as well as numerous discriminatory social norms, laws, and cultural practices.

14.3 THE COVID-19 PANDEMIC'S EFFECT ON GENDER EQUALITY

Gender equality has been significantly impacted by the COVID-19 pandemic, with women being more severely affected than men in a number of sectors. A few of the pandemic's major effects on gender equality are as follows:

- **Health:** Women have been more likely to face barriers in accessing healthcare services during the pandemic. Due to their caregiving responsibilities and lack of financial resources, women have been more likely to avoid seeking healthcare services, leading to health disparities. Women also make up the majority of frontline healthcare workers, putting them at higher risk of contracting the virus.

- **Education:** The pandemic has had a significant impact on education, with schools closing and classes moving online. Girls are more likely to miss out on education during times of crisis, with many forced to drop out of school due to poverty, early marriage, or caregiving responsibilities. The pandemic has exacerbated these challenges, making it even harder for girls to access education.
- **Employment:** Women have been disproportionately affected by job losses and reduced working hours due to the pandemic. Women in low-wage jobs have been particularly hard hit, with many losing their jobs entirely or being forced to work reduced hours. Women have also been overrepresented in industries that have been most affected by the pandemic, such as hospitality and retail.
- **Unpaid Care Work:** Women have been expected to take on extra tasks like childcare and domestic work because schools and childcare centers had to close due to the pandemic. Women have experienced a dramatic decline in their economic engagement as a result, along with increased stress and burnout. Due to their frequent lack of access to paid leave or flexible work schedules, women who work in low-paying jobs have been disproportionately impacted.
- **Reduced Working Hours:** Women are more likely to have flexible schedules or part-time jobs, which are more susceptible to the effects of the recession. Women's wages and capacity to care for themselves and their families may be significantly impacted by the reduction in working hours.
- **Increased Caregiving Responsibilities**: With the closure of schools and childcare facilities, women have been expected to take on additional caregiving responsibilities. This has led to increased stress and burnout and has made it more challenging for women to work outside the home.
- **Increased Risk of Poverty**: Women in low-wage jobs are more likely to experience poverty, and the loss of income due to the pandemic can make this even more challenging. Women who are single parents or who live in households with other dependents may be particularly vulnerable to poverty.

- **Limited Opportunities for Career Advancement:** Women in low-wage jobs often have limited opportunities for career advancement, which can make it difficult for them to move out of poverty. The pandemic has made it even harder for women in these jobs to access training or education opportunities, which could help them to develop new skills and progress in their careers.

14.4 PRIORITIZING GENDER EQUALITY IN POLICY RESPONSES TO THE PANDEMIC

Women often face unique challenges in accessing affordable and quality healthcare services, and the COVID-19 pandemic has further highlighted the need to prioritize gender equality in policy responses. Here are some examples of policy interventions that can help ensure women have access to affordable and quality healthcare services and policy interventions that can help reduce the gender gap in employment and entrepreneurship:

- **Addressing Reproductive Health Needs:** Women have specific reproductive health needs, including access to contraception, prenatal care, and maternal health services. Policies that promote access to these services, such as expanding health insurance coverage, increasing funding for family planning programs, and providing free or low-cost reproductive healthcare services, can help to ensure that women can access the care they need.
- **Promoting Mental Health Services:** Women are more likely than men to experience mental health issues, and the pandemic has had a significant impact on mental health. Policies that promote access to mental health services, including counseling and therapy, can help to address this issue.
- **Removing Financial Barriers to Healthcare:** Cost can be a significant barrier to accessing healthcare services, particularly for women who are more likely to live in poverty than men. Policies that remove financial barriers to healthcare, such as expanding Medicaid, providing subsidies for health insurance premiums, and offering free or low-cost healthcare services, can help to ensure that women can access the care they need.
- **Providing Culturally Competent Care:** Women from different ethnic and cultural backgrounds may have unique healthcare needs

and preferences. Policies that promote culturally competent care, such as increasing funding for language translation services and training healthcare providers in cultural competency, can help to ensure that women receive high-quality healthcare services that meet their specific needs.

- By implementing these policy interventions, governments can help ensure that women have access to affordable and quality healthcare services, promoting gender equality and women's health and well-being.
- **Investing in Education and Training:** Women often face a skills gap that limits their employment opportunities. Policies that invest in education and training programs, particularly in fields that are traditionally male-dominated, can help to reduce the gender gap in employment and entrepreneurship.
- **Supporting Women Entrepreneurs:** Women entrepreneurs often face unique challenges, including limited access to capital and networks. Policies that support women entrepreneurs, such as providing access to financing and business development support, can help to reduce the gender gap in entrepreneurship.
- **Promoting Work-Life Balance:** Women are more likely than men to take on caregiving responsibilities, which can limit their employment opportunities. Policies that promote work-life balance, such as flexible work arrangements and paid family leave, can help to reduce the gender gap in employment and entrepreneurship.
- **Addressing Gender Bias and Discrimination:** Women often face gender bias and discrimination in the workplace and in entrepreneurial ecosystems. Policies that address gender bias and discrimination, such as promoting gender diversity and inclusion in hiring and promoting women's leadership, can help to reduce the gender gap in employment and entrepreneurship.

14.5 ADDRESSING THE ROOT CAUSES OF GENDER INEQUALITY

To achieve long-term gender equality, it is crucial to address the root causes of gender inequality. Addressing the root causes of gender inequality requires a multifaceted approach that addresses the complex ways in which gender, race, class, and other social structures intersect. Some strategies that have been proposed include:

- **Challenging Harmful Gender Norms and Stereotypes:** Many gender inequalities are reinforced by societal expectations and stereotypes about gender roles. Challenging and changing these norms can help promote gender equality and empower individuals of all genders to pursue their goals and aspirations.
- **Promoting Equal Access to Education:** Education is a powerful tool for promoting gender equality and empowering women and girls. Providing equal access to education, particularly in developing countries, can help break the cycle of poverty and increase opportunities for women.
- **Addressing Workplace Discrimination and Promoting Work-Life Balance:** Women continue to face discrimination in the workplace, including unequal pay, limited opportunities for advancement, and lack of support for work-life balance. Promoting policies that address these issues, such as paid parental leave and flexible work arrangements, can help level the playing field.
- **Increasing Women's Representation in Leadership and Decision-Making Roles:** Women are underrepresented in positions of leadership and decision-making, both in the public and private sectors. Increasing women's representation in these roles can help promote gender equality and ensure that women's perspectives are reflected in important decisions.
- **Addressing Violence Against Women:** Gender-based violence is a pervasive problem around the world, and addressing it is essential to promoting gender equality. This includes not only providing support for survivors but also challenging the societal attitudes and beliefs that contribute to violence against women.
- **Flexible Work Arrangements:** Governments and employers can implement policies that allow workers to have greater control over their schedules, such as telecommuting or flexible work hours. This can help address gender disparities in work and family responsibilities and allow for greater work-life balance.
- **Social Protection Measures:** Providing access to social protection measures such as unemployment insurance, health care, and

childcare can help alleviate the burden of uncertainty on individuals and families, particularly for those who are most vulnerable to economic shocks.

- **Gender-Responsive Budgeting:** Governments can use gender-responsive budgeting to ensure that budgetary allocations consider the specific needs and priorities of women and girls, and that gender equality is integrated into all policy decisions.
- **Strengthening Women's Access to Finance:** Policy interventions can focus on providing women with greater access to finance, such as microcredit schemes or targeted financing for women-led businesses. This can help women weather economic uncertainty and contribute to their economic empowerment.
- **Addressing Gender-Based Violence:** During times of uncertainty and stress, gender-based violence can increase. Policies and interventions that address and prevent gender-based violence can help ensure the safety and well-being of women and girls.

Overall, addressing the root causes of gender inequality requires a comprehensive approach that addresses the many factors that contribute to gender-based discrimination and inequality. By promoting policies and programs that support women's empowerment and gender equality, we can work towards a more just and equitable society.

14.6 GENDER AND RESILIENCE

Gender and resilience are closely intertwined concepts. Resilience refers to the ability of individuals, communities, and systems to withstand, adapt to, and recover from shocks and stresses. In the context of uncertain times, building resilience is crucial to reducing the negative effects of uncertainty on gender equality. Women and girls play a vital role in building resilient communities.

They are often the first responders to crises and have unique knowledge, skills, and networks that can help to build community resilience. However, they also face unique challenges during and after crises, including increased risk of violence, reduced access to resources, and limited decision-making power.

For resilience to be increased and sustainable development to be promoted, gender equality must be attained. Communities' capacity to anticipate shocks and respond to pressures is limited by gender disparity. Women's unequal access to resources, services, and decision-making authority can worsen the effects of crises, while their involvement in decision-making and leadership can increase community resilience.

In order to advance gender equality and foster resilience, civil society, the private sector, and the government all have significant roles to play. Organizations in civil society can support and assist women and girls during and after crises, speak out in favor of laws and initiatives that advance gender equality, and make it easier for women to participate in decision-making. The private sector may help supply chains that take gender diversity into account, offer flexible work schedules to employees, and make investments in women's economic empowerment. Governments can implement laws and plans that advance gender equality, provide aid to women and girls during and after crises, and make sure that women's opinions are taken into consideration when making decisions.

14.7 CONCLUSION

In conclusion, uncertain times can have significant negative impacts on gender equality, but there are steps that can be taken to mitigate these effects. Best practices and policy interventions such as flexible work arrangements, social protection measures, and investments in education and training can help ensure that women and girls are not left behind. Civil society, the private sector, and the government all have a role to play in promoting gender equality and building resilience in communities. Women and girls themselves also have an important role to play in building resilience, and efforts should be made to ensure that their voices and perspectives are included in decision-making processes. Finally, promoting gender equality is not only a moral imperative but also essential for achieving sustainable development. As such, all stakeholders should prioritize gender equality in uncertain times and work towards building a more resilient and equitable world for all.

The chapter has also highlighted best practices and policy interventions that can help promote gender equality during uncertain times, including measures to address gender-based violence, support women's economic empowerment, and provide access to healthcare and education. The role of civil society, the private sector, and the government in promoting gender equality has been discussed, and the need for collaboration and multi-stakeholder engagement emphasized.

Finally, we recommend future research and policy interventions to better understand and address the gendered impacts of uncertainty. This can be achieved by gathering more data and evidence on the gendered impacts of uncertainty, as well as investing in research that explores the relationship between gender equality, resilience, and sustainable development. By prioritizing gender equality in uncertain times, we can build more resilient and sustainable communities for all.

KEYWORDS

- **COVID-19**
- **discrimination**
- **gender equality**
- **gender gaps**
- **gender-based violence**
- **gender-responsive policies**
- **social norms**
- **sustainable development goal**

REFERENCES

Antonopoulos, Rania, The Unpaid Care Work-Paid Work Connection (July 25, 2008). Levy Economics Institute, Working Papers Series, Available at SSRN: https://ssrn.com/abstract=1176661 or http://dx.doi.org/10.2139/ssrn.1176661

Carranza, E., Dhakal, C., & Love, I. (2018). Female entrepreneurs. Retrieved from: https://documents1.worldbank.org/curated/en/400121542883319809/pdf/Female-Entrepreneurs-How-and-Why-are-They-Different.pdf (accessed on 19 June 2024).

Cubrich, M., Tengesdal, J. A., Ugueto-Rey, G., Stahl, R., & Crow Brauer, M. (2022). Pandemics and precarious work: Translating research to practice for marginalized workers. *Translational Issues in Psychological Science, 8*(3), 416–430. doi:10.1037/tps0000327.

Errami, E., Ochir, G., & Peppoloni, S. (2021). Achieve gender equality and empower all women and girls. In G. di Capua, L. Becerra Valdivia, & S. Peppoloni (Eds.), *Geosciences and the Sustainable Development Goals* (pp. 105–126).

Ferrant, G., Pesando, L. M., & Nowacka, K. (2014). Unpaid care work: The missing link in the analysis of gender gaps in labor outcomes. Boulogne Billancourt: OECD Development Center.

Kabeer, N., & Natali, L. (2013). Gender equality and economic growth: Is there a win-win? *IDS Working Papers, 2013*(417), 1–58. doi:10.1111/j.2040-0209.2013. 00417.x.

Kabeer, N., Razavi, S., & van der Meulen Rodgers, Y. (2021). Feminist economic perspectives on the COVID-19 pandemic. *Feminist Economics, 27*(1–2), 1–29. doi:10.1080/13545701. 2020.1856494.

Mahajan, D., White, O., Madgavkar, A., & Krishnan, M. (2020). Don't let the pandemic set back gender equality. *Harvard Business Review, 16*, 1–3.

Welter, F., & Smallbone, D. (2011). Institutional perspectives on entrepreneurial behavior in challenging environments. *Journal of Small Business Management, 49*(1), 107–125. doi:10.1111/j.1540-627X.2010. 00317.x.

CHAPTER 15

INDIAN WOMEN ENTREPRENEURS: CHALLENGES AND EMERGING ISSUES

SEEMA GARG

AIBS, Amity University, Noida, Uttar Pradesh, India

ABSTRACT

In recent years, there has been a growing interest in women's entrepreneurship in India. Despite the challenges faced by women entrepreneurs, there has been a significant increase in the number of women-led businesses in the country. However, women entrepreneurs continue to face a range of challenges that inhibit their growth and success. The purpose of this chapter is to explore the challenges faced by women entrepreneurs in India and to identify emerging issues that may impact their businesses. The chapter aims to provide a comprehensive overview of the current state of women's entrepreneurship in India and to suggest strategies to support women entrepreneurs. This paper is based on a review of existing literature and data on women's entrepreneurship in India. The literature review included academic articles, reports from international organizations, and news articles. In addition, interviews were conducted with women entrepreneurs in India to gain a better understanding of their experiences and challenges.

The findings of this chapter highlight the challenges faced by women entrepreneurs in India, including access to finance, networking opportunities, and cultural barriers. Women entrepreneurs in India also face challenges related to social and family expectations, which can limit their ability to devote time and resources to their businesses. Additionally, emerging issues such as the digital divide, the impact of the COVID-19 pandemic, and the changing nature of work present both challenges and opportunities for

Subverting Social Inequalities: Gender as a Social Reality.
Akanksha Srivastava, Disha Maheshwari, Chitra Krishnan (Eds.)

women entrepreneurs in India. To support women entrepreneurs in India, it is necessary to address the challenges they face and to provide targeted support in areas such as access to finance, networking opportunities, and skill-building. Strategies such as mentorship programs, training, capacity-building initiatives, and policy interventions can also play a critical role in supporting women's entrepreneurship.

15.1 INTRODUCTION

Entrepreneurship is often viewed as a driving force for economic growth and development, with entrepreneurs playing a key role in creating new businesses, generating employment, and driving innovation. This is a widely accepted view among scholars, policymakers, and business leaders around the world (Scott, 1986). Entrepreneurship plays a crucial role in creating opportunities for future performers and is considered an essential component of globalization. By creating new businesses and innovative products and services, entrepreneurs help to stimulate economic growth and job creation, while also driving innovation and technological advancement. Moreover, entrepreneurship has the potential to address social and environmental challenges by developing new solutions that promote sustainability and inclusivity. Thus, entrepreneurship is increasingly recognized as a key driver of economic and social development, both at the national and international levels (Mitra, 2002).

Women entrepreneurship is a growing phenomenon in India, with more and more women stepping into the world of business and creating successful enterprises. Women entrepreneurship refers to the process of women starting and running their own businesses, with the goal of creating successful and sustainable enterprises. According to various reports and studies, women entrepreneurs make up approximately 10% of all business owners in India, and this number is gradually increasing year by year. While women have traditionally faced a range of social, cultural, and economic barriers to starting and growing their own businesses, the Indian government and various organizations have been implementing several measures and initiatives to encourage and support women's entrepreneurship. These include providing financial and technical assistance, creating networks and mentorship programs, and promoting gender-inclusive policies and practices. As a result, there has been a growing interest among women in pursuing entrepreneurship as a viable career option, which is expected to further contribute to the growth of the Indian economy. One of the sources that support this claim is the Sixth Economic Census conducted by the Ministry of Statistics and Program Implementation, Government of India in 2013. The report states that out of the 58.5 million establishments in India, around 8.05 million were owned by women, which accounts for around 14% of the total.

In recent years, there has been a significant increase in the number of women entrepreneurs in India, with women accounting for approximately 14% of all entrepreneurs in the country (Global Entrepreneurship Monitor, 2020–2021). Despite this growth, women entrepreneurs in India continue to face a number of challenges, including limited access to funding, lack of support networks, and social and cultural barriers. However, studies have shown that women entrepreneurs tend to be more innovative, customer-oriented, and resilient than their male counterparts. Rajvanshi (2017) conducted a study on women entrepreneurs in India, examining the challenges and opportunities they face in starting and running their own businesses. The study found that while there has been a significant increase in the number of women entrepreneurs in India in recent years, they continue to face a range of challenges, including limited access to finance and markets, lack of social support, and cultural biases against women in business. The study also identified a number of opportunities for women entrepreneurs, including the growing demand for women-led businesses, the availability of government schemes and initiatives to support women entrepreneurs, and the emergence of new technologies and platforms that make it easier for women to start and grow their businesses.

A woman is referred to as a woman entrepreneur if she manages, owns, and takes risks with a business. Women entrepreneurs refer to women or a set of women who start, plan, and have their own businesses. They have capabilities like a strong will, talent, skill, and a desire for economic development. Therefore, a woman entrepreneur is a strong, imaginative, and creative lady. Also considered an individual with economic independence while also producing work. According to Butner & Moore (1997), a woman entrepreneur has the potential to drive economic growth and development in various ways, such as creating new jobs, boosting local economies, promoting innovation, and increasing diversity in the business world. Studies have shown that supporting women entrepreneurs can have significant economic and social benefits, both in developed and developing countries.

Despite facing various challenges, women entrepreneurs have been able to make significant contributions to the Indian economy, creating jobs, promoting innovation, and driving growth. In this chapter, we will provide an overview of the current status of women entrepreneurship in India, discuss the challenges faced by women entrepreneurs, and highlight the emerging issues in the field. We will also examine successful case studies of women entrepreneurs in India, such as Chitra Gurnani Daga and Shradha Sharma, to better understand the qualities and characteristics that have enabled them to succeed. Finally, we will explore the various government schemes and initiatives that have been launched to support women entrepreneurs in India. By examining the opportunities and challenges faced by women entrepreneurs in India, we hope to provide insights and guidance to aspiring women entrepreneurs, policymakers, and stakeholders, to promote and support the growth of women entrepreneurship in the country.

15.2 LITERATURE REVIEW

Khan et al. (2021) stressed the crucial role that women play in economic development and suggested looking into the elements that contribute to Pakistani women entrepreneurs' success. They made use of information gathered from 181 registered SMEs doing business in Pakistan using structured surveys. They created a conceptual model and conducted an analysis using SPSS and AMOS software. They cited numerous types of research to examine the effects of various variables on women's success as entrepreneurs, but they also looked into other related variables such as religion, culture, etc. Ritwik & Remya (2020) tried to raise awareness of women's entrepreneurship, grasp what it means, and highlight how crucial it is for the rational, economic, and overall growth of the globe. An extensive literature review on female entrepreneur-related studies is conducted. Indian women entrepreneurs encounter, their successes, the factors that influence women entrepreneurs, and the viewpoints of various social groups on women entrepreneurs have all been noted at the conclusion. After economic liberalization and globalization, women entrepreneurs have increased, according to 2003 research by Vijayakumar et al. (2013). They discussed how important women-owned businesses are to the economy and society. Sharma (2013)'s essays on comprehending female entrepreneurs and particularly for the purpose of their role-taking and making new directions and routes, will fall short. According to García-Palma and Sánchez-Mora Molina (2016), female entrepreneurs need to have marketing knowledge and skills in order to succeed in their businesses. The entrepreneurial approach is guided by market information (García-Palma & Sánchez-Mora Molina, 2016). A true understanding of entrepreneurship and its causes is crucial since it plays a significant role in innovation, economic development, and the reduction of poverty (Wahba, 2012).

Specifically focusing on female entrepreneurs, Bowen & Hisrich (1986) discussed and examined the idea of women's entrepreneurship in their study. Through the lens of career development, their work played a crucial role in bringing together research and methodologies on women entrepreneurs that had previously been fragmented. Through a thorough examination of the effects and influences on women's capacity and decision-making regarding entrepreneurship, they provided a comprehensive framework for comprehending the entrepreneurial behavior of women. The study concluded that, while generally speaking, female entrepreneurs have reasonably good educations, they lack proper management skills, have a higher internal locus of power than other women, and are more likely to have had fathers who were also business owners.

Family plays a very critical role in the economy of any country. Studies related to this show that female entrepreneurs achieve a reputation at an official place or even in their personal life and network related to it through existing living society family (Hanson, 2009). The significance of family support, self-confidence, motivation, risk-taking, and motivation, and a lack of business skills are additional findings from earlier research (Azmi, 2017) (Muhammad, McElwee, & Dana, 2017). While the performance of women-run businesses is heavily impacted by policies of government, culture, and legislation (Muhammad et al., 2017). What (Modarresi, Arasti, Talebi, & Farasatkhah, 2016) concluded based on their research is that company performance is significantly influenced by employee behaviors, culture, economic variables, and environmental factors. Singh (2008) concentrated on the causes and determining elements of women's entry into entrepreneurship. He described the traits of their businesses in the context of India, as well as the difficulties and challenges. In addition, he noted that barriers to women's entrepreneurship growth include gender discrimination, a lack of engagement with successful businesspeople, and family obligations. Bankers also give women entrepreneurs a low priority when it comes to providing loan-like facilities. He advised corrective actions such as supporting micro-businesses, dismantling institutional frameworks, projecting and pulling to grow and support motivated and influential winners, etc. There are several nations where the proportion of female entrepreneurs is less than half that of male entrepreneurs. These nations include Sweden, Slovenia, Greece, Turkey, the United Kingdom, and Switzerland. They provide an overview of female entrepreneurship across 49 nations. The Total Entrepreneurial

Activity for women is below 5% in a number of countries in Europe and North America (Bosma & Kelley, 2019).

Swarnalatha (2014) focused on Indian women who confront numerous challenges and other limitations when trying to advance in life and business. They should look into the possibility of starting a new business and take chances because based on a study by Guzman & Kacperczyk (2019), women entrepreneurs are 63% less likely than male entrepreneurs to receive finance from external sources in terms of risk capital, with gender disparities accounting for the majority of the disparity. Additionally, women must lead well in all business-related fields, coordinate administration, and propose innovations in new companies.

Vinothalakshmi & Ganesan (2013) underlined all the additional facets of Indian female entrepreneurs and the challenges associated with it that must be overcome. In India, there is a clear indication of the rise and contribution to the economy. Women's participation in the employment of a business firm is based on how the Indian government defines women entrepreneurs. Families are made up of women, which creates social and family.

According to Shah (2012), there needs to be a larger pool of female entrepreneurs if economic growth is to be accelerated. In her study, Veena S. Samani (2008) focused on a particular group of working women in the food processing industry. According to the report, the majority of women in Gujarat are skilled and knowledgeable in food preparation and processing. Regardless of the quantity and type of food being processed, whether or not these businesses are connected to homes, they have been shown to be quite successful. The current study also provides information on their activities, expertise, attitudes, and issues. All of the selected women identified stress as their main issue. The researcher discovered that the majority of women business owners were Hindus, about 65% of women were raised in nuclear homes, and only a small percentage of women had completed formal education.

A literature review on Indian women entrepreneurs reveals a complex and diverse set of challenges and opportunities facing women entrepreneurs in India. Some of the key themes that emerge from the literature are discussed below:

- **Socio-Cultural Factors:** Traditional gender roles and societal norms can create obstacles for women entrepreneurs in India. Cultural expectations and biases can make it difficult for women to secure funding, access business networks, and overcome other challenges.
- **Access to Finance:** One of the biggest challenges faced by women entrepreneurs in India is access to finance. Many women

entrepreneurs struggle to secure loans or other forms of financing due to a lack of collateral or other financial resources.

- **Access to Markets and Networks:** Women entrepreneurs in India often face barriers to accessing markets and business networks. Limited access to business networks can make it difficult for women entrepreneurs to gain visibility, build relationships, and identify new opportunities.
- **Technology and Infrastructure:** Limited access to technology and infrastructure can be a significant challenge for women entrepreneurs in India. Poor internet connectivity, unreliable power supply, and inadequate transportation infrastructure can limit the ability of women entrepreneurs to operate and grow their businesses.
- **Support Networks and Resources:** There is a growing recognition of the importance of support networks and resources for women entrepreneurs in India. This includes access to mentoring, training, and other resources to help women entrepreneurs build their skills and expand their businesses.

Overall, the literature suggests that while women entrepreneurship in India faces a range of challenges, there are also many opportunities for growth and success. As the Indian government and other organizations continue to invest in women's entrepreneurship initiatives and support networks, there is hope that the sector will continue to grow and thrive in the years ahead.

15.3 OBJECTIVES OF THE STUDY

Women entrepreneurs in India have made significant strides in recent years, but they still face a range of challenges that can make it difficult for them to succeed. This chapter will explore some of the most pressing challenges facing Indian women entrepreneurs, as well as some of the emerging issues that need to be addressed to support their success.

15.4 WOMEN ENTREPRENEURS

Women entrepreneurs refer to women who initiate, manage, and own their own businesses. Women entrepreneurship has been on the rise in recent years, with more and more women starting their own businesses. However, women entrepreneurs still face a range of challenges, including limited access to finance, lack of networks and mentoring, and social and cultural barriers. There are five categories of women entrepreneurs, including rural entrepreneurs, wealthy entrepreneurs, self-employed entrepreneurs, push factors, and urban women with pull factors. Nowadays, practically all economies are seeing an increase in the number of female entrepreneurs. With increased awareness of women's roles and economic standing in any community, both their hidden and evident business potentials have grown. The main factors encouraging women to start their own businesses are their expertise, aptitude, compliance, and capacity in the field. Due to push and pull elements that give women the courage to have a self-sustaining career and stand on their own, women become entrepreneurs. For the advancement of women entrepreneurs and their increased participation in entrepreneurial activities, appropriate and timely initiatives in all sectors are crucial.

15.4.1 CHARACTERISTICS OF WOMEN ENTREPRENEURS

Babu (1978) identified the social elements that support the growth of small business owners. A woman entrepreneur is someone who develops new ideas, uses them as the foundation for her business, and adds value to society via her own initiative. Women entrepreneurs come from diverse backgrounds and have a variety of personal and professional characteristics. Here are some common characteristics of women entrepreneurs:

- **Resilience:** Women entrepreneurs often have to overcome a range of obstacles to succeed, including social and cultural barriers and limited access to resources. As a result, they tend to be highly resilient and determined.
- **Creativity:** Women entrepreneurs often bring a fresh perspective and unique ideas to their businesses. They are often highly creative and innovative in their approach.
- **Collaboration:** Women entrepreneurs tend to be highly collaborative and willing to work with others to achieve their goals. They often build strong networks of support and are willing to seek out advice and guidance from others.
- **Passion:** Women entrepreneurs are often passionate about their businesses and the impact they can make on their communities. They are driven by a desire to make a positive change and leave a legacy.

- **Flexibility:** Women entrepreneurs need to be flexible and adaptable to changing circumstances. They are often able to pivot and adjust their strategies as needed to respond to market changes and other challenges.

These characteristics can help women entrepreneurs to succeed, but they also need access to resources and support to overcome the challenges they face. Governments, organizations, and communities can help by providing funding, mentorship, training, and other resources to support women's entrepreneurship.

15.4.2 CHALLENGES IN THE JOURNEY

Women entrepreneurs face a range of challenges in their entrepreneurial journey. Here are some of the main challenges:

- **Limited Access to Finance:** Women entrepreneurs often have difficulty securing financing for their businesses, as they may have limited collateral and face discrimination from lenders. This can limit their ability to invest in their businesses and grow.
- **Lack of Networks and Mentoring:** Women entrepreneurs may have limited access to networks and mentors, which can limit their ability to learn from others and build relationships with potential customers, partners, and investors.
- **Social and Cultural Barriers:** Women entrepreneurs may face discrimination and bias based on their gender, which can limit their opportunities and access to resources. They may also face pressure to conform to traditional gender roles, which can make it difficult to balance their personal and professional lives.
- **Balancing Work and Family Responsibilities:** Women entrepreneurs may face challenges in balancing their work and family responsibilities, particularly if they have caregiving responsibilities for children or elderly relatives.
- **Managing Growth:** Women entrepreneurs may struggle with managing growth, particularly if they have limited access to resources and support. They may need to make difficult decisions about hiring, financing, and expanding their operations.

Despite these challenges, women entrepreneurs have been shown to be highly resilient and determined, and they have made significant contributions to the economy. Efforts to support women's entrepreneurship, including policies and programs that address these challenges, can help to promote gender equality and economic growth.

15.4.3 SUCCESSFUL WOMEN ENTREPRENEURS

There are many successful women entrepreneurs in India who have made significant contributions to the economy and to society. Here are some examples:

1. **Falguni Nayar:** One of the case studies of a successful woman entrepreneur in India is Falguni Nayar, the founder of Nykaa, an e-commerce platform that specializes in beauty and wellness products. Before launching Nykaa in 2012, Nayar spent over two decades working in the corporate sector, including senior roles at companies like Kotak Mahindra and the consulting firm A.T. Kearney. Despite her successful career, Nayar felt a strong desire to pursue her entrepreneurial dreams and to create a business that would disrupt the beauty and wellness industry in India.

   Nayar faced a number of challenges in launching Nykaa, including limited access to funding and the need to build a new brand in a crowded and competitive market. However, she was able to leverage her experience in the corporate sector and her keen understanding of the Indian consumer to build a company that has been successful beyond her wildest dreams.

   Today, Nykaa is one of the largest beauty e-commerce platforms in India, with over 1,500 brands and 130,000 products. The company has also expanded into brick-and-mortar retail, with more than 50 stores across India. Nayar's success as a woman entrepreneur in India highlights the importance of experience, vision, and a willingness to take risks. Her story serves as an inspiration to women entrepreneurs around the world and underscores the potential for women to disrupt even the most established industries.

2. **Kiran Mazumdar-Shaw**, one case study of a successful women entrepreneur in India is Kiran Mazumdar-Shaw, the founder of Biocon Limited. Biocon is a biotechnology company that specializes

in the development and manufacture of pharmaceuticals, including biosimilars, which are similar to existing biologic drugs but are produced by different companies. Kiran Mazumdar-Shaw founded Biocon in 1978 with just Rs. 10,000 ($140) and a small team of employees. Today, Biocon is one of the largest biotech companies in India, with a market capitalization of over $8 billion. Mazumdar-Shaw faced a number of challenges as a woman entrepreneur in India, particularly in the male-dominated field of biotechnology. She struggled to secure funding and gain credibility in a field that was largely dominated by men. However, she persevered and built a successful company by leveraging her scientific expertise and business acumen.

Today, Mazumdar-Shaw is recognized as a leading figure in the Indian biotechnology industry and has received numerous accolades for her contributions to science and entrepreneurship. She has also become a prominent philanthropist, using her wealth and influence to support a range of causes, including healthcare and education. Mazumdar-Shaw's success as a woman entrepreneur in India highlights the potential for women to succeed in even the most challenging fields. Her story serves as an inspiration to women entrepreneurs around the world and underscores the importance of persistence, creativity, and a strong vision for success.

3. **Aditi Gupta:** A third case study of a successful woman entrepreneur in India is Aditi Gupta, the founder of Menstrupedia. Menstrupedia is a website and comic book series that provides information and resources on menstruation and women's health. Gupta's inspiration for Menstrupedia came from her own experiences growing up in India, where menstruation was often considered a taboo topic and access to information and resources was limited. She saw a need for a platform that could provide accurate information and support for young girls and women who were dealing with issues related to menstruation.

   Gupta faced a number of challenges in launching Menstrupedia, including limited funding and cultural barriers to discussing menstruation in public. However, she was able to leverage social media and other digital platforms to raise awareness and build a community of supporters around her brand. Today, Menstrupedia is a widely recognized platform for women's health, with a range of resources and tools that have been translated into multiple languages and used by millions of people around the world. Gupta's success as a woman entrepreneur in India highlights the importance of addressing unmet needs in the market and the potential for social entrepreneurship to drive positive change in society. Her story serves as an inspiration to women entrepreneurs around the world and underscores the power of technology and digital media in enabling new forms of entrepreneurship and social impact.

4. **Richa Kar:** A fourth case study of a successful woman entrepreneur in India is Richa Kar, the founder of Zivame, an e-commerce platform that specializes in lingerie and intimate wear for women. Kar started her career as an IT consultant but soon became interested in the e-commerce sector and identified a gap in the market for women's intimate wear. She launched Zivame in 2011 with the aim of creating a platform that would provide women with access to high-quality, comfortable, and stylish lingerie tailored to their needs.

   Kar faced a number of challenges in launching Zivame, including the need to build a new brand in a market dominated by established players, as well as the need to educate Indian women about the importance of wearing well-fitted lingerie. However, she was able to leverage digital marketing and other innovative strategies to build a strong brand and attract a loyal following.

   Today, Zivame is one of the largest lingerie e-commerce platforms in India, with over 5 million customers and more than 2,000 products. The company has also expanded into brick-and-mortar retail, with over 30 stores across India. Kar's success as a woman entrepreneur in India highlights the importance of identifying unmet needs in the market and the potential for digital platforms to disrupt established industries. Her story serves as an inspiration to women entrepreneurs around the world and underscores the potential for women to drive innovation and growth in the e-commerce sector.

5. **Vandana Luthra** is the founder of VLCC, one of India's largest health and wellness companies. Luthra started her career as a homemaker, but after struggling with weight issues, she became interested in exploring different ways to stay healthy and fit. In 1989, Luthra launched VLCC, with the aim of providing affordable and accessible health and wellness services to women across India. She faced

a number of challenges in launching VLCC, including the need to build a new brand and find a loyal customer base. However, Luthra was able to leverage her expertise in health and wellness and her passion for helping others to create a strong brand that resonated with Indian women. Today, VLCC is a widely recognized brand in the health and wellness sector, with a range of services that include weight management, skincare, and haircare. Luthra's success as a women entrepreneur in India highlights the potential for women to drive innovation and growth in the health and wellness sector and underscores the importance of pursuing one's passions and interests in building a successful career.

6. **Shahnaz Husain:** Shahnaz Husain is the founder of the Shahnaz Husain Group, which produces a range of herbal beauty products. She is often called the "queen of herbal beauty" and has been recognized with numerous awards for her contributions to entrepreneurship and the beauty industry.

7. **Shradha Sharma** is the founder and CEO of Your Story, India's largest media platform for startups and entrepreneurs. Sharma started her career as a journalist, working for leading publications such as the Times of India and CNBC TV18. In 2008, Sharma launched YourStory, with the aim of creating a platform that would tell the stories of India's emerging startups and entrepreneurs. She faced a number of challenges in launching YourStory, including the need to build a new brand and establish credibility in a market that was dominated by established media players. However, Sharma was able to leverage her experience in journalism and her knowledge of the Indian startup ecosystem to create a platform that resonated with Indian entrepreneurs. Today, Your Story is the go-to source for news and insights on the Indian startup ecosystem, and is widely recognized for its role in promoting entrepreneurship in India. Sharma's success as a woman entrepreneur in India highlights the potential for women to drive innovation and growth in the media and tech sectors, and underscores the importance of following one's passions and interests in building a successful career.

8. **Chitra Gurnani Daga:** Chitra Gurnani Daga is a successful woman entrepreneur in India who is the founder and CEO of Thrillophilia, India's largest online platform for booking adventure activities and experiences. Daga was born and raised in Rajasthan, and after

completing her MBA, she worked for several years in the corporate sector before deciding to start her own venture. In 2009, Daga launched Thrillophilia, with the aim of providing a one-stop-shop for adventure activities and experiences across India. She faced a number of challenges in launching Thrillophilia, including the need to build a new brand in a market that was largely unorganized and fragmented. However, Daga was able to leverage her expertise in marketing and her passion for adventure travel to create a platform that resonated with Indian consumers. Today, Thrillophilia is the leading platform for booking adventure activities and experiences in India, with a wide range of offerings that include trekking, camping, water sports, and more.

Daga's success as a woman entrepreneur in India highlights the potential for women to drive innovation and growth in the travel and tourism sector, and underscores the importance of following one's passions and interests in building a successful career. She has been recognized for her achievements and has received several awards and honors, including the Economic Times Women Ahead Award and the Business Today Most Powerful Women in Business Award.

The success stories of the aforementioned female business owners show that nothing is out of the question for a woman. They stand out now after overcoming all obstacles, realizing their goals, and motivating many people.

15.5 EMERGING ISSUES

The government has made the advancement of women a priority from its inception. The idea of women's development up until the 1970s was mostly welfare-oriented. The 1980s embraced a multidisciplinary strategy with a focus on the three fundamental areas of work, education, and health. In every industry, including the SSI sector, women were given priority. Government and non-government organizations are increasingly focusing on the economic contribution that women make through their own businesses and industrial endeavors. The field of women entrepreneurship is constantly evolving, and there are several emerging issues that are likely to shape the future of women's entrepreneurship in India. Here are some of the key emerging issues:

- **Digital Entrepreneurship:** The growth of digital technologies and e-commerce platforms has created new opportunities for women entrepreneurs to start and grow businesses. However, there are also challenges associated with digital entrepreneurship, including the need for digital skills and the risks associated with online security and privacy.
- **Social Entrepreneurship:** Social entrepreneurship, which involves using business to create social or environmental impact, is becoming an increasingly important area of focus for women entrepreneurs. Social entrepreneurship can help to address some of the key social and environmental challenges facing India, while also creating economic opportunities for women.
- **Access to Funding:** While there have been some positive developments in recent years in terms of improving access to funding for women entrepreneurs, there is still a long way to go. Emerging issues related to funding include the need for more venture capital and angel investment, as well as the potential for crowdfunding and impact investing to support women entrepreneurs.
- **Scaling Up:** Many women entrepreneurs in India face challenges in scaling up their businesses, including the need for more support and resources to help them navigate the growth process. Emerging issues related to scaling up include the need for mentorship, access to markets, and opportunities for collaboration and networking.
- **Globalization:** As the Indian economy becomes increasingly integrated with the global economy, there are new opportunities and challenges for women entrepreneurs. Emerging issues related to globalization include the need for more international partnerships and collaborations, as well as the need for women entrepreneurs to navigate new and complex regulatory environments.

These emerging issues, along with others, will continue to shape the field of women's entrepreneurship in India in the years to come. It will be important for policymakers, business leaders, and other stakeholders to work together to address these issues and support the growth and success of women entrepreneurs in India.

15.5.1 SCHEMES OFFERED BY THE INDIAN GOVERNMENT

The government of India has provided the following programs to support an ecosystem for female entrepreneurs. Government, non-government, promotional, and regulatory organizations must step up to support female entrepreneurs in India. The Indian government has launched several schemes and initiatives to support and encourage women entrepreneurship in the country. Here are some of the key schemes offered by the Indian government:

- **Annapurna Scheme:** This scheme is offered by the State Bank of Mysore and provides loans of up to Rs. 50,000 to women entrepreneurs who want to start a food catering business. The loan is repayable in 36 monthly installments.
- **Mahila Udyam Nidhi Scheme:** This scheme is offered by the Small Industries Development Bank of India (SIDBI) and provides financial assistance of up to Rs. 10 lakhs to women entrepreneurs. The loan can be used to set up a new business or expand an existing one.
- **Sree Shakti Package for Women Entrepreneurs:** This scheme is offered by the State Bank of India and provides loans to women entrepreneurs at a reduced rate of interest. The scheme also provides for a concession on collateral.
- **Trade Related Entrepreneurship Assistance and Development (TREAD) Scheme for Women:** This scheme is offered by the Ministry of Micro, Small, and Medium Enterprises and provides training, counseling, and financial assistance to women entrepreneurs who want to start or expand a small business.
- **Mudra Yojana:** This scheme is offered by the government of India and provides loans of up to Rs. 10 lakhs to small business owners, including women entrepreneurs. The loan can be used for a variety of purposes, including starting a new business, expanding an existing one, or buying equipment and machinery.

These are just a few examples of the many schemes and initiatives offered by the Indian government to support women's entrepreneurship. Other schemes include the Stand-Up India scheme, the National Small Industries Corporation (NSIC) Women Entrepreneurship Program, and the Women Entrepreneurship Platform, among others. Women entrepreneurs in India are encouraged to explore these schemes and take advantage of the support and resources available to them.

15.6 CONCLUSION

In almost every economy, the number of female business owners is steadily increasing. The rise of female entrepreneurs in the 20th century has been dubbed the quiet revolution. Women's untapped entrepreneurial potential has been growing as social awareness of their responsibilities and economic status has grown. Women have become aware of their rights and employment opportunities due to the media. Women now work in every industry, from household activities like pickles to new-generation technologies like telecommunications. They have a vital and considerable impact on the overall economic growth of any nation. Women who are in their own businesses are being praised and admired internationally as well as nationally. The topic of entrepreneurship has always generated the most discussion, and the economic difficulties facing the world today have only increased its importance. More than ever, developing nations like India need to support female entrepreneurs since they have the workforce on hand right away to take advantage of untapped economic opportunities. Entrepreneurs have the power to bring changes in the style of how to work and live.

Their ideas have the potential to raise our standard of living, and in addition to generating wealth through their business ventures, they also contribute to a thriving society by creating job opportunities. They must also be able to sustain and compete in the local economic environment. As rights to education and work were established in the post-independence era, equality was promised and women gained prominence. Following independence and more recently, the government has implemented several programs to support female entrepreneurs. However, only a small number of women have benefited from these programs. Women are eager to start their own businesses and contribute to the nation's growth. Currently, women own 20% of all enterprises in India. Women entrepreneurs in India are breaking barriers and inspiring other women to take the lead and succeed in various ventures. By creating job opportunities in the country, women-owned businesses are actively contributing to society. Startup India is committed to promoting women's entrepreneurship in India through initiatives, programs, the development of supportive networks and communities, and the establishment of partnerships among different stakeholders in the startup ecosystem. This commitment is aligned with the organization's vision to promote the sustainable development of women entrepreneurs for the nation's overall growth. If you believe in your talent, you will undoubtedly be able to succeed through hard work and focused effort. With women playing a significant role in our economy each year, it is evident that more women entering the startup and small business sector will greatly enhance India's entrepreneurial landscape.

KEYWORDS

- **challenges**
- **COVID-19 pandemic**
- **Female Entrepreneurship**
- **literature review**
- **National Small Industries Corporation**
- **Related Entrepreneurship Assistance and Development**
- **Small Industries Development Bank of India**

REFERENCES

Abd Rani, S. H., & Hashim, N. (2017). Factors that influence women entrepreneurial success in Malaysia: A conceptual framework. *International Journal of Research in Business Studies and Management, 1*(4), 16–23.

Azmi, I. A. G. (2017). Muslim women entrepreneurs' motivation in SMEs: A quantitative study in Asia Pacific countries. *Asian Economic and Financial Review, 7*(1), 27–42.

Babu, P. (1978). A Study on Sociological Characteristics of Small Scale Industrialist. Margaret Meaning and Anne Jardin (1979) The Managerial Women-Pan Books London Sidney, 14–15.

Bosma, N., & Kelley, D. (2019). Global Entrepreneurship Monitor 2018/2019. Global Report. Babson Park, MA, London: Babson College and London Business School. Retrieved from: https://www.gemconsortium.org/report/gem-2018-2019-global-report (accessed on 19 June 2024).

Chaturvedi, N., Garg, S., & Jeswal, R. (2019). Challenges & Emerging Issues with Women Entrepreneurs-an Indian Context. *Amity Global Business Review, 54–64.*

Ferreira, J. J. M., Fernandes, C. I., Peris-Ortiz, M., & Ratten, V. (2017). Female entrepreneurship: A co-citation analysis. *International Journal of Entrepreneurship and Small Business, 31*(2), 325–340.

Ganesan, S. (2003). Status of women entrepreneurs in India. *Women Empowerment and Gender Equality.* Kanishka Publishers.

Global Entrepreneurship Monitor. (2021). Global Entrepreneurship Monitor India 2020-2021 Report. Retrieved from: https://www.gemconsortium.org/report (accessed on 19 June 2024).

Gould, S., & Perzen, J. (Eds.). (1990). Enterprising women organization. *Local Initiatives for Job Creation,* pp. 20–30

Guzman, J., & Kacperczyk, A. O. (2019). Gender gap in entrepreneurship. *Research Policy, 48*(7), 1666–1680.

Hanson, S. (2009). Changing places through women's entrepreneurship. *Journal of Women's Entrepreneurship and Education, 1–2*, Retrieved from: https://doi.org/10.1111/j.1944-8287.2009.01033.x.

Jahanshahi, A. A., Pitamber, B. K., & Nawaser, K. (2010). Issues and challenges for women entrepreneurs in global scene, with special reference to India. *Australian Journal of Basic and Applied Sciences, 4*(9), 4347–4356.

Khan, R. U., Salamzadeh, Y., Shah, S. Z. A., & Hussain, M. (2021). Factors affecting women entrepreneurs' success: A study of small-and medium-sized enterprises in emerging market of Pakistan. *Journal of Innovation and Entrepreneurship, 10*(1), 1–21.

Kirve, J. (2020). Women entrepreneurship in India–Problems and prospects. *International Research Journal of Marketing & Economics, 7*(2), 328–334.

Mattu, A. (2004). Women Entrepreneurship–Key to Development. In *Research Paper Presented at National seminar on Women Entrepreneurship–A Need for Training and Curriculum Development held by Development of Home Science Extension and communication, Faculty of Home Science, MS University, Feb.* (p. 256).

Mitra, R. (2002). The growth pattern of women-run enterprises: An empirical study in India. *Journal of Developmental Entrepreneurship, 7*(2), 217.

Modarresi, M., Arasti, Z., Talebi, K., & Farasatkhah, M. (2016). Women's entrepreneurship in Iran: How are women owning and managing home-based businesses motivated to grow?. *International Journal of Gender and Entrepreneurship*, *8*(4), 446–470.

Muhammad, N., McElwee, G., & Dana, L. P. (2017). Barriers to the development and progress of entrepreneurship in rural Pakistan. *International Journal of Entrepreneurial Behavior & Research, 23*(2), 279–295.

Rajvanshi, A. (2017). Women entrepreneurs in India: Challenges and opportunities. *IOSR Journal of Humanities and Social Sciences, 22*(4), 1–9.

Robson, P. J., & Bennett, R. J. (2000). SME growth: The relationship with business advice and external collaboration. *Small Business Economics, 15*, 193–208.

Scott, C. E. (1986). Why more women are becoming entrepreneurs. *Journal of Small Business Management, 24*(4), 37–44.

Sharma, V., et al. (2014). Women entrepreneurship: The emerging economic in the 21st century. *International Journal of Commerce, Business, and Management, 3*(4), 543–548.

Swarnalatha, K., & Anuradha, R. K. (2013). Women entrepreneurship in India – Problems and prospects. *International Journal of Science and Research, 5*(3), 1289–1291.

Vijay, B. (1997). Problems and prospects of women entrepreneurs. *The Indian Journal of Commerce, 193*(IV), 218–221.

Vijayakumar, A., & Jayachitra, S. (2013). Women entrepreneurs in India – Emerging issues and challenges. *International Journal of Development Research, 3*(4), 12–17.

CHAPTER 16

GENDER EQUALITY: THE NEED OF THE HOUR IN TIMES OF UNCERTAINTY

SHIKHA KAPOOR

Professor, Amity International Business School, Amity University, Noida, Uttar Pradesh, India

ABSTRACT

The issue of gender equality has been a longstanding concern, with progress made in recent decades in some areas, but significant gaps and disparities persist. The COVID-19 pandemic has further highlighted the urgent need for action to address gender inequalities, as women have been disproportionately affected by the crisis. The purpose of this chapter is to examine the importance of gender equality in times of uncertainty, particularly in the context of the COVID-19 pandemic. The chapter aims to highlight the impact of the pandemic on gender disparities and to discuss the need for action to promote gender equality. This chapter is based on a review of existing literature and data on gender inequality, with a focus on the impact of the COVID-19 pandemic on gender disparities.

The literature review contained academic articles, reports from international organizations, and news articles. The COVID-19 pandemic has had a disproportionate impact on women, exacerbating existing gender disparities and revealing new ones. Women are overrepresented in low-paid and insecure jobs, which have been hit hardest by the pandemic. They also shoulder a disproportionate burden of unpaid care work, which has increased with the closure of schools and childcare facilities. Lockdowns and social distancing

Subverting Social Inequalities: Gender as a Social Reality.
Akanksha Srivastava, Disha Maheshwari, Chitra Krishnan (Eds.)

measures have led to a rise in domestic violence against women and girls. To address these issues, it is essential to act to promote gender equality and empower women and girls.

This includes challenging gender stereotypes, promoting women's economic empowerment, ensuring equal access to education and healthcare, and addressing the root causes of gender-based violence. Men and boys also have a critical role to play in promoting gender equality by challenging harmful gender norms and behaviors. In conclusion, promoting gender equality is essential in building resilient and sustainable societies, particularly in times of uncertainty such as the COVID-19 pandemic. Action is urgently needed to address gender disparities and empower all genders to contribute to the development and well-being of their communities.

16.1 INTRODUCTION

"Gender equality is not just a target in and of itself. For the challenge of eradicating poverty, advancing sustainable development, and fostering good governance, it is a requirement."

— *Kofi Annan, Former Secretary-General of the United Nations*

Organizational structures, procedures, and practices can all be affected by the complex phenomena of gender inequality. Some of the most damaging gender inequities for women are implemented *via* HR procedures. This is due to the fact that women's hiring, training, salary, and promotion are impacted by HR practices (i.e., policies, decision-making, and their implementation). We offer a theory of gender bias in HR that stresses the reciprocal nature of gender inequality inside businesses. Gender directly affects the effectiveness of national and international organizations in implementing their policies, programs, and projects, which in turn affects how society develops. Gender has an impact on every aspect of an individual's and society's very dynamic, social, every day, and private lives as well as the numerous roles that society assigns to men and women. Equal rights for men and women are a fundamental human right and a requirement for a prosperous, stable, and sustainable global community. Governments and development organizations have long given gender issues the utmost consideration in development planning and policy. All recent international meetings have had a prominent discussion about gender equity as it relates to resource access and allocation as well as opportunities for social and economic advancement. These meetings have also looked into the fundamental relationship between gender equity and sustainable development, defining specific mechanisms and goals for global cooperation.

The Preamble, Fundamental Rights, Fundamental Duties, and Directive Principles of the Indian Constitution all mention the idea of gender equality. In accordance with the Constitution, the government is prohibited from enacting laws that support discrimination against women. Long-term progress is required to eradicate discrimination against women and provide equal opportunities for both education and employment. Gender equality is crucial because it promotes economic development. International organizations describe gender-equal opportunity in terms of economic development and human constitutional rights, notably women's constitutional rights.

This chapter discusses the present state of gender equality, workplace equality, the gender pay gap, and the need for women's independence. It has been observed that this movement for gender equality became even more important and crucial during the period of global uncertainty in the COVID and post-COVID era. The circumstances that made this action necessary have been investigated and discussed.

A clear indication of the world's greatest democracy's dedication to social justice, gender equality, and the equitable advancement of each section of its people is the election of a deserving woman from the tribal community to the position of India's highest office as President of India is a recent example of Women Equality in India. Although it is a goal, gender equality is not the sole one. It is crucial to tackling the issue of lowering poverty, boosting sustainable development, and establishing good governance. Gender equality is the condition of having an equal approach to resources and prospects, as well as financial involvement and policymaking, including the regard for each one's particular performances, goals, and needs. Equal pay for comparable work is referred to as gender equality in the workplace. Furthermore, it implies that a woman who leaves her career for a period of time—like maternity leave—won't face any consequences after she returns.

India's total score in 2021 was 0.625, and in 2022 it was 0.629. Since the measurement's introduction, the gender gap rating for India has varied from 135th to 135th, between 0.593 and 0.683. The study found that India's 2022 score of 0.629 was the 7th highest in the preceding 16 years. The World Economic Forum's Global Gender Gap Report 2022 released on 15th July places India 135th out of 146 countries. It is a considerable dip from its rating of 105th out of 135 countries in 2012, even though it is an improvement over its 140th place out of 156 in 2021. In the initial publication of the gender gap report in 2006. India came in at number 98 out of 115 countries. In the World Economic Forum's (WEF) annual Gender Gap Report 2022, which was released in Geneva India performs poorly for gender parity on July 13. Out of 146 nations, India is placed 135th. Following India on the list of 146 countries are only 11 other countries.

To achieve UNICEF's mission of defending the rights of all children, gender equality is required. The UNICEF Gender Action Plan (GAP), 2022–2025, operationalizes the UNICEF Gender Policy, 2021–2030, by outlining how UNICEF will achieve gender equality across all its drivers and workstations. It asserts that regardless of organizational level, everyone has a responsibility to promote gender equality and women's and girls' emancipation. In addition to concrete indicators and monitoring tools to measure development, the GAP outlines the procedures necessary to hasten the accomplishment of gender equivalence inside institutional structures and processes, as well as throughout the five focus sections of the 2022–2025 UNICEF Strategic Plan.

The GAP is based on the growing body of information about gender equality, including the most recent data on how the 2019 (COVID-19) coronavirus illness has impacted different genders. It is a result of comprehensive worldwide consultation with employees, partners, and youth as well as insights acquired through the implementation of past GAPs. Based on the non-discrimination and equality principles of human rights, it describes UNICEF's role in advancing the 2030 Agenda for Sustainable Development as a partner with governments and other stakeholders.

Gender implications of the COVID-19 pandemic must be considered in every response strategy, recovery plan, and resource budgeting. Among other things, this entails (1) Planning and decision-making by including women and their organization in the COVID-19 response; (2) addressing the inequities of voluntary by developing a new, inclusive care economy that benefits everyone; and (3) evolving socioeconomic plans with an intentional emphasis on the present and future of vulnerable populations. In order to lessen the COVID-19 crisis' effects on women and girls and to ensure that long-term recovery benefits, UN Women has created a swift and concentrated response that is focused on five priorities.

1. Domestic violence, which includes gender-based violence, is lessened and decreased;

2. Economic stimulus plans and social protection programs benefit women and girls;
3. Supporters and practitioners of equitable caregiving;
4. Girls and women are in charge of and actively engage in COVID-19 response planning; and
5. Data and coordination methods take gender into account.

16.2 THE GROWING GAP

A crucial factor in the gap's increase is India's position in the world in terms of women's political empowerment. The current world ranking for India is 48. Despite what would seem like a positive, the country's global ranking in 2016 was eighth. In the years that followed, the position fell to 15, 19, and finally 51 in 2021. The latest evaluation states that "Political Empowerment displays a declining score (in India) due to the declining proportion of time over the previous 50 years that women have held the position of head of state."

India is placed 135th out of 146 countries in the World Economic Forum's Global Gender Gap Index 2022. (WEF). In the "health and survival" sub-index, where it is ranked 146, it has the worst overall performance. India does poorly compare to its neighbors as well, coming in last place after Sri Lanka (96), Bangladesh (71), Bhutan (117), Bangladesh (110), and the Maldives (110). (110). (126). Only Iran, Pakistan, and Afghanistan perform worse than India in South Asia (143, 145, and 146, respectively).

16.3 ACTION NEEDED TO STOP THIS DECLINE

The growing gender disparity in India's representation of women in leadership positions is criticized in the report. This issue might be resolved by the Women's Reservation Bill, where 33% of seats are kept for women. Additionally, steps might be implemented to lessen the gender wage gap in all industries. According to estimations from the World Inequality Report 2022, men make up 82% of the labor force in India, while women make up 18%. It would also be possible to raise funding for the gender budget, which strives to guarantee that men and women have equal access to socioeconomic benefits. 23.7% of the parliamentary seats are held by women, far short of parity, notwithstanding recent increases in the number of women vying for office, including those won through the establishment of particular quotas. In the private sector, where less than a third of senior and middle management roles are held by women globally, the situation is not much better.

UN Women seeks to elevate the opinions of women and girls via all its initiatives and programs. Along with more aggressive action on gender equality, the world can go in the direction of sustainable progress by 2030, leaving no one behind.

16.4 ACTION BY UNICEF TO ADVANCE GENDER EQUALITY

Reducing inequality strengthens communities, enhances economies, and allows everyone—especially boys and men—to realize their full potential. UNICEF collaborates with international organizations to advance gender equality. Every area of our work incorporates strategies to combat discrimination and disadvantage based on gender. This entails working with the country's health sectors to increase access to maternity care and assist the professionalization of most female public well-being individuals. Women's involvement in the layout and execution of WASH ecosystems must be encouraged. It also includes working together with the informative sector to make certain that both boys and girls attain educational accomplishments and discover roads to rewarding jobs. UNICEF collaborates with international organizations to advance gender equality. Every area of our work incorporates strategies to fight bias and disadvantage centered on gender.

16.5 2022–2025 GENDER ACTION PLAN (UNICEF)

According to gender parity, boys and girls should get equal opportunities, resources, and protections. A new gender policy (2021–2030) detailing UNICEF's objectives for attaining gender equality in all of our programs, workplaces, and practices was introduced in 2021. The Gender (2022–2025) Action Plan outlines the direction of UNICEF for the future with a variety of objectives and due dates that benefit young people, women, and children globally. The numerous root causes of discrimination that continue to limit women's constitutional rights in both the public and private spheres must be addressed if gender equality is to be achieved by 2030. For instance, it is necessary to amend discriminatory laws and enact new legislation in order to actively promote equality. 39 nations ban equal inheritance rights for girls and boys, and 49 nations still lack domestic violence protection legislation.

According to reports from 87 countries, one in five women and girls under the age of 50 would have undergone physical or sexual abuse.

Women are not only the demographic most badly impacted by the epidemic, but they also lay the groundwork for social healing. The world will be better able to accomplish Sustainable Development Goals by placing women and girls at the center of the financial system, and everyone will benefit from stronger and further sustainable development outcomes. The COVID-19 pandemic offers a chance to act swiftly and effectively to address chronic disparities in a variety of aspects of adult female lives and create a more equitable and resilient society. A substantial increase in cruelty against women has been caused by the epidemic. Many women are unable to seek the services that are being cut because lockdown policies prevent them from leaving the homes of their violent husbands. Recent statistics show that since the pandemic began, domestic violence against women and girls has grown.

16.6 IMPORTANCE OF GENDER EQUALITY IN THE WORK

A nation's total economic performance depends on gender equality in the workplace. Gender equality at work is associated with national productivity growth and economic development. But other companies are making the effort to fix that "broken rung" and guarantee that women who work there are ready for career growth from the outset. Young women who wish to start their careers with an employer who cares about their success would do well to get to know these companies. It is not surprising that Abbott is still a top employer for women today given that it was formed in the late 1800s and has always had female CEOs. Thanks to Abbott's organized year-long mentoring program and dedication to assisting women, specifically mothers, to achieve their full capacity at work, many of the company's female senior and executive personnel began their careers there and progressed up the corporate ladder.

On Cognizant's website, you can meet a ton of women executives and read their biographies, but they all have one thing in common: they've all had fantastic support from their employers. Cognizant workers have access to networking opportunities, meals, forums, and even a book club through Women Empowered, all of which are intended to connect women and offer insight into the workplace. Additionally, Cognizant has committed to eliminating the gender pay gap and plans to hire 100,000 women in the near future. Unilever, a multinational consumer goods corporation with a goal to better consumers' lives and communities, places just as much importance on its staff as it does on all of the company's purpose-driven products. Unilever announced in March 2020 that it had achieved gender equality throughout its executive team globally, one full year before its goal. The company is dedicated to eliminating the gender pay gap throughout the organization; non-executive board members and management-level staff are now equally split between men and women, whereas supply chain, finance, operations, and tech engineering were traditionally underrepresented. The climate for women employees at Honeywell is fantastic. From networking opportunities just for women to an extensive Return to Work program created to assist women with lengthier maternity breaks and a smooth return to work after giving birth. Younger workers have role models within the firm to connect with and model careers thanks to the several women executives who are fueling Honeywell's success.

16.7 IMPLEMENTATION OF WORK PLACE GENDER EQUALITY

Establishing a gender-inclusive workplace, creating better job descriptions to advance gender equality, making the interview panel diverse, and aggressively seeking out a pipeline that is gender diverse. Businesses may focus on organizational and cultural reforms in addition to legislative measures to minimize gender inequality. Even if this is a positive start, simply adding more women to the workforce is insufficient. Businesses must work to close the gender gap and create truly diverse workplaces because diversity does not guarantee inclusive environments by itself.

16.7.1 DURING THE EMPLOYMENT PROCESS, GIVE DIVERSITY CONSIDERABLE CONSIDERATION.

The first phase toward attaining gender parity at work is the hiring process. Work toward establishing a different and reasonable workplace by producing comprehensive and precise job descriptions, developing a line-up of candidates with a diversity of gender identities, and conducting unbiased interviews. Make sure there is no internal prejudice in your hiring process. These guidelines should be followed regardless of the degree of seniority, while leadership positions have higher expectations. Males currently hold roughly 60% of management responsibilities, while women hold about 40% of similar positions, according to McKinsey statistics. The representational disparity gets worse as one moves up the corporate ladder. For instance, just about one in four C-suite executives are women, and fewer than one in 25 of them are women of color. Businesses may support gender equality by putting more women in positions of leadership.

16.7.2 CREATE AN EMPLOYEE COMPENSATION PLAN THAT IS TRANSPARENT, EQUAL, AND FAIR

Regardless of gender, offer equal compensation for equal work to all your workforce. This is one of the truly understandable and uncomplicated ways to advance gender parity at work. Another great tactic to recruit and retain top talent is to offer fair and competitive remuneration. Make a thorough plan for employee remuneration that includes both direct and indirect payment methods. Businesses should give qualified women who are internally promoted a priority. To assist deserving women in advancing their professions, create uniform evaluation and promotion procedures. Transparent assessment and promotion processes benefit everyone, not just women, and can help close the gender gap that currently exists.

i. **Supportive and Flexible Benefits Offer:** Employee burnout is one of the stresses at work that women are currently facing the most, according to a McKinsey report. Due to the epidemic, women are more prone than men to experience burnout, stress, and exhaustion. Additionally, 1 in 3 women reported having considered quitting their jobs or reducing their vocation.

ii. **Teach Your Employees How to Behave Professionally:** Encourage your workers to take part in a diversity training program created especially for your business to address any biases and prejudices that may exist in the organization. This might also motivate your staff to put their newfound awareness of all into practice.

iii. Make businesses brave about gender diversity and consider it as a key element of their business strategies.

iv. **Promote a Diverse Workplace Atmosphere**: If businesses want to close the gap, they must create a culture where employees feel valued and at home. They should focus on developing business cultures to increase inclusivity and improve the experience and engagement of their employees. Price claimed that in addition to advancing gender equality, doing so might promote creativity, retain critical personnel, and reduce attrition rates.

v. Establish a training program on diversity and inclusion.

16.8 GENDER INEQUALITY DURING PANDEMIC TIMES

There have been a variety of reactions to the new coronavirus epidemic worldwide. One of the toughest measures was taken by India, which imposed significant restrictions on people's freedom of travel and business transactions. The lockdown, initially intended to continue for 21 days but then extended to May 31, was announced by the Indian Prime Minister on March 24. By mid-April, the nation had been split into three distinct regions: red districts, where COVID-19 cases were most prevalent, which had very strict movement controls for non-essential work; orange districts, where COVID-19 cases were less prevalent; many economic activities were restricted; and green districts, which were free of COVID-19 and thus had much greater freedom than their red and orange counterparts.

The repercussions of the COVID-19 pandemic rolled back India's gains in women's equality. The coronavirus occurrence exacerbates now occurring inequalities for women and girls in every area, from security and social security to health and the economy. In the fight against the coronavirus, women were disproportionately represented among healthcare workers and household carers. Due to school closings and the increasingly complex requirements of the elderly, women's unpaid caregiving has considerably expanded. For working or single mothers, carving out a little "me" time has proven challenging in this pervasive pandemic condition. As a result, individuals were denied the essential element needed to sustain a healthy lifestyle. Women were disproportionately represented among frontline healthcare workers and household carers in combatting the coronavirus. Due to school closings and the increasingly complex requirements of the elderly, women's voluntary caregiving has significantly increased. Additionally, domestic aggression against women and girls had abruptly improved because of the pandemic.

Women were stranded at home with their abusers because of lockdown measures, not capable of gaining access to help due to cuts and limitations. New evidence indicates that violent behavior against women and girls, mostly household abuse, has intensified since the pandemic outbreak. Small enterprises, the hospitality sector, and the service sector—which employ largely women—were among the traditional industries that were severely damaged by the pandemic. Many female workers in these industries run the risk of being permanently ejected from the labor force or compelled into more precarious positions. The economic effects of COVID-19 were equally worse on women because they labor disproportionately in unstable markets and platforms. About 60% of women work in the unorganized sector of the economy, which increases their vulnerability to poverty. COVID-19, which amplifies pre-existing disparities, frequently had an unfavorable effect on women's employment. Additionally, women are more likely to be forced out of their professions and into the less stable informal sector.

16.9 CONCLUSION

In conclusion, the COVID-19 pandemic has highlighted the urgency of addressing gender inequality, as women have been disproportionately affected by the crisis. The pandemic has exacerbated existing gender disparities and revealed new ones, including in the areas of employment, unpaid care work, and gender-based violence. To promote gender equality, it is crucial to challenge harmful gender stereotypes, promote women's economic empowerment, ensure equal access to education and healthcare, and involve men and boys in efforts to promote gender justice. Gender equality is not only a human rights issue, but it is also a crucial factor in building resilient and sustainable societies, particularly in times of uncertainty. Therefore, action is urgently required to tackle gender disparities and empower all genders to contribute to the development and well-being of their communities.

> "Women must be freed from all forms of oppression in order to obtain freedom."
>
> — *Nelson Mandela*

KEYWORDS

- **COVID**
- **empowerment**
- **equality**
- **gender action plan**
- **growing gap**
- **UNICEF**
- **World Economic Forum's**

REFERENCES

Chancel, L., Piketty, T., Saez, E., & Zucman, G. (Eds.). (2022). *World inequality report 2022*. Harvard University Press.

Daly, M. (2005). Gender mainstreaming in theory and practice. *Social Politics: International Studies in Gender, State & Society, 12*(3), 433–450.

Deshpande, A. (2020). *The Covid-19 pandemic and lockdown: First effects on gender gaps in employment and domestic work in India* (No. 30). https://ideas.repec.org/p/ash/wpaper/30.html.

Field, E., Krivkovich, A., Kügele, S., Robinson, N., & Yee, L. (2023). Women in the workplace 2023. *McKinsey & Company*.

LeMoyne, R. (2011). Promoting Gender Equality: An Equity-based Approach to Programming (PDF). Operational Guidance Overview in Brief. UNICEF. Retrieved from: https://www.unicef.org/gender-equality/gender-action-plan-2022-2025 (accessed on 19 June 2024).

McGhee, T. J. (2023). *The Role and Contribution of Rural North Carolina Community Colleges in Social Capital Development* (Doctoral dissertation, Old Dominion University).

Rinehart, Jane & Lorber, Judith. (2002). Gender Inequality: Feminist Theories and Politics. Teaching Sociology. 30. 128. 10.2307/3211533.

Sharma, R. R., Chawla, S., & Karam, C. M. (2021). Global gender gap index: world economic forum perspective. In *Handbook on diversity and inclusion indices* (pp. 150-163). Edward Elgar Publishing.

UNICEF. (2022). *Gender Action Plan 2022–2025*. Retrieved from: https://www.unicef.org/gender-equality/gender-action-plan-2022-2025 (accessed on 19 June 2024).

World Economic Forum. (2022). *Global Gender Gap Report 2022*. Retrieved from: https://www.weforum.org/reports/global-gender-gap-report-2022 (accessed on 19 June 2024).

World Economic Forum. (2022). Virtual media briefing on the global gender gap report 2022. Retrieved from: https://www.weforum.org/agenda/2022/07/virtual-media-briefing-on-the-global-gender-gap-report-2022/ (accessed on 19 June 2024).

INDEX

D

E

N

T